AF411536

Populism and Foreign Policy

Populism and Foreign Policy

Sandra Destradi
Johannes Plagemann

OXFORD
UNIVERSITY PRESS

Oxford University Press is a department of the University of Oxford.
It furthers the University's objective of excellence in research, scholarship,
and education by publishing worldwide. Oxford is a registered trade mark of
Oxford University Press in the UK and in certain other countries.

Published in the United States of America by Oxford University Press
198 Madison Avenue, New York, NY 10016, United States of America.

© Oxford University Press 2025

All rights reserved. No part of this publication may be reproduced, stored in a retrieval system,
transmitted, used for text and data mining, or used for training artificial intelligence, in any form or
by any means, without the prior permission in writing of Oxford University Press, or as expressly
permitted by law, by license or under terms agreed with the appropriate reprographics rights
organization. Inquiries concerning reproduction outside the scope of the above should be sent
to the Rights Department, Oxford University Press, at the address above.

You must not circulate this work in any other form
and you must impose this same condition on any acquirer.

CIP data is on file at the Library of Congress.

ISBN 9780197694985

ISBN 9780197694978 (hbk.)

DOI: 10.1093/9780197695012.001.0001

Paperback Printed by Integrated Books International, United States of America

The manufacturer's authorized representative in the EU for product safety is
Oxford University Press España S.A. of Parque Empresarial San Fernando de Henares,
Avenida de Castilla, 2 – 28830 Madrid (www.oup.es/en or product.safety@oup.com).
OUP España S.A. also acts as importer into Spain of products made by the manufacturer.

Contents

Acknowledgements

This book is the result of several years of collaborative work in the context of the research project 'Populism and Foreign Policy', funded by a generous grant from the German Research Foundation (project number 451375110). We thank our colleagues working with us in the project. Hakkı Taş read large parts of the manuscript and greatly improved its analysis and empirics. Ferit Belder and Ege Hüsemoglu helped us with data collection and analysis on the case of Turkey. Elena Dressler, Carlos Heras Rodríguez, and Liliana Oropeza supported us with the analysis of the Bolivia case study. Liliana was of great support by performing the interviews in Bolivia. Alyssa Santiago was in charge of the case study of the Philippines in our project. She carried out the first round of field research in Manila, managing to speak to high-ranking government officials and experts. We are also grateful to Ronald Schleehauf, who worked on data collection for the case of Italy, and to Vihang Jumle, who supported us with the analysis of the Indian case.

Yonatan Etzion-Rosenberg coded the speeches by the selected non-populist and populist governments of Bolivia, India, the Philippines, and Turkey at the United Nations General Assembly. Moreover, we would like to thank Jule Schürmann, Victória Silveira Novaes, Jessica Blumberg, Houssein Al Malla, and Alma Lurie for outstanding research assistance.

Sandra Destradi thanks the Lauder School of Government, Diplomacy and Strategy at Reichman University, where she worked on this manuscript in 2024, for being such a supportive and inspiring environment. She is particularly grateful to Assaf Moghadam and Lesley Terris for all their help. This publication is also closely related to the research agenda of the MSCA doctoral network 'The International Dimensions and Effects of Populism' (IDEoPOP, Project 101168714), led by Sandra Destradi at the University of Freiburg.

Johannes Plagemann thanks the German Institute for Global and Area Studies (GIGA) in Hamburg and especially colleagues in Research Program 4 'Global Orders and Foreign Policies' for stimulating discussions and collegial support.

This book is the result of an abductive research process that started in 2017 and led to the publication of a number of articles and chapters, from the first plausibility probe of hypotheses for the case of India (Plagemann and Destradi 2019) to a first comparative analysis of Global South countries

(Destradi and Plagemann 2019), the establishment of a more systematic research agenda on populism and foreign policy (Destradi, Cadier, and Plagemann 2021) and international politics (Wajner, Destradi, and Zürn 2024), and several side projects on issues ranging from the politicization of foreign policy in India and Turkey (Destradi, Plagemann, and Taş 2022), populist mobilization around foreign policy issues in Bolivia (Plagemann, Heras Rodríguez, and Destradi 2022), populist foreign policy rhetoric (Destradi et al. 2022), populism and status seeking (Destradi 2023), and populist patterns of centralization in foreign policy institutions (Jumle et al. 2025) to the advantages of theorizing populism and foreign policy based on the ideational approach (Destradi 2025). Large parts of Chapter 3 are based on the following article: Destradi, Sandra, and Johannes Plagemann (2024), 'Do Populists Escalate International Disputes?', *International Affairs* 100 (5): 1919–40. Relevant permissions were obtained, as this is an Open Access article distributed under the terms of the Creative Commons Attribution License (https:// creativecommons.org/licenses/by/4.0/). Further, we reproduced minor parts of the following publications and obtained permissions for that: Plagemann, Johannes, Carlos Heras Rodríguez, and Sandra Destradi (2022), 'Populist Foreign Policy and Mobilization in Bolivia', *Política* 60 (2): 9–32; Destradi, Sandra et al. (2023), 'Populists' Foreign Policy Rhetoric: More Confrontational, Less Consensual?', in C. Lacatus, G. Meibauer, and G. Löfflmann (eds) *Political Communication and Performative Leadership* (Cham: Springer), 279–98 (license number 5872510369095).

Over the years, our thinking benefited tremendously from the feedback and input by colleagues who attended our presentations and read our papers at several workshops, seminars, and conferences. We presented earlier versions of our work starting from 2017, with the first presentation being held at the workshop 'Populist Mobilization in Asia: Causes, Contours, Consequences' at Monash University Malaysia. We gave lectures and presentations, among others, at the GIGA in Hamburg, Catholic University of Eichstätt-Ingolstadt (May 2019), Helmut Schmidt University (December 2019), MERICS (January 2020), University College Dublin (online, December 2020), Central University of Kashmir (online, February 2021), CERI SciencesPo (online, March 2021), Brigham Young University (online, October 2021), De La Salle University Manila (online, January 2022), at the Robert Schuman Centre for Advanced Studies of the EUI (September 2022), University of Trieste (April 2023), University College Freiburg (May 2023), Reichman University (April 2024), Hebrew University of Jerusalem (May 2024), University of Palermo (May 2024), LMU in Munich (October 2024), and the University of the Philippines Diliman (November 2024). Further, the EWIS Workshops in

Groningen (2018) and in Thessaloniki (2022) as well as the workshops for the special section 'The Effects of Global Populism' in *International Affairs* stand out as particularly inspiring events, besides several presentations at international conferences. We are grateful to the colleagues who invited us and engaged with our papers. Among those who particularly helped us sharpen our thinking about populism and foreign policy are David Cadier, Angelos Chryssogelos, Leslie Wehner, Daniel Wajner, Cora Lacatus, Hakkı Taş, Stephan Fouquet, and Bertjan Verbeek. It is a true privilege to be surrounded by such a collegial and dynamic community of scholars.

We also would like to thank the anonymous reviewers who gave feedback on our book proposal and draft manuscript at OUP, and Dave McBride for believing in this project.

Finally, we are especially grateful to the experts and practitioners with first-hand experiences who agreed to share their knowledge and insights with us in the 114 interviews that we conducted for this book.

List of Interviewees

Bolivia

B01   career diplomat under Morales, La Paz, 12 January 2023

B02   former diplomat and academic, La Paz, 15 January 2023

B03   international affairs expert and foreign policy advisor under Morales, La Paz, 16 January 2023

B04   senior career diplomat under Veltzé and Morales, La Paz, 16 January 2023

B05   senior career diplomat, La Paz, 16 January 2023

B06   senior career diplomat, La Paz, 18 January 2023

B07   Carmen Capriles, civil society expert in climate change, La Paz, 20 January 2023

B08   Bolivian foreign relations scholar, Zoom, 25 January 2023

B09   senior career diplomat, Zoom, 27 January 2023

B10   diplomat under Morales, La Paz, 30 January 2023

B11   Eduardo Rodríguez Veltzé, former Bolivian president (2005–2006), Zoom, 30 January 2023

B12   Soledad Enríquez, Bolivian expert in agroforestry and natural resource management, Zoom, 1 February 2023

B13   acting senior diplomat, La Paz, 2 February 2023

B14   former career diplomat, La Paz, 6 February 2023

B15   former senior diplomat, La Paz, 6 February 2023

B16   acting senior diplomat, La Paz, 9 February 2023

B17   senior political appointee under Morales, La Paz, 13 February 2023

B18   David Agramont, Research Associate at the Peace Research Institute Frankfurt, Zoom, 15 February 2023

B19   acting senior diplomat, La Paz, 20 February 2023

B20   former diplomat (pre-2006), La Paz, 24 February 2023

B21   Bolivian academic and former diplomat, La Paz, 1 March 2023

B22   former senior diplomat, Zoom, 3 March 2023

B23   academic and former senior diplomat, La Paz, 6 March 2023

B24   journalist and former senior diplomat, Zoom, 8 March 2023

B25   Daniel Robison, Bolivian academic and environmentalist, Zoom, 8 March 2023

B26   former career diplomat, La Paz, 8 March 2023

B27   Nataly Reguerin, Bolivian foreign relations analyst and former diplomat, La Paz, 9 March 2023

B28   former diplomat, La Paz, 22 March 2023

B29   Bolivian foreign relations analyst and former senior diplomat, La Paz, 22 March 2023

B30   Javier Murillo de la Rocha, former foreign minister (1997–2001), La Paz, 14 February 2023

India

I01   expert on India's foreign policy, New Delhi, 20 February 2023
I02   Indian journalist, New Delhi, 21 February 2023
I03   Indian journalist, New Delhi, 22 February 2023
I04   Indian academic, New Delhi, 22 February 2023
I05   retired Indian diplomat, New Delhi, 28 February 2023
I06   Indian scholar and observer, New Delhi, 28 February 2023
I07   retired Indian diplomat, New Delhi, 1 March 2023
I08   retired Indian diplomat, New Delhi, 1 March 2023
I09   senior retired Indian diplomat, New Delhi, 1 March 2023
I10   Indian strategic analyst, New Delhi, 2 March 2023
I11   retired Indian diplomat, New Delhi, 2 March 2023
I12   retired Indian diplomat at think tank, New Delhi, 2 March 2023
I13   Indian analyst, online, 2 March 2023
I14   Indian academic, New Delhi, 6 March 2023
I15   retired Indian diplomat at think tank, New Delhi, 6 March 2023
I16   Indian journalist, New Delhi, 7 March 2023
I17   European diplomat posted to India, New Delhi, 7 March 2023
I18   retired Indian diplomat, New Delhi, 7 March 2023
I19   Indian academic, New Delhi, 8 March 2023
I20   Indian security expert, New Delhi, 9 March 2023
I21   Indian scholar, New Delhi, 9 March 2023
I22   Indian scholar, New Delhi, 9 March 2023
I23   former high-ranking government official from India, online, 23 March 2023

Italy

IT01   Italian scholar, Florence, 12 September 2022
IT02   Italian academic, online, 19 September 2022
IT03   Italian journalist, online, 20 September 2022
IT04   Italian academic, online, 21 September 2022
IT05   retired Italian diplomat, telephone interview, 22 September 2022
IT06   expert of Italian politics, Florence, 22 September 2022
IT07   Italian academic, Florence, 26 September 2022
IT08   retired Italian ambassador, telephone interview, 3 October 2022
IT09   senior Italian official, Florence, 5 October 2022
IT10   former high-ranking officer, Italian Ministry of Foreign Affairs and International Cooperation, online, 12 October 2022

The Philippines

P01   former high-ranking government official, Manila, 26 September 2022
P02   former senior diplomat, Manila, 28 September 2022

P03   senior staff to opposition senator under Duterte, Manila, 29 September 2022

P04   three members of Senate Committee Secretary on Foreign Relations under Duterte, Manila, September 29, 2022

P05   Filipino scholar, Manila, 30 September 2022

P06   senior military official, Manila, 4 October 2022

P07   Filipino senator 2007 to 2019, Manila, 5 October 2022

P08   Filipino military affairs journalist, Manila, 7 October 2022

P09   Filipino academic, Manila, 10 October 2022

P10   former high-ranking government official, Manila, 10 October 2022

P11   senior military official, Manila, 11 October 2022

P12   former senior navy official, Manila, 11 October 2022

P13   senior government official, Manila, 12 October 2022

P14   senior government official, Manila, 12 October 2022

P15   former senior navy official under Aquino and Duterte, Manila, 13 October 2022

P16   foreign affairs journalist, Manila, 13 October 2022

P17   e-mail communication with former senior national security official under Aquino, 8 December 2022

P18   UN official in the Philippines, Zoom, 13 September 2023, Zoom

P19   senior civil society activist, Zoom, 17 September 2023

P20   Filipino environmental affairs journalist, Zoom, 18 September 2023

P21   Filipino environmentalist, Zoom, 21 September 2023

P22   Filipino climate activist, Zoom, 22 September 2023

P23   Filipino environmentalist and former DENR official, Zoom, 23 September 2023

P24   e-mail communication with Filipino scholar, 22 June 2024

P25   senior staff at foreign NGO, Manila, 21 November 2024

P26   Filipino scholar, Manila, 21 November 2024

P27   Prof. Herman Joseph S. Kraft, University of the Philippines Diliman, 22 November 2024

P28   Filipino scholar, Manila, 22 November 2024

P29   former government official during the Duterte administration, Manila, 23 November 2024

P30   Filipino scholar, Manila, 23 November 2024

P31   Filipino academic, Manila, 27 November 2024

P32   Filipino academic, Manila, 27 November 2024

P33   former Filipino justice, Manila, 27 November 2024

P34   Marites Danguilan Vitug, editor at large, *Rappler*, Manila, 28 November 2024

P35   Filipino academic, Manila, 28 November 2024

P36   Filipino academic, Manila, 28 November 2024

Turkey

T01   Turkish academic, Istanbul, 8 March 2023

T02   Prof. Emre Erşen, Marmara University, Istanbul, 9 March 2023

T03   Prof. Semra Cerit Mazlum, Marmara University, Istanbul, 9 March 2023

T04   retired Turkish diplomat, Istanbul, 23 March 2023

1
Introduction

What are the implications of the rise of populist governments all over the world for international affairs? Prominent episodes from the recent past like US President Donald Trump's plans to occupy Greenland, the Panama Canal, and Gaza or his retreat from the Paris Agreement on climate change, suggest that populists, once elected, subvert traditional foreign policy stances and overthrow pre-existing international commitments. Populist governments are often considered to reject multilateralism and global governance and to pursue less cooperative foreign policies than their non-populist predecessors. At first glance, the global rise of populism therefore has the potential to change world politics profoundly. Indeed, populism has been labelled as one of the most fundamental challenges to the principles and institutions of the 'liberal international order' (Lake, Martin, and Risse 2021; Adler-Nissen and Zarakol 2021; Börzel and Zürn 2021, 2; Colgan and Keohane 2017; Jahn 2018; Bunde et al. 2017). At the same time, a closer look at populists in power calls for a more nuanced assessment. Ultimately, as of 2025, only the UK has left the European Union, despite widespread Euroscepticism and criticism of European integration among several European right- and left-wing populist parties and governments, and recurring fears of a 'Grexit', 'Italexit', or 'Polexit' (Szczerbiak 2017). Venezuela's Hugo Chávez used the UN General Assembly as a stage for his anti-US rants, but he did not call into question the usefulness of multilateralism and created new regional organizations to strengthen his influence in Latin America. Similarly, not all populists have undermined climate change mitigation: while former right-wing populist Brazilian President Jair Bolsonaro was a climate change denialist, dismantling competent institutions (Queiroz-Stein et al. 2023), India's right-wing populist Prime Minister Narendra Modi promoted renewable energies.

Clearly, populism has become a phenomenon that matters in international politics. At the same time, as these examples show, there seems to be considerable variation in how populists approach a range of foreign policy issues. Not all populist governments bring dramatic change to the foreign policies of their countries, nor do they all follow a Trumpian 'populist playbook' in international affairs. While the literature on the international dimensions of

Populism and Foreign Policy. Sandra Destradi and Johannes Plagemann, Oxford University Press.
© Oxford University Press (2025). DOI: 10.1093/9780197695012.003.0001

populism has been burgeoning in recent years, we still lack a systematic effort at theorizing what is distinctive of the foreign policies of populist governments. This book aims to fill this gap. It asks the following question: *how and why does the formation of populist governments lead to changes in foreign policy?* Its key contention is that, to understand how populism impacts world politics, we need a better understanding of what is distinctive of the foreign policies of populists in the first place. To this end, we explore changes brought about by populists after they come to power and form governments. In fact, while it has been shown that populist parties, even in the opposition, have ample influence on political discourses, societal polarization, and indirectly also on the policies of mainstream parties in government (Rooduijn 2014; Rooduijn, de Lange, and van der Brug 2014), the most direct impact on foreign policy will be observed if populists are in government and thus have the means to directly steer their countries' foreign policy course.

The Study of the International Dimensions of Populism: A Rapidly Growing Field

Until recently, populism was almost exclusively discussed in the fields of Comparative Politics and Political Theory. Since the 1960s, comparativists and political theorists had been exploring alternative conceptualizations of populism as well as its consequences for domestic politics, often with reference to Latin American cases (Germani 1978; Hofstadter 1965; Ionescu and Gellner 1969; Laclau 1977; for overviews, see Moffitt 2020; Mudde and Rovira Kaltwasser 2017). Thus, although populists had been in power time and again in various world regions since then—from the second wave of populism in Latin America in the 1990s to prominent figures like Silvio Berlusconi in Italy in the 1990s or Hugo Chávez in Venezuela in the 2000s— the question of how populist rule impacts foreign policy remained surprisingly unaddressed for decades. It was only in 2017 that some first systematic attempts at analysing the peculiarities of populist foreign policy were published (Verbeek and Zaslove 2017; Chryssogelos 2017).[1] From then onwards, the field has literally boomed. As Wajner and Giurlando (2024) show in their mapping of this developing research programme, the number of publications on populism and foreign policy exploded after the BREXIT referendum and the US presidential election of Donald Trump in 2016. Special issues or

---

[1] Two exceptions are a study of the foreign policy preferences of right-wing populist parties in Europe edited by Liang (2007a) and an analysis of the Lega's influence on foreign policy as a populist junior coalition partner in Italy by Verbeek and Zaslove (2015).

forums on the international dimensions of populism were published in *Comparative European Politics* (Destradi, Cadier, and Plagemann 2021), *British Journal of Politics and International Relations* (Löfflmann 2022b), *Política. Revista de Ciencia Política* (Escudero and Wehner 2022), *International Studies Review* (Chryssogelos et al. 2023), and *International Affairs* (Wajner, Destradi, and Zürn 2024). Moreover, three edited volumes collected case studies of populist foreign policy in different world regions (Stengel, MacDonald, and Nabers 2019; Giurlando and Wajner 2023), one of them with a distinctive focus on populist communication in international politics (Lacatus, Meibauer, and Löfflmann 2023), and a handbook of populism and foreign policy summarizes findings around theoretical approaches, actors, and factors in the foreign policy of populists (Cadier, Chryssogelos, and Destradi 2025).

Over the past years, the field has developed in manifold directions, making important theoretical advances into issues such as the relationships between populism and nationalism and how this impacts foreign policy revisionism (Jenne 2021); how populists relate to international courts (Voeten 2020) and international institutions more broadly, and under what conditions they delegitimize them (Söderbaum, Spandler, and Pacciardi 2021; Spandler and Söderbaum 2023; Pacciardi, Spandler, and Söderbaum 2024); or how populism affects the development of grand strategies (Krebs 2021). Some studies have addressed in greater depth issues like populists' discursive use of history to justify their foreign policies (Cadier and Szulecki 2020) or the impact of populism on foreign policy issue areas such as defence (Henke and Maher 2021; Ceccorulli, Coticchia, and Gianfreda 2023) or trade policy (Skonieczny 2018; Meislová and Chryssogelos 2024; Skonieczny and Sherel 2024). Large parts of this literature have worked with single case studies or with small-N comparisons, drawing on a broad range of world regions, from Latin America (Wajner 2021; Wajner and Wehner 2023; Wehner and Thies 2021; De Sá Guimarães and De Oliveira E Silva 2021; Wajner and Roniger 2019; Farias, Casarões, and Wajner 2024) to Europe (Coticchia and Vignoli 2020; Diodato and Niglia 2019; Cadier 2021; Monteleone 2021; Chryssogelos 2021; Giurlando 2021; Visnovitz and Jenne 2021; Giurlando and Monteleone 2024) to South and Southeast Asia (Plagemann and Destradi 2019; Arugay 2022; Magcamit and Arugay 2024) and the Middle East (Taş 2020; Holliday 2019), but rarely venturing into cross-regional comparisons to detect broader patterns (among the exceptions are Söderbaum, Spandler, and Pacciardi 2021; Spandler and Söderbaum 2023; Destradi and Plagemann 2019; Özdamar and Yanik 2024; Destradi and Plagemann 2024). Moreover, given the prominence of the case, a large number of analyses have focused on the first Trump administration (Wojczewski 2020c; Löfflmann 2022a; Lacatus 2021; Boucher and Thies 2019), even if drawing conclusions from this very peculiar case for populist foreign policy more generally is risky. In any case, the burgeoning literature on the international effects of populism has so far not been able to identify what a genuinely 'populist foreign policy' would consist of.

However, research by scholars from different theoretical traditions and focusing on various world regions is coalescing around two broad themes that relate to how foreign policy is made in populist governments, and which also form the basis of the theoretical framework of this book: *mobilization* and *personalization*.

In fact, one topic on which there is some broad agreement in the recent literature also in terms of empirical findings is the deep interconnectedness between domestic politics and foreign policy under populist governments. For instance, Wajner (2022) highlights how populists use foreign policy to bolster their domestic legitimacy, and Cadier (2024) shows that populists end up using foreign policy issues in their domestic discourse, thus politicizing foreign policy in different ways: according to him, populist foreign policy is a 'continuation of domestic politics by other means'. Destradi et al. (2022) have shown that populist politicization of foreign policy can take different shapes, depending on whether the people-centric or the anti-elitist dimension of populism is emphasized. Studies in the discursive tradition have analysed how populists construct the 'people' in opposition to various domestic and foreign 'others', thereby also addressing how international issues are deeply intertwined with domestic politics (Wojczewski 2020b; 2023; 2020a; Löfflmann 2022a; Subotic 2022; Bonansinga 2022). Thus, despite differences in ontology and epistemology, there is an agreement that one characteristic of populist foreign policy is a stronger-than-usual link between the domestic and the international, with populists literally bringing foreign policy to the people.

The second emerging area of agreement among scholars studying the international implications of populism concerns the more procedural aspects of how foreign policy is made, and by whom. In line with much research from Comparative Politics and Political Theory (see Chapter 2), recent studies have highlighted the centrality of individual leaders in decision-making processes, pointing towards a stronger-than-usual personalization in how decisions are made by populists (Destradi and Plagemann 2019; Özdamar and Yanik 2024). Several scholars have started applying approaches from the Foreign Policy Analysis tradition to the study of populist foreign policy, asking about individual populist leaders' leadership traits (Thiers and

Wehner 2022; Fouquet and Brummer 2023), operational codes (Özdamar and Ceydilek 2020), or roles and national identity conceptions (Friedrichs 2022; Wehner 2023). At the same time, a number of studies have dealt with how populist governments reshape foreign policy bureaucracies, usually marginalizing diplomats and experts. For example, Drezner (2019) traced efforts at dismantling the State Department during Trump's first presidency and Lequesne (2021) analysed variations in European populist governments' efforts towards marginalizing 'elitist' diplomats via the political capture of foreign ministries. A different strand of research, which builds on theorizations of populism as a 'style' (Moffitt 2016; Moffitt and Tormey 2014), has started to look into the performative aspects in populist leaders' foreign policy and discourses about international issues (Lacatus and Meibauer 2022; Aiolfi 2023). Also in this case, scholars from different theoretical and methodological traditions, working with various understandings of populism, ultimately concur in the assessment about a feature of populists' foreign policies: that leaders will play a disproportionate role in shaping foreign policy in populist governments, and that this will marginalize other actors such as traditional foreign policy bureaucracies. The purpose of this book is to build upon these insights, and to bring them together by developing a novel theory able to explain commonalities and differences in populists' foreign policies across space, time, and issue areas.

Theorizing Populist Foreign Policy

To theorize populist foreign policy, we proceeded in an abductive way. Abduction is a particularly useful approach to theorizing that combines deduction and induction in an iterative way (Tavory and Timmermans 2014). This means that, in several rounds of hypothesis testing and theorizing via a back-and-forth between theory and empirical data, a theoretical framework is progressively refined. As it is applied to a growing number of cases, the theory is modified, and new insights are integrated into it in the course of the research process. In fact, this book is the outcome of a longer research process, which started from the development of some basic hypotheses on the impact of populism on foreign policy, for which we carried out a first plausibility probe with the case of India (Plagemann and Destradi 2019). On that basis, we refined our hypotheses, and via a first comparative analysis of populist governments' foreign policies in India, the Philippines, Turkey, and Venezuela, we identified some contextual conditions that help make sense of variations in populists' foreign policy. Moreover, we found that the personalization and centralization of decision making are important common traits of populists' foreign policies, which lead to some degree of unpredictability (Destradi and Plagemann 2019). At the same time, our early work also alerted us to the importance of international context conditions shaping a populist's foreign policy repertoire. On the basis of those initial findings, in this book we develop our theory of populist foreign policy and we test the expectations derived from it in four detailed cases, each of which includes the transition from a non-populist to a populist government. Moreover, as another step in our abductive research process, in Chapter 7 we contrast our findings from cases in the Global South with a set of European cases (see below).

In line with much contemporary research, we understand populism in ideational terms. More specifically, populism for us is a 'thin-centered ideology' (Mudde 2004a, 544), a set of few core ideas about what society should look like (as opposed to a full-fledged, 'thick' ideology). According to this conceptualization, populism is 'an ideology that considers society to be ultimately separated into two homogeneous and antagonistic groups, "the pure people" versus "the corrupt elite", and which argues that politics should be an expression of the volonté générale (general will) of the people' (Mudde 2004a, 543, emphasis removed). This thin-centred ideology is usually combined with an accompanying 'thick' ideology such as socialism or some variant of ethno-nationalism (e.g., Hindu nationalism or Muslim nationalism). We believe this parsimonious ideational understanding of populism is particularly well suited to develop concrete expectations about how populism impacts foreign policy change. At the same time, as we discuss in more detail in Chapter 2, alternative conceptualizations of populism—for example, as a discourse, strategy, or style—would not lead to radically different expectations about how populism plays out in foreign policy (Destradi, Cadier, and Plagemann 2021).

The question guiding this book is: *How and why does the formation of populist governments lead to changes in foreign policy?* Thus, we want to explain foreign policy change, and our theory of populist foreign policy focuses on the different ways in which the formation of populist governments (*explanans*) leads to changes in foreign policy (*explanandum*). In a nutshell, our theory argues that populism in power will lead to changes in foreign policy that derive from the very features of populism as a thin-centred ideology (people-centrism and anti-elitism). Among the many aspects and issue areas of foreign policy, we focus on four broad fields, in which populism is sometimes expected to lead to major disruptions: conflict behaviour, and especially the escalation of bilateral disputes; contributions to global governance, and specifically the readiness to provide global public goods; approaches to multilateralism, focusing on engagements in international institutions; and a reorientation of their countries' international partnerships towards fellow populist as well as authoritarian governments. In terms of the classic typology of foreign policy change by Hermann (1990), for the first three issue areas, we mostly focus on 'program changes', that is, on shifts 'in the methods or means by which the goal or problem is addressed' (Hermann 1990, 5) after populist government formation, but we also differentiate intensities of change. In the last field, addressed in Chapter 6, we analyse under what conditions populism brings about broader shifts in a country's 'international orientation' (Hermann 1990, 5–6), distinguishing between partial and radical reorientation.

Overall, based on the definition of populism as a thin-centred ideology, we expect a country's foreign policy to change after populists come to power, and specifically to become more confrontational (conflict behaviour), more 'egoistic' (global public goods), more sovereigntist (multilateralism), and more independent (diversification of partnerships, reduction of dependence on traditional partners or allies)—in line with the preliminary theorizing we did in our previous work (Plagemann and Destradi 2019; Destradi and Plagemann 2019; Destradi, Cadier, and Plagemann 2021). However, as we briefly illustrated above, these changes do not take place in the same way across the board: not all populists are always more belligerent or less willing to compromise, not all of them refuse to contribute to global public goods or indiscriminately undermine international institutions, and not all populists have aligned with Russia and China in some sort of populist-authoritarian 'international'. We argue that, to make sense of these variations, we need to take into account how foreign policy decisions are made by populist governments. We therefore base our theoretical framework on the two features that have been identified as being characteristic of populist foreign policy making: personalization and mobilization. More specifically, we argue that variations in the intensities of mobilization and personalization explain variations in the intensity of foreign policy change under populist governments across different fields. The combination of these two mechanisms also captures populism's democratic ambiguity and its repercussions for foreign policy: whereas mobilization refers to populists' desire to rally public support, personalization refers to their dislike of intermediating institutions and democratic oversight. It is indeed this ambiguity that warrants an original theory of populist foreign policy.

Mobilization is a key feature of populist foreign policy not the least because, as the literature on populism has argued, populists in power are forced to find new ways of generating support after they have become themselves the much-despised political 'elite'. Since populists' goal is to get re-elected, they are continuously on the campaign trail, even after having formed a government (Urbinati 2019a; J.-W. Müller 2016). Foreign policy issues are well suited for mobilization as they easily allow to rally support by pitting the 'people' against some external 'other' connected to domestic elites, or by claiming that contributions to global governance or to multilateral institutions undermine putting the people 'first'. As populist mobilization promises to break with the establishment's past policies, calling for changes in foreign policy is a likely consequence. The often elitist nature of foreign policy and the actors traditionally involved in crafting it may pose another reason for populists to visibly change its course. At the same time, populists who use a foreign policy issue to mobilize support will need to follow up on the expectations they generated among the public if they want to remain credible. Mobilization can thus be a powerful impetus for foreign policy change. Variations in mobilization around foreign policy issues can be driven by the salience of specific issues to the domestic public. Moreover, they will depend on how well certain issues resonate with populists' thin and thick ideologies, as mobilization will only work well if it relates to the more general set of ideas and policy justifications propagated by populists.

Personalization, in turn, is the other important trend in populist decision making. It relates to populists' peculiar understanding of democratic representation as 'embodiment' of the popular will—something that will ultimately weaken democratic institutions. Like mobilization, personalization can be a powerful driver of change in foreign policy: leaders who take decision making in their own hands sideline traditional bureaucracies. They will thus be less constrained by them and they will be less exposed to alternative viewpoints expressed by foreign policy advisors and experts. Typically, they present themselves as men of action who do not shy away from difficult decisions based on 'common sense solutions' (Mudde and Rovira Kaltwasser 2017, 64). In other words, personalized leadership involves marginalizing precisely those actors who usually stand for continuity and moderation in foreign policy. Thus, it makes foreign policy change more likely. While we expect populist leaders to personalize foreign policy decision making more than non-populist leaders, there are variations in personalization across issues. These depend on how much interest a leader takes in a specific issue but also on the ability of foreign policy bureaucracies to resist excessive personalization and to constrain the leader.

In any case, we expect foreign policy under populist governments to be both more personalized and more prone to be used for mobilization purposes than under non-populist governments. Yet, mobilization and personalization each occur to different degrees. Depending on the combination of mobilization and personalization, we expect different intensities of foreign policy change in each issue area. While the intensities of mobilization, personalization, and foreign policy change should be thought of as continuums, in Chapter 2 we propose a simplified model that expects strong foreign policy change to occur if both mobilization and personalization are strong. In such cases, the leader is less constrained, and the issue lends itself for populist mobilization along the lines of thin and thick ideology. If only either personalization or mobilization is strong but the other dimensions is weak, we expect foreign policy change to be less pronounced. Finally, our theoretical model also allows us to explain instances of foreign policy continuity after the formation of populist governments. This is the case if neither mobilization nor personalization is strong—for example, in issue areas that do not matter much, neither to the public nor to the leader. This allows us to make sense of those instances in which populists' foreign policy continues as 'business as usual', for example on technical matters, or in uncontentious bilateral relations with far-away states, or when it comes to membership in issue-specific international organizations that do not have the potential to impinge on state sovereignty.

Our theory of populist foreign policy develops testable hypotheses and predictions about the kind and intensity of foreign policy change that we can expect under populist governments. Importantly, we also consider contextual factors that influence populist governments' ability to introduce changes in foreign policy. A key context condition is a populist government's perception of its own vulnerability in international politics. As in other theories of foreign policy, we assume that a state's perception of its relative strength affects its foreign behaviour. In fact, populists are political entrepreneurs, and as such, they are unlikely to pursue entirely erratic and irrational policies that are bound to politically harm them. As a consequence, for instance, it is unlikely that they will escalate militarily a bilateral conflict with a clearly superior adversary, even if this could be valuable for mobilization purposes in the short term. This implies that populist mobilization and the personalization of foreign policy play out more forcefully (and foreign policy change will be more intense) in strong states, where governments feel less restrained, than in weaker ones. We return to this in the Conclusion.

Empirical Analysis

After outlining in greater detail our theory of populist foreign policy in Chapter 2, we move on to apply it to the empirical analysis of foreign policy change in four broad issue areas: conflict behaviour (Chapter 3), contributions to global governance (Chapter 4), approaches to multilateralism (Chapter 5), and the reorientation of international partnerships (Chapter 6). In each chapter, we focus on transitions from non-populist to populist governments in four countries: Bolivia, India, the Philippines, and Turkey. In order to identify how populism impacted foreign policy change, we perform in-depth qualitative within-case comparisons between non-populist and populist governments for each of these countries, as well as a cross-case and cross-regional comparison among them for each issue area.

We deliberately focus our main empirical analysis on cases from the Global South, as populism has become a truly global phenomenon but large parts of existing research are still focused on cases from the Global North, most notably Trump's United States and (mostly right-wing) populism in Europe. We thus aim to move beyond the still-conventional canon of theorizing based on Global North cases and mostly just applying such theories to the Global South. Moreover, the presidency of Evo Morales in Bolivia, the governments led by Prime Minister Narendra Modi in India, the presidency of Rodrigo Duterte in the Philippines, and large parts of the rule of Recep Tayyip Erdoğan in Turkey are particularly prominent and undisputed cases of populism in power (see below).[2]

We explicitly chose cases that display a high amount of variation along several theoretically relevant dimensions. First of all, these cases belong to four different world regions: South America, South Asia, Southeast Asia, and the Middle East. Further, they display different thick ideologies that are combined with populism: socialism in the case of Bolivia's President Morales and his Movimiento al Socialismo (MAS); different right-wing ideologies (Hindu nationalism in the case of Modi's Bharatiya Janata Party, BJP, in India; Muslim nationalism in the case of Erdoğan's Adalet ve Kalkınma Partisi, AKP, in Turkey); and one case with an inconsistent and unclear thick ideology (Duterte in the Philippines). By focusing on cases with varying thick ideologies we aim to identify what is common to populists, and to theorize the impact of populism 'as such' (that is, not just of right- or left-wing populism) on foreign policy. Our four countries also occupy very different

---

[2] We validated our qualitative assessments by taking into consideration the populism index in the Varieties of Party Identity and Organization (V-Party) data set (Lührmann et al. 2020). The populism index directly relates to the definition of populism as thin-centred ideology as it entails both anti-elitism and people-centrism. The data derive from an expert survey assessing each party's position on the basis of documents such as election manifestos, press releases, official speeches, and media interviews (see Lührmann et al. 2020 for more information). For an opposing view on the selected cases, see Pappas (2019, 4): To him, Duterte, Modi, and Erdoğan are not representative of what he calls 'modern populism' as they operate within political systems in which 'political liberalism never put down roots' (Philippines, India) or which, according to Pappas, never qualified as democratic (Turkey). Hence, they are not considered comparable to populists in Europe or the Americas. We argue, by contrast, that the definition of populism as a thin-centred ideology can be applied to them.

positions in the international system, from a comparatively small state with limited international reach, Bolivia; to an important regional player such as the Philippines; to Turkey and India, both powers aspiring for a more prominent global role. Also, the degree of authority ceded to international organizations by these countries varies. Turkey is a member of NATO and held accession talks with the European Union during the period analysed; the Philippines and Bolivia are members of comparatively active regional organizations; while India's region, South Asia, is the world's least institutionalized. Moreover, the populists in power differed in terms of their forms of government, with presidential (Bolivia, the Philippines, Turkey since the transition to a presidential system in 2018) and parliamentary systems (India, Turkey until 2018). Besides, they also differed in terms of their duration in power, with Duterte serving a single six-year term (in line with the Philippines' Constitution) and the other populist leaders being in power for longer time periods.[3] At the end of this chapter, we introduce the defining features of the non-populist and populist governments analysed for the four countries, providing some more detail on populists' thick ideologies, their understandings of the 'people' and the 'elite', as well as an assessment of their overall levels of personalization of decision making.

In our qualitative analyses of foreign policy change under populist governments in Bolivia, India, the Philippines, and Turkey we sought to identify to what extent foreign policy change was driven by different degrees of mobilization and personalization. To perform this kind of analysis, deep insights into the single cases are required. We had the opportunity to delve into our four empirical country cases thanks to a grant by the German Research Foundation, which allowed us to work with a team of native-speaking research assistants, junior scholars, and more senior colleagues with profound expertise on the four countries. Together, our project team members supported us with the collection and analysis of data in Spanish, Hindi, Tagalog, and Turkish. Besides primary sources from the respective governments, from international organizations, national and international media, as well as publications by think tanks and the secondary literature, we gathered new primary data via expert interviews. We had the privilege of carrying out a total of 114 interviews with experts, both on-site, including in the context of extensive field research, as well as remotely. Among the experts interviewed were high-ranking serving and former government officials, retired diplomats, academics, journalists, members of NGOs, and civil society activists.

---

[3] Yet, we paid attention to select only contemporary or recent cases of populists in power since historical cases with grossly different context conditions (e.g., alliance systems in the Cold War) would have included different constraints that would have limited the applicability of findings to current international affairs.

We used the expert interviews to complement other data, for instance by gaining more immediate insights into the processes of foreign policy decision making, and to discuss alternative hypotheses and explanations along our abductive research process. The possibility of carrying out interviews varied depending on the local context, with access to interviewees being particularly difficult in India and Turkey due to tighter government control, suspicion of foreign assessments of the respective governments' performance, and growing limitations to academic freedom. Luckily, those were the cases for which there is greater availability of secondary literature. Conversely, we gained extensive insights from thirty interviews with experts and (former) foreign policy decision makers for the case of Bolivia, thus complementing the otherwise scarce secondary literature. In the Philippines, too, our interviews include several former officials immediately involved in President Duterte's inner decision-making circle. All interviewees expressed their consent to the interview. We anonymized all interviews, with the exception of those for which we were explicitly given the consent to mention the interviewee's name. For the interviews performed in foreign languages, as well as for all other non-English sources, the translations are ours or by our team members. For the analysis of non-populist and populist governments' approaches to the United Nations in Chapter 5, we also performed a qualitative content analysis (Schreier 2012) of all speeches given during the relevant time periods by the representatives of our four main country cases at the UN General Assembly.

Finally, in response to the insights from the application of our theoretical framework to Bolivia, India, the Philippines, and Turkey, we added another step in our abductive process of theory building. In Chapter 7, we discuss our theory's applicability beyond our cases from the Global South, and if it maintains its explanatory power when it comes to analysing populist governments in the Global North. We do so by contrasting our findings with additional analyses of transitions to populist governments in three European countries: to the right-wing populist government of Viktor Orbán in Hungary (2010–2024), to the government of Boris Johnson in the UK (2019–2022), and to the all-populist 'yellow-green' alliance government in Italy (2018–2019). By including additional findings from a diverse set of cases that were not part of our theorizing previously, we improve our empirical work's overall persuasion. In the Conclusion (Chapter 8), we discuss how empirical insights from these very diverse sets of cases confirm the overall explanatory power of our theory, but also which contextual factors need to be taken into account to make sense of cases that do not conform to our expectations. Finally, we outline avenues for the further development of the research programme on the international dimensions and effects of populism.

Introducing Populist Governments: Bolivia, India, the Philippines, and Turkey

We want to theorize the impact of populism on foreign policy change. Thus, we compare the policies of populist governments with those of their non-populist predecessors in the cases of Bolivia, India, the Philippines, and Turkey. Table 1.1 provides an overview of the non-populist and populist governments studied in the four countries.

Table 1.1 Populist governments and non-populist predecessors

	Period	Government
Bolivia	2002–2006	Presidents Gonzalo Sánchez de Lozada, Carlos Mesa (both from Movimiento Nacionalista Revolucionario, MNR), and Eduardo Rodríguez Veltzé (independent)
	2006–2019	President Evo Morales (Movimiento al Socialismo, MAS)
India	2004–2014	Prime Minister Manmohan Singh (Indian National Congress, INC)/United Progressive Alliance (UPA I and II)
	2014–2024	Prime Minister Narendra Modi (Bharatiya Janata Party, BJP)/National Democratic Alliance (NDA I and II)
The Philippines	2010–2016	President Benigno Aquino III (Liberal Party)
	2016–2022	President Rodrigo Duterte (Partido Demokratiko Pilipino—Lakas ng Bayan, PDP)
Turkey	1999–2002	Prime Minister Bülent Ecevit (Democratic Left Party)/ANASOL-M coalition
	2003–2011	Prime Minister Recep Tayyip Erdoğan, non-populist phase (Adalet ve Kalkınma Partisi, AKP)
	2011–2014	Prime Minister Erdoğan, AKP
	2014–2018	President Erdoğan, AKP
	Since 2018	Executive President Erdoğan, AKP

Bolivia

In the case of Bolivia, our focus is on the populist presidency of Juan Evo Morales Ayma of the Movimiento al Socialismo (MAS) (2006–2019). In 2005, the MAS was the first party to win a single-party majority (53% in the first round) in a national election since the restoration of democracy in Bolivia in the 1980s. The MAS had been founded ten years earlier by peasant unions and had a strong support base among coca growers from the central region of Cochabamba (Grisaffi 2019; Anria 2019; Zuazo 2009). The campaign that brought Morales to power in 2006 had circulated around topics such as the defence of indigenous rights and an increase in their political representation, the nationalization of natural gas fields and other strategic assets, and the redistribution of wealth via direct transfers.

Bolivia under Morales is almost a textbook example of left-wing populism (Carrión 2022, 16). Morales claimed to speak in the name of the 'people', identified as marginalized indigenous communities and the poorer sections of the population, with a particular focus on the community of coca grow-ers. In his discourse, this 'people' was opposed to an elite represented by the established political parties that had been governing the country up to that point and that had been relying on neo-liberal policies, coca-eradication cam-paigns, and cooperation with the United States. Relatedly, as we will discuss in greater detail in the empirical analysis, the 'elite' was also projected to the international level, with the United States and other great powers depicted as imperialist actors aiming to subjugate the deprived people in South Amer-ica and beyond. Morales's speech at the UN General Assembly in 2014 is illustrative:

> We must eradicate violence and war and denounce the imperialist warmongering of the world Powers that arrogantly believe they embody the ideals of freedom. The imperial Powers use their communication media to manipulate the wills and the emotions of the people. They lie and deceive with impunity. They divide and pit nations and communities against one another to promote wars, control strate-gic resources and put them at the service of their foreign capitals. (United Nations General Assembly 2014, 3–4)

The MAS's socialist thick ideology gave a clear imprint to the definition of the 'people' and the 'elite' in Morales's populism, and one that already entailed an international dimension. Populist mobilization under Morales took place along the lines of his thin and thick ideology, which allowed the MAS to both mobilize support through bottom-up campaigning in rural areas, and in urban areas via more top-down mechanisms (Anria 2013, 21). At the same time, overall, decision making became more personalized even if, at first sight, this does not seem to be the case. In fact, the MAS introduced the notion of 'people's diplomacy' for a foreign policy directly reflecting the people's interests. Although ill-defined in practice, according to our interviews with senior diplomats under Morales, people's diplomacy foresaw the inclusion of social movements in the making and execution of Bolivia's foreign policy, especially in the environmental sector.[4] Moreover, in 2009 Morales introduced a new constitution that included a number of plebiscitary mechanisms as well as a recall provision for elected public officials by the Bolivian people (Wolff 2012). On foreign policy, the new constitution envisaged referendums for the approval of international treaties concerning border issues, monetary and economic integration, as well as the granting of authority to international institutions in processes of integration, or for any other issue if requested by 5 per cent of the electorate or 35 per cent of the representatives of the Pluri-National Legislative Assembly (Plurinational State of Bolivia 2009). Yet, despite these vertical control mechanisms, the new constitution ended up strengthening the executive branch and centralizing decision making (Schilling-Vacaflor 2011, 13). Thus, although the level of personalization varied across issues, overall our interviewees confirmed that on foreign matters, decision making under Morales was highly personalized (see Chapters 3–6). As the free press, the judiciary's independence, and other forms of democratic oversight deteriorated, Bolivia under Morales's 'caudillo-style leadership shifted toward authoritarianism and a politics of division that ultimately led to his ouster as president' (McKay and Colque 2021, 1) in 2019.

To assess whether Bolivia's foreign policy changed under Morales's populist government, we compare his foreign policies with those under the preceding non-populist presidencies of Gonzalo Sánchez de Lozada, elected in 2002, his successor Carlos Mesa in power until June 2005, and Eduardo Rodríguez Veltzé, the Supreme Court's chief justice who took over from the unpopular Mesa on an interim-basis to hold elections. Together, these three presidencies ultimately reflected the end of a long tradition of market-oriented policies that had been in place in Bolivia since the mid-1980s, sustained by an elite consensus often described as Bolivia's 'pacted democracy' (Carrión 2022, 64–68). They also stand for a particularly unstable period in Bolivian politics with unresponsive political institutions leading to massive civil society protests met by violent state repression (the so-called Gas Wars; see Chapter 3). In

---

[4] Interviews B04, senior career diplomat under Veltzé and Morales, La Paz, 16 January 2023; B13, acting senior diplomat, La Paz, 2 February 2023.

foreign policy terms, the predominantly white elites' dominance in Bolivia's politics throughout the preceding decades of Bolivia's 'pacted democracy' translated into a high degree of cooperation with the United States, especially in the field of counter-narcotics and concomitant efforts to eliminate the cultivation of coca. Further features of Bolivia's foreign policy during the years preceding Morales's rise to power were dependency on the IMF and World Bank given Bolivia's high foreign debt, cooperation in regional organizations, and efforts to achieve access to the ocean in a long-standing dispute with Chile (Crabtree 2013; Torres Armas 2004).

India

In the case of India, our analysis focuses on the right-wing populist government of Prime Minister Narendra Modi of the Bharatiya Janata Party (BJP). We address Modi's first two terms in office at the helm of the BJP-led National Democratic Alliance (NDA) coalition, that is, what are usually referred to as the NDA-I (2014–2019) and NDA-II (2019–2024) governments. We ask about changes in foreign policy as compared to the preceding decade (2004–2014), during which the Indian National Congress (INC) led the United Progressive Alliance I and II governments, with the economist Manmohan Singh as a prime minister. In fact, the contrast between the technocratic Singh and the populist Modi could not be starker. Anti-elitism was one of the core components of Modi's populism ever since he was a chief minister of the state of Gujarat. At that time, he referred to the central government led by the INC as the 'Delhi Sultanate' (Express News Service 2008), thus condemning the political establishment and associating it with historical Muslim invasions of India, a trope that resonated with his Hindu-nationalist thick ideology. The campaign that brought Modi to power in 2014 denounced the corruption of the political establishment of the INC, highlighting the dynastic character of that party, which had ruled India with only few interruptions since independence in 1947 (Chakravartty and Roy 2015). In particular, Modi mocked Rahul Gandhi, the INC's top candidate and a grand-grandson, grandson, and son of Indian prime ministers, as 'naamdaar' (dynast) (Ghose 2018) or 'shehzada' (prince of a Muslim dynasty) (Tharoor 2019). After coming to power, the idea of combatting corrupt and impure elites remained a key component of Modi's discourse. He stylized himself 'as the ultimate outsider to the elite establishment' (Roy 2024, 3), an ascetic celibate devoted exclusively to the service of the people, a self-made man, the son of a tea seller, who through hard work and perseverance managed to achieve the highest position in the country. To underscore the contrast with established elites, in 2016 Modi for example declared: 'On one hand, there are these intellectuals who talk about Harvard, and on the other, there is this son of a poor mother, who is trying to change the economy of the country through hard work' (quoted in Rodrigues and Pradhan 2017). At the same time, people-centrism and the notion of literally embodying the 'popular will' is evident in Modi's rhetoric, as for instance in one of his Independence Day speeches: 'I am merely an instrument. It is not one single person who makes that address, but it is the collective voice of 1.25 billion of my countrymen that resounds from the Red Fort. I try to give words to their dreams' (Modi 2017b). Ahead of the 2024 elections, Modi went so far as to hint at a possible divine character of his persona:

> When my mother was alive, I used to believe that I was born biologically. After she passed away, upon reflecting on all my experiences, I was convinced that God has sent me. This energy could not be from my biological body, but was bestowed upon me by God. I believe God has given me abilities, inspiration, and good intentions for a purpose. . . . I am nothing but an instrument. That's why, whenever I do anything, I believe god is guiding me. (The Wire Analysis 2024)

Direct communication with the 'people' was performed by Modi via a series of tools, from extensive use of social media (as of June 2024, Modi had 99.6 million followers on X), to his 'NaMo' (Narendra Modi) app, to monthly radio addresses called Mann Ki Baat ('talking from the heart') aimed at sections of the population who do not have access to the internet. After the BJP's electoral victory in 2014, all this led to another massive success for Modi in 2019, when his BJP won an absolute majority in the Lok Sabha, the lower house of Parliament. Albeit losing the BJP's absolute majority in the 2024 elections, Modi started his third term as prime minister with coalition partners in June 2024.

The thick ideology that Modi combined with his populism was Hindu nationalism, a variant of ethno-nationalism that identifies the true people with India's Hindu majority (Jaffrelot 2010; 2021). The notion of *Hindutva* ('Hinduness'), introduced in colonial times by ideologues like V. D. Savarkar and M. S. Gowalkar, ultimately equates India's nationhood with Hinduism, understood as a broad cultural-religious tradition (Rowe 2012, 132; Khilnani 2010). Several other aspects flow from this basic idea, including a claim of civilizational superiority, the idealization of a golden Vedic era preceding Muslim invasions (Jaffrelot 2010), but also fears of succumbing to Muslims (Jaffrelot 2021). Based on such ideology, a whole 'family' of Hindu-nationalist organizations (called Sangh Parivar) emerged in India, spearheaded by the Rashtriya Swayamsevak Sangh (RSS), a cadre-based movement founded in the 1920s, of which the BJP is the political arm. It was in the RSS that Narendra Modi's political formation took place (I. Hall 2021), and thus it is not surprising to see the influence of the organization throughout Modi's terms in office, with RSS members being appointed to leadership positions in all fields (Andersen and Damle 2019; O'Brien 2024).

Overall, decision making under Modi became much more personalized than it had been before—and this despite a long tradition of personalized decision making on foreign policy matters in India, which dates back to the times of Jawaharlal Nehru, the country's founding father and first prime minister (as well as minister of external affairs), who decisively shaped India's Cold War foreign policy (I. Hall 2019). While the BJP, a relatively well organized party from the outset, and the wider Hindu-nationalist eco-system were essential for campaigning, once in power Modi's personal authority was clearly stronger than party networks (Jaffrelot and Tillin 2017, 187). In fact, Modi personalized and centralized decision making. This was confirmed by all our interviewees, who pointed to a 'presidentialization' of power under Modi.[5] Decision making on foreign policy issues was also centralized in the Prime Minister's Office, and Modi consulted closely mostly with Minister of External Affairs Subrahmanyam Jaishankar and with National Security Advisor Ajit Doval.[6] The appointment of Jaishankar, described by one of our interviewees as 'a career diplomat, a cosmopolitan, not exactly part of the [Hindu-nationalist] family',[7] as minister of external affairs in 2019 seems to contradict our expectation about populists marginalizing traditional foreign policy elites.[8] However, Jaishankar's elevation to Modi's inner decision-making circle did not increase the Ministry of External Affairs' (MEA) authority. In fact, the MEA was excluded from the most important foreign policy decisions.[9] Yet, according to some interviewees, the MEA did

---

[5] Interview I18, retired Indian diplomat, New Delhi, 7 March 2023.

[6] Interviews I17, European diplomat posted to India, New Delhi, 7 March 2023; I19, Indian academic, New Delhi, 8 March 2023.

[7] Interview I19.

[8] According to two Indian scholars interviewed, the BJP did not have qualified individuals to be appointed to important positions ('there are no good people in the party', Interview I21, Indian scholar, New Delhi, 9 March 2023), so Modi was forced to resort to the appointment of technocrats like Jaishankar (Interviews I21; I06, Indian scholar and observer, New Delhi, 28 February 2023). Another interviewee pointed to the fact that the nomination of Jaishankar was seen with much scepticism within the BJP since he did not come from the party (I03, Indian journalist, New Delhi, 22 February 2023).

[9] Interviews I02, Indian journalist, New Delhi, 21 February 2023; I08, retired Indian diplomat, New Delhi, 1 March 2023.

not entirely lose its relevance[10] and, despite tighter control by the Prime Minister's Office (PMO) and an unprecedented readiness by the government to remove senior bureaucrats ('something the previous governments would not have dared to do'[11]), 'normal diplomacy goes on'.[12] This all points precisely to the variations in the personalization of decision making that we study in more detail in Chapters 3–6. In any case, Modi deliberately marginalized India's more cosmopolitan, Nehruvian-inclined strategic community. In an interview with an expert on foreign policy carried out at the India International Centre, an elite club in Delhi where retired diplomats mingle with academics, jurists, former high-ranking army officers, and other members of the Indian capital's intelligentsia, an interviewee told us: '[Modi] has deliberately cut out the elite class. The people in this room now have nothing. They are not invited to government events, he does not come to their events, he doesn't meet them. They have been totally cut off. They suffer from a total loss of relevance'.[13] By contrast, the experts consulted by Modi were increasingly 'not Delhi-based [and] not necessarily English-speaking'.[14] Also traditionally influential think tanks were ignored or, according to the same interviewee, reduced to the role of event managers.[15]

Parallel to this personalization and centralization of foreign policy decision making, mobilization around foreign policy issues also became prevalent under the Modi government. We assess in greater detail how this played out in various fields in Chapters 3–6. Suffice to say here that Modi in his public appearances emphasized those foreign policy activities that highlighted India's global status. Thereby Modi brought foreign policy—or aspects of it—to the people. As one Indian scholar told us in Delhi:

> As a smart politician, [Modi] realized the value of foreign policy for domestic projection. Immediately after he came to power, he brought foreign policy 'out of Delhi'. He went to Ahmedabad with Xi Jinping, took Abe to Benares, the BRICS meeting was in Goa. He met Xi Jinping in Chennai. In Delhi, people are used to such visits, but in the rest of the country, it makes a difference.[16]

At the same time, as a journalist interviewed put it, foreign policy became focused on 'what works. We only look at success stories'—another form of

---

[10] Interviews I19, Indian academic, New Delhi, 8 March 2023; I21.

[11] Interview I18.

[12] Interview I18.

[13] Interview I01, expert on India's foreign policy, New Delhi, 20 February 2023.

[14] Interview I18

[15] Interview I18.

[16] Interview I06.

prioritization by a populist leader with a carefully cultivated image as a competent manager.[17]

Philippines

In the Philippines, the election of President Rodrigo Duterte in 2016 marked the return to a populist government after a non-populist phase under President Benigno Aquino III, in power from 2010 to 2016. A former mayor of Davao City on the southern island of Mindanao, Duterte presented himself as an outsider of the Manila-based political elite and as the only leader strong enough to save the country from crime and drug abuse (Timberman 2019). In fact, his 'war on drugs' was his signature policy agenda, which also shaped his understanding of the 'people'. In his view, the main danger to the people of the Philippines, and the main internal enemy, were drug dealers as well as drug users, who would have to be combatted with all means, even if that implied violating human rights (Canovan 1999; Curato 2016; C. Ramos 2020). Duterte went so far as to call for citizens to execute drug users: 'If you know of any addicts, go ahead and kill them yourself' (Human Rights Watch 2017). Accordingly, Curato (2016) defines Duterte's approach as 'penal populism', with the leader trying to attract voters by focusing on the fight to criminality via short-term and punitive approaches. Ultimately, Duterte's brutal war on drugs killed between 12,000 and 30,000 civilians in the less than three years from July 2016 to March 2019 alone (The Economist 2021). The 'elite' in Duterte's discourse was mainly represented by the political establishment of the capital city Manila, sometimes called 'imperial Manila' to signify the intrusiveness of the central government. Compared to our other cases, however, the 'elite' in Duterte's populism remained somewhat nebulous. Besides the political establishment, it included the 'oligarchs'[18] who, enabled by the central government, controlled some mines near Davao City, which Duterte said was like 'fighting a monster' (Macaraig 2016). His attempt to curtail the capital's power via the introduction of federalism (Heydarian 2018), however, was not successful. Ultimately, as a prominent journalist we interviewed put it, 'The US was our enemy, [and] the drug lords'.[19]

While anti-elitism and people centrism are easier to identify, Duterte did not adhere to any coherent thick ideology. This is much in line with the

---

[17] Interview I02.

[18] Interview P36, Filipino academic, Manila, 28 November 2024.

[19] Interview P34, Marites Danguilan Vitug, editor at large, Rappler, Manila, 28 November 2024.

Philippines' politics and history, in which political parties in general display a low degree of ideological commitment and patronage politics is pervasive (Kenny 2020; Kreuzer 2020). Duterte himself had been a student of the founder of the Communist Party of the Philippines[20] and defined his ideology as socialist, stating: 'I am a socialist, not a communist. We, socialists, are for the people' (Cinco 2016). Yet, his economic policies were much in line with the neo-liberal approach followed by his predecessors (Thompson 2020, 8). At the same time, his emphasis on drugs and crime reflected an illiberal right-wing approach (Thompson 2016, 51; Heydarian 2017) labelled by some as 'Dutertismo' (David 2016). Ultimately, we argue that Duterte did not combine his populism with any clearly defined thick ideology. Instead, time and again, Duterte strategically combined ideological elements that can be attributed to the right and to the left in order to gain support from different domestic groups (Thompson 2016, 53).

As ruled by the Supreme Court of the Philippines, the president is the 'sole organ and authority in external relations' and the 'chief architect of foreign policy' (Supreme Court of the Philippines 2005). It is thus not surprising that Duterte played a key role in the foreign policy of the Philippines. Beyond such legal provisions, personalization as well as centralization were extremely strong, as confirmed by our interviews in the Philippines. For one, Duterte personally shaped foreign policy with his distinctive style and bad manners. Both contributed to his performance of the role as an outsider to high politics (McCargo 2016; Arugay 2022). However, the imprint of Duterte's personality on the Philippines' foreign policy went far beyond style. As an academic expert with close relations to key decision makers under Duterte told us: 'It's normal to expect that the [foreign policy] preferences would be affected by the [president's] personal desires and attitudes but what's different about Duterte was it was unmitigated and unrestrained'.[21] Consider that Duterte tried to change the most fundamental tenets of the Philippines' foreign policy single-handedly: in 2019, he introduced a new doctrine of 'independent' foreign policy (IFP), primarily driven by his dislike of the United States (see Chapter 3).[22] As explained to us by two cabinet members under Duterte, personalization shaped the way foreign policy was made.[23] For instance, the IFP 'was just suddenly declared. [. . .] It was more of the President thinking about it and then saying it to the media'.[24]

---

[20] Interview P36.

[21] Interview P05, Filipino scholar, Manila, 30 September 2022.

[22] Interview P13, senior government official, Manila, 12 October 2022.

[23] Interviews P01, former high-ranking government official, Manila, 26 September 2022; and P10, former high-ranking government official, Manila, 10 October 2022.

[24] Interview P10.

In fact, Duterte consulted few advisors, and even they were struggling to cope with his personalistic approach. According to the former member of cabinet: 'We couldn't address [Duterte] head-on because he might get angry. [. . .] We don't talk to him at the same time, we do it bilaterally'.[25] As a result, meetings of the National Security Council took a peculiar turn under Duterte, as recalled by a senior diplomat: 'Secretaries were actually avoiding the chances of [Duterte] talking about certain things. Because for them if Duterte said something on record then they would have difficulty in backing out. So you would just present something to him and you would immediately divert his attention. [. . .] Us there [in the Office of the President] were just surviving day to day. Every day was like "what fresh hell is this?"'[26]

A senior military official confirmed the observation. Whereas Aquino was willing to listen to expert advice, including by his cabinet, under Duterte secretaries would simply implement what the president instructed them to do: 'Whatever Duterte says, that's it. There is no advising happening because they were scared to talk'.[27] In fact, the personalization of decision making was paralleled by a weakening of most cabinet members (i.e., secretaries) and the Department of Foreign Affairs (DFA) in particular. Duterte appointed inexperienced Secretaries of Foreign Affairs (four of them in six years),[28] most notably including Alan Peter Cayetano (2017–2018), to whom the bureaucracy of the DFA reportedly was staunchly opposed (CNN 2018). At the same time, the president surrounded himself with a small group of advisors, mostly coming from Davao: 'It became an even smaller circle, with less deep expertise [. . .]. [And] some very influential Chinese individuals got into that circle'.[29] Meanwhile, established research institutes were increasingly sidelined, while numerous small pro-China think tanks 'popped up'.[30]

Naturally, personalization also determined the foreign policy issues the president would pay attention to—and which not. As laid out in more detail in Chapters 3–6, numerous issues failed to attract Duterte's interest and thus saw little change at all. Our interviewees agreed that Duterte generally had limited interest in foreign and strategic affairs and the IFP's genesis—devoid of wider debates or any written outline of its strategic contents—was exemplary of this.

---

[25] Interview P10.

[26] Interview P13.

[27] Interview P11, senior military official, Manila, 11 October 2022.

[28] By contrast, the secretary of national defense, Delfin Lorenzana, served a full six years.

[29] Interview P32, Filipino academic, Manila, 27 November 2024.

[30] Interview P31, Filipino academic, Manila, 27 November 2024.

Moreover, even in the issues dear to the president—for instance, security relations with China—state agencies, and especially mid-level bureaucracies and the military, retained a certain leeway in the implementation of foreign policy directives (see Chapter 3).[31]

Unlike what we describe for our other three cases, Duterte hardly used foreign policy for the mobilization of public support. For one, foreign policy has limited salience to most Filipinos. A prominent exception to this are matters related to Overseas Filipino Workers (OFW). As OFWs were an important constituency for Duterte, he spoke about their plight frequently, established a new ministry for them (the Department of Migrant Workers, DMW), and prominently included their concerns in his bilateral agenda with respective governments. Here, we see Duterte most closely in line with what our theory of populist foreign policy would lead us to expect. Another exception was his sensitivity to criticism of his war on drugs and related human rights violations. As laid out in more detail in Chapters 3 and 5, Duterte viciously attacked both international actors and individual country representatives in response. Finally, a key cause for the limited use of foreign policy for mobilization purposes was the lack of popularity that the changes he sought to bring about had with the wider public. In fact, his Independent Foreign Policy, his rapprochement with China, as well as, arguably, his abusive language vis-à-vis international organizations all stood in contrast to Filipinos' generally positive predispositions towards the West, their preference of the United States over China, and comparatively positive feeling towards international institutions (see Chapter 3–6).

The non-populist government to which we compare the presidency of Duterte is that of Benigno Simeon Aquino III of the Liberal Party, who was president between 2010 and 2016. Aquino came from a political dynasty that had been active in the Philippines for decades. During his presidency, the Philippines displayed remarkable growth rates, propelled by a range of policies addressing corruption, increasing transparency, and promoting sectors such as IT and business process outsourcing (Lanzona 2016; Schnabel 2016). In foreign policy, Aquino relied on the long-established alliance with the United States and resisted Chinese expansionism in the South China Sea by bringing a lingering maritime dispute with Beijing to the Permanent Court of Arbitration in The Hague (see Chapter 3).

---

[31] Interviews P34, P36; P35, Filipino academic, Manila, 28 November 2024.

Turkey

In the case of Turkey, our main focus is on Recep Tayyip Erdoğan of the Justice and Development Party (Adalet ve Kalkınma Partisi, AKP), who has profoundly reshaped Turkish politics since the early 2000s. Erdoğan served as prime minister from 2003 to 2007 (Erdoğan I),[32] from 2007 to 2011 (Erdoğan II), and from 2011 to 2014 (Erdoğan III). In 2014, Erdoğan became the first directly elected president, following a reform that was devised under his auspices. After a failed coup attempt in 2016, Erdoğan pushed for a constitutional referendum to replace the existing parliamentary system with a presidential one, removing the figure of the prime minister and concentrating executive power in the presidency. In April 2017, the referendum was held under a state of emergency and amid allegations of fraud (Adar and Seufert 2021), ultimately leading to the planned constitutional changes. After the presidential elections in 2018, Erdoğan took over the executive presidency, further consolidating his power. He was re-elected in 2023.

Erdoğan's populism combines people-centrism and anti-elitism with a thick ideology that has been labelled as Muslim nationalism (Jenny White 2013). The 'people' in the understanding of Erdoğan and of the AKP are Turkey's 'deprived ordinary people' (Özpek and Tanriverdi Yaşar 2018, 206), especially the Anatolians, who are pitted against 'Kemalist' elites supported by the military (Günay 2016; Cop and Zihnioğlu 2017)—with Kemalism referring to the republican, secular, statist, and modernist ideology established by the country's founding father Mustafa Kemal Atatürk (Mardin 1973). Over time, Erdoğan sought to eliminate the old elites, and especially the so-called system of 'tutelage' that had seen the Turkish military enjoy de facto veto powers and repeatedly intervene in Turkish politics since 1960 (Sakallioğlu 1997). Taking heed of the European Union's calls to curtail the military's say in Turkish politics, Erdoğan's predecessor as prime minister, the centre-left politician Bülent Ecevit, had already amended Article 118 of the Constitution to increase the number of civilian members of the National Security Council, a military-dominated organ overseeing Turkey's foreign and security policy. Erdoğan's government built upon such efforts by, for instance, reducing the council's executive authorities (Kars Kaynar 2017, 13).

After the Kemalist establishment challenged his government, among other things by the 2007 e-memorandum and the 2008 closure case at the

---

[32] The AKP came to power in 2002, but Erdoğan could only become prime minister on 14 March 2003, after Abdullah Gül, who had been the initially appointed prime minister, lifted a political ban on Erdoğan (Strategic Survey 2003).

Constitutional Court, Erdoğan's government reacted by launching criminal proceedings, most notably the 2008 'Ergenekon' and 2010 'Sledgehammer' trials, which saw hundreds of retired and active-duty military officers indicted on charges of plotting to topple the government. Reforms driven by the negotiations for accession to the European Union further contributed to limit the role of the military in politics (Balta 2018). In parallel, constitutional reforms following the 2010 constitutional referendum allowed the AKP government to alter the Kemalist dominance in the judiciary (Bechev 2022; Taş 2015). A potentially severe challenge to Erdoğan's rule came in 2013, when the Gezi protests erupted. What had started as a protest against an urban development plan in central Istanbul soon turned into a countrywide series of protests against the AKP government, ongoing democratic backsliding, and the erosion of individual freedoms and secularism. The protests, which took place between May and August 2013, overlapped with the fall of the Muslim Brotherhood–led government under Mohamed Morsi in Egypt—a political ally for Erdoğan—and the subsequent military coup there. It is thus not surprising that Erdoğan perceived the Gezi protest as a threat to his rule (Özkırımlı 2014).

There is some disagreement in the literature on Turkish politics as to whether Erdoğan was always a populist politician (Aytaç and Elçi 2019; Balta 2018; Taş 2022a), or whether he became populist at a later point. Ultimately, as we discuss in the following chapters with reference to concrete examples, changes were gradual. Yet, we argue that, during his first two governments, Erdoğan should not be considered a populist. We thus consider the period 2003–2010 as non-populist, and the years from 2011 onwards as populist. As Çınar puts it:

> during the first period, which roughly lasted until 2010/2011, the AKP represented a gradually fading hope for a genuinely moderate Muslim political force, advocating a non-authoritarian practice of secularism, furthering Turkey's alignment with the political norms of the European Union and pursuing a pro-Western foreign policy while maintaining an Islam-sensitive identity. At least since 2011 elections, however, the AKP has turned away from further democratization and undermined the existing electoral democracy in Turkey. It has adopted a populist vote-maximization strategy that does not make room for other gray shades in the socio-political realm. It has dismissed critics and opponents by disqualifying them as self-interested, ill-intended, illegitimate, unnecessary, redundant and manipulative. This was accompanied by a unilateralist, imposing, moralistic and combative political style that denigrated, if not interfered with, secular lifestyles. (2019, 176–77)

To further validate our assessment for the non-populist period, we include in our comparative analysis the non-populist, technocratic (but nationalist) ANASOL-M coalition government led by Bülent Ecevit of the Democratic Left Party (DSP), and also consisting of the Nationalist Movement Party (MHP) and the Motherland Party (ANAP) (1999–2002) (Balkan and Savran 2002; Kınıklıoğlu 2002; Örmeci 2011). Despite shifts and frictions in foreign policy, the ANASOL-M represented the last chain of the evolving traditional approach of the 'Old Turkey'—in other words, precisely the policies of the 'establishment' that Erdoğan later sought to break with.

As Erdoğan became more populist over time, the anti-elitist and people-centric elements of his ideology became more visible, also acquiring a transnational dimension. His appeals to the people started reaching beyond the Turkish state, as in his victory speech after the 2011 elections, when he claimed that his success was that of 'the victims and the oppressed' Muslim populations, not just in Turkey: 'The Middle East, the Caucasus and the Balkans have won, just as Turkey has won' (Quoted in: Alpan 2016, 21). Moreover, especially after the 2013 Gezi protests, Erdoğan began claiming that obscure international forces, referred to as the 'mastermind' (*üst akıl*), were trying to divide and conquer the nation (Destradi, Plagemann, and Taş 2022). Allegedly these forces comprised 'Western imperialists', 'interest lobbies', and 'Crusaders'—and Erdoğan called for a war of liberation against them (Taş 2022c, 567). As the traditional Kemalist establishment had been weakened over the course of his first two terms as prime minister already, he elevated the corrupt 'elite' to the international level via conspiracy theories. In foreign policy, this corresponded to a growing mobilization over time. According to one retired diplomat we interviewed, 'the extensive use of foreign policy as an integral part of domestic politics and as a complementary tool began after 2011'.[33] In Chapters 3–6, we outline in greater detail how this played across various fields of Turkey's foreign relations.

Likewise, the personalization of decision making intensified over time. During the non-populist phase, foreign policy was still prominently shaped by Erdoğan's foreign ministers, including the nonconfrontational AKP foreign minister Abdullah Gül (2003–2007), and by the bureaucracy itself, albeit less so over time. In fact, frictions between the AKP government and the Ministry of Foreign Affairs already emerged prior to 2011. For instance, following a loud verbal exchange between Erdoğan and then Israeli Prime Minister Shimon Peres during a panel discussion at the World Economic Forum 2009

[33] Interview T06, Ambassador (retired) Fatih Ceylan, former permanent representative to NATO, Istanbul, 28 March 2023.

in Davos, several retired ambassadors publicly accused Erdoğan of battering Turkey's image abroad (Vatan 2009). He responded by saying, 'I came from politics; I don't know about the ways *mon chers* [*sic*] behave. And I don't want to know' (Aras 2011). '*Mon chers*' subsequently became a frequently used derogatory term for the diplomatic corps. As a retired diplomat put it:

> In its early years, due to the AKP limited knowledge in the field, the Ministry of Foreign Affairs continued to have an influence on the formulation and implementation of foreign policy. Abdullah Gül, an experienced statesman, had a good working relationship with the foreign ministry staff and frequently consulted them. In the years to follow, [the] AKP chose to take matters into their own hands. Ahmet Davutoğlu was the first figure who took control of foreign affairs. Even if he was at the forefront as a foreign minister, the foreign ministry became increasingly sidelined. He led the processes, and the foreign ministry followed him. He was not like his predecessors. Thus, personalization in foreign policy began with Davutoğlu.[34]

Indeed, in 2010, the Turkish government embarked on a reform aimed at transforming the organization of the foreign ministry. Initiated by Davutoğlu,[35] Erdoğan's foreign policy advisor from 2003 to 2009, and minister of foreign affairs from 2009 to 2014, the reforms allowed the appointment of non-ministerial individuals as ambassadors and the recruitment of graduates from a broader range of fields, including theology. These and other institutional changes coincided with the start of the populist phase with significant repercussions for Turkey's foreign relations. According to a Turkish journalist we interviewed, especially after Davutoğlu left the foreign ministry to become prime minister in 2014, Erdoğan started personally playing an active role in foreign policy.[36] The introduction of the executive presidency in 2018 further reinforced Erdoğan's personal control. Within few days, Erdoğan issued several presidential decrees that reshaped state institutions and led to increased personalization across fields (Yılmaz 2020). As a result, foreign policy actors outside the presidency have lost most of the influence on decision making they once had.[37]

As a retired diplomat interviewed in March 2023 put it:

> Today, [. . .] foreign policy is managed directly and decisively by the president. Perhaps, opinions are sought from the Ministry of Foreign Affairs on some fundamental

---

[34] Interview T04, retired Turkish diplomat, Istanbul, 23 March 2023.
[35] Interview T04.
[36] Interview T10, Gürkan Emre Melikoğlu, Turkish journalist, Istanbul, 10 April 2023.
[37] Interview T06.

issues, but it is governed directly by the presidential complex [. . .]. Now, we see the leader's diplomacy. The influence of ambassadors declined in general as a result of a change in traditional diplomacy in the world, but Turkey experienced this more intensely.[38]

In Chapters 3–6, we address how such shifts in mobilization and personalization over time and across issue areas contributed to different intensities of foreign policy change in the case of Turkey.

---

[38] Interview T04.

2

Theorizing Populist Foreign Policy

What happens to a country's foreign policy when populists win elections and form governments? In other words, what are the effects of populist government formation on foreign policy, to what extent does this lead to foreign policy change, and what does a 'populist foreign policy' look like? These questions are at the centre of this book. In this chapter, we outline a novel theory of populist foreign policy, which explains the different ways in which populism impacts foreign policy. We developed our theory in an abductive research process (Tavory and Timmermans 2014), bringing together different strands in the literatures on populism, International Relations, Foreign Policy Analysis, and foreign policy decision making. Additionally, we incorporated insights from related fields such as diplomatic studies and social movements theories, along with rich qualitative empirical data.

We begin with an introduction of the concept of populism, focusing on the ideational approach to populism. Since the literature on populism is a crowded field that has developed over several decades, there is no dearth of conceptualizations of populism. This makes it all the more important to clearly outline what notion of populism we borrow from the fields of Comparative Politics and Political Theory. After all, this choice is consequential for the development of expectations concerning the impact of populism on foreign policy. We understand populism as a set of ideas, or more precisely a thin-centred ideology, and we consider this ideology to be the main driver of foreign policy change. The chapter proceeds with a discussion of how the ideology of populism influences the way in which foreign policy is made. We argue that two features of populist foreign policy making matter the most: personalization and mobilization. We elaborate on how these characteristics of the process through which foreign policy is made relate to the ideational understanding of populism and in which ways we can expect them to shape foreign policy. In a nutshell, we expect the intensity of foreign policy change on a specific issue after the formation of a populist government to depend on the degree to which foreign policy in that area has become personalized as

Populism and Foreign Policy. Sandra Destradi and Johannes Plagemann, Oxford University Press.
© Oxford University Press (2025). DOI: 10.1093/9780197695012.003.0002

well as on the degree to which this issue is used for domestic political mobilization by the populist government. If both personalization and mobilization are strong, foreign policy change will be more radical. If just one of the two elements is strong and the other is weak, this will lead to only moderate foreign policy change. By contrast, we expect foreign policy continuity if both mobilization and personalization are weak. In Chapters 3–6, we will build upon this general framework to develop concrete expectations about the impact of populism on foreign policy change in the four policy fields addressed in each of those chapters: conflict behaviour or, more specifically, dispute initiation or escalation; the provision of global public goods, with a particular focus on climate change mitigation, the promotion of peace, and development aid; engagement in multilateral institutions, with a particular focus on the UN and relevant regional organizations; and the diversification of international partnerships. The final part of this chapter discusses context conditions that might mitigate the impact of populism.

Populism as a Thin-Centred Ideology

The systematic study of populism goes back to the 1960s and has produced a rich variety of sometimes competing but also partially complementary conceptualizations of populism. What most approaches to populism have in common is that they emphasize how populism makes a fundamental distinction between 'the people' and 'the elite'. However, they differ widely in their ontological assumptions.

Early studies of populism in Latin America that emerged in the 1960s–1980s viewed this political phenomenon through an economic-structuralist lens, mostly associating it with responses to modernization such as financially 'irresponsible' distributive policies (e.g., Germani 1978; Cardoso and Faletto 1979; for an overview, see Weyland 2001, 4–9). However, with a new generation of populist leaders in Latin America who did not follow the same kind of fiscal policies, populism came to be understood as a 'political strategy in which a personalistic leader seeks or exercises government power based on direct, unmediated, uninstitutionalized support from a large number of mostly unorganized followers' (see Weyland 2001, 4–9). The strategic perspective has the advantage of addressing the actual policies adopted by populists and it captures the often essential role of individual populist leaders, but it also has limitations. For one, critics have pointed out that it runs the risk of equating populism with demagoguery, thereby hampering conceptual clarity (Aslanidis 2016, 96). Moreover, the assumption of an unmediated link between a leader and unorganized masses does not capture well the reality of contemporary populism, in which we see instances of populist movements without a strong leader, such as the Occupy Wall Street movement (Gerbaudo 2023), as well as many instances of very well-organized political parties. For instance, the 'Law and Justice' party (PiS) in Poland played a paramount role in the eight years of populist government that ended in 2023—without a strong leader at the top. In India, the personalistic and charismatic populist leader Narendra Modi is supported by a well-organized political party apparatus and by a network of Hindu-nationalist organizations, with his Bharatiya Janata Party (BJP) and organizations like the Rashtriya Swayamsevak Sangh (RSS) playing a key role in his electoral successes (P. Jha 2017). In Bolivia, Evo Morales was a towering figure with a strong personal mandate as president (2006–2019); yet, like Modi, his success also relied on the effective employment of ideology and his ties to grassroots political movements were strong, at least initially. Moreover, the focus on populist leaders that is typical of the strategic approach has been criticized by scholars who point out that 'populism is neither defined by nor wedded to a specific type of leader' (Mudde and Rovira Kaltwasser 2017, 77).

Another approach to populism considers it to be a discourse. According to Laclau (2005), populism should be understood in discursive terms, as a 'political logic' that 'simplifies' the 'political space' by creating a 'stark dichotomy' (Laclau 2005, 18) between the 'people' and a 'power bloc'. This approach, however, has the disadvantage of being 'extremely abstract' (Mudde and Kaltwasser 2012, 7). It complicates empirical analyses because it ends up equating populism with 'politics' in general (Moffitt and Tormey 2014, 384–85). Yet, some studies on the international dimensions of populism have constructively adopted a discursive approach, for example to analyse how discursive reinterpretations of history can contribute to foreign policy change (Cadier and Szulecki 2020), or how populist actors have used foreign policy issues to reproduce people vs. elite antagonisms and their own claim to represent the people (Wojczewski 2020b).

In recent years, populism has also been conceptualized as a political style that involves appealing to 'the people', highlighting and performing crises and threats, and resorting to 'bad manners' (Moffitt and Tormey 2014; Moffitt 2015). The stylistic approach has the advantage of encompassing both left- and right-wing populists, and it highlights several interesting commonalities shared by populist leaders. By building bridges to disciplines such as political communication but also performance studies (Aiolfi 2023), it helps us reflect on some key elements in populist mobilization. At the same time, an emphasis on the style and performance of populists ends up downplaying their shared ideological elements as well as the ideational connections to populist voters and, by extension, to populist attitudes among the public.

Currently, in the literature on populism, the predominant approach is an ideational one, which understands populism as a set of ideas (Hawkins et al. 2018). According to Mudde (2004a, 544), populism is a 'thin-centered ideology', a rather narrow set of ideas about the essential features of society. We argue that this approach is the most suitable for our theorization of the impact of populism on foreign policy and the development of concrete expectations about how this plays out. The theorization of populism as a thin-centred ideology was developed by Cas Mudde. According to him, populism is 'an ideology that considers society to be ultimately separated into two homogeneous and antagonistic groups, "the pure people" versus "the corrupt elite", and which argues that politics should be an expression of the volonté générale (general will) of the people' (2004a, 543, emphasis removed). This thin-centred ideology is usually combined with a 'thick', full-fledged ideology such as socialism, or some variant of ethno-nationalism like Hindu-nationalism. People-centrism and anti-elitism are therefore the constitutive dimensions of populism. However, what the 'people' and the 'elite' mean in a specific case largely depends on the respective thick ideology. Thanks to its parsimony, this understanding of populism allows us to capture what is common to a broad range of actors across the political spectrum and in very different political and institutional contexts. Regardless of populists' idiosyncratic economic policies, strategic moves, or stylistic features, understanding populism as a thin-centred ideology helps us in theorizing the more general impact of populism on foreign policy.[1]

According to the ideational approach we employ, *anti-elitism* is the first constitutive component of populism. Populist leaders claim to speak on behalf of a morally upright and unified people. The people are contrasted to a detached and exploitative elite. The moralistic nature of populist discourses implies a Manichean, black-and-white worldview, where the 'people' are portrayed as virtuous and the elites as malevolent (Mudde 2004a, 543;

---

[1] The conceptualization of populism as a thin-centred ideology has also been variously criticized. For example, Bonikowski (2016, 13) argues that populism should not be considered as a feature of actors but just as a speech-level phenomenon, since 'the assumption of ideological stability is problematic for the simple reason that it cannot account for the dynamic nature of populism'. Katsambekis (2022) points to the dangers of normative bias that emerge from a strand of populism research that tends to equate populism with illiberalism. At the same time, thanks to its broad applicability, the ideational definition has become the most widespread in populism studies. On the advantages of using the ideational approach, see Plagemann and Destradi (2019b), Destradi and Plagemann (2019a), and Destradi (2025a). Beyond such conceptual debates, however, most theoretical approaches to populism ultimately lead to similar expectations when it comes to the impact of populism on foreign policy, despite diverging ontological assumptions (see Destradi, Cadier, and Plagemann 2021).

Hawkins 2009, 1043–44). Consequently, populists often depict themselves and the people as victims within their own societies, so that ultimately 'majorities act as mistreated minorities' (J.-W. Müller 2016, 42). As was mentioned above, who exactly counts as the evil and predatory elite depends on the specific thick ideology embraced by populists. For instance, European populists routinely blame the EU bureaucracy as a far-away elite, US President Trump targeted the Washington establishment with his 'drain the swamp' rhetoric (Biegon 2019), and leftist Latin American populists took aim at transnational capitalist entities, particularly those from or with links to the 'imperial' United States. Anti-elitism frequently leads to demands for a radical departure from the past policies of the 'establishment' and can therefore be a driver for change. Some sections of the literature have indeed highlighted that populists call for a '"rupture" with the existing unjust order' (Panizza and Miorelli 2009, 40) constructed by past elites at the expense of the people.

The second constitutive component of populism, *people-centrism*, is in many ways the other side of the coin. Populists claim that the 'people' are inherently good and morally pure. Again, who belongs to the people depends on the thick ideology that is combined with populism. Therefore, the people can be hard-working white Christian Americans for Trump, the oppressed victims of capitalism for left-wing populists in Latin America or Europe, or the Hindu majority in India's Prime Minister Modi's Hindu-nationalist variant of populism. In all cases, such constructions of the people involve an emphasis on presumed moral differences between various groups (J.-W. Müller 2016; Hawkins and Rovira Kaltwasser 2017; McKibben 2023) and the exclusion of specific segments of society from what is considered to be the 'true people'. The dimension of people-centrism also has consequences for populists' understanding of democratic representation. As Mudde points out in his definition, populists assume that a 'popular will' exists and should determine political outcomes. This ideational element translates into a peculiar understanding of democratic representation, which according to political theorist Nadia Urbinati is focused on the notion of 'embodiment': the leader literally comes to embody the popular will. This implies that 'populism epitomizes not so much the claim of "a part" representing "the whole" (pars pro toto) . . . but instead, and much more radically, the claim to embody one part only—the "authentic" part, which, for this very reason, deserves to rule for its own good against the excluded, inauthentic part' (Urbinati 2019a, 45).[2] This

---

[2] Urbinati, who is specifically interested in populism in power, criticizes elements of the conceptualization of populism as a thin-centred ideology, which she argues misses some important elements. Among

notion of democratic representation is also inherently anti-pluralist because 'populists claim that they, *and only they,* represent the people' (J.-W. Müller 2016, 20, emphasis in original), thereby implicitly or explicitly discrediting any form of opposition as unrepresentative of the true people. And since the pure and virtuous people is always right, any opposition to populist leaders is illegitimate.[3]

Anti-pluralism and populists' specific understanding of democratic representation, in turn, have implications for democratic institutions once populists form governments. With democratic representation understood as an embodiment of the popular will in the person of the leader, populists will be extremely suspicious of all institutions intermediating—and thereby interrupting the presumed direct link—between them and the 'people'. This will lead to a weakening of checks and balances and the rule of law, established independent media, and other intermediary institutions such as political parties, and ultimately to the disfiguring of constitutional democracy (Urbinati 2019a). Pappas (2019, 1) relatedly argues that populism should be understood as a 'form of modern democratic politics that is antagonistic towards established liberal democracy'. Numerous examples, from Donald Trump's unwillingness to cede power in 2020 to Recep Erdoğan's establishment of a presidential system in Turkey—with him at the top—support this view. Also the literature on democratic backsliding emphasizes the majoritarian and illiberal tendencies of populist rule, and the ensuing detrimental effects of populism on democracy (Haggard and Kaufman 2021).

Populism and Foreign Policy Making: Personalization and Mobilization

As outlined in the Introduction, the growing body of literature on the international effects of populism has not been able to unequivocally establish a set of foreign policy outcomes that would characterize a genuinely 'populist foreign policy'. Being a thin-centred ideology that only entails the notions of anti-elitism and people-centrism as well as a basic understanding of representation

them is the notion of charismatic leadership, which she considers important to distinguish populism in power from populism as a protest movement. According to Urbinati (2019a, 50), populism as a thin-centred ideology 'seems too broad and unpolitical to capture the form of representation that qualifies populism in its relation to democracy'. Yet, despite such criticism, her understanding of populism is ultimately compatible with the ideational approach, which is why we are widely referring to her work to develop our theorization of populist foreign policy.

[3] According to Mudde and Kaltwasser (2013), there is variation between inclusionary and exclusionary types of populism. Yet, the binary opposition of people vs. elite mostly ends up delegitimizing political actors described as elitist and sections of society associated with them.

focused on the 'general will', populism does not offer any direct prescription about how to act in foreign affairs. In this regard, populism is different from other, thicker ideologies, which allow more concrete predictions about foreign policy (see Maynard and Haas 2021). This makes it so important to study the conditions under which populism has an impact on foreign policy (see Destradi and Plagemann 2019).

In fact, previous research has shown that the impact of populism is most immediate when it comes to the *procedures and practices* of foreign policy (Plagemann and Destradi 2019; see also Jenne 2021). These, in turn, will affect the very substance of foreign policy. And, in fact, the literature in the field of Foreign Policy Analysis has abundantly shown that the way decisions are made and the influences of various domestic actors matter greatly in shaping foreign policy outcomes (Farnham 2004; Brummer and Oppermann 2024; Kaarbo and Thies 2024b).

We argue that there are two features of foreign policy that can be derived from the thin-centred ideology of populism and that are indeed characteristic of populist foreign policy: personalization and mobilization. What do we mean by personalization and mobilization, and how do these two characteristics impact foreign policy change once a populist government is formed?

Personalization

Populist leaders tend to personalize decision making, including when it comes to foreign policy decisions. While personalized decision making is not an exclusive feature of populists, there are good reasons to expect it to characterize populism in power as it closely relates to both the people-centric and the anti-elitist dimensions in populism.

The centrality of the leader is one aspect that most approaches to populism highlight, albeit to various degrees. The strategic approach to populism goes so far as to reduce populism to precisely this unmediated link between a single leader and masses of followers (Weyland 2001). But also approaches that focus on stylistic (Moffitt 2015) or performative aspects emphasize the importance of personalized leadership. Another interesting conceptualization of populism in this regard is the one developed by Ostiguy (2017), who understands populism as a particular form of political relationship between leaders and their social basis focused on the 'flaunting of the low' in socio-cultural and politico-cultural terms. Largely compatible with the ideational approach (Ostiguy 2017, 74), populism in politico-cultural terms is about personalism, with populist leaders exercising personal authority, frequently in the form of 'strong (virile or affectionate)' leadership (Ostiguy 2017, 79). This will also translate into a preference about policy making that is clearly personalist and concrete, as opposed to the proceduralist and formalist nature of non-populists' decision making (identified with the conventional 'high' dimension of politics) (Ostiguy 2017, 80). The literature that contrasts populism with technocracy has similarly highlighted how populists' decisions are centred on the leader and the embodiment of the popular will (Caramani 2017). For Urbinati (2019a), the very notion of populist leaders literally embodying the pure and virtuous people, thereby incarnating a presumed popular will, automatically puts the populist leader centre stage in foreign policy as well as other policy domains.

The anti-elitist dimension of populism, in turn, reinforces personalization because the actors traditionally entrusted with the debate and conduct of foreign policy—diplomats, business representatives, foreign correspondents, and other members of a country's 'strategic community'—are typically identified as elitist par excellence (Destradi and Plagemann 2019; Plagemann and Destradi 2019). According to Lequesne (2021, 781), 'populist governments have a structural conflict with career diplomats'. Career diplomats are usually recruited via a highly selective procedure, they tend to come from prominent families in the respective national context, and they undergo a tough training in small cohorts (Berridge 2011; Binder, Davis and Bloom 2016). In their job, they move in highly secluded circles detached both from public scrutiny and the living realities of most ordinary citizens. Through their frequent relocations and the professional and private networks they build in the course of their careers, they become cosmopolitan almost by definition. It is little wonder, then, that members of the diplomatic corps are frequently identified as elitist by leaders who claim to speak in the name of the 'people' and who often take pride in behaving like the 'common man'. According to Ostiguy, populists leaders' 'flaunting of the low' entails precisely the adoption of forms of behaviour that distinguish them from the elitist foreign policy 'establishment': '"Betrayed" by a current or previous well-educated and proper elite—often painted as hypocritical or false—the populist politicians and parties claim, loudly, politically incorrectly, and often vulgarly, to be that (truly) authentic people's "fighting hero"' (Ostiguy 2017, 76). Examples of this attitude abound—think of Silvio Berlusconi's sexist jokes that found broad appeal among his supporters in Italy, or of Donald Trump's innumerable abuses and regular use of offensive language (Winberg 2017). Populists consciously try to set themselves apart from established elites. Moreover, the structural conflict with elite diplomats is fuelled by the fact that diplomats consider themselves to be experts of foreign policy due to their training and specialized knowledge (Lequesne 2021), while populists disdain expertise. The same logic applies to other members of the 'strategic community': populists reject established foreign policy think tankers' or trade economists' views, often denigrate media opinions, and are loath to consider advice by human rights groups and other 'globalist' civil society movements. In fact, as they claim to be close to the 'people', populists often denigrate expert knowledge and juxtapose it to common sense or to alternative expertise (Ylä-Anttila 2018). As Michael Gove, then Lord Chancellor in the UK, famously said ahead of the Brexit vote in 2016: 'I think the people of this country have had enough of experts with organisations with acronyms saying that they know what is best and getting it consistently wrong' (Mance 2016). This became particularly visible during the Covid-19 pandemic, when several (but notably not all) populists in power expressed their scepticism over protective measures recommended by medical experts (Lasco 2020; Belder et al. 2023). Relatedly, populism has come to be frequently associated with post-truth politics, understood as a disregard for facts and expertise (Montgomery 2017; Waisbord 2018).

In foreign policy, populists' disdain for career diplomats is often extended to the bureaucracies to which diplomats belong: foreign ministries. Populist personalization of foreign policy making will thus be accompanied by *centralization*, understood as the institutional concentration of power with a small circle of advisors around the populist leader, away from the institutions traditionally tasked with addressing foreign policy issues.[4] A caveat is necessary, however: the trend towards a centralization of foreign policy decision making and a marginalization of foreign ministries is not exclusive to populist governments. In an age of globalization, or of what Habermas (1998, 12) calls 'world domestic politics' (*Weltinnenpolitik*), international interactions cannot just be managed as state-to-state relationships in the exclusive purview of diplomats. All over the world, this has led to a diffusion of competencies on external affairs towards a number of line ministries as well as, via paradiplomacy, to subnational actors like city administrations or states in federations (Cason and Power 2009; Rachman 2017, 91; C. K. Sharma, Destradi, and Plagemann 2020). Paradoxically, the redistribution of competencies associated with these

---

[4] Like personalization, centralization under populist governments is not limited to foreign policy, as for example studies on the management of the Covid-19 pandemic have revealed that it was highly centralized in India under populist Prime Minister Narendra Modi (Mukherji 2020) or in Turkey under populist President Erdoğan (Kemahlıoğlu and Yeğen 2021). For a more detailed discussion of possible patterns of centralization, see Jumle et al. (2025).

processes, and the concomitant diffusion of authority, have often led to a centralization of decision making. At the same time, the fragmentation of global governance, the declining authority of many international organizations, and an ever more multipolar distribution of power globally led to a resurgence of international clubs, from the G-20 to a revived G-7 and an expanding BRICS, with individual national leaders as key protagonists. For instance, unrelated to populism in power, in the Unites States, it was the Obama administration that 'created an array of special envoys while centralizing foreign policy power within the White House to bypass the State Department' (Drezner 2019, 724), thereby already setting in motion a trend that was later exacerbated under the first Trump administration.

Yet, overall, we expect the centralization of power and the marginalization of foreign ministries to be more pronounced under populist governments. And in fact, various case studies of populism in power have revealed that populist leaders have systematically weakened their countries' foreign ministries. This took place in different ways: in Israel, Prime Minister Benjamin Netanyahu governed for almost four years (2015–2019) without a foreign minister, taking over the portfolio himself (Gülen 2019). During his first administration, Trump dismantled the foreign policy bureaucracy, including by leaving numerous posts vacant and by cutting funds (Drezner 2019). During the early stages of his second administration, he installed his personal friend, real estate investor and billionaire Steve Witkoff, as special envoy, essentially running ceasefire negotiations over Gaza and Ukraine thus bypassing the US State Department. Others, like the PiS leadership in Poland, sought to politically capture the foreign ministry by substituting career diplomats with loyalist political appointees (Lequesne 2021). In India the populist government marginalized the foreign policy bureaucracy and, at the same time, exercised pressure on it to act in line with the populist government's thick ideology (Huju 2022). These findings resonate with an emerging strand of literature on public administration, which shows that populists adopt a range of strategies to transform state bureaucracies, from the strengthening of top-down decision making to budget cuts, the reduction of accountability and participation, as well as purges to eliminate ideologically unaligned staff (Bauer 2024, 1022).

Overall, therefore, we expect the personalization of foreign policy making to be accompanied by centralization, meaning that populist leaders will surround themselves with small circles of advisors, often recruited among party members, ideologues with connections to the respective thick ideology, or family, long-time friends and companions not necessarily selected due to their foreign policy expertise.[5] While we expect populists in power to personalize foreign policy making, we are not claiming that all populist governments will do so in the same way and to the same extent. Moreover, the same populist leader is unlikely to personalize foreign policy making evenly across foreign policy issues. For example, a populist leader might be particularly invested in some key bilateral relationships, while showing little interest and personal involvement in other, less salient (see below) ones.[6] Those rather secondary relationships would then be left to the 'business as usual' management on the part of the foreign ministry. By contrast, populist leaders might be particularly engaged in one policy field that speaks to their political agenda and to the thick ideology of their party—think of the migration issue for right-wing populists in Europe, for example. Other fields from which there might be less to gain politically would be left to the competent ministries to manage. In other words, it is important to keep in mind that the personalization of foreign policy does not occur evenly across foreign policy issues and over time. Our theoretical framework aims to capture precisely these variations and to assess their consequences for foreign policy change.

Mobilization

The second characteristic feature of foreign policy under populist government is mobilization. In a nutshell, this implies that foreign policy issues are often used by populist leaders to mobilize support, thereby creating a closer-than-usual connection between domestic politics and foreign policy.

As we discussed at the beginning of this chapter, the thin-centred ideology of populism puts great emphasis on the notion of politics as an expression of the 'general will' of the 'people'. Hence, populism is in many ways a genuinely democratic phenomenon in the sense that populists claim to speak for

[5] There are exceptions, of course: the populist politician Benjamin Netanyahu was a career diplomat himself before entering politics. In Brazil, populist President Bolsonaro's first choice as foreign minister was career diplomat Ernesto Araújo. Populist prime minister Modi in 2019 selected a cosmopolitan career diplomat, Subrahmanyam Jaishankar, as the new minister for external affairs and involved him in his close circle of decision making. However, these episodes expose how technocrats too can adopt the populist playbook. Another example is Nikos Kotzias, a technocrat who was appointed foreign minister by populist prime minister Alexis Tsipras in Greece in 2015. Kotzias ended up using a personalistic foreign policy style, politicizing foreign policy, and antagonizing diplomats. Like Araújo in Brazil, the appointment of a low-profile technocrat revealed the populist government's disdain for the foreign ministry (Chryssogelos 2021, 734).

[6] The recent literature on populism and foreign policy has pointed out that leaders prioritize specific issues depending on their party's ideology (Verbeek and Zaslove 2017), on their national identity conceptions (Friedrichs 2022), or on the issues that resonate most with their support base (Wojczewski 2020c).

the people. Populists believe in the notion of representation of the popular will, even if they are hostile towards liberal or constitutional democracy (see Mudde 2004, 561). They therefore emphasize holding and winning elections, but they end up using them 'as a celebration of the majority and its leader, rather than as a competition among leaders and parties that facilitates assessment of the plurality of preferences' (Urbinati 2019a, 8). Indeed, 'electoral legitimacy is a key defining dimension of populist regimes' (Urbinati 2019a, 20). Thus, it is not surprising that mobilization has been analysed by several strands in populism research as an important political mechanism. According to the strategic understanding of populism by Weyland (2001), mobilization plays a crucial role in establishing the direct link between the populist leader and the masses. Jansen (2011, 82) even claims that mobilization constitutes the very essence of populism—with populist mobilization being understood as a political project that combines popular mobilization (the publicly visible activation of marginalized sections of society) with anti-elitist populist rhetoric.

In this book, we focus on populists in power. They have already successfully mobilized their followers to win elections. Once they form governments and lead a country, however, these populists come to face a new, complex challenge: having become themselves the 'political establishment', they need to find new ways to mobilize support in order to get re-elected. As a consequence, as J.-W. Müller (2016, 42) points out, '[p]opulists in office continue to polarize'. They keep mobilizing, for example by blaming any failures to conspiring elites allegedly guided from abroad and aiming to harm the 'people'. Thus, despite having been in power for several years in some cases, populists continue to resort to an underdog narrative. Ultimately, 'populism in power [is] like a permanent electoral campaign, which the leader and its majority wage in order to prove they are not—and never will be—a new establishment. Persuading the people is paramount, since faith in the leader is the only guarantee the populist has that his or her power will last' (Urbinati 2019a, 191). Actual practices of mobilization depend on country-specific circumstances. In India with its never-ending succession of regional elections, Prime Minister Modi was never far from the next public rally. By contrast, President Rodrigo Duterte in the Philippines not only enjoyed a comparatively long presidency of six years, he also had to contend with a constitutional one-term limit. Both Evo Morales in Bolivia and Erdoğan in Turkey held referenda over major constitutional changes that would entrench their grip on power, thereby creating further opportunities for mobilization.

Foreign policy issues can easily be used for domestic political mobilization. They can be brought into the domestic political discourse and connected to domestic issues to generate support for the populist government. Correspondingly, we expect populists to politicize some aspects of foreign policy, with politicization being defined as 'the demand for, or the act of, transporting an issue or an institution into the sphere of politics—making previously unpolitical matters political' (Zürn 2019, 977–78). Populists in power will therefore be particularly inclined to break with the notion that 'politics stops at the water's edge' (Rathbun 2004) and that foreign policy should not be the object of domestic political quarrels. Quite to the contrary, they tend to politicize foreign policy issues in order to mobilize political support (Zürn 2014, 50–51). According to Cadier (2024), 'populism translates into a greater proclivity to use foreign policy as the continuation of domestic politics by other means'. More specifically, Cadier (2024) identifies three patterns of foreign policy politicization by populist governments: a greater tendency, as compared to non-populist governments, to highlight differences in foreign policy as compared to that of the previous, 'elitist' government; a tendency to use foreign policy issues to battle domestic political opponents; and a tendency to over-prioritize domestic issues as compared to foreign ones, ultimately putting the greatest emphasis on domestic political gains.

This politicization of foreign policy on the part of populists is often made easier because the very success of populist parties and leaders in many parts of the world is at least in part driven by international issues, with populists harnessing fears of globalization. In many Western countries, contemporary populism is understood as a reaction to the increasing influence of 'international bureaucracies' (Zürn 2004, 285). Think of European populists' criticism of 'Brussels' as a code word for a far-detached bureaucracy impinging on ordinary people's lives, but also of populists' more general scepticism of cosmopolitan elites and the competencies of transgovernmental policy networks and supranational institutions in what Chryssogelos (2020) calls the 'internationalized state'. In other parts of the world, the success of populism might have a different international dimension related to resentment towards Westernization (Krastev and Holmes 2019). Anti-Americanism, with its opposition to a hegemonic power imposing its preferences on the people in distant parts of the world, has long been an important component in both left- and right-wing populism—from Latin America, where it has driven left-wing populists' discourses for decades, to a Cold War populist like Greek Prime Minister George Papandreou (Chryssogelos 2021, 727), to contemporary European right-wing populist parties (e.g., Lemke 2020; Ostermann and Stahl 2022), or a populist without a clearly defined thick ideology like Duterte in the Philippines (see Chapter 3). Anti-imperialism as well as anti-colonialism have been successfully used by populists, especially in the Global

South, to mobilize support. For example, in his Independence Day speech of 2023, Narendra Modi drew a link between Mughal-era and British colonial domination, as opposed to a brighter future for his country under his leadership: 'We are at the milestone between 1000 years of slavery and 1000 years of grand future that is about to come' (The Indian Express 2023).

In sum, we therefore expect populist governments to be more inclined than their non-populist predecessors to use foreign policy to mobilize support. The precise content of mobilization will depend on the specificities of each case, but also on which element of populism (anti-elitism vs. people-centrism) will be more prominent in a populist government's thin ideology. In fact, previous research (Destradi, Plagemann, and Taş 2022) has shown that not all populists use foreign policy issues for domestic mobilization in the same way. If a populist government emphasizes the anti-elitist dimension of populism, it will end up politicizing foreign policy in a more negative way, conjuring up external threats and enemies conspiring against the 'people' and aiming to harm it. By contrast, populists who put greater emphasis on the people-centric dimension of populism will rather politicize foreign policy via a more 'positive' discourse, by underlining the greatness and strength of the 'people' and the country in international politics.

In any case, populists can be expected to use foreign policy issues for domestic political mobilization to different degrees. In fact, not all issues will be similarly suitable for mobilization. The broad literature on mobilization tells us that mobilization is most successful if it can build upon a set of ideas that are appealing to the audience (Gerhards and Rucht 1992; Rosenstone and Hansen 1993). Mobilization will therefore work particularly well if it resonates with both the thin and the thick ideologies espoused by populists, thus giving coherence to populists' frames and narratives. We therefore expect mobilization around foreign policy issues to be particularly strong either on issues that reflect the people-elite divide, or on those that can be discursively related to key elements of the populist government's thick ideology. Thus, it is not surprising that the issue of migration has been a central element around which right-wing populist governments in Europe like that of Viktor Orbán in Hungary or of the Law and Justice (PiS) in Poland have mobilized support: by pitting migrants against the 'people' and presenting themselves as the protectors of the latter, these governments have harnessed their ethno-nationalist ideology to rally support while intertwining domestic and international issues and blaming domestic and foreign elites for failures in migration policy (Dymek 2016; Coman and Leconte 2019; Gross 2023).

At the same time, to be successful, populist mobilization around foreign policy needs to refer to issues that are salient to the respective audience

(Oppermann and Viehrig 2011; Bornschier 2017; Ernst et al. 2019). Voter salience varies a lot across foreign policy issue areas (Wlezien 2005; Walgrave and Lefevere 2013; Hellwig 2014). Broadly speaking, a foreign policy issue that is highly salient for relevant domestic constituencies is more likely to be used for mobilization, and, in turn, mobilization will likely further increase salience (Oppermann and Viehrig 2011, 9). Yet, systematic knowledge about the conditions under which 'playing the foreign policy card' is a successful campaigning strategy is limited and mostly confined to specific cases (Narang and Staniland 2018). Having said that, a populist government is unlikely to try mobilizing public support by referring to issues that do not attract the attention of either its support base or the wider public. For example, more technical issues in European regulation—from agriculture to consumer safety—have not been used by populist parties to mobilize support to the same extent as migration or the broader call to 'take back control' from an overbearing Brussels. At the same time, the literature on public opinion and elite cuing tells us that leaders can play an important role in shaping public attitudes on foreign policy issues (Jacobs and Shapiro 1999; Strezhnev, Simmons, and Kim 2019; Santoro et al. 2021). Indeed, scholarship on the public's influence on foreign policy that came to be known as the 'limited responsiveness view' observed that, rather than responding to public opinion, leaders sought to modify it, thereby maintaining popularity despite their pursuit of essentially unpopular policies (Foyle 2017, 4).[7] So we can expect populists to increase the salience of certain foreign policy issues or of foreign policy in general by actively promoting this issue vis-à-vis the public or by making foreign policy 'more visible'. According to Cadier (2024), populists indeed distinguish themselves from non-populists because they will not so much use foreign policy to distract from domestic politics, as suggested by the diversionary theory of war (see Tir 2010), but rather do the opposite. Instead of deflecting attention from domestic politics, they use foreign policy to 're-focus attention on domestic politics' (Cadier 2024, 5). For example, although foreign aid used to be of low salience in US domestic politics, the radical dismantling of USAID under the second Trump administration both vastly increased public attention to it and framed development aid in decidedly domestic terms, as a target of cost-cutting policies aimed at a superfluous domestic bureaucracy. Similarly, the Brexit campaign in the UK turned the dissociation from the European Union into a promise for investments in health care.

Finally, to be suitable for domestic political mobilization, a foreign policy issue ideally would also allow for differences to be highlighted between

---

[7] Also see Jacobs and Page (2005) and Canes-Wrone (2021).

opposing domestic political camps. As Zürn (2004, 50–51) points out, the politicization of a foreign policy issue implies the contestation of the policies of political opponents, not just of technocrats and the bureaucracy. For populists who claim to speak for the 'people' against the 'elite', the foreign policy issues would especially need to be connected to this fundamental cleavage. This kind of mobilization will work particularly well around issues that allow for a clear and comprehensible differentiation between the populist government's approach and that of the 'elite', that is, issues that can be easily conveyed to the public, without getting lost in technical details. For example, Modi's BJP habitually describes the opposition Congress party as 'weak' on India's long-term rival Pakistan, and critics of the government are portrayed as 'anti-national' appeasers versus the BJP's supposedly 'muscular' security policy vis-à-vis Pakistan (Jaffrelot and Verniers 2020).

Foreign Policy Change

The overarching goal of this book is to theorize how populism impacts foreign policy by focusing on shifts from non-populist to populist governments. Therefore, we ultimately aim to explain how populism leads to foreign policy change. Although the idea of making sense of changes in foreign policy is at the core of the field of Foreign Policy Analysis as well as of many works in International Relations, the notion of foreign policy change has received relatively little attention in the literature. Surprisingly, not much effort has been made since the 1990s to further refine the theorization and operationalization of foreign policy change (see Haesebrouck and Joly 2021).[8]

The existing FPA literature distinguishes four dimensions of foreign policy change, whose overlaps complicate definitions of change. These are (a) the nature of change; (b) the intensity of change; (c) the scope of change; and (d) the outcomes of change. First of all, when it comes to the nature of change, the literature points to various aspects of foreign policy that can be modified. The most established classification of this kind is the typology of foreign policy change by Hermann (1990). Defining foreign policy as 'a goal-oriented or problem-oriented program by authoritative policymakers (or their representatives) directed towards entities outside the policymakers' political jurisdiction', Hermann (1990, 5) distinguishes four types of change. 'Adjustment change' does not involve any shifts in the main goals and means

---

[8] For instance, the recently published *Oxford Handbook of Foreign Policy Analysis*, a key reference work in the field, does not include a specific chapter on the issue of foreign policy change (see Kaarbo and Thies 2024b).

of foreign policy, but just changes in the 'level of effort (greater or lesser) and/or in the scope of the recipient (such as refinement in the class of targets)' (Hermann 1990, 5). 'Program changes' involve shifts 'in the methods or means by which the goal or problem is addressed' (Hermann 1990, 5), thereby implying that the goals remain the same, but are pursued in a different manner. 'Problem/goal changes', by contrast, involve a change of the objectives of foreign policy. And finally, 'international orientation change' concerns a broader redirection of a country's overall approach to international politics, with several policies being changed at the same time (Hermann 1990, 5–6). The typology by Hermann thus mainly addresses the nature of foreign policy change (a), that is, whether change referred to the goals of foreign policy, to its means, or to both (Haesebrouck and Joly 2021, 484). At the same time, this typology entails a more quantitative dimension, as its ideal-types are meant to depict variations in the 'magnitude of the shift' (Hermann 1990, 3). Thus, Hermann's categories also refer to the intensity of foreign policy change (b).[9] This category is only implicitly acknowledged by large parts of the literature, even though most empirical analyses have traditionally focused on particularly dramatic and visible instances of foreign policy change (for a recent example and a discussion of this aspect, see Brummer 2024). By contrast, incremental foreign policy changes that only display a cumulative effect in the long term have mostly been neglected (Haesebrouck and Joly 2021, 484; for an exception, see Wehner 2025). Another dimension that some studies take into account is the scope or extensiveness of change (c), that is, whether changes take place in single issue areas or, instead, across a broad range of sectors. This dimension is also implicit in Hermann's typology, with 'international orientation change' depicting a shift across policy domains. This latter type of change is similar to foreign policy 'restructuring' (see Volgy and Schwarz 1991), that is, changes in the '*total* pattern' (emphasis in original) of countries' external relations (Holsti 2015, 2)—something the early works on foreign policy change tended to focus on. Finally, also the outcome of foreign policy change (d) is a category that needs to be taken into account, distinguishing between foreign policies that are successfully implemented (i.e., that achieve the actor's goals) and those that are not. Here, going back to the definition of 'foreign policy' is crucial. As we mentioned above, Hermann (1990, 5) understands foreign policy as a 'program by authoritative policymakers (or their representatives) directed towards entities outside the

---

[9] To illustrate this, Hermann (1990, 6) refers to US policy towards Vietnam, which changed in several ways over time. For example, increasing military assistance during the 1950s and early 1960s amounted to adjustment changes, while the deployment of American combat troops in 1965 constituted a programme change.

policymakers' political jurisdiction'. Another definition by Morin and Paquin puts greater emphasis on foreign policy practices as they define foreign policy as 'a set of actions or rules governing the actions of an independent political authority deployed in the international environment' (Morin and Paquin 2018, 3).[10] In any case, the focus is clearly on the actors and on the processes of foreign policy making. In order to identify foreign policy change, we thus need to focus on shifts in the goals and means adopted by the government we analyse. A 'changed' foreign policy is thus not necessarily one that has achieved its goals. For example, Russia's shift to the attempt of a full-scale invasion of Ukraine in February 2022 constituted a drastic change in foreign policy, even if Russia did not achieve its war aims. While this might sound obvious, it is important to emphasize that foreign policy change is an actor-centred category, and that we can observe a changed foreign policy even if this ultimately fails to achieve its goals in the strategic interaction with external actors and, because of this, the key tenets of a bilateral relation remain constant. In other words, we do not focus so much on the outcome, but primarily on the process of foreign policy change.

In this book, we are interested in how the formation of populist governments leads to foreign policy change, and our understanding of change is closely connected to our object of inquiry. In Chapters 3–5, we address three specific policy fields: approaches to international disputes, the provision of global public goods, and contributions to multilateralism. In Chapter 6, we take a broader approach by asking whether populists were inclined towards re-directing their countries' foreign policies towards a different set of international partners, especially towards populist governments and/or authoritarian regimes.

As a consequence, in Chapters 3–5, when it comes to the nature of change (a), we focus primarily on programme changes as conceptualized by Herman. Thus, we primarily explore shifts in foreign policy means, but we also came across more profound changes in goals (problem/goal changes). The scope of change (c) is limited to each specific issue area, and we are primarily interested in the actor-centred aspect; that is, we do not make the 'success' of a foreign policy the precondition for identifying change (d). Moreover, we go beyond Herman's definition by taking into account different intensities of change (b). As we will discuss below, we distinguish between strong

---

[10] Another widespread definition of foreign policy that emphasizes its goal-oriented character is that by Carlsnaes: 'foreign policies consists of those actions which, expressed in the form of explicitly stated goals, commitments and/or directives, and pursued by governmental representatives acting on behalf of their sovereign communities, are directed toward objectives, conditions and actors—both governmental and non-governmental—which they want to affect and which lie beyond their territorial legitimacy' (Carlsnaes 2002, 335).

foreign policy change, moderate foreign policy change, and no foreign policy change (i.e., foreign policy continuity). In other words, we acknowledge that changes in foreign policy means and goals can have different intensities. For example, if a government chooses to escalate a bilateral dispute, this can happen in very different ways: it may introduce sanctions, but it may also employ more aggressive means, for example by threatening to use force, or by using it. These varying intensities within the classic category of 'programme change' are important and need an explanation. In each of the empirical chapters, we provide issue-specific operationalizations of different intensities of change.

In Chapter 6, we take a broader look at countries' reorientation of international partnerships towards authoritarian and populist regimes. Here, we focus on changes of a different nature (a); that is, we are closer to Herman's category of 'international orientation change'. Again, we do not consider a successful outcome of such policies to be a precondition for change (d). And also in this case, we focus on and seek to explain variations in the intensity of change (b), which we operationalize in Chapter 6.

How Personalization and Mobilization Lead to Foreign Policy Change

Our explanation for foreign policy change under populist governments focuses on personalization and mobilization, which we discussed above as being the key features of populist foreign policy.

The personalization (and concomitant centralization) of foreign policy making can be expected to impact foreign policy in a number of important ways. First, the marginalization of foreign policy bureaucracies can contribute to foreign policy change simply because of the declining influence of precisely those actors who were tasked with keeping the country's foreign relations going. Foreign ministries are, almost by definition, in charge of guaranteeing continuity in a country's foreign relations, with the embassies forming the connection to foreign governments and respective political elites. Foreign policy bureaucracies, like all bureaucracies, have a very important function in cultivating an institutional memory about a country's foreign policy and in upholding lines of communication even in crisis situations (Drezner 2000; He 2015). Research in FPA has long claimed that bureaucratic incrementalism is a major source of foreign policy continuity and that bureaucratic constraints tend to prevent major foreign policy changes (Neumann 2007; Haesebrouck and Joly 2021, 487). More than that, diplomats typically understand themselves as 'intermediators' who seek 'to reduce the separation between distinct, even opposing worlds' (Lequesne 2021, 782). Embassies serve as important sources of knowledge around the political impediments in bilateral relations with foreign countries, especially those which are culturally and geographically farther away. Think tanks, foreign correspondents, and prominent academics may serve a similar function in some cases. By delegitimating their advice as elitist and corrupt, populists steering bilateral relations may fall back on their personal relations with foreign leaders while, essentially, ignoring the internal politics of foreign countries, including potential red lines.

The personalization of foreign policy and the marginalization of diplomatic elites and strategic communities are thus liable to break with past foreign policy conventions and to ultimately lead to a less predictable foreign policy. For populists specifically, the literature suggests that they are interested in deliberately breaking with the past policies of the 'establishment' and to provoke a 'rupture' in key policy areas (Panizza and Miorelli 2009, 40). They have much greater leeway to do so if they face a limited number of veto players and are less constrained in the decision-making process.

Second, strong personalization of power ultimately amounts to insulated decision making. As we have seen, populists disdain expertise. Therefore, we can expect populists to marginalize not only career diplomats, but also foreign policy advisors with expert knowledge, allowing only individuals close to the populist party or the leader to serve as advisors. Among the marginalized actors are think tanks, academics such as area specialists, foreign correspondents, retired diplomats, or, in some countries, retired high-ranking army officers, as well as NGOs focusing on fields that are relevant to foreign policy, from human rights to environmental issues. All these actors form a broader 'strategic community' interested in international affairs providing expertise or advice on foreign policy making. This can happen quite directly, for example in the case of government-funded think tanks, but also indirectly, for example via various media contributions, from the publication of opinion pieces in newspapers to the appearance in talk shows on television or via a presence on social media (Baum and Potter 2008; D. Stone 2015; Zaytsev, Kuskova, and Kononova 2021). By delegitimating these actors as elitist or corrupt, populists end up prioritizing the advice of a more limited number of trusted individuals.

Especially for upsurge populist parties or leaders winning power for the first time—and often unexpectedly—the choice of potential foreign policy advisors may be small and confined to fringe figures, as demonstrated by Jair Bolsonaro's first minister of foreign affairs, Ernesto Araújo, or Donald Trump's very first National Security Advisor, Michael Flynn. We may also expect populists in power to replace established foreign policy think tanks with new, partisan ones staffed with loyalists following the government line.

Populists may also place loyalists at the helm of existing institutions, seeking to control the discourse there, inevitably stymying critical debate on the government's foreign policy. As a consequence, populists will end up relying more on fringe figures or ideological hardliners close to their party with often very limited understanding of foreign countries' politics. They are unlikely to hear a broader spectrum of voices and positions on foreign policy matters and less likely to be confronted with dissenting opinions. In fact, it has been abundantly shown in empirical research that aides to a leader, whose careers are entirely dependent on the leader's goodwill, are very unlikely to challenge the leader's positions (Edwards, Mayer, and Wayne 2022, 266). Ultimately, this may lead to more marked foreign policy change since these advisors tend to reinforce populists' inclination to choose policies that are at odds with the traditional foreign policy consensus of previous years. Moreover, populists might end up hardening their stances due to a lack of counterarguments and dissent.

Relatedly, high personalization and centralization can promote groupthink within the populist leader's small circle of advisors, and this phenomenon has been shown to be liable to lead to foreign policy change (Badie 2010, 293). Groupthink has been studied in FPA as a 'pathology' in foreign policy making: if decisions are made in small groups, a high degree of conformity will emerge (Irving 1982; Walker and Watson 1989; Schafer and Crichlow 2010). The results are phenomena like pressure on dissenters, mindguarding, and corresponding self-censorship. Moreover, groupthink may lead to an illusion of invulnerability, to the formation of stereotyped views of enemies, and to a belief in the inherent morality of the in-group (see Irving 1982). Most likely, in a populist government that already sees itself as representing a morally superior 'people' against corrupt and evil elites, these dynamics will be further strengthened and exacerbated. The beliefs and attitudes promoted by groupthink can ultimately contribute to a stronger tendency towards foreign policy change, or towards more intense forms of foreign policy change because of the strengthened conviction that the choices made by the leader and this small group of advisors are right. Additionally, t'Hart (1990, 49) points out that status differences within a group can lead to increased pressure on decision makers and to an even greater tendency towards conformity—and indeed this would be the case if a strong populist leader claiming to individually embody the popular will is surrounded by a small circle of advisors who cannot claim to be similarly infallible.

Finally, a high degree of personalization can lead to more intense foreign policy change because of the very visibility the leader gains in the process. Showing resolve in foreign policy matters can be important to strengthen the leader's credibility and popularity, all the more so if the leader claims that the 'national interest' is at stake. Research from prospect theory has argued that individuals tend to suffer from losses more than they value gains, and this might lead to more risk-taking in the face of negative prospects. Research on autocratic regimes has also revealed that personalistic leaders ultimately tend to be more likely to use military force because they will not face any significant consequences for initiating wars unwisely or leading their countries to defeat (Weeks 2012). However, while populists gradually weaken democratic institutions and checks and balances once they are in power, they are fundamentally different from personalistic autocrats as they claim to speak in the name of the 'people' and thus care more about their potential audience costs. Ultimately, the very visibility of the leader and his imprint on foreign relations may also lead to more prudent behaviour if there is a high risk for the leader to be held personally responsible for failures. In fact, personalization changes the 'accountability environment' of foreign policy (Narang and Staniland 2018), with personalistic leaders being more liable to be held directly accountable for their respective foreign policies' success or failure. This is where personalization is also closely related to mobilization: the direct involvement of the leader in a foreign policy issue will likely create awareness about it and it will be accompanied by its politicization. However, as we contend here, personalization and mobilization do not always go hand in hand.

Mobilization around foreign policy issues takes place with different intensities. We argue that strong mobilization around a certain foreign policy topic will increase the likelihood of foreign policy change under populist governments. For one, mobilization is about bringing a foreign policy issue into the sphere of domestic political debates. This frequently involves bashing the 'political establishment' or the 'elites' of the previous government for wrong policies not benefitting the 'people'. A call for a different approach, for foreign policy change, is a natural consequence. In his typology of populist politicization of foreign policy, Cadier (2024, 6) also points out that populists will try to distinguish their approach from that of their non-populist predecessors (what he calls, 'counter-step' foreign policy). Donald Trump's vocal opposition to any of his predecessor's foreign policy achievements—from the Transpacific Partnership to dealing with North Korea or Iran—is exemplary. Radical change is an almost natural conclusion if mobilization relies on the highly moralistic (Hawkins et al. 2018) distinctions that are peculiar to populism.

Moreover, the populist understanding of the 'people' and the elite entails a Manichean distinction between an in-group and an out-group, usually expressed in moral terms. Depending on the specific context, populists might associate a certain out-group with a foreign country or an international institution (Destradi and Plagemann 2019). For example, depicting their political approach as a struggle against 'Brussels' and predatory elites, populists in Europe almost automatically commit themselves to foreign policy change. Donald Trump's animosity towards traditional US allies Mexico and Canada in part stemmed from the latters' association with migrants and domestic liberal critics. Also in this case, stronger populist mobilization is likely to contribute to more marked changes in foreign policy: the more vocal a populist's critique of his or her country's adherence to cooperative relations with foreign partners, the more likely he or she will change such practices once in power. For instance, in her study of populism and nationalism, Jenne (2021, 330) points out that populist mobilizational frames lead to pressures for 'systemic revisionism'. This means that populist leaders aim to break with traditional foreign policy practices of previous elites and 'claw back sovereignty from domestic and foreign elites by rejecting the authority of supranational organizations such as the EU or UN or excluding transnational advocacy networks, foreign NGOs or other foreign actors that frustrate self-governance. It might also mean turning away from traditional allies who are seen as limiting the sovereignty of the political in-group over the affairs of the state' (Jenne 2021, 331–32).

Importantly, mobilization can have unintended consequences that contribute to explaining foreign policy change. If populists heavily politicize a foreign policy issue and mobilize around it, they create potential audience costs. In order to maintain their domestic political credibility, they will ultimately be forced to live up to their rhetoric. As a result, for example, domestic politics may incentivize a tougher foreign policy posture, thus contributing to escalating tensions and eventually complicating a potential agreement. Thus, if a populist had used an international dispute to mobilize domestic support, making concessions in such dispute would look like surrendering to the enemy. This underscores that foreign policy change will be more pronounced if a populist government strongly uses an issue for domestic political mobilization.

Intensities of Change

Based on the previous discussion of why we should expect various intensities of personalization and mobilization to lead to more or less intense foreign policy change, we now bring these two elements together. Our core argument is that populism in power leads to foreign policy change, but that this change will not take place in the same way across the board. Instead, it will vary across foreign policy issues or even single bilateral relationships, and such variation will be driven in large parts by different intensities of personalization and mobilization. While these concepts, as well as populism itself and its components, are usually considered to be continuous (e.g., Akkerman, Mudde, and Zaslove 2014; Destradi, Plagemann, and Taş 2022), for the sake of simplicity here we distinguish between strong and weak personalization and mobilization, leading to strong, moderate, or no foreign policy change (see details on the operationalization below).

As is illustrated in Table 2.1, we expect foreign policy change to be strong if both personalization and mobilization are strong. With the notion of programme change by Hermann (1990) as a frame of reference, we understand strong foreign policy change as a shift to entirely different means in addressing an issue. In each of the Chapters 3–6, we start by outlining what this means specifically for the foreign policy issue addressed in that chapter. For example, in Chapter 3, we define strong foreign policy change as a shift to a more conflictive foreign policy, operationalized as the use of more conflictive foreign policy means (measured on a modified Goldstein scale of conflict-cooperation; see Goldstein [1992]). As was mentioned above, strong foreign policy change can also involve a clear shift in the very objectives of foreign policy, that is, what Hermann (1990) labels 'problem/goal changes'. This will be relevant especially in Chapter 4 on the provision of global public goods,

Table 2.1 Populism and foreign policy change

		Personalization	
		Strong	**Weak**
Mobilization	**Strong**	*Strong foreign policy change*: leader less constrained by bureaucratic apparatus and therefore free to break with the past + leader able to mobilize support along the lines of thin and thick ideology	*Moderate foreign policy change*: leader more constrained by bureaucratic apparatus, but trying to generate support along the lines of thin and thick ideology
	Weak	*Moderate foreign policy change*: leader free to break with the past, but unable to use the issue for mobilization	*No foreign policy change*: leader constrained by bureaucratic apparatus, and unable to use the issue for mobilization

where strong foreign policy change might also involve a rather fundamental shift in understanding global public goods provision in an issue area as an important first goal. In Chapter 6, where we focus on populist governments' shifts towards new international partners, we understand strong foreign policy change as the abandonment of traditional international partnerships and the formation of new ones—something that ultimately amounts to a reorientation in foreign policy, a redirection of a country's overall approach to international politics (Hermann 1990, 5–6). According to our theory of populist foreign policy, strong personalization and strong mobilization will lead to particularly marked foreign policy change. Leaders who clearly personalize decision making in a specific issue area will have much greater leeway for promoting change, and if they strongly mobilize around that same foreign policy issue, they will be further forced to live up to their own mobilizing discourse.

If personalization is weak but mobilization is strong (upper-right quadrant in Table 2.1), we also expect foreign policy change under a populist government, but this change will be more moderate. This will be the case because the leader will whip up expectations about change via mobilization, but will be more constrained by the bureaucratic apparatus, which will guarantee greater foreign policy continuity. Such more limited personalization may be driven by the resilience of bureaucracies. As is documented by Lequesne (2021), for example, diplomats from Austria and Italy managed to withstand populist pressures towards a weakening of the respective foreign services. The relatively strong presence of so-called grown-ups from the United States' traditional strategic community throughout the first years of Trump's first administration tempered some of his instincts and thus stood in the way of more radical foreign policy changes (Sanger 2024). Another constraint leading to more limited personalization might be represented by the resilience of the strategic community, possibly with strong connections to civil society. This might prevent the populist leader from personalizing power excessively, ultimately forcing the populist government to allow some influence to individuals and organizations not immediately affiliated with the leader. For example, in Israel after the Hamas attack of 7 October 2023 and ahead of the start of the military campaign in Gaza, populist Prime Minister Netanyahu was pressurized to form a national unity government and ultimately won the support of the National Unity party including two prominent figures of that party, Benny Gantz and Gadi Eizenkot, in his war cabinet.

Similarly, if personalization is strong but mobilization is weak (lower-left quadrant in Table 2.1), we expect foreign policy to change, but to a moderate extent. While in this case the leader will be able to sideline foreign policy bureaucracies and personalize foreign policy making, the specific foreign policy issue will not be used for mobilization beyond a certain point. This will be the case, for example, in foreign policy issues that do not resonate particularly well with either the populist's respective thin or thick ideology. Despite a personal interest in an issue, a populist leader will not be able to capitalize on it for domestic political gains. This may reduce pressure for change since the public does not expect or welcome a turnabout in foreign policy on an issue that the populist government does not emphasize much in public discourse.[11]

Finally, if both mobilization and personalization are weak, we expect continuity in foreign policy. This will be the case because the populist leader is constrained by the bureaucracy, advisors from the traditional establishment, or by other actors such as the military at the same time as there is little public attention generated around a foreign policy issue via mobilization.

Context Conditions

Our theory of populist foreign policy develops testable hypotheses about the nature and intensity of foreign policy change that we expect under populist governments. As is always the case in foreign policy analysis, we should be aware of the simplifying assumptions made while emphasizing a specific set of explanatory factors. Foreign policy is the outcome of different factors and forces operating at various levels of analysis (see Haesebrouck and Joly 2021; Kaarbo and Thies 2024a). For example, structural factors like the relative power capabilities of a country will of course play an important role in shaping its government's room for manoeuvre in international politics (Blavoukos and Bourantonis 2014; Wivel 2024). Moreover, foreign policy always entails a relational component (think of the literature on two-level games, e.g., Putnam 1988), so that many decisions emerge as reactions to a third party's foreign policy, adding an idiosyncratic element to any foreign policy decision (see also Blavoukos and Bourantonis 2014). Especially external shocks have been identified as a major driver of foreign policy change in the literature (Haesebrouck and Joly 2021, 486). In order to keep as many contextual factors as similar as possible, in this book we chose a diachronic within-case comparative approach. In other words, we are interested in whether the formation of a populist government leads to foreign policy changes as compared to the course followed in the same country by

[11] Note that according to liberal theories of international politics the absence of public interest ascribes the leader or government more leeway in its foreign policy conduct as opposed to issues with high voter salience and, correspondingly, significant audience costs (Oppermann and Viehrig 2011, 8). We think this underlines the necessity of an original theory of populist foreign policy.

a preceding non-populist government. In the empirical chapters, following a most-similar-systems logic, we try to address issues that are as similar as possible to identify whether the populist government reacted differently as compared to the preceding non-populist one under similar conditions. For instance, in studying India's dispute with Pakistan in Chapter 3, we address specifically Indian governments' reactions to attacks carried out on Indian soil by Pakistan-sponsored terrorist groups, which occurred both under the non-populist government and under its populist successor.

One context condition that we take into account specifically in our theoretical framework and that needs to be highlighted at this stage is a populist government's perception of its own vulnerability in international politics. We focus on this factor starting from the assumption that populists are not irrational mavericks inevitably driving their countries into disaster, but political actors keen to get re-elected (see above). Even though highly personalistic populist leadership may be prone to misjudgements, for example via the overestimation of the country's capabilities, populists in principle are still unlikely to pursue policies that are bound to harm their political careers. This means that they will be sensitive to the structural constraints their country is faced with—all the more so if they lead relatively small or weak states (Wivel 2024). In particular, populist leaders take into account their country's limitations in dealing with international adversaries and partners, and they will not ignore the constraints but also the opportunities arising from its embeddedness in regional or global multilateral institutions. This is why, for example, we do not expect a populist government to escalate a dispute with a neighbouring country from a position of clear military inferiority, even though in the short term the escalation of such a dispute could be useful for domestic mobilization. As we will see in the case of India's approach towards China, in some cases it is precisely the awareness of these structural constraints and of a country's vulnerability that induces populist governments to refrain from mobilizing too much around a specific dispute. This also contributes to explain why personalization and mobilization do not always go hand in hand. Similarly, we expect a populist government that perceives its country to be in a vulnerable position not to challenge a useful security alliance, even if mobilizing against it would fit with its thin and thick ideology. This is why, for example, populist Greek Prime Minister Papandreou never implemented his threats to withdraw from NATO during the Cold War (Chryssogelos 2021, 727). Moreover, the desire to make use of the benefits of multilateralism, including of substantial financial transfers, might also ultimately explain why, despite all Euroscepticism of their populist governments, central-eastern European countries like Hungary and Poland have not left the EU. Likewise, Recep

Erdoğan's habitual bashing of the West and diplomatic overtures to Putin's Russia notwithstanding, the Turkish prime minister and later president has shown no sign of abandoning NATO, the quintessential Western alliance.

In any case, depending on a populist's sensitivity to the major constraint of his or her country's vulnerability in international politics, we can expect to see some of the effects of personalization and mobilization to be mitigated. As a consequence, we hypothesize that it will make a difference whether populists govern in strong states, where they will be less restrained in their foreign policy choices by structural conditions, or in weak states with limited capabilities, where they will be forced to adjust their desired foreign policy to the realities of international affairs. Personalization and mobilization will play out more forcefully in strong states, and this is where we expect populism to have the most tangible effects. We will discuss this aspect based on our cross-country comparative insights in the Conclusion.

Finally, another important element to take into account is a temporal one. Some populist governments stay in power for several consecutive terms, and we hypothesize that this aspect also makes a difference in shaping the impact of populism on foreign policy. From the literature in Comparative Politics and Political Theory, we know that populists in power tend to weaken checks and balances and to undermine democratic institutions (Pappas 2019; Urbinati 2019a). Ultimately, populism leads to democratic backsliding.[12] The room for foreign policy change might grow quite substantially as time passes because there will be fewer institutions able to counter populist personalization. Moreover, populist mobilization around foreign policy issues will become more and more ingrained and normalized, as people are constantly exposed to it and the independent media is sidelined, silenced, or persecuted (Ernst et al. 2019; Sehl, Simon, and Schroeder 2022). For these reasons, we expect that, the longer populists are in power, the stronger foreign policy change will be as compared to the preceding non-populist government. This is in line with recent research on foreign policy change in democracies vs. autocracies, which finds that the foreign policies of democracies are characterized by greater continuity than those of nondemocracies (Leeds and Mattes 2022). Democratic checks and balances such as the oversight of the legislature and the judiciary, but also the constraining powers of bureaucracies play an important role in preventing leaders from pursuing radical foreign policy turnovers (Leeds and Mattes 2022).

---

[12] On democratic backsliding, see e.g., Waldner and Lust (2018), Grzymala-Busse (2019), Hyde (2020), Bauer and Becker (2020), Leon (2022), and Huber and Pisciotta (2023).

On the other hand, being in power for longer periods of time may also rub off the revolutionary zeal of some populists. Once a certain course of foreign policy has been established, some changes have been realized and many obstacles have been encountered, the original impetus for fundamental change may lessen and the more systemic factors co-determining a country's foreign relations come to the fore again. Moreover, in some cases it is very difficult to assess foreign policy change over very long periods of time—think of climate change mitigation policies, which overall had much less salience worldwide two decades ago: how would we be able to study the impact of populism on foreign policy change in this issue area, particularly if some governments have been in power for many years? We address this issue by also focusing on whether the foreign policy of a populist government that has been in power for many years changes over time, asking whether mobilization and personalization intensify over time and produce more marked shifts in foreign policy.

3

Escalation of International Disputes

Are populist governments more likely than non-populist ones to escalate or initiate international disputes?[1] Conflict behaviour is one of the most significant aspects of foreign policy, and anecdotal evidence suggests that populists in power are prone to use more conflictive rhetoric and foreign policy means. Venezuelan President Chávez verbally attacked the United States, US President Trump threatened North Korea with 'fire and fury', President Rodrigo Duterte in the Philippines called US President Obama a 'son of a whore', and Brazil's Jair Bolsonaro joked about French President Macron's wife on social media (Baker and Sang-Hun 2017; Gayle 2016; France24 2019). Going beyond rhetoric, Trump started a 'trade war' with China; Turkey under Erdoğan intervened militarily in Syria, Libya, and via crucial arms exports in the conflict between Armenia and Azerbaijan; India's Prime Minister Modi ordered air strikes on Pakistani territory ahead of Indian elections in 2019; and Benjamin Netanyahu made opposing Palestinian statehood official Israeli policy (Shaheen 2016; Reuters 2024). All this seems to point towards a proclivity on the part of populists to adopt aggressive rhetoric, if not policies. Beyond anecdotal evidence, however, we do not know much about whether populists are really a danger to international peace as some authors claim (e.g., Meier and Vieluf 2021). Indeed some studies have shown that populist parties have mixed attitudes on the use of force, depending more on their thick ideologies and on the specificities of national strategic cultures (Falkner and Plattner 2020; Henke and Maher 2021) than on the thin ideology of populism. Moreover, comparative research has found that not all populists in power pursue more conflictive policies (Destradi and Plagemann 2019). Özdamar and Ceydilek (2020), in turn, found that European populist radical right leaders ultimately pursued foreign policies that were similar to

---

[1] Large parts of this chapter are based on the following article: Sandra Destradi and Johannes Plagemann (2024), 'Do Populists Escalate International Disputes?', *International Affairs* 100 (5): 1919–1940, https://doi.org/10.1093/ia/iiae172. Relevant permissions were obtained as this is an Open Access article distributed under the terms of the Creative Commons Attribution License (https://creativecommons.org/licenses/by/4.0/).

Populism and Foreign Policy. Sandra Destradi and Johannes Plagemann, Oxford University Press.
© Oxford University Press (2025). DOI: 10.1093/9780197695012.003.0003

the average in terms of propensity to conflict, despite holding more conflictive worldviews.

We argue that there are several theoretical reasons to expect populists to be more prone to escalate or initiate international disputes as compared to non-populists. We develop our expectation based on the understanding of populism as a thin-centred ideology as outlined in Chapter 2. First of all, populists will find it more difficult to compromise in international disputes because of their Manichean worldview and of their very claim of embodying the popular will. In fact, seeing the world in highly moralistic binary oppositions of good vs. evil or us vs. them will make it more difficult for populists to justify any compromise with the 'enemy'. Such binaries inevitably reduce the room for negotiation, making the choice of non-diplomatic means in international disputes more likely. People-centrism and the notion of representation as embodiment of the popular will also make compromises more difficult to achieve: populists tend to assume that the 'true people' is always right and, by extension, that the populist leader is practically infallible. This inevitably makes it more difficult for populists to acknowledge mistakes or to backtrack on previous promises or commitments. Populist leaders, feeling less constrained by the diplomatic traditions and established positions of their countries, may be more inclined to generate or exacerbate tensions. Besides these theoretical expectations at the level of populist governments, some recent findings from empirical research on individual attitudes similarly point towards populism being associated with a propensity to escalate disputes. In fact, such research has found that individuals with populist attitudes also tend to be more likely to consider it acceptable to use violence to achieve political goals (Piazza 2024).

However, in line with our more general theoretical framework outlined in Chapter 2, we do not expect populists to escalate all kinds of disputes all the time. In fact, we argue that populists' tendency to adopt more conflictive foreign policy means plays out more or less forcefully depending on the intensity of personalization and mobilization around specific foreign policy disputes. In our empirical analysis in this chapter, we focus on existing or latent bilateral disputes. To assess whether the foreign policy means adopted by a populist government were more or less conflictive as compared to those of a preceding non-populist government, we resort to an operationalization of foreign policy means based on the classic conflict-cooperation scale by Goldstein (1992). This scale provides a classification of sixty-one types of non-verbal and verbal action that reach from military attack, the most conflictive, to the provision of military assistance, the most cooperative. Our qualitative case study analysis aggregates the Goldstein indicators into a more limited number of categories placed on a conflict-cooperation continuum: use of force, military threats, sanctions, public criticism, neutral interactions, compliance, diplomatic support, material support, and military support. We are interested in whether populists in power escalate international disputes and we consider escalatory behaviour to be the shift towards more conflictive foreign policy means. A strong foreign policy change corresponds to a 'more conflictive' foreign policy, operationalized as a move of at least two steps towards the 'conflict' end of the continuum in these categories. A moderate foreign policy change corresponds to an only 'somewhat more conflictive' foreign policy, which is operationalized as a shift of one step towards the more conflictive end of the continuum.

We expect populists to pursue a more conflictive foreign policy in a (latent) dispute if both mobilization and personalization are strong. This is the case for various reasons. While the politicization of foreign policy does not make it more conflictive per se, the way populists mobilize support suggests a greater likelihood of escalation. In fact, populists typically rally support by pitting the 'people' against domestic 'elites' and other groups outside the true people. Depending on the precise context, these elites and out-groups may also be associated with foreign countries or governments, or they may be identified as international or transnational elites—and this may then transport the domestic struggle between good and evil into international politics. Moreover, as populist mobilization promises to break with the establishment's past policies, calling for changes in foreign policy is a likely consequence. This may turn latent disputes into escalating ones. If a dispute resonates with a populist government's thick ideology and allows for the discursive construction of a friend-enemy dichotomy, mobilization will likely be strong: The populist leader will use the dispute's salience to mobilize domestic support while resorting to both thin and thick ideology to justify it. This often happens in highly moralistic terms, the dispute being framed as a battle of good vs. evil and with some external enemy often linked to corrupt domestic elites. Ultimately, mobilization by populist leaders reshapes their audiences' views about the relative benefits of pursuing a more conflictive foreign policy. It harnesses pre-existing popular enthusiasm for escalation—or reduces resistance to it—and makes foreign policy change towards a more conflictive foreign policy likely. However, such mobilization may also have unintended consequences, as populists may be forced to live up to their hostile rhetoric if they want to uphold their domestic credibility. In other words, mobilization increases domestic audience costs (Fearon 1994) and thus potentially makes backtracking vis-à-vis a foreign adversary politically costly. By contrast, if a dispute does not resonate with the thin and thick ideology of the populist government, if it lacks voter salience, or if the thick ideology in itself is vague or inconsistent, mobilization will be weak, and the populist government will not substantially reshape the public's preferences towards escalation.

We also expect the personalization of foreign policy making to contribute to the use of more conflictive foreign policy means for several reasons. Highly insulated decision making is more likely to lead to risky and confrontational foreign policy since the leader is free to ignore professional advice and is more likely to sideline domestic actors that commonly stand for a more accommodative behaviour, such as bureaucracies, but also civil society groups, or (some) opposition parties. Moreover, by crowding out establishment elements, fringe figures and/or ideological hardliners become more influential. Ideological zealots not only tend to be less pragmatic than the foreign policy establishment. They also often have only a limited understanding of foreign countries' politics and capabilities. Ignorance increases the likelihood of more confrontational policies, not necessarily by design but by accident. Groupthink within such small groups of non-establishment advisors is likely to exacerbate conflictive behaviour, too (see Chapter 2). Finally, a highly personalized foreign policy will also make the leader's foreign policy activities particularly visible. Thus, the attribution of success or failure to the leader will be more direct. All this makes it more difficult for populist leaders as compared to non-populist ones to compromise in international negotiations or to backtrack as compared to their previous uncompromising stances. In sum, we expect a more conflictive approach, the more foreign policy is personalized. Herein, our theory speaks to research on personalist autocrats, who have been found to be particularly likely to initiate conflicts (Weeks 2012).

Different intensities of mobilization and personalization will impact foreign policy change in governments' approaches to international disputes in various ways, summarized in Table 3.1. For the sake of simplicity, we only distinguish between strong and weak mobilization and personalization, even though both are conceptualized as continua. Mobilization is strong if populists explicitly and consistently connect an actual or latent bilateral dispute to domestic politics along the lines of thin and thick ideology. It is weak if the populist government only implicitly or sporadically refers to the dispute in domestic discourse. Personalization is strong if foreign policy decisions are made personally by the leader and a very restricted group of advisors, while the foreign ministry and/or other relevant ministries as well as civil society actors and the strategic community are largely excluded from the process. It is weak if more inclusive procedures constraining the leader's impulses remain in place.

Table 3.1 Populism and international conflict behaviour

		Personalization	
		Strong	**Weak**
Mobilization	**Strong**	*More conflictive*	*Somewhat more conflictive*
	Weak	*Somewhat more conflictive*	*Not more conflictive*

First, we expect the approach to a dispute to become more conflictive (that is, to involve means located two or more categories further towards the 'conflict' end of the continuum) after populist government formation if both personalization and mobilization around a dispute are strong.

Populist leaders who are more constrained by the bureaucratic apparatus and/or experts, advisors, and members of civil society will pursue a less confrontational foreign policy as compared to those who strongly personalize foreign policy making. Similarly, populists who do not extensively use a foreign policy issue for domestic mobilization will be less prone to adopting a more conflictive approach. We therefore expect weak personalization combined with strong mobilization (Table 3.1, upper-right quadrant) to also lead to a more conflictive foreign policy, but less so than in the case of both strong personalization and strong mobilization: Populists will shift to only somewhat more conflictive foreign policy means. Likewise, strong personalization combined with weak mobilization leads to an only somewhat more conflictive foreign policy (lower-left quadrant). If neither personalization nor mobilization with reference to a specific dispute is strong, we do not expect populists to pursue a more conflictive foreign policy. This helps us make sense of cases in which populist foreign policies display continuity with the policies of preceding non-populist governments.

Our Findings

The core contention of our theoretical framework is that the combination of different degrees of mobilization and personalization leads to variations in foreign policy change with the transition from a non-populist to a populist government. Table 3.2 summarizes our findings for all cases, which we discuss below.

Table 3.2 Summary of findings

		Personalization	
		Strong	**Weak**
Mobilization	**Strong**	*More conflictive* India-Pakistan Bolivia-US Turkey-Greece Turkey-Germany	*Somewhat more conflictive* Bolivia-Chile
	Weak	*Somewhat more conflictive* Philippines-US India-China	*Not more conflictive* Philippines-China

However, populist foreign policy, like all foreign policy, does not take place in a vacuum. The international context in which populists engage their partners and adversaries matters. As discussed in Chapter 2, we presume that a state's perception of its relative strength or vulnerability affects its foreign behaviour. Populists are therefore unlikely to escalate bilateral conflicts militarily vis-à-vis clearly superior adversaries, even if this was valuable for mobilization purposes in the short term. Similarly, in such circumstances, populist governments tend to maintain established security alliances even if they do not fit with their thick ideology. Consequently, we can expect populist mobilization and personalization of foreign policy to play out more forcefully (and to lead to more extensive foreign policy change) in strong states, where governments feel less restrained by foreign forces, than in weaker ones.

In our abductive theory-building process, we focused on four country cases that experienced a shift from a non-populist to a populist government (see Chapter 1; Table 3.3). To study the impact of populism on the propensity to escalate bilateral disputes, for each country, we chose two pre-existing or latent bilateral disputes, asking to what extent foreign policy became more conflictive in each of them. We included long-standing territorial disputes (with Chile for Bolivia, with Pakistan for India, with China for the Philippines, with Greece for Turkey) and disputes with one important extra-regional power with which some potential for bilateral tensions existed before the formation of the populist government (US for Bolivia, China for India, US for the Philippines, and Germany for Turkey). The analysis of those eight bilateral disputes was based on a broad range of primary and secondary sources such as official statements and documents, newspaper articles, think tank reports, grey literature, and so forth, and it was complemented by expert interviews (see Chapter 1).

Table 3.3 Country cases and bilateral disputes under non-populist and populist governments

	Time period	Non-populist and populist governments	Bilateral disputes
Bolivia	2002–2006	Presidents Sánchez de Lozada, Mesa (both from Movimiento Nacionalista Revolucionario), and Rodríguez Veltzé (independent)	Chile (territorial dispute ocean access) US (counternarcotics)
	2006–2019	President Evo Morales (Movimiento al Socialismo)	
India	2004–2014	Prime Minister Manmohan Singh (Indian National Congress)/United Progressive Alliance (UPA I and II)	Pakistan (territorial dispute Kashmir) China (border issues, regional competition)
	2014–2024	Prime Minister Narendra Modi (Bharatiya Janata Party)/National Democratic Alliance (NDA I and II)	
The Philippines	2010–2016	President Benigno Aquino III (Liberal Party)	China (territorial dispute South China Sea) US (security dependence)
	2016–2022	President Rodrigo Duterte (Partido Demokratiko Pilipino—Lakas ng Bayan)	
Turkey	1999–2002	Prime Minister Bülent Ecevit (Democratic Left Party)/ANASOL-M coalition	Greece (territorial dispute, minority issues) Germany (EU accession, diaspora, human rights)
	2003–2011	Prime Minister Erdoğan (non-populist phase), AKP	
	2011–2014	Prime Minister Erdoğan, AKP	
	2014–2018	President Erdoğan, AKP	
	Since 2018	Executive President Erdoğan, AKP	

Strong Personalization, Strong Mobilization

India-Pakistan

Under the populist government led by Prime Minister Modi of the Hindu-nationalist Bharatiya Janata Party (BJP) since 2014, India's approach to Pakistan has become clearly more conflictive as compared to that of the non-populist predecessor United Progressive Alliance (UPA) I and II governments under the leadership of Prime Minister Manmohan Singh of the Indian National Congress (INC).

India and Pakistan have been arch-enemies since independence in 1947. The two countries emerged from the partition of British India, a traumatic event that displaced 15 million, 'the largest forced migration of the twentieth century', and caused a death toll ranging between 200,000 and 2 million victims (Talbot and Singh 2009, 2). One born as a secular state and the other as the homeland for the Muslims of South Asia, India and Pakistan fought wars over Kashmir, a Muslim-majority region in the Himalayas which both claim as their respective territory, in 1947–1948 and in 1965. Moreover, in 1971 India supported Bangladesh's independence movement, with the war ultimately leading to Pakistan's loss of its entire eastern territory.[2] In 1999, India and Pakistan, which by then had both acquired and tested nuclear weapons, fought the Kargil war, a high-altitude conflict unleashed by Pakistani forces crossing the de facto border called Line of Control (LoC). The hostilities ultimately ended also thanks to pressure by the US on Pakistan (Ganguly 2016, 41–42). The following years were marked by efforts towards a rapprochement, to a large extent driven by the Hindu-nationalist (but not populist) Indian prime minister Atal Bihari Vajpayee (1998–2004).[3] The so-called Composite Dialogue with Pakistan aimed at improving bilateral ties by discussing a broad range of disputed issues beyond just Kashmir, from water sharing to border demarcation (Gul 2008).

When the non-populist UPA I government under the leadership of the economist Manmohan Singh took over in 2004, it continued the dialogue with Pakistan via official and back-channel negotiations (Lambah 2023). According to a retired diplomat directly involved in India's Pakistan policy during the UPA years, at that time India's policy 'was focused on building a calm periphery', including via the South Asian Association for Regional

---

[2] For overviews of India-Pakistan relations, see e.g., Ganguly (2002) and Bose (2005).
[3] For an additional comparison of Modi's and Vajpayee's government, see Plagemann and Destradi (2019b).

Cooperation (SAARC).[4] The back-channel talks were reportedly quite successful in producing 'an understanding that any potential peace would involve two key ideas. First, the LOC would become an international border with only minor, mutually-agreed adjustments. Second, the border would be a soft one; that is, a border permitting maximum movement of Kashmiris between the two states' (Riedel 2009, 114). However, in 2008 a major coordinated terrorist attack by Lashkar-e-Taiba, an Islamist organization from Pakistan, hit Mumbai. The terrorists targeted iconic sites in India's main business metropolis such as the Chhatrapati Shivaji Maharaj Terminus railway station, and the Taj Mahal hotel. Parts of the city were held hostage for several days, and over 150 people were killed. The UPA I government reacted in a very moderate way: the Composite Dialogue was interrupted, but Prime Minister Singh withstood domestic pressures for retaliatory military measures, thus displaying 'remarkable restraint' (Riedel 2009, 111). During the following years, India's approach to Pakistan continued in a way that Bajpai (2017, 69) calls a 'slow-to-anger bilateral diplomacy'. According to a retired diplomat, 'the idea was not to break up everything. The focus was on the trial [of Mohammed Ajmal Amir Qasab, the only terrorist who survived]'.[5]

Things changed under the populist BJP-led government of Prime Minister Modi. Initially, he surprised observers with a phase of bonhomie towards Pakistan, epitomized by Modi's theatrical visit to Pakistan for Prime Minister Nawaz Sharif's birthday in December 2015. However, this rapprochement ended abruptly as the Pakistan-based Islamist militant group Jaish-e-Mohammad (JeM) attacked an Indian airbase at Pathankot in January 2016 and killed 19 Indian soldiers in another attack in Uri, Jammu and Kashmir, in September 2016. After a failed attempt to promote a joint investigation of the Pathankot attack, the Indian government changed its approach.[6] For one, in interactions with Pakistan, Modi emphasized more strongly the topic of terrorism, while 'avoid[ing] the subject of Kashmir's future altogether' (Bajpai 2017, 75). Moreover, Modi's rhetoric became clearly more confrontational. For instance, he broke a taboo by mentioning separatism in Pakistan's Balochistan province during his Independence Day speech in August 2016 (Haidar 2021) – a thinly veiled threat of Indian support for separatists in response to Pakistani misbehaviour. Most remarkably, after the Uri attack, Indian special forces carried out operations against militants on territory controlled by Pakistan. Although similar operations had occurred before,[7]

---

[4] Interview I05, retired Indian diplomat, New Delhi, 28 February 2023.

[5] Interview I05.

[6] Interview I20, Indian security expert, New Delhi, 9 March 2023.

[7] This was confirmed to us by a retired diplomat who had extensive first-hand insights: Interview I07, retired Indian diplomat, New Delhi, 1 March 2023

Modi in contrast to his predecessors publicized the raids widely (Clary 2022, 288) and thereby used them for domestic mobilization in line with his thin and thick ideology. Even the Bollywood movie industry picked up the topic, producing a military action blockbuster titled *Uri: The Surgical Strike* that came out in 2019.

Indeed, mobilization around the conflict with Pakistan was well in line with *Hindutva*, the ideology espoused by the BJP that ultimately aims to transform India into a Hindu nation, thus excluding India's sizeable Muslim minority from its understanding of the 'people' (Jaffrelot 2021). In this kind of discourse, a deep connection is created between India's Muslims and Pakistan. As Wojczewski (2020b, 408–9) puts it:

> Pakistan plays a crucial role in the Hindu nationalist imaginary. It serves as the prime external Other against which India is discursively constructed and reproduced as a Hindu space. Accordingly, Pakistan symbolizes the conquest and subjugation of the ancient Hindu *rashtra* through Islamic invaders and the later partition of "Akhand Bharat" [undivided India] into two separate states. By Islamizing the Pakistani threat and representing it as an aggressive, irredentist, and cultural enemy, the discourse seeks to communalize the Indo-Pakistani conflict and unite Hindus in a common front.

For instance, Modi during the election campaign of 2024 called India's Muslims the Congress Party's 'Jihadi Vote Bank' (Bharatiya Janata Party 2024). Examples such as this one illustrate how India's Muslim minority has been more or less explicitly despised as Pakistan's 'fifth column', all the while implicating political forces outside the Hindu-nationalist fold as traitors or 'anti-nationals'.[8] Mobilization further intensified after another attack on Indian security personnel took place, in Pulwama in Indian-administered Kashmir in February 2019, leading to over forty victims. Days later, the prime minister authorized air strikes on a suspected JeM facility near Balakot in Pakistan proper. Despite its dubious operational success, the strikes represented a major break with past precedent not to strike Pakistani territory. As Sridharan (2020, 166–67) puts it: 'Although an Indian pilot in a MiG-21 fighter was shot down, captured, and then returned without conditions by Pakistan (a development in which the Trump administration might have played a discreet role), the BJP government won the media battle in the election campaign on this issue, putting the opposition on the defensive'. Domestically, air strikes were widely celebrated as a decisive move by the prime minister, underscoring his image as a daring leader ahead of the April–May 2019 general

---

[8] Interview I05.

elections. According to an interviewee, 'the media coverage was as if Indian jets were flying through all of Pakistan [while] in reality, the incursion into Pakistan was small and short'.[9] In his 2019 campaign speeches, Modi often referred to the strikes, highlighting his qualities as a *chowkidar* (watchman) protecting the country, as opposed to an allegedly 'anti-national' opposition:

> When we entered the homes of these terrorists and killed them, was it then right to question the army this way? [. . .] the Congress 'nobles' say that Modi shouldn't say all this. Modi shouldn't talk about Balakot, Modi shouldn't talk about India's national security, terrorism? Should Modi just keep mum? Should Modi be scared of terror threats? Friends, this *chowkidar* does not have the *sanskar* [values] of being scared. (Hindustan Times 2019)

Addressing a rally in Maharashtra in April 2019, Modi appealed to first-time voters to dedicate their vote to the victims of the Pulwama attack and the executors of the Balakot air strikes (The Times of India 2019). Indeed, according to an Indian journalist we interviewed, 'The 2019 election was driven by the idea that we were teaching Pakistan a lesson'.[10]

A few months after Modi's re-election with an absolute majority for the BJP in the lower house of parliament, the Indian government in August 2019 revoked the special status of the state of Jammu and Kashmir (Sridharan 2020). Articles 370 and 35A of the Indian Constitution, which had granted a substantial degree of autonomy to the state were abolished, and Jammu and Kashmir was divided into two Union Territories to be administered directly by the central government. This change of the status quo in the disputed region was heavily criticized by Pakistan's Prime Minister Imran Khan, who expelled India's High Commissioner and set the revocation of those reforms as a precondition for the restoration of bilateral relations (The Economic Times 2019). Unsurprisingly, India's populist government was unwilling to give in to such demand, since the reform of Kashmir's status was one of the core points in its Hindu-nationalist agenda. As a result, bilateral relations worsened only further from 2019 onwards. Although the BJP reduced its mobilization against Pakistan after its electoral victory[11] and a ceasefire on the line of control separating the two countries was restored via back-channel talks in 2021 (Haidar and Bhattacherjee 2021), New Delhi continued to seek to isolate Pakistan internationally. At the regional level, India ignored the ailing South Asian Association for Regional Cooperation (SAARC) and instead

[9] I09, senior retired Indian diplomat, New Delhi, 1 March 2023.
[10] Interview I02, Indian journalist, New Delhi, 21 February 2023.
[11] Interview I05.

promoted alternative sub-regional schemes that exclude Islamabad such as the Bay of Bengal Initiative for Multi-Sectoral Technical and Economic Cooperation (BIMSTEC) or the Indian Ocean Rim Association (IORA) (see Chapter 5). Moreover, as a form of sanctioning, India revoked Pakistan's most-favoured-nation status in trade relations (India Today Web Desk 2019).

Besides mobilization, these shifts to more conflictive foreign policy means can also be related to strong personalization of foreign policy making in India under Modi. Indian prime ministers had always played an important role in managing bilateral relations with Pakistan. According to Lambah (2023, 36), who was a special envoy for Prime Minister Singh in back-channel negotiations with Pakistan, '[t]he Prime Minister is the final arbiter'. Under populist Prime Minister Modi, however, the trend towards personalization of power was clearly reinforced, all the more so in key bilateral relationships like those with Pakistan and China, as our interviewees confirmed. The Ministry of External Affairs (MEA) was increasingly sidelined—according to one interviewee, basically relegated to dealing with soft power and diaspora issues,[12] and with less salient relationships. Modi also abandoned past consultative practices. According to a retired diplomat with first-hand insights into India's Pakistan policy during the UPA governments, Manmohan Singh usually sought bipartisan consensus on delicate foreign policy matters: 'When there were issues with Pakistan, Manmohan Singh would call [BJP leaders] Sushma Swaraj, Advani and consult with them'.[13] This did not happen anymore under Modi, who managed relations with Pakistan personally, together with his National Security Advisor Ajit Doval[14]—something that likely contributed to an abandonment of dialogue efforts.[15] The high degree of personalization initially allowed Modi to make some surprising conciliatory moves, most notably his birthday visit to the Pakistani prime minister in late 2015. However, personalization arguably also increased the pressure on Modi as public opinion and his own support base called for a tougher stance vis-à-vis Pakistan, especially so following Pakistan-sponsored terrorist attacks in India. In fact, in October 2015, survey results by the PEW Research Centre gave Modi high marks on everything except his dealings with Pakistan (Donthi 2017). After the Uri attack of September 2016, '[f]acing a clamor at home, Prime Minister Modi opted to escalate' (Clary 2022). Ultimately, this case shows how populists in power may deepen the interrelation between domestic and

---

[12] Interview I18, retired Indian diplomat, New Delhi, 7 March 2023.
[13] Interview I05.
[14] Interviews I21, Indian scholar, New Delhi, 9 March 2023; I22, Indian scholar, New Delhi, 9 March 2023.
[15] In the specific case of the Balakot strike, a retired diplomat familiar with the decision-making process told us that the decision was made by the Cabinet Committee on Security and the NSA. Interview I07.

international politics, with high mobilization and personalization at times almost forcing a government to pursue a more confrontational foreign policy approach.

Bolivia-US

Another case of a shift towards a significantly more conflictive foreign policy was that of Bolivia in its approach to the United States under populist President Morales from 2006 onwards. Driven by a high degree of domestic mobilization and personalization, relations with the US turned sour around the latent dispute over counternarcotics and coca cultivation, in particular (Plagemann, Heras Rodríguez, and Destradi 2022).[16] The shift towards a more conflictive foreign policy was remarkable because Bolivia's approach to the US had been friendly throughout the preceding twenty-year period of market-oriented multiparty democracy. Bolivia never was among Washington's priorities within the region, as, for instance, Cuba, Venezuela, or Nicaragua had been at times. Yet, the US had been a key donor during the Cold War, it had supported relieving Bolivia of most of its bilateral debts in the late 1990s, and aid continued to flow in the early 2000s helped by Bolivia's association with the US' 'war on drugs' (Zambrana Marchetti 2017). Moreover, the US was Bolivia's leading supplier of arms. In fact, a key component of the country's 'pacted democracy' throughout the late 1980s until the end of Sánchez de Lozada's presidency in 2003 (Carrión 2022) was an elite-consensus around liberal economics along the 'Washington Consensus' and amicable relations with the US. Ironically, both elements greatly contributed to the political rise of Morales, thus foregrounding the breakdown of relations post-2006. While Morales was campaigning for the presidency for the first time in 2002, the US ambassador threatened the withdrawal of US aid in the case of Morales winning elections, a statement that only increased his wider appeal (he won a surprising 20.9% of the vote). A year later and facing a severe fiscal crisis, Bolivian President Sánchez de Lozada pushed for the expansion of liquefied gas exports to the US via a Chilean port, a manoeuvre that was so unpopular that it led to violent protests, which came to be known as the 'Gas War', and, eventually, to Lozada's resignation in late 2003 (Carrión 2022, 66–67). His replacement by Carlos Mesa deepened Bolivia's political instability but did not fundamentally alter the country's relations with the US. Eduardo Rodríguez Veltzé's short interim-presidency, in turn, was primarily

---

[16] Parts of this section are based on this article. Relevant permissions have been obtained.

focused on holding elections to re-establish political stability. In many ways, the 2005 elections represented a stark choice between Morales's Movimiento al Socialismo (MAS) and its opposition to what Bolivia's 'pacted democracy' stood for, on the one hand, and the US-friendly elites on the other hand, the '"winners" of the economic model and those who have traditionally ruled Bolivia' (Carrión 2022, 90).

US-Bolivian relations changed course after the MAS won the 2005 elections with the first single-party majority since the 1980s. The MAS has roots in Bolivian peasants' unions and coca growers from the central region of Cochabamba. Given their dissatisfaction with the 'war on drugs', changes in relations with the US were widely expected. Indeed, the latent dispute over coca cultivation had been used by Morales for mobilization during the election campaign along with opposition to 'neoliberalism' and free trade with the US.[17] Ahead of entering office, Morales called himself the Bush administration's 'worst nightmare' (Kohl 2010, 117) and he kept mobilizing around anti-US sentiments, often framed as anti-imperialism, after coming to power. The defence of national sovereignty was intertwined with allegations of US intervention in domestic affairs (Plagemann, Heras Rodríguez, and Destradi 2022, 19–24). Moreover, personalization became a prominent feature of foreign policy making under Morales, especially with regards to the relationship with the US. While Morales claimed to rule 'by obeying' to what the people wanted and indeed introduced mechanisms for greater civil society participation (Anria 2013), these had an impact on policy fields like environmental issues, but much less so on key bilateral relations. According to one of our interviewees, 'Evo was the head in what mattered to him' and this prominently included 'anti-imperialism' and the rejection of US influence in Bolivia.[18] A former Bolivian diplomat concurred that it was Morales calling the shots on relations with the US and that 'Evo had a particular personal animosity [against the US]'. Moreover, 'politically, this deterioration [of bilateral relations] has been exploited for domestic purposes'.[19] As phrased by a Bolivian scholar speaking with us, 'there is a flat Bolivian view of the governments in the United States and there is an anti-imperialism that is almost granite-like, it does not change in the slightest'.[20] A reason for this consistency was that Morales surrounded himself with a small circle of advisors (Ranta 2014). The constitutional reform of 2009 further strengthened the executive branch and

---

[17] Interview B18, David Agramont, Research Associate at the Peace Research Institute Frankfurt, Zoom, 15 February 2023.

[18] Interview B18.

[19] Interview B14, former career diplomat, La Paz, 6 February 2023.

[20] Interview B24, journalist and former senior diplomat, Zoom, 8 March 2023.

centralized decision making (Schilling-Vacaflor 2011). Against the backdrop of anti-US mobilization and personalization, Bolivia under Morales's populist government adopted a clearly more conflictive approach towards the US.

Within his first year in office, Morales introduced several measures ending previous cooperation on drugs. Particularly contentious was his opposition to US-led forced eradication of coca crops. Instead, the Morales government aimed to substantially expand coca cultivation legally, following a 'coca yes, cocaine no' approach (Grisaffi 2019). In 2006, the Bush administration reduced military aid to Bolivia by 96% in response to the refusal of the Bolivian Congress to ratify a bilateral agreement exempting US military personnel from the jurisdiction of the International Criminal Court. One year later, Bolivia announced its exiting from the Western Hemisphere Institute for Security Cooperation, previously known as the US Army School of the Americas (St John 2020, 172–73). In 2007, the US Embassy announced a substantial cut in counter-narcotics aid to Bolivia (Gamarra 2007, 29). While the EU and the United Nations Office on Drugs continued their cooperation with Bolivia, the US cancelled the preferential trade agreement with Bolivia under the Andean Trade Preferences Act (ATPA) (Seelke 2014, 7). From 2008 onwards, the US State Department designated Bolivia as a country that 'failed demonstrably' to adhere to the obligations undertaken under international counternarcotic agreements (Johnson 2008). In a context of growing bilateral tensions, Bolivia in September 2008 expelled the US ambassador, accusing him of 'dividing the country' (Azcui 2008). At that time, domestic political disputes around the Constituent Assembly, the autonomy of Eastern regions, and the distribution of oil revenues escalated in violent clashes between supporters of the government, opposition protesters, and security forces (Centellas 2013). The expulsion of the US ambassador was triggered by the fact that he had met with opposition governors of some of Bolivia's regions (*departamentos*). The US responded by expelling the Bolivian ambassador to Washington. The two countries have not exchanged ambassadors since then despite an intent of rapprochement during the Obama years. In line with his thick ideology, Morales explained the ambassador's expulsion to his supporters in this way:

> We have taken a decision, of course, a political one, to defend our dignity [. . .]. We realize that it has been an external conspiracy headed by the ambassador of the United States; without consulting anybody, neither the cabinet nor the social movements, I decided that that conspiring ambassador goes to his country. (Morales 2009)

Other domestic speeches further illustrate how Morales politicized relations with the US by discursively associating his domestic political opponents with foreign interests. For instance, during months of mounting political tensions in 2008, Morales said:

> The rich, the transnational companies, the oligarchs, they also have their political instrument that defends the latifundium, the privatizations. And these days I have heard, comrades, some prefects, some civic committees that publicly say that the Government, that the President should sign a Free Trade Agreement with the US. (Morales 2008a)

In 2008, Morales also declared the suspension of activities by the US Drug Enforcement Agency (DEA) in Bolivia, accusing it of meddling in domestic politics, funding opposition groups and spying (La Opinión/Agencias 2008). In that context, Morales described Bolivian politics before he came to power as essentially run by the US Embassy thus describing his political rivals as little more than US proxies. For instance, in Morales's inauguration speech after his re-election in 2009, referring to the time when he was expelled from parliament in 2002, he claimed that:

> The expelling of Evo Morales was also broadcasted in [State TV] Channel 7, I asked myself why because I thought that people would react as they did [increasing support to the MAS] but this broadcast was made so the [US] ambassador from his Embassy could control who voted and who did not vote. (Morales 2009)

Over the years, relations with the US were further cut to a minimum, as in 2013 Morales asked USAID to end its operations in the country entirely, accusing it of 'conspiring' against the government and of funding opposition activities (Azcui 2013; Seelke 2014, 7). Bad already, relations suffered another blow following an apparently spontaneous remark by Morales to *Russia Today* in July 2013. In Russia to attend an energy conference, Morales in an interview stated he might be willing to offer asylum to the former US intelligence analyst and whistle-blower Edward Snowden, who was at that time holed up at an airport near Moscow. Suspecting Snowden was accompanying Morales on his way back to Bolivia, some European governments denied the presidential plane to traverse their airspace so that Morales had to land in Vienna, waiting for hours to reroute. The diplomatic fallout of the episode was considerable, not the least since Snowden, despite reports to the contrary, had not left Moscow (Gladstone and Newman 2013). By the end of 2013, the US State Department also decided to close its Bureau of International Narcotics and Law Enforcement Affairs office in Bolivia, citing the lack of cooperation by the local authorities (Seelke 2014, 7).

As Morales and his MAS faced growing domestic opposition from 2016 onwards, the president intensified mobilization efforts around US-relations. With a divided public opinion ahead of a referendum on constitutional changes that would have allowed him to participate in the next presidential elections, in his discourse he increasingly associated his internal opponents with the US. For instance, days before the referendum of 2016, Morales accused the US Embassy of leaking information about a private scandal, and he depicted the referendum as a fight between the Bolivian people and 'the empire':

> To begin the campaign in favor of the Yes, I said: this campaign is against the empire, the empire's money, I would tell you about the information we have [. . .]. The No was born in Washington and the instructions come from there, the Bolivian people are confronted with a superpower. (Morales 2016)

Morales also accused the opposition of being incapable of autonomous action without US support, as in this speech of 2017, in which he threatened to expel the highest-ranking US diplomat remaining in the country: 'From the US Embassy, they have planned to attack the government, our democratic and cultural revolution, using corruption and narcotraffic. The right has no idea about how to attack us. Who does prepare it so they attack us? The US Embassy' (Agencia EFE 2017). This type of bellicose language continued after Morales lost the referendum and ahead of his controversial participation in the 2019 presidential elections.

In sum, Morales in his discourse throughout the entire fourteen years of his presidency depicted the US as a threatening force against which the Bolivian people ought to unite. By repeatedly presenting his domestic opponents as US puppets, he narrowed the scope for compromise further. The combination of a high degree of personalization and anti-US mobilization under the populist leader Morales uprooted existing cooperation with the US and led to a substantially more conflictive foreign policy as compared to that of preceding non-populist governments.

Turkey-Greece

Turkey's relations with its NATO ally Greece also fall in line with our expectations. Bilateral relations had been tempestuous throughout the twentieth century, given protracted disputes over Cyprus, maritime boundaries in the Aegean, and minority issues (Özerdem and Öztürk 2023; Grigoriadis 2022, 805). Among these, Cyprus proved the most intractable issue. Erdoğan's predecessor, Bülent Ecevit (1999–2002), had overseen Turkey's invasion of the Mediterranean island in 1974 as prime minister and was, at times, a vocal critic of Greece. Despite some attempts to improve relations (Efe 2000), under Ecevit Turkey did not compromise on the Cyprus issue, threatening to annex Northern Cyprus if the EU were to admit the republic before a settlement was reached (Christou 2001).

Compared to his immediate predecessor, Erdoğan during his non-populist phase starting in 2003 demonstrated more flexibility in resolving long-standing disputes with Greece. Elected on a pro-European platform, the AKP focused on advancing Turkey's EU membership and market liberal-ization. The conflictive course in relations with EU member state Greece, preferred by hardliners in the Kemalist security establishment, would have created new obstacles. Meanwhile, support for the EU, which demanded increasing civilian oversight, not only ensured the AKP's survival in a chal-lenging political landscape but also garnered new international allies at a time when foreign policy was heavily influenced by the military-dominated National Security Council (Cizre 2003, 221–22). Foreign policy making in the early Erdoğan years was shaped by Ahmet Davutoğlu, a former International Relations professor. At the centre of his new foreign policy approach were his 'Strategic Depth' doctrine marked by economic interdependence, public diplomacy, and the principle of 'zero problems with neighbors', all leading to his neo-Ottoman dream of a Turkey-led benign regional order (Tüysüzoğlu 2014). The AKP fully endorsed this self-confident yet mostly nonconfronta-tional foreign policy outlook, thus replacing the more rigid visions of Turkey's foreign policy cultivated by the Kemalist security apparatuses.[21]

Thus, Erdoğan's ascent to power created a new opportunity for a politi-cal settlement in Cyprus (Asmussen 2004). Reversing past policy (Altunışık 2022, 172), Erdoğan put pressure on the intransigent Turkish Cypriot leader Rauf Denktaş into accepting his government's more accommodating agenda over Cyprus (Yeni Şafak 2004). Prior to this, Denktaş had joined forces with Turkish generals to subvert the UN's 'Annan Plan' for the reunification and demilitarization of Cyprus (Bianet 2003). Thus, Erdoğan's attempts to resolve tensions over Cyprus came along with serious domestic political risks. Ulti-mately, the Annan Plan failed due to Greek Cypriots' resistance, and Cyprus

---

[21] Also see the article by Erdoğan's first foreign minister Abdullah Gül from 2004 proposing a 'Turkish vision' that assigned the country the role of a bridge-builder between Europe and the Middle East (Gül 2004).

became a member of the EU in 2004. Nonetheless, Turkish-Greek relations moved into a peaceful phase, later emboldened by Davutoğlu's 'zero problems with neighbors' doctrine.

In contrast to this, relations with Greece worsened considerably under an increasingly populist Erdoğan from 2011 onwards, as Turkey adopted increasingly conflictive foreign policy means, up to military threats. On a visit to Northern Cyprus in 2011, Erdoğan backtracked from all his concessions over Cyprus made over the 2004 Annan Plan (Voice of America 2011). The stalemate deepened when Greece harboured military suspects from the failed 2016 coup attempt and after the failure to reach a negotiated settlement on Cyprus during the Crans-Montana talks in Switzerland from 2015 to 2017 (Dizdaroğlu 2023, 150). An even more severe blow to bilateral relations came from a maritime dispute over gas fields in the Eastern Mediterranean. As Erdoğan publicly declared to make 'no concessions on that which is ours' (Hincks 2020) and Greek and Turkish naval vessels collided in the Aegean Sea in August 2020 (J. Sharman 2020), the crisis appeared perilously close to military escalation. Observers saw the standoff, which was ultimately resolved diplomatically, as a diversionary tactic to deflect public attention from Turkey's predicament in Syria (Fraser and Gatopoulos 2020). For Grigoriadis (2022, 806), mobilization was also the driver of another crisis in the Turkish-Greek borderlands, when in 2020 Turkey bussed thousands of refugees to the border and encouraged them to cross into Greece. Reports of Greek pushbacks were used by the AKP as evidence of the hypocrisy and moral decline of Western civilization (Grigoriadis 2022, 813). All told, Turkish-Greek relations by the early 2020s reached a low not seen in decades.

The wider evolution of a new Turkish foreign policy outlook in the populist phase also impacted Turkey's approach to Greece. The coming to the fore of the AKP's Muslim nationalist ideology precipitated worsening relations with both Israel (over Gaza) and Egypt under Sisi. Greece and the Republic of Cyprus used this to their advantage by forging the East Mediterranean Gas Forum (EAST-MED) in 2019 meant to facilitate energy exploration and the construction of undersea pipelines between the four countries, with the notable exclusion of Turkey. The initiative was anathema to Ankara as it fuelled old fears of encirclement. Under the label 'Blue Homeland', in 2019 Turkey conducted its largest-ever naval exercises in the Eastern Mediterranean, the Marmara, and the Aegean Sea, thus contributing to the '[re-]securitization' of relations with Greece—this time led by the civilian leadership rather than the security establishment (Dizdaroğlu 2023, 158). In fact, militarization and securitization under Erdoğan since the Gezi protests of 2013 go far beyond relations with Greece, as 'the military has become a crucial pillar of his anti-Western, autonomy-seeking foreign policy' (Taş 2024, 79).[22] In any case, as the EU accession process had reached a dead end by the early 2010s (see Chapter 5), an important pull factor for a rapprochement with EU-member state Greece practically ceased to exist, thus making the relationship more vulnerable to 'shocks emanating from the strategic shifts in the Eastern Mediterranean as well as domestic political factors' (Grigoriadis 2022, 814). One component of the shift to clearly more conflictive foreign policy means was also an increase in Turkey's criticism of Greece, with Erdoğan's rhetoric becoming more hostile, albeit returning to more conciliatory tones occasionally. For instance, in December 2017, Erdoğan made the first presidential visit to Greece in sixty-five years. There, he stated: 'The aim of our visit is to build our future together in a distinct way and to promote unity and solidarity' (Presidency of the Republic of Turkey 2017). By contrast, in 2022 the Turkish president made headlines threatening Greece that Turkey 'may come one night all of a sudden', adding that Athens should avoid messing with Ankara (Presidency of the Republic of Turkey 2022b). Yet, after elections in the same year, Erdoğan returned to a more benign discourse, stating, for instance, that Turkey had been striving for normalization in its relations with Greece (and other members of the EAST-MED) and claiming that his government 'displayed a strong will to settle our issues' with Greece (Presidency of the Republic of Turkey 2023).

All this was driven, domestically, by Erdoğan and his AKP turning increasingly populist with a more distinctively anti-elitist and anti-pluralist discourse, and concomitantly shifting to strong mobilization and strong personalization in foreign policy making. With the Kemalist elite out of the picture almost entirely and the EU accession process in a dire state (see Chapter 5), the AKP from 2011 onwards began mobilizing against an allegedly hostile West as the primary enemy of the Turkish people. As such, 'foreign policy became a major instrument for gaining a competitive edge in domestic politics, enhancing the AKP's popularity' (Balta 2018). As relations suffered from new and old tensions, the post-2011 populist discourse depicted Greece as a puppet (Presidency of the Republic of Turkey 2022a) of a hostile West, now seen as the primary adversary. The centralization of power at the party level following the dismissal of Davutoğlu in 2016, and at the state level after the transition to the presidential system in 2018, allowed Erdoğan to exercise

---

[22] On the increasing importance of the military in Turkish foreign policy, see in particular Heibach and Taş (2024b, 16–19; 2024a).

unprecedented control over foreign policy (Akkoyunlu 2021). As a result, 'Ankara's foreign policy has grown ever more executive-oriented with few oversight mechanisms that would give more room to inter-agency consultation' (Balta 2018). As a former diplomat we interviewed concurred: 'The actors involved in foreign and security policy decision-making and implementation have largely been erased [. . .] The institutional base of diplomacy has also weakened significantly'.[23] Consequently, not only his personal characteristics and convictions but also personal motives matter more under the populist Erdoğan than in previous phases (Ülgül 2019). As one commentator pointed out, 'the most powerful determinant of Turkish alliance behaviour has become the calculation as to which outside power is most likely to do what is necessary to keep the current regime in power' (Balta 2018). As a journalist we spoke with put it: 'there is no separation between foreign policy and domestic politics for Erdoğan,'[24] explaining the considerable back and forth in Erdoğan's personal diplomacy. In fact, although at times close to escalating militarily, the Erdoğan government went along mediation initiatives repeatedly, and at times expressed its willingness to resolve outstanding issues diplomatically.

Thus, the considerable worsening of relations in the populist phase came about as a consequence of increased mobilization and personalization, along with modifications in the international context. Whereas the pre-populist Erdoğan era saw significant improvements in bilateral relations with Greece—the 'desecuritization' of it (Dizdaroğlu 2023)—relations became more tense after 2011 and especially so after the aborted coup in 2016.

Turkey-Germany

Turkish relations with Germany post-2011 are another instance in which Erdoğan's populist turn contributed to more conflictive relations. With a trading volume of €55 billion in 2023, Germany is Turkey's biggest export market and among its most important sources of imports (Bundesministerium für Ernährung und Landwirtschaft 2024). Turks also form the largest ethnic minority in Germany, playing a significant part in the country's domestic politics. Moreover, as the EU's largest member state, relations with Berlin have been key in Turkey's attempts to gain EU membership. Sharing a history of close diplomatic and economic relations that date back to the Ottoman

---

[23] Interview T06, Ambassador (retired) Fatih Ceylan, former Permanent Representative to NATO, Istanbul, 28 March 2023.
[24] Interview T11, senior Turkish journalist, Istanbul, 13 April 2023.

and German empires, people-to-people ties are stronger than with any other western European state. Yet, we selected this case because it also entailed contentious issues and latent disputes, from German chancellor Angela Merkel's cold view on Turkish EU membership to Turkey's concerns over opposition forces finding refuge in Germany.

Similar to relations with Greece, the scholarship broadly concurs around three distinctive phases in Turkey's relations with Germany, from the 'golden years' throughout Erdoğan's first mandate as prime minister, to a 'phase of stagnation' roughly until 2016, and a rapid deterioration post-2016 (Tekin and Schönlau 2022, 111). It was thus under the populist and increasingly autocratic Erdoğan that relations with Germany worsened to a degree unseen since the end of World War II. Indeed, a systematic analysis of official statements by the Ecevit and Erdoğan governments reveals a clear pattern (Destradi et al. 2023, 287).[25] The non-populist government of Bülent Ecevit typically adopted a friendly tone vis-à-vis Germany, emphasizing the close trade relationship and the strong bonds emerging from the presence of Turkish migrant workers in Germany. After Turkey's formal recognition as a candidate for EU membership at the Helsinki summit in 1999, the rhetoric became even more friendly, presumably due to the support by German chancellor Gerhard Schröder for Turkey's EU accession—and it remained so throughout the early years of the AKP government, as Turkey's EU accession process accelerated (see Chapter 5).

In the populist era, however, the foreign policy means used by the Turkish government in its interactions with Germany moved (according to our conflict-cooperation continuum) from the category of 'compliance' to 'public criticism' and even the adoption of punitive measures ('sanctions') via the arrest of German human rights activists. Despite a number of transactional agreements, which allowed for a continuation of a working relationship with Germany, this ultimately constituted a shift to a more conflictive foreign policy.

The Turkish government's criticism of Germany increased dramatically, driven by Erdoğan's domestic mobilization strategy. With the abandonment of the liberal intelligentsia as a support base, a more competitive domestic political context, and the EU accession process in disarray, Erdoğan from 2011 onwards started describing Turkey as a victim of obscure foreign enemies from a hostile West (Destradi, Plagemann, and Taş 2022). At the same time, the AKP's changes to Turkey's electoral law, which allowed Turkish citizens abroad to vote in Turkish referenda and national elections from 2008

---

[25] Parts of the following paragraphs are based on this chapter. Relevant permissions have been obtained.

onwards (Alemdar 2021, 7), made mobilization of Turks in Germany more relevant. Thus, the Islam-West dualism and the disadvantageous treatment of Turks emerged as recurring themes in presidential speeches. Although foreign ministers Davutoğlu and Çavusoğlu (2015–2023) also picked up on this narrative, they usually employed a more sober and technocratic language than Erdoğan himself. Meanwhile, we found the most bellicose language in his speeches about Germany held after the failed coup attempt in 2016, as in this example:

> I have difficulty understanding how come a democratic country, which is one of the leading countries of the EU, can defend members of an organization which it designates as a terrorist organization. And now they attempt to give us advice. They express 'concern'! Germany, we are concerned about your stance! [...] We are concerned because Germany, which has taken members of such terrorist organizations as the PKK, DHKP-C, FETO, etc., under its wing, is now turning into FETO's backyard. As I have always said, terrorist organizations are like scorpions, sooner or later they will bite whoever carries them on their back. (Presidency of the Republic of Turkey 2016)

Besides Erdoğan's furious public statements, the pro-government media spread fabricated content and cultivated conspiracy theories regarding Germany's hidden agenda (Tekin and Schönlau 2022; Dalaman 2023). For instance, seemingly absurd theories around Germany instigating the 2013 Gezi Park protests in Istanbul or its support for the failed coup proliferated. Yet, a fundamentally different political climate did not preclude transactional political agreements between the two countries in the 2010s, the most consequential of which was the Turkey-EU refugee deal sealed in March 2016. Under the leadership of German chancellor Merkel, the EU promised billions of Euros in return for Turkey closing the migration route from Syria to Europe (European Council 2016). Ostensibly as an additional reward, Merkel in late 2015 and 2016 argued for opening new chapters in Turkey's EU accession talks (Alemdar 2021, 8). The migration deal helped greatly reducing the number of refugees in Germany and Europe and cemented Merkel's own reputation as an apt crisis manager. But these improvements in bilateral ties did not last long, as the coup attempt of July 2016, official German reactions to it, a subsequent exodus of Turks to Europe, as well as critical press coverage in Germany contributed to new tensions. Among such tensions was the German and Dutch governments' refusal in early 2017 to allow members of the AKP to campaign ahead of the constitutional referendum over the replacement of Turkey's parliamentary system with a presidential system, a move Erdoğan described as 'fascism' (Yeni Şafak 2017). Moreover, he called for the sizeable number of voters with Turkish origins in Germany not to vote for 'Turkey's enemies', that is, candidates from parties criticizing Turkey's democratic credentials or him personally, and in a speech in March 2017 he stated, 'I thought Nazism was over in Germany, [. . .] but it still continues' (Hintz 2019). In July 2017, Turkey placed German human rights activist Peter Steudtner under arrest. He and other activists, including the director of Amnesty International in Turkey, were charged with aiding terrorist organizations. On top of that, the prominent German journalist Deniz Yücel, as well as seven other Germans, were already in jail for similar reasons (Hintz 2019). With both the German and Turkish press following events closely, Berlin in an unprecedented move made veiled threats about curtailing economic cooperation, travel and investments, and imposing sanctions. Moreover, Merkel in September 2017 called for an end to Turkey's bid for EU membership and Germany, Turkey's second-largest arms supplier at that time, declared a hold on arms exports (Deutsche Welle 2017a; News Wires 2017).

After the 2017 national elections in Germany and the referendum in Turkey, both sides sought to mend fences at Erdoğan's three-day presidential visit to Berlin in September 2018. By that time, arms exports had resumed, Yücel and Steudtner had been freed, and the German side sought reassurance with regard to Turkey hosting a continuous flow of Syrian refugees. Again, the international context matters. The Turkish economy at that time was under pressure with soaring inflation. Turkey's relations with the US had worsened over a variety of issues, from new US tariffs to the Turkish decision to buy Russian S-400 air defence missiles, the arrest of pastor Andrew Brunson, a US citizen, in Turkey, and the US refusal to extradite Fethullah Gülen (Martin 2019) (see Chapter 6). Thus, Turkey was suddenly more interested in a rapprochement with Germany, even though Erdoğan tempered his language only intermittently. In fact, he continued to mobilize, as, for instance, at the inauguration of Germany's largest mosque in Cologne in 2018 (Deutschlandfunk 2018). Besides helping him secure electoral and financial support from the Turkish diaspora in Germany and elsewhere, the exploitation of anti-Western sentiments for electoral gains was fuelled by the AKP's reliance, since 2015, on its junior coalition partner, the Nationalist Movement Party (Milliyetçi Hareket Partisi or MHP). The ultra-right MHP, among other things, called for ending EU accession talks (Hintz 2019). Thus, mobilization clearly drove Turkey's adoption of more conflictive foreign policy means and, as a consequence, the sinking of bilateral affairs.

Also, personalization of decision making was high in Turkey's approach to Germany. Erdoğan unquestionably was deeply involved in the management of relations with Germany, thus crowding out alternative channels of communication (Kutlu et al. 2021). His combative personality negatively affected German policymakers' trust in Turkey as a partner as well as Turkey's image in Germany more widely, to the extent that he was habitually portrayed as the quintessential strongman in German media. An apt illustration of this was German comedian Jan Böhmermann's satire of Erdoğan in 2016, which created a massive media storm on both sides, fuelled by fears around Böhmermann's safety in Germany and his month-long disappearance from the public (Frankfurter Allgemeine Zeitung 2016; Zeit 2016). Thus, 'Erdoğan's tendency to personalize politics as well as his emotional and polarizing language' (Kutlu et al. 2021, 6) strongly affected Turkey's conduct of relations with both Germany and the EU (Görener and Ucal 2011, 375). Western governments' scepticism vis-à-vis Erdoğan in his populist phase was aggravated by Erdoğan's increasingly militarized foreign policy elsewhere, most notably vis-à-vis the Kurds domestically and in Turkey's military intervention in Syria from 2016 onwards. Moreover, Erdoğan's forceful personal outreach to the Turkish diaspora in Germany was widely perceived as an assault on German domestic politics that left him virtually without allies among German policymakers and the strategic community. At the same time, his foreign manoeuvring was frequently described as quintessentially transactional, with his personalized leadership also allowing for pragmatic agreements and sudden turns in Turkey's approach to Germany (Haugom 2019; Bashirov and Yilmaz 2020). In this, Erdoğan found a partner in German chancellor Merkel, who for long regarded Turkey as a necessary but not necessarily aligned partner to deal with. As a result, Erdoğan and Merkel were able to restore relations so that cooperation over key issues—economics and migration—remained intact (Kutlu et al. 2021, 9258). Meeting Merkel on her farewell trip to Turkey in October 2021, Erdoğan even called her his 'friend', a stark contrast with his Nazi-comparisons of past years (Dalaman 2023). In the meantime, he continued resorting to accusatory narratives, combined with calls for 'cooperation and friendship under different [foreign policy] dimensions' (Tekin and Schönlau 2022). And yet, the longer-term consequences of Turkey's more conflictive approach to Germany were severe. As Lisel Hintz described it in 2019: 'relations cannot usefully be classified as warmed or normalised; this is wary and opportunistic transactionalism, not cordial rapprochement' (Hintz 2019, 173).

Strong Mobilization, Weak Personalization

Our second expectation concerned cases in which personalization was weak, but mobilization was strong. Here, we expect a somewhat more confrontational foreign policy under populist governments as compared to non-populist ones (Tables 3.1/3.2, top-right quadrant).

Bolivia-Chile

Bolivia's approach towards Chile is a case in point. Relations between the two countries had long been tense due to a dispute over Bolivia's access to the sea, which the landlocked country had lost in the Pacific War of 1879–1883. The two countries have not maintained full diplomatic relations since 1978, as the demand for a Bolivian land bridge to the Pacific Ocean had become a national cause that virtually every government preceding Morales had called for. Thus, unlike relations with the US, the maritime issue was a matter of national consensus spanning from the phase of Bolivia's 'pacted democracy' to the populist government of Evo Morales. The new constitution adopted in 2009 declares the 'inalienable and imprescriptible right over the territory giving access to the Pacific Ocean and its maritime space' (Plurinational State of Bolivia 2009, art. 267). References to the maritime issue were prominent in the MAS electoral manifestos in 2009, 2014, and 2019. Under Morales, domestic political mobilization around the issue reached its climax with the so-called *banderazo* in 2018, a giant human chain holding a 200 km long blue flag visualizing Bolivia's demand for an independent access to the sea (BBC Mundo 2018). However, as will be seen below, personalization in this case was not prominent.

Bolivia's attempts to reverse the status quo under Morales can be separated into two distinct phases. During the first phase from 2006 to 2010, the Morales government sought 'a very deep rapprochement'[26] with the leftist Chilean government of Michelle Bachelet. The two governments established the so-called thirteen-point agenda to deal with a broad range of bilateral issues. This process was driven by President Morales, but career diplomats played an important role in it.[27] In fact, the thirteen-point agenda and subsequent discussions were structured negotiations, not leader-level personal interactions.

---

[26] Interview B24, journalist and former senior diplomat, La Paz, 8 March 2023.
[27] Interview B01, career diplomat under Morales, La Paz, 12 January 2023.

Moreover, initially, the Bolivian government sought to involve a larger spectrum of societal actors in foreign policy making vis-à-vis Chile in the name of 'people's diplomacy'.[28] Correspondingly, Morales's public references to the dispute with Chile during this phase were mostly conciliatory and constructive (Plagemann, Heras Rodríguez, and Destradi 2022). Yet, the negotiations never came close to resolving Bolivia's core demand, and with the election of a new centre-right government in Chile in 2010, the process stalled.

During the second phase, Morales increasingly used the dispute for domestic mobilization. In line with his populist thin and his leftist thick ideology, he described the Pacific War as the result of oligarchic and foreign interests, emphasizing its negative economic consequences for the Bolivian people (Plagemann, Heras Rodríguez, and Destradi 2022, 23). However, personalization remained limited and the dispute with Chile was portrayed as a national struggle that went beyond ideological differences (St John 2020, 187). In his frequent public references to the issue, Morales highlighted a national consensus and appealed to domestic elites associated with the opposition. For instance, Morales in 2015 started a speech by thanking three former presidents who collaborated with him on the maritime cause but otherwise had not been sympathetic to the MAS. This was remarkable, as Morales at previous occasions had heavily criticized the very three ex-presidents as part of Bolivia's corrupt elite (Plagemann, Heras Rodríguez, and Destradi 2022, 23). Further, in a major shift, the Bolivian government in 2013 called upon the International Court of Justice (ICJ) in The Hague for resolving the issue. This decision broke with past precedence focused on bilateral negotiations. Importantly, at this stage, Morales invited a group of former Bolivian presidents and foreign ministers from opposition parties as advisors. Former President Carlos Mesa for some years became the international speaker for the maritime cause. As former interim President Eduardo Rodríguez Veltzé stated in an interview with us, '[the] maritime claim was not only a political decision, it was a State decision to find a path consistent with International Law'. Moreover, '[it] was not an improvisation, far from it, the arguments of international law were worked with great rigor'.[29] Meanwhile, Bolivia also invested in an international campaign in support of its claims. Morales thus involved a broad set of actors, including former opposition politicians, specialized technocrats from within the Ministry of Foreign Affairs and international lawyers.[30] The result was a policy that we classify as

---

[28] Interview B13, acting senior diplomat, La Paz, 2 February 2023.

[29] Interview B11, Eduardo Rodríguez Veltzé, former Bolivian President (2005–2006), Zoom, 30 January 2023.

[30] Interview B01.

only somewhat more conflictive as compared to that of previous non-populist governments, as it shifted from negotiations ('neutral interactions', in our classification of foreign policy means on a conflict-cooperation continuum) to public criticism. On the one hand, devolving dispute resolution to an international body was in many ways a moderate policy we would not expect from a populist leader (Voeten 2020). Notably, Morales also recognized the ICJ ruling of 2018, which was not favourable to Bolivia (International Court of Justice 2018). At the same time, Morales frequently highlighted the problems deriving from his country's landlocked situation in his domestic speeches while accusing Chile of acting in bad faith (Plagemann, Heras Rodríguez, and Destradi 2022, 24). Moreover, by moving from bilateral negotiations to an intensification of the diplomatic campaign and ultimately to the deferral to the ICJ, Morales internationalized the dispute and clearly increased diplomatic pressure. Doing so with the advice of experts and in a bipartisan way (that is, combining high mobilization with low personalization), foreign policy became only somewhat more conflictive.

Weak Mobilization, Strong Personalization

The bottom-left quadrant of Tables 3.1/3.2 concerns cases in which a bilateral relationship mattered a lot to a populist leader and was therefore strongly personalized. However, such cases had a low salience to the domestic public or were not clearly related to the populist's thin or thick ideology and therefore had a low potential for mobilization. In those cases, we expected a populist government to pursue an only somewhat more conflictive foreign policy as compared to a non-populist one.

Philippines-US

Within our sample, we find evidence for this logic in the Philippines' populist President Duterte's approach to the US. Under him, the Philippines' relations with the US became somewhat more confrontational than under his non-populist predecessor Benigno Aquino III (2010–2015), who had strengthened existing defence treaties and regularly referred to the US—a long-standing ally with considerable military presence in the country—as 'a true friend' (Official Gazette 2013). In fact, driven by an increase of Chinese incursions into Philippine waters and aided by the Obama administration's 'pivot to Asia' and by the US military's rapid response to the Typhoon

Yolanda in 2013, Aquino further deepened ties with the US. This happened through joint military exercises, defence procurements, and close leader-level relations (Avila and Goldman 2015). Ultimately, under the non-populist government of Aquino, the Philippines stood firmly in the US camp.

When Duterte came to power in 2016, he initially tried to take an entirely different approach to the US, referring to it as a 'former colonial master' (Department of Foreign Affairs 2016a), calling for 'shackling dependency' on Washington (Department of Foreign Affairs 2016b), and personally offending President Obama (Rappler 2016). Further, Duterte tried to launch what he called an 'Independent Foreign Policy'—something that mainly meant veering away from the US and drawing the Philippines closer to China (and Russia) (for more details, see Chapter 6). This included threats to abrogate the Visiting Forces Agreement (VFA), a treaty from 1999 that regulates the stationing of US military and civilian personnel in the Philippines. In 2016, Duterte warned of an 'eventual repeal or abrogation' of the agreement after the US deferred an aid grant to the Philippines (A. Romero 2016b)—but he ultimately did not follow up on that threat. Years later, a similar episode occurred. In 2020, after the US cancelled the visa of the Filipino Senator Ronald dela Rosa, a close friend of Duterte (Castro 2020), the president instructed his secretary of foreign affairs to send out an official letter of termination of the VFA (Merez and Sabillo 2020). Yet, such letter was retracted in 2021 and efforts towards a parallel rapprochement with China (see below) ceased. According to an expert we interviewed in Manila, these threats were mostly symbolic, as the alliance with the US had returned to stability already in 2018. As Islamist militants put under siege the city of Marawi on Mindanao island for five months in 2017, Duterte had initially asked China for weapons, but ultimately the Americans provided more substantial support, thus mitigating Duterte's aversion towards the US.[31] Moreover, as revealed in our interviews with some of his cabinet members, senior diplomats, and military officials, the foreign and security apparatus was almost entirely opposed to Duterte's change of course vis-à-vis the US. Finding creative ways to undermine several of the president's decisions, the security establishment thus contributed to 'moderating the swing'[32] and to de facto continuity.[33] Especially members of the middle bureaucracy, 'because they were under

---

[31] Interview P30, Filipino scholar, Manila, 23 November 2024.
[32] Interview P35, Filipino academic, Manila, 28 November 2024.
[33] Interviews P01, former high-ranking government official, Manila, 26 September 2022; P02, former senior diplomat, Manila, 28 September 2022; P06, senior military official, Manila, 4 October 2022; P11, senior military official, Manila, 11 October 2022; P12, former senior navy official, Manila, 11 October 2022; P15, former senior navy official under Aquino and Duterte, Manila, 13 October 2022.

the radar, were able to prevent any major excesses.[34] The same applies for the military—and indeed remarkably, 'the biggest Balikatan [the yearly major US-Philippines military exercise] happened under Duterte.[35] Moreover, according to one interviewee, Duterte himself 'realized his appeasement policy [vis-à-via China] wasn't working when Chinese money wasn't coming in and Chinese grey-zone operations continued against the military.[36] Thus, we consider the Philippines' relationship with the US to have become only somewhat more confrontational: the shift to public criticism was paralleled by a continuation of the previous policies of compliance with the US alliance, and the deep existing cooperation de facto was not revoked.

The mostly symbolic and short-lived changes in the Philippines' approach towards the US make sense once we consider the highly personalistic management of such relations by Duterte, combined with their limited potential for mobilization. As we discussed in the Introduction, personalization under Duterte was generally extremely strong. More specifically, Duterte's anti-Americanism appeared to be primarily a personal sentiment rooted in his experience as a provincial statesman in Mindanao, an impoverished southern island that had been a site of US military interventions throughout the past century (Heydarian 2021).[37] This was exacerbated, according to our interviewees, by a number of episodes that Duterte perceived as personal offences against him, such as a US immigration officer treating him rudely and bringing him to a detention room in the early 2000s,[38] or US President Obama not shaking his hand at an event and criticizing him:[39] 'he felt so insulted.[40]

However, mobilization over relations with the US was not a viable strategy for Duterte, mainly because Filipinos are generally well disposed towards the US. For instance, a PEW Research Center survey from 2019 found that 80% of Filipinos have a positive view of the US—compared to 40% with a positive view of China (Cha 2020). US military presence has at times provoked animosities but resentment about colonial history is relatively low (Hincks 2016), American culture—from basketball to Hollywood—figures

[34] Interview P35.

[35] Interview P34, Marites Danguilan Vitug, editor at large, *Rappler*, Manila, 28 November 2024.

[36] Interview P09, Filipino academic, Manila, 10 October 2022. Another interviewee pointed out that less than 5% of Chinese projects ultimately materialized. Interview P33, former Filipino justice, Manila, 27 November 2024.

[37] According to Duterte's sister, for the people of Mindanao, the US colonial experience had left deep scars, and Duterte's grandmother taught him that Washington was guilty of crimes during invasion and colonization (Moss 2016).

[38] Interview P34.

[39] Interview P30.

[40] Interview P34. See also Chapter 6 for more details.

prominently in the daily lives of Filipinos, and people-to-people contacts are intense. We also found no indication of Duterte's narrower support base deviating from such widespread pro-American sentiments. As one of our interviewees put it, 'There has always been an anti-American sentiment among the Filipino elites, intellectuals [and especially the left, which is a nationalist left]. But ordinary Filipinos have always had a soft spot for the US, a sense that the US are good friends'.[41] Unlike in Bolivia or Turkey, mobilization was further complicated by the absence of a well-defined 'thick' ideology involving anti-American elements that would accompany the 'thin' ideology of populism in the case of Duterte(see Introduction).

In sum, strong personalization of decision making under Duterte explains the somewhat more confrontational policy vis-à-vis the US, which led to a short-lived attempt to subvert this traditional partnership. However, since this issue was not helpful to mobilize domestic support, Duterte eventually reverted to a more conventional course, opting not to put at risk a relationship that remained of fundamental importance for the Philippines' security.

India-China

Another bilateral relation in the bottom-left quadrant of Table 3.1/3.2 is the one between India and China. After an initial phase of bonhomie post-independence spearheaded by India's first Prime Minister Jawaharlal Nehru in the 1950s, China's surprising attack on India in 1962 marked the beginning of tensions which have lasted until today. The two countries have a number of major unresolved border disputes. Most notably, China claims the entire territory of India's state of Arunachal Pradesh, which it calls South Tibet. Also, the high-mountain area of Aksai Chin is disputed, thus making China a party in the protracted dispute over Kashmir. Under Prime Minister Manmohan Singh, India-China relations were initially relatively harmonious. However, as time passed, they came to be shaped by increasingly hostile policies on the part of Beijing. Among other things, China denied visa to Indian citizens from Arunachal Pradesh; it carried out military incursions in Demchok in 2009 and in Daulat Beg Oidi in 2013; and it deepened its ties with India's South Asian neighbours, thus increasing its presence in India's traditional sphere of influence (Bajpai 2017; Destradi 2012c). The INC-led governments under

---

[41] Interview P27, Prof. Herman Joseph S. Kraft, University of the Philippines Diliman, 22 November 2024. According to another expert we interviewed, 'the Filipino left is anti-American, but always marginalized'. Interview P30.

Manmohan Singh responded to these challenges by stepping up India's military capabilities, improving border roads and infrastructure, and developing closer ties with the US, ASEAN, and other Asia-Pacific countries (Bajpai 2018). Overall, however, under Manmohan Singh India's approach remained relatively conciliatory, as illustrated by his signing of a Border Defence Cooperation Agreement, besides several other agreements, at a three-day state visit to Beijing in 2013 (Panda 2013).

However, under Prime Minister Modi India's policy towards China became more confrontational. Against the backdrop of growing Chinese pressure, but also as a result of a 'growing strategic exasperation with China' (Bajpai 2018, 246), India's approach hardened. Yet, change was not radical in the sense of the unilateral adoption of clearly more confrontational policies. This is remarkable as tensions over land borders between the two countries escalated on the ground. During the Doklam standoff between Indian and Chinese troops in 2017 and during the border conflict of 2020 in Ladakh—the most serious military confrontation between India and China since 1962—India pursued a policy that may be termed more decisive than that of the preceding government. Nonetheless, the Modi government also showed restraint in responding to what appear to have been Chinese provocations: It clearly sought to avoid an all-out confrontation even if this included silently ceding territory to the People's Liberation Army (PLA). Although the precise events in Doklam remain shrouded in secrecy, credible news reports and scholarship describe a chain of events starting with a Chinese military excursion into Doklam, leading to a seventy-three-day military standoff (Ganguly, Pardesi, and Thompson 2023, 116–22). Whereas the ultimate withdrawal of PLA forces was described by some Indian commentators as a 'diplomatic victory' and a proof of the Modi government's resolve (Sajjanhar 2017), Chinese troops returned to the disputed area later in the same year and resumed the construction of roads and shelters (Ruser and Grewal 2022). India's response included an informal summit between Xi and Modi in Wuhan early in the following year but no actual escalation on the ground.

Similarly, in 2020 Chinese forces occupied several positions in the Galwan Valley in Ladakh. Tensions culminated in a clash involving hundreds of Chinese and Indian soldiers in hand-to-hand combat that killed at least twenty Indian soldiers (Ganguly, Pardesi, and Thompson 2023, 119–21). Contrary to an agreement from the 1990s that sought to isolate the border dispute so that it would not disrupt progress in other bilateral issues, the Modi government in 2020 reportedly made the withdrawal of PLA forces from the area a precondition for cooperation in other fields (The Times of India 2020).

Ostensibly at least in part as a reaction to the border clashes, India also slowly intensified relations with Taiwan, 'worked hard to stymie Chinese initiatives in both multilateral and minilateral settings' (I. Hall 2023), and became a proactive member of the Quad, a security forum with the US, Japan, and Australia (see Chapter 6)—all policies that irk Beijing. Yet, these shifts and Indian protests notwithstanding, the PLA continued to strengthen its presence in the disputed areas via new infrastructures (Ganguly, Pardesi, and Thompson 2023, 22).

Overall, therefore, India's approach to disputes with China was somewhat more conflictive. Responses to Chinese escalation led to the adoption of more confrontational means, but not to military escalation on the part of Modi's populist government. In this case, the context condition of a country's vulnerability played a prominent role. India's relatively moderate responses appear closely linked to the government's decision not to use the border clashes for domestic political mobilization beyond a certain point. As public anger in India flared up in 2020 (Ellis-Petersen 2020), with images circulating of Indians throwing their China-produced TV sets from their balconies and calling for boycotts of Chinese goods, the government refrained from heating up the debate (Destradi et al. 2023). For instance, Modi did not even mention China in his 2020 Independence Day speech despite the ongoing dispute and fierce domestic debates around it. The Indian government must have been aware of the risks of a more serious military confrontation with China, and indeed our Indian interviewees confirmed that Modi paid attention not to mobilize excessively around the China issue: as an Indian observer told us, 'the nationalism card hasn't been whipped up, it's too dangerous. While you are riding a tiger, you cannot jump off'.[42] Notably, New Delhi pursued a moderate course despite centralized and personalized decision making by the prime minister and the National Security Advisor plus, from 2019 onwards, by External Affairs Minister Jaishankar.[43] Ostensibly, India's sense of vulnerability vis-à-vis China prevented officials from mobilizing public support over China[44] thus resulting in an only moderately more confrontational foreign policy.

---

[42] Interview I19, Indian academic, New Delhi, 8 March 2023.

[43] According to an expert interviewed, Jaishankar shaped India's approach towards China: 'Since March 2020, Jaishankar's line is prevailing: until the Chinese step back, [there is] no movement [from our side]. All we see is the Jaishankar line'. Interview I19. According to a retired diplomat, the MEA has been marginalized when it comes to decisions on important bilateral relations like those with China. Interview I18, retired Indian diplomat, New Delhi, 7 March 2023.

[44] A former high-ranking government official argued that thick ideology driven mobilization was prevalent in relations with Pakistan, but not in those with China: '[Pakistan] is an example where the ideology is [...] I would even say the driver of policy, while with China it's non-ideological'. Interview I23, former high-ranking government official from India, online, 23 March 2023.

Weak Mobilization, Weak Personalization

Philippines-China

The case of the Philippines' approach towards China did not become more conflictive. For one, both mobilization and personalization were relatively weak (bottom-right quadrant, Tables 3.1/3.2). Moreover, given the geopolitical context with an intensifying Sino-US rivalry at that time, a more friendly approach towards China almost naturally followed from Duterte's attempted rupture with the United States.

Relations between the Philippines and China were tense due to a long-standing dispute over maritime boundaries in the West Philippine Sea/South China Sea. Duterte's predecessor Aquino had taken a clearly anti-China approach, filing a case with the Permanent Court of Arbitration, which dismissed China's claim in the disputed territories (see also Chapter 5). Aquino vocally criticized China's expansionist activities in the area as 'illegal' and he sought to internationalize the issue via debating it within ASEAN and other fora (Destradi et al. 2023).

By contrast, Duterte already during the election campaign dismissed the arbitration case and called for a reopening of direct negotiations with China (Krejsa 2016). Once in government, Duterte downplayed the Permanent Court of Arbitration's ruling—a surprising move, given that its outcome was widely seen as a major victory for the Philippines. Moreover, he described the territorial dispute as a bilateral affair, visited China more frequently than Aquino had done, and employed a more friendly rhetoric when addressing China (Destradi et al. 2023). Philippine naval forces were also asked to apply greater restraint than under Aquino. According to a former senior military official, 'That was the policy. [. . .] It was clear that we are pro-China.'[45] Such rapprochement with China was presented as beneficial in economic terms, as Duterte hoped for Chinese investments, mainly in the infrastructure sector.[46] However, these rather radical changes notwithstanding, Duterte's overtures to China ultimately did not yield the economic and political gains he may have hoped for, and the Philippines eventually reverted to their traditional partnership with Washington (see above and Chapter 6 for more details on the Philippines' efforts towards a reorientation of international partnerships).

Importantly, Duterte's rapprochement with China was not popular at the domestic level. Given the rather negative views of China among Filipinos,

---

[45] Interview P11.
[46] Interview P09.

mobilization did not drive the policy changes described above. As a former high-ranking government official put it, 'Duterte's turn to China never became a popular issue; it was mostly indifference.'[47] Neither was it the result of a personal interest in the territorial dispute by Duterte. While Duterte's attempted shift to China has been described as personal 'unrequited love' (Vitug and Elemia 2024) and some of our interviewees pointed out that Duterte surrounded himself with Chinese-Filipino and mainland Chinese businessmen[48] and might have even been bribed by China,[49] personalization seems less marked than in the case of relations with the US. According to one interviewee, in contrast to Aquino, Duterte would channel all communication over China via his National Security Advisor, an indication of a lack personal engagement.[50] Others describe his approach to China as transactional. 'He was closer to Japan than to China.'[51] The bonhomie in Philippines-China relations at the beginning of Duterte's presidency can be interpreted as an illustration of populists' instinctive desire for 'independence' in foreign policy and for a break with the past approaches of established elites (see Chapter 6). More than that, however, Duterte's turn to China was a corollary of him personally detesting the US. As a former senior government official stated, Duterte's motivation for his 'Independent Foreign Policy' was 'really personal—his experience with the Americans. It's really just him and his fetish for saying that he's not Uncle Sam's puta.'[52] Relatedly, interviewees described his reformulation of the Philippine's foreign policy doctrine as 'shallow' and merely 'rhetorical'.[53] Duterte 'simply has a personal grudge against the US' and then 'put an economic spin on, that's to have China finance his Build, Build, Build projects.'[54] Wider geopolitical context conditions as well as the Philippines' perception of vulnerability as a comparably weak state also contribute to explaining these shifts: the Philippines could not have antagonized both the US and China, therefore temporary efforts to distance the country from the US were bound to result in a rapprochement with China. Meanwhile, the foreign policy and defence establishments, instinctively pro-US and anti-Chinese, sought ways to limit the fallout.[55]

As a result of this curious combination of a relative disinterest by the populist leader in the territorial dispute, virtually no anti-Chinese mobilization

---

[47] Interview P01.
[48] Interview P34.
[49] Interviews P33; P36, Filipino academic, Manila, 28 November 2024.
[50] Interview P14, senior government official, Manila, 12 October 2022.
[51] Interview P13, senior government official, Manila, 12 October 2022.
[52] Interview P13.
[53] Interviews P09, Filipino academic, Manila, 10 October 2022; P13.
[54] Interview P09.
[55] Interviews P09; P12.

efforts over the issue, and strong perceptions of the Philippines' vulnerability, bilateral relations with China throughout the first years of Duterte's presidency improved markedly. However, as relations with the US recovered (see above) and substantive benefits from the Chinese side were not forthcoming, the warming up of relations ended and the territorial dispute retained its original status as a lasting stain on bilateral relations.

Conclusion

Our theory of populist foreign policy expects populists in power to escalate ongoing or latent international disputes if these are suitable for domestic mobilization and if decision making on them is highly personalized. Across the eight disputes we looked into, we found substantive evidence in support of our theory. Turkey's foreign policy was increasingly used by Erdoğan for domestic political mobilization and was managed in a personalized way after 2011, thus leading to a worsening of bilateral ties with Greece as well as with Germany. Also, India's populist government led by Prime Minister Modi mobilized public support around relations with Pakistan at the same time as he centralized decision making. Overall, also in this case, populist foreign policy led to a worsening of bilateral relations. Similarly, the escalation of Bolivia's disputes with the United States was clearly driven by the long-standing anti-US and anti-imperialist mobilization that populist leader Evo Morales had relentlessly and personally adopted.

Importantly, our theory also makes sense of variations. Where bilateral relations are less salient for mobilization and leader-level involvement is relatively limited, foreign policy did not become more conflictive. Moreover, our in-between cases are instructive. India's populist government pursued only slightly more conflictive policies vis-à-vis China, despite their potential for mobilization and the high degree of personalization. Here, New Delhi wisely chose not to mobilize around territorial disputes with China in order to avoid a larger conflict with a vastly superior rival. In Bolivia, Morales used the age-old dispute with Chile over his country's access to the sea for domestic mobilization, but he refrained from turning it into a personal affair—perhaps because, similar to the India-China case, a decisive victory was out of reach. Thus, the populists in our sample clearly were aware of the political dangers of foreign confrontations.

This points to another finding that nuances previous work on the importance of thick ideologies in populist foreign policy. Populist leaders in India, Bolivia, and Turkey held strong and fairly cohesive thick ideologies—Hindu-nationalism, Bolivarian socialism, and Muslim nationalism respectively. These are the three cases where we found more meaningful and substantive changes than in the case of Duterte in the Philippines, where change was short-lived. However, we also found that geopolitical considerations and possible threats may outweigh potentials for mobilization, as is most visible in Modi's approach to China but also Morales's policy vis-à-vis Chile.

Another qualification concerning all four cases is warranted here. Beyond this chapter's empirical focus on individual bilateral relations, data from the Stockholm International Peace Research Institute show that in none of our four cases the populist government, once in power, substantially increased military expenditures as share of GDP (SIPRI, n.d.).[56] An important observation in its own right, this implies that even in those cases where we found significantly more tense bilateral relations following the election of populist leaders, none of them appeared to be prepared to mobilize new resources away from other domestic needs so much so that it would significantly alter the respective country's offensive capabilities. Future research should explore in greater detail how populists relate to the military (Taş 2024; Krebs 2025), as this relationship has the potential to influence governments' approaches to international conflicts in the long term.[57]

---

[56] Bolivia in 2010 saw an increase of military expenditures as share of GDP to 2.8 per cent but expenditures then returned to below 2.0 per cent of GDP in the years thereafter. In India, expenditures barely changed despite the notable increase in tension at its northern borders. In the Philippines, expenditures increased only slightly from 1.0 per cent in 2016, when Duterte took over the presidency, to 1.4 and 1.3 in his penultimate and ultimate budgets, respectively. In Turkey, notwithstanding an increasingly interventionist foreign policy—from Syria to Azerbaijan and North Africa—military expenditure as share of GDP slightly decreased from the non-populist to the populist Erdoğan.

[57] We thank our colleague Hakkı Taş for alerting us to this matter.

4
Provision of Global Public Goods

Populists are often considered to hamper the provision of global public goods. Several prominent examples of populists in power challenging key global governance mechanisms in various ways have contributed to this perception—from US President Trump leaving the Paris agreement on climate change mitigation in 2017 and again initiating the procedure to withdraw the US from it in 2025, to Brazilian President Bolsonaro undermining global health governance during the Covid-19 pandemic[1] or climate change mitigation via policies that led to sharp increases in deforestation and greenhouse gas emissions (Observatório do Clima 2023).

However, looking at a broader spectrum of populist governments again leads us to call into question this generalization. For example, India's populist prime minister, Narendra Modi, forcefully declared his government's support for climate change mitigation efforts; Turkey's President Erdoğan offered himself as a mediator in the Russian war against Ukraine; and Venezuela at the heyday of Chávez's presidency was a major donor of foreign aid to ideologically aligned countries. It therefore seems too easy to claim that populism will automatically lead to policies that are detrimental to global governance and that undermine the provision of public goods.

Global governance has been defined as 'the exercise of authority across national borders justified with reference to common goods or transnational problems' (Zürn 2018, 138). As Dingwerth and Pattberg (2006) point out, global governance thus entails systems of rule aimed at governing 'without government' that (a) involve a broad range of actors in world politics, not just nation states; (b) span across levels, with 'local, national, regional, and global political processes [being] inseparably linked' (Dingwerth and Pattberg 2006, 192); (c) entail different forms of governance that coexist, without a clear hierarchy among them; and (d) do not always imply a pre-eminence

---

[1] As laid out in detail in a Brazilian parliamentary investigation committee from 2021 (Comissão Parlamentar de Inquérito da Pandemia 2021).

Populism and Foreign Policy. Sandra Destradi and Johannes Plagemann, Oxford University Press.
© Oxford University Press (2025). DOI: 10.1093/9780197695012.003.0004

of sovereign nation states in those emerging spheres of authority. What all these interrelated systems of rule have in common is ultimately the justification of authority with reference to common goods (Zürn 2018). In other words, they aim to resolve global problems via the provision of global public goods. Do populists navigate global governance differently as compared to non-populist governments? More specifically, under what conditions are populists less willing to provide global public goods, as suggested by some of the examples above?

There are several theoretical reasons to expect populists to be less inclined than non-populists to contribute to global public goods provision. The first reason is derived from people-centrism and it has to do with the essence of global public goods. By definition, these are non-excludable, which means that single actors cannot be effectively excluded from using such goods. Moreover, they are non-rivalrous in consumption, which means that the use by one actor does not reduce the availability of these goods to others. Their 'global' features moreover imply that their 'benefits reach across borders, generations and population groups' (Kaul, Grunberg, and Stern 2004, xxi). All this makes global public goods particularly challenging to provide since problems of collective action and the phenomenon of free-riding almost inevitably emerge (Ostrom 1990). When it comes to populist governments, we may expect them to be even less inclined to contribute to the provision of global public goods as compared to non-populist counterparts, first and foremost because populists claim to speak in the name of a narrowly defined 'people'. Such people is usually defined in opposition to some 'other', which, depending on the 'thick ideology' that accompanies populism, will be a domestic or transnational elite, and sometimes some external 'other', such as foreign countries or elements within them (Löfflmann 2020a; Wojczewski 2020a). In populists' Manichean, black-and-white view of the world (Hawkins 2009), there will be little space for the notion that the government of a narrowly defined 'people' should accept costs for something that ultimately benefits everybody, including the 'others' out there. Slogans like Trump's 'America first' or Bolsonaro's *Brasil acima de tudo* epitomize this logic.

Another reason to expect populists to be averse towards global governance is more deeply related to anti-elitism and specifically to populists' profound scepticism of the elites that have driven the agenda of global public goods provision, for example in climate change mitigation or aid. These are not just the technocratic elites of international organizations, which many populists believe undermine the sovereignty of the true 'people' and the state (Chryssogelos 2020; Zürn 2018)—we will discuss in greater detail populists' approaches to international organizations in Chapter 5. Global governance also entails a transnational dimension and the engagement of actors beyond the nation state, including NGOs, transnational corporations, or civil society groups of various kinds. If decision making on global issues moves to spheres of authority unrelated to a narrowly defined people, populists may understand this shift as weakening the pre-eminence of the 'people' and its preferences. While the literature on populism points to the importance of social movements in populist mobilization and for populism in general (Aslanidis 2017), this refers to groups supporting populist leaders or promoting populist ideas. But this is unlikely to apply to non-state actors or transnational social movements that populists do not control. Besides episodes like Trump's quarrels with climate activist Greta Thunberg (Taylor 2019), there is much evidence of populists cracking down on transnational NGOs (e.g., Frangie-Mawad 2024; Limaye 2020; Bayer 2017). All this, together with the notion of populists 'embodying' the popular will and establishing a direct connection with the people, leads us to expect populists to be sceptical of global governance, with its complex actor constellations, multi-level decision making, and diffuse authority.

We therefore expect populists in power to be less inclined to contribute to the provision of global public goods as compared to non-populist governments. More concretely, we expect a change towards less cooperative policies in various fields of global governance after populists come to power. Yet, as was mentioned above, we need to make sense of variations in populists' readiness to contribute to global public goods in specific fields (Destradi and Plagemann 2019). We argue that a combination of strong mobilization and strong personalization allows populists' aversion for global governance to play out most forcefully, leading to a clearly reduced readiness to contribute to global public goods. This is the case because highly personalized decision making reduces path dependencies in approaches to global governance: populists will be better able to break with the past policies of the 'establishment' and with some of the main conventions in their countries' approaches to various fields of global governance if they are less restrained by bureaucracies, experts, and civil society. This is particularly relevant in issue areas that require a high degree of technical knowledge and expertise. Climate change mitigation is a case in point. The very agenda of this global governance field has been driven to a large extent by epistemic communities that many populists distrust, as well as by transnational civil society (R. A. Huber, Greussing, and Eberl 2022).

A high level of mobilization, at the same time, will further enable and ultimately force populists to break with past policies and turn their back to global public goods provision, or at least reduce engagement in them. As happened in the case of Trump in the US, mobilization against contributions to global public goods is framed in terms of high costs to be paid by the 'people' to address problems caused by others.[2] Moreover, populists may highlight the problem of free riding, condemning contributions to global governance as a waste of resources for the people that ultimately just benefits strangers.

As outlined in the Introduction and in Chapter 3, we expect a combination of either strong personalization and weak mobilization, or strong mobilization and weak personalization, to lead to a somewhat reduced readiness to provide global public goods. Finally, we expect populist governments that do not strongly mobilize around the issue of global public goods provision, or strongly personalize decision making over global governance issues, to pursue a policy of continuity vis-à-vis their predecessors, and not to significantly reduce the readiness to contribute to global public goods. Table 4.1 summarizes these expectations.

We focus on the 'readiness' to contribute to global public goods since this allows us to develop a more fine-grained operationalization that involves both the dimension of rhetoric and the actual contributions made by non-populist vs. populist governments. We consider a 'clearly reduced readiness to provide global public goods' to be in place if populists stop or drastically cut contributions to global public goods in a specific field as compared to the contributions made by the preceding non-populist government, and if such shift is paired with statements playing down or dismissing the importance of this field. A 'somewhat reduced readiness to provide global public goods' is observed if populist governments slightly reduce their country's contributions in that field or if the shift is mainly rhetorical, with strong statements

Table 4.1 Populism and the readiness to contribute to global public goods

| | | Personalization | |
		Strong	**Weak**
Mobilization	**Strong**	*Clearly reduced readiness to provide global public goods*	*Somewhat reduced readiness to provide global public goods*
	Weak	*Somewhat reduced readiness to provide global public goods*	*Continuity: no reduced readiness to provide global public goods*

[2] This is well illustrated in a press statement titled 'Climate Ideology Fights [against the Principles of] Physics on Taxpayers' Money' by the populist *Alternative für Deutschland* (AfD) from Thuringia, Germany (Winzer 2023).

indicating disengagement and criticism of the policy field but no substantial impact in terms of reduced contributions. Finally, continuity is in place if we see neither a decline in actual contributions nor criticism of global governance in a specific field.

When it comes to concrete global public goods, there is a broad variety of issue areas one could focus on, from the freedom of the seas to the stability of financial markets, from the fight against transnational terrorism to the control of infectious diseases (Nye 2002). We chose to specifically address the following global public goods and, relatedly, fields of global governance: (a) climate change mitigation; (b) peace; and (c) development.

We selected climate change because it is frequently considered to be one of the main challenges in world politics given its global implications, but it also is an issue area that has seen denialism and lots of scepticism on the part of populists from Trump to Bolsonaro to various populist parties in Europe (Lockwood 2018), and thus merits particular consideration.

The promotion of peace is another suitable issue area because of its high salience, at least potentially. Here, we analyse specifically contributions to UN peacekeeping missions and other multilateral peace missions as well as populist governments' initiatives in the field of mediation in violent conflicts. Mediation is defined as 'a process of conflict management where disputants seek the assistance of, or accept an offer of help from, an individual, group, or state, or organization to settle their conflict or resolve their differences without resorting to physical force or invoking the authority of law' (Bercovitch, Anagnoson, and Wille 1991, 8). Serving as a mediator in a violent conflict can be considered an important contribution to the global public good of peace—and offering to mediate indicates a readiness to provide such public good. While mediation obviously implies lower financial costs as compared to sending troops to peacekeeping missions, it still generates costs for the mediator: Given the high stakes in violent conflicts, mediation not only requires substantial time and political capital, it also risks the loss of reputation or potentially a deterioration of relations with actors involved in a conflict (Vukovic 2014).

The third global public good we analyse is development, and specifically the provision of development aid. This is an issue area in which the 'global' dimension of the public good is perhaps less visible, while the bilateral dimension stands out. Economic development and welfare in form of public health, education, and other fundamental capabilities are first and foremost domestic matters. However, fighting poverty in foreign lands and providing humanitarian aid can be, and frequently are, considered contributions to humanity on a global scale (Culp 2018). Moreover, in a more indirect way, development is related to policy fields such as peace and migration. These connections are also sometimes discursively constructed by populists. For example, right-wing populists in Europe, such as Marine Le Pen in France, have supported development cooperation as a tool to prevent migration from Africa (Caramel 2017; Roberts 2024). This all makes it especially interesting to explore the provision of development assistance besides more conventional global public goods such as peace and climate change mitigation.

In our theoretical framework we again take into account context factors that might mitigate the impact of populism on contributions to global public goods. Most obviously, we consider the capabilities of the countries in our sample. Not all states are able to contribute to the high costs of global public goods provision in the same way. Specifically, this means that we will not include an analysis of development cooperation for the cases of Bolivia and the Philippines, which do not have their own development aid programmes.

Our Findings

We argued that various intensities of mobilization and personalization lead to variations in foreign policy change when it comes to governments' readiness to contribute to the provision of global public goods. In Table 4.2, we summarize our findings from all four cases.

Strong personalization, strong mobilization

Against our theoretical expectations, we did not observe clearly reduced contributions to global public goods in any of the cases, not even in those that displayed a combination of strong personalization and strong mobilization. Quite to the contrary, we observed an *increased* readiness to engage in the provision of selected global public goods on the part of populist governments in Turkey and India, accompanied by strong personalization and mobilization.

Turkey and Development Aid

Turkey has been a donor of development assistance since the 1990s. While it is not a member of the Development Assistance Committee (DAC) of the OECD, it has submitted its statistics voluntarily to the body since 1992. With the creation of the Turkish Cooperation and Coordination Agency

Table 4.2 Summary of findings

		Personalization	
		Strong	**Weak**
Mobilization	**Strong**	*Clearly reduced readiness to provide global public goods* None	*Somewhat reduced readiness to provide global public goods* Bolivia: peace
		Increased readiness to provide global public goods, against our expectations Turkey: development Turkey: peace India: climate	
	Weak	*Somewhat reduced readiness to provide global public goods* Philippines: climate	*Continuity: no reduced readiness to provide global public goods* Turkey: climate India: peace India: development Philippines: peace Bolivia: climate

(TIKA) in the same year, the country established an agency specifically tasked with development cooperation. Over time, foreign aid became a major priority in Turkey's projection as an emerging power (Gök and Dal 2016). While foreign aid expenses started increasing from 2003, they rose much more remarkably during Erdoğan's populist period, after 2011 (see Figure 4.1). Official Development Aid (ODA) disbursements declined again after 2021, possibly due to increasing domestic critique from opposition parties and within a more difficult budgetary situation in Turkey following the economic upheavals of the Covid crisis. In any case, by the mid-2010s development aid had become a major political goal under the AKP government. Whereas before 2011, foreign aid was only mentioned in election manifestos as a rather minor point, the AKP manifestos of 2015 and 2018 included it much more prominently, framing Turkish aid as a contribution to a global development agenda (AKP 2015) and under the title 'humanitarian and conscientious foreign policy: foreign aid and refugees' (AKP 2018, 300).

In terms of geographical priorities, Turkey's ODA traditionally focused on Balkan countries and Central Asian Turkic Republics, that is, on territories historically linked to the Ottoman Empire or having close ethnic or cultural

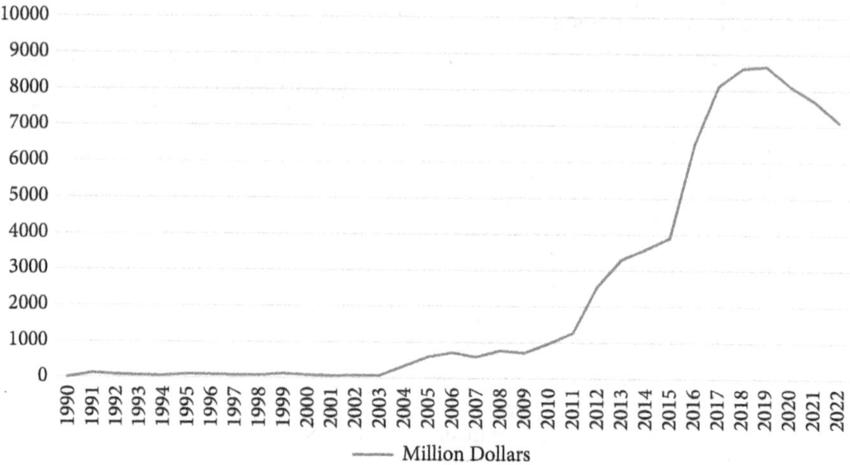

Figure 4.1 Turkey's net ODA (disbursement) (million dollars)
Source: OECD, https://stats.oecd.org/qwids/ (last accessed 25 June 2024).

connections to Turkey (Hausmann and Lundsgaarde 2015, 2). From 2011, the biggest portion of Turkey's development assistance was spent for humanitarian purposes due to the ongoing civil war in Syria, mainly supporting 'Syrian guests' in Turkey (Tüyloğlu 2021, 8). Given that the Turkey-EU deal over migration compensated Turkey for hosting Syrian refugees and closing their pathway towards Europe (Hacaoglu 2022; Karnitschnig and Barigazzi 2016), understanding that part of aid as a genuine public good would be a distortion. Yet, the fact remains that with an estimated 6 million refugees in 2022 Turkey over the years hosted the world's largest refugee population (Karnitschnig and Barigazzi 2016) and the Erdoğan government had to fend off domestic criticism—increasing over time—because of its largesse vis-à-vis Syrian refugees in particular (Glinski 2024). It did so, among others, with reference to the 'alleged Ottoman tradition of giving shelter and protection to the oppressed regardless of their ethnic or religious backgrounds' (Morgül 2023, 33). However, Turkish aid also increasingly targeted African countries, serving mainly as a tool to pursue Turkey's ideological, political, and economic interests: fulfilling its self-ascribed role of a humanitarian power, gaining support in international platforms, for example in its bid for membership in the United Nations Security Council, and pursuing free trade agreements with African countries (Belder and Dipama 2018).

Turkey's growing engagement as a donor was driven by both strong personalization and strong mobilization. Especially after 2011, Turkey's development assistance was highly personalized. Erdoğan started to appear in Turkey's international aid activities, for example through visits to Mogadishu in 2011 and 2015, as Ankara massively increased its aid to Somalia in the context of a famine crisis (Turkey's ODA to Somalia jumped from $5.8 million in 2010 to $93.3 million in 2011 and up to $314 million in 2015; see Ozkan and Orakci 2015). More generally, Erdoğan had visited as many as thirty African countries by the end of 2021 (Heibach and Taş 2024a, 320). After the transition to the presidential system in 2018, TIKA was downgraded and affiliated to the Ministry of Culture and Tourism by presidential decree (Tüyloğlu 2021, 20), something that Heibach and Taş (2024a, 320) describe as the 'institutional reflection of [. . .] personalization of power'.

Overall, the notion of Turkey's 'humanitarian diplomacy', introduced by Ahmet Davutoğlu (2013), was embraced by Erdoğan to underscore Turkey's rise in international politics. Development aid was therefore explicitly linked to status seeking, including references to Turkey's glorious past and its self-ascribed civilizational mission as the representative of the oppressed world and helping 'the victims, the homeless and the poor' (TIKA 2020). In a recent book titled *The Friendly Hand of Turkey: Humanitarian Diplomacy* published by the Presidency's Directorate of Communications, foreign aid is defined as an instrument of 'nation branding' (Cumhurbaşkanlığı İletişim Başkanlığından 2022). In line with the AKP's ideological turn away from the West, Erdoğan repeatedly emphasized how Turkey's efforts differed from those of Western donors, highlighting Turkey's history as a non-colonial power (a dubious claim) and its desire to build cooperation based on notions of equal partnership, mutual respect, and win-win principles (Al Jazeera 2017). In this sense, development aid over time also played an increasingly important role for domestic political mobilization. Especially Turkey's development assistance to Muslim countries was used to project an image of Erdoğan's Turkey as the vanguard of the Muslim world and a voice of the oppressed (Haber7 2016). Importantly, the increasing readiness to provide aid survived the dismissal of Davutoğlu and the parallel substitution of his foreign policy ideas with the more anti-Western Muslim nationalism championed by Erdoğan in the populist era (see Chapter 3). A decline in aid disbursements after 2021 notwithstanding, overall we consider this case as one in which a populist government engaged much more actively as compared to its previous non-populist phase in the provision of aid as a public good. This was accompanied by both strong personalization and mobilization, which, contrary to our expectation, did not decrease Turkey's readiness to contribute to public goods for years. Instead, Erdoğan's populist government resorted to development cooperation as a tool for status seeking, and clearly emphasized this aspect by making the issue a personal priority and by using it to gain domestic political support.

Turkey and Peace

Among our cases, we observed a similar dynamic in Turkey's readiness to provide the global public good of peace. However, in this case the shift towards greater engagement is less explicit, as we rather see a different, more personalized form of engagement with Erdoğan's mediation efforts.

Turkey was very active in UN peacekeeping after the end of the Cold War, sending troops to several missions in the Balkans (Tarik Oğuzlu and Güngör 2006, 476). Moreover, it joined missions like the UN Iraq-Kuwait Observation Mission (UNIKOM, 1991–2003), to East Timor (UNMISET, 2000–4), and Georgia (UNOMIG, 1994–2009) (Satana 2013, 359). Over the years, Turkey was also engaged in a number of NATO missions, most notably in the International Security Assistance Force (ISAF) mission in Afghanistan, which it led twice (2002–2003 and 2005–2006) (Oğuzlu and Güngör 2006, 477).

As Figure 4.2 shows, Turkey's troop contributions to UN peacekeeping missions rose sharply during the non-populist years but started declining from 2008 onwards. During the populist period, we observe another steep decline, followed by rather constant contributions of between 100 and 200 troops from 2014 onwards. According to Parlar Dal and Kurşun (2018, 1785), this decline was related to Turkey's own domestic and regional security environment and increasing challenges by, among others, the PKK and ISIS. As we show in Chapter 5, it was not paralleled by a fundamental rejection or by

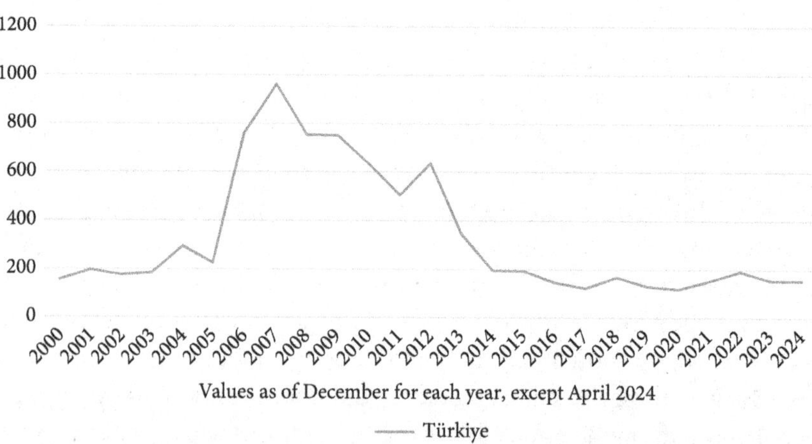

Figure 4.2 Turkey's total UN peacekeeping staff contributions
Source: United Nations Peacekeeping, https://peacekeeping.un.org/en/troop-and-police-contributors (last accessed 1 July 2024).

particularly strong criticism of the United Nations, and it should thus not be interpreted as a sign of a clearly reduced willingness to contribute to peace.

In fact, despite decreasing engagement in UN peacekeeping, Erdoğan was an active mediator in international conflicts. Clearly driven by personalization in foreign policy making, this allowed him to increase his international visibility while mobilizing support at home. Arguably, the idea of devising a new international role for Turkey came from Ahmet Davutoğlu, who in the early 2000s presented Turkey as having key features that made it an ideal mediator in its neighbourhood (Arkan and Kınacıoğlu 2016). In 2010, Turkey and Finland launched the 'mediation for peace' initiative at the United Nations, which aimed to promote coordination among international mediators and led to the formation of the 'Group of Friends of Mediation'. While these initiatives were devised by Davutoğlu, they were embraced by Erdoğan. Among his mediation initiatives were those between Israel and Syria in 2008 (Stratton 2008); with Brazil on the Iranian nuclear programme in 2010 (Hafezi 2010); and assistance in direct talks between Somali and Somaliland administrations from 2011 onwards, even though this last facilitator role was not much publicized in the domestic discourse (Donelli 2024). More recently and visibly, Turkey mediated in the Russian war against Ukraine. In 2022, the UN and Turkey brokered the so-called grain deal to allow Ukraine to export its grain through the Black Sea. Additionally, Turkey also hosted direct talks between Ukraine and Russia, with Russia's foreign minister Lavrov and Ukraine's foreign minister Kuleba meeting in Antalya in 2022 (Republic of Türkiye Ministry of Foreign Affairs 2022). Importantly, these mediation initiatives were used by Erdoğan to underscore his government's image as peace-loving, and Turkey's responsibility for the global public good of peace, as evidenced by this 2022 speech at the UN General Assembly:

> Our foreign policy vision has been always peace-oriented. We have worked tirelessly, beginning in our region, to ensure that peace prevails in the entire world. [. . .] We seek to act as a mediator or facilitator in order to settle disputes once and for all. Our country is located in the heart of a region surrounded by conflict, but we seek to be a part of the solution rather than a part of the problem, which is possible only through the initiatives that we choose to undertake. (Erdoğan 2022)

Mediation was also clearly used to mobilize support domestically, as revealed by Erdoğan's 2023 presidential election manifesto: 'Could the Ukraine-Russia crisis be solved? As Turkey, we stepped in there as well. Since we are the only country that can speak with both sides and is trusted by both, Turkey's role emerged as irreplaceable' (Erdoğan 2023, 8). Erdoğan also highlighted that under his leadership '[w]e are closer than ever to a Turkey whose voice is listened to in regional and global politics' (Erdoğan 2021), and the pro-government media presented him as 'the world's hope' (Usta 2023). Yet, it also is important to note the concrete geo-economic and political benefits related to the supposedly neutral role as a mediator, especially in the case of the Ukraine war. While Turkey's involvement in the civil war in Syria required a functioning working relation with Russia, the Turkish economy also bene-fitted tremendously from staying firmly outside the Western sanctions against Russia (Bechev 2024).

India and Climate

A similar logic applies to India's climate policy. Modi domestically and on the international stage endorsed the global climate agenda much more than his predecessor Manmohan Singh had done. Not only did this help him increase his global visibility, but it also came along with attempts to use climate change in the mobilization of public support. Although domestically climate policies changed only incrementally, overall, we observe an increasing willingness to contribute to climate change mitigation as a global public good under Modi compared to the non-populist predecessor government.

India traditionally is seen as a difficult partner in global climate politics. Since the beginning of global negotiations at the Rio Earth Summit in 1992, it has remained steadfast in its principled rejection of binding emission tar-gets that would hamper domestic development efforts. The Indian position was industrialized countries had grown rich on polluting the climate while depriving their former colonies of the same benefits; relatedly, Western calls for reducing emissions in the developing world were described as 'environ-mental colonialism' (Agarwal and Narain 2019; Vihma 2011). This approach was consistently followed by the first UPA government (2004–2009), with a temporary exception in the beginning of UPA-II under the leadership of environment minister Jairam Ramesh (2009–2011) (Plagemann and Prys-Hansen 2020). The relative stasis in India's international climate policies in the pre-Modi era was driven by institutional as well as domestic political factors. For long, India's climate policies were shaped by bureaucrats, with a core group of officials from the Ministry of External Affairs (MEA) and the Ministry of Environment and Forests (MoEF) holding 'a near-monopoly in terms of determining what India's interests on this issue were, and what its negotiating position should be' (Sengupta 2020, 183). The bureaucracy's hold was further strengthened by the low salience of climate issues in Indian elections (Pillai and Dubash 2021, 93). Nonetheless, with global pressure for climate action increasing during the 2000s, India embarked on its first National Action Plan on Climate Change just before the Copenhagen summit of 2009. Moreover, a new narrative of 'co-benefits' slowly but steadily took hold, underlining the interlinkages between energy security, efficiency, renewables, and economic development (V. Jha 2022, 283).

The Modi government built on such changes and combined them with its penchant for political branding to create an impression of Indian leadership on the global scene. Indeed, Modi's appearance as prime minister at the historic COP-21 in Paris 2015 was a departure from past precedence. Global attention had increased in the lead-up to Paris, and India in particular was facing considerable public critique by, among others, US climate envoy John Kerry. As usual, New Delhi was widely expected to complicate negotiations, but, to the surprise of many, around the summit India engaged in what its chief negotiator at that time called a 'massive outreach' campaign (Lavasa 2019, 178). The *Financial Times* published an opinion piece by Modi on the summit's first day and the prime minister inaugurated the first India Pavilion at a COP. India unexpectedly announced an ambitious domestic goal of 175 GW renewable energy by 2022 and, together with France, launched the International Solar Alliance, which was widely regarded as an original and ambitious Indian contribution (V. Jha 2022, 286). Moreover, the Modi government ratified the Paris Agreement emanating from the negotiations early on, thus helping to bring it into force (V. Jha 2022). According to his more sympathetic observers, Modi replaced India's essentially 'reactive' climate policy, its 'trade union-style politics at global forums' with a 'forward-looking, agenda-setting India' (Saran and Jones 2017, 119), an India that was a 'problem solving rule shaper' by seeking 'global solutions on climate change' (Sidhu 2015). Post-Paris, India was credited for shedding its traditional role of being 'obstructionist' (A. Mohan and Wehnert 2019, 275), instead exhibiting a flexibility and progressiveness unseen so far (A. Mohan 2017, 53). A former US negotiator is quoted as saying, 'I noticed clear shifts in the negotiators pre-2014 and post-2014. There was a marked uptick in India's engagement [on issues of climate change] with the beginning of the Modi government' (V. Jha 2022, 289). According to the same source, a subgroup of Indian negotiators, empowered by the Prime Minister's Office, proactively sought to make deals and find pragmatic solutions in Paris, rather than sticking to India's traditional positions (V. Jha 2022, 290). In stark contrast to Kerry's pre-Paris remarks, the White House after Paris praised India for its 'leadership' on climate issues (The Times of India 2016).

Notwithstanding this clearly increased readiness to engage in international climate change negotiations, the populist Modi government did not radically subvert the key planks of India's climate policy.[3] For instance, in the run-up to Paris, Modi had adopted 'climate justice' as a motif for the domestic justification of India's negotiating position, arguing that 'advanced countries must leave enough room for developing countries to grow' (Sengupta 2020, 188). Also, the new Indian flexibility in Paris might have been driven by the desire to emulate China, which prior to the summit had declared that its emissions would peak by 2030. As India's lead negotiator in Paris wrote, the Modi government reacted by displaying a similar willingness to act, but it also sought to ensure that India's 'developmental space will not be constricted by a top-down approach, and also that [India's] contributions to counter climate change will remain nationally determined in years to come' (Lavasa 2019, 184).

The years following Paris exposed a similar dynamic of widely publicized global action at least partially driven by external pressure (Pillai and Dubash 2021, 111). At the COP-26 in Glasgow 2021, Modi unexpectedly pledged to cut India's emissions to net zero by 2070, a first-time promise of this kind. Yet, 2070 is twenty years later than what the EU and US promised, and ten years later than China's pledge to reach net zero emissions. Moreover, at the same summit, India in a last-minute intervention watered down the language on phasing out coal (V. Jha 2022, 292). India's reliance on coal also prohibited New Delhi from agreeing to a Just Energy Transition Partnerships (JETP), a key mechanism supposed to resolve the tension between climate change mitigation and economic growth in the developing world.[4] Whereas oil and gas are mostly imported, coal is a domestically available resource in India. As Sengupta and Jindal note: 'Any international deal perceived to reduce India's sovereignty in energy will face political hurdles to its adoption' (Sengupta and Jindal 2024). As a result, the scholarship on Indian climate policies observed 'a significant mismatch between India's current domestic energy realities and the pledges submitted towards the Paris Agreement' (A. Mohan and Wehnert 2019, 280). Other leading scholars of Indian climate policies describe Modi's India as 'an intriguing case of active mitigation policymaking in the absence of overt national climate politics' (Pillai and Dubash 2021, 93). Thus, domestic

---

[3] Interview I09, senior retired Indian diplomat, New Delhi, 1 March 2023.

[4] The Just Energy Transition Partnerships through a combination of loans and private finance for clean energy from G-7 countries are supposed to create employment for workers in the fossil fuel sectors in countries such as South Africa or Indonesia while also retiring coal-powered plants. As the world's third largest emitter, India would be a prime candidate for a large JETP deal. Yet, given both the geoeconomic imperative of energy sufficiency and political resilience in India's coal rich states, no such deal has materialized so far (Sengupta and Jindal 2024). Due to growing consumption of coal and gas, the Climate Action Tracker, a not-for-profit site, rates India's climate targets and actions as 'highly insufficient' (Climate Action Tracker 2023).

development concerns continued to shape India's climate policy, as visible for instance in India's country targets, kept deliberately low for India to be able to overachieve them (Bhatt et al. 2018). Still, the MoEF was renamed Ministry of Environment, Forest and Climate Change (MoEFCC) in 2015, and India under Modi introduced new policies incentivizing the use of eco-friendly technologies domestically, with remarkable success in some areas, such as the expansion of LEDs and photovoltaics (Mathur 2019).

India's overall greater readiness to contribute to public goods in the field of climate change mitigation was driven by high personalization, as well as mobilization. First, some observers indeed identified a 'personal ambition to lead on climate-related issues' on the part of Modi (V. Jha 2022, 292). Already when he was chief minister of Gujarat, Modi took interest in climate change, writing a book titled *Convenient Action: Gujarat's Response to Challenges of Climate Change* (Sengupta 2020, 188; Modi 2011). As an expert pointed out to us, Gujarat under Modi was the only Indian state to have a climate minister.[5] Modi personally engaged in climate change mitigation in line with his self-stylization as *vishwaguru* (teacher) to the world (Pathak and Parris 2021). Such personalization of decision making around climate and the new approaches taken by Modi were met with hostility by India's 'climate bureaucracies', especially by the energy ministry, according to the same expert.[6]

The issue of climate change was also used for domestic mobilization, using the Hindu-nationalist thick ideology as a frame of reference and a reservoir of metaphors and justifications for such engagement. The extent to which the rephrasing of climate concerns in terms of the BJP's thick ideology increased its salience to the wider public is debatable.[7] However, in purely discursive terms, the colonization of environmental issues by Hindu-nationalist terminology surely facilitates references to it. For instance, an in-depth exploration of *The Organiser*, a key Hindu-nationalist news magazine, illustrated the extent to which the BJP's thick ideology adopted environmentalism as an element in its striving for a purified nation (M. Sharma 2023). Since 2014, governmental initiatives for cleanliness, the protection of cows, and the environment more generally have multiplied, thus increasing the political prominence of climate change and renewable energy (M. Sharma 2023, 102). The RSS, the BJP, and other Hindu-nationalist outfits participated in this,

---

[5] Interview I06, Indian scholar and observer, New Delhi, 28 February 2023.

[6] Interview I06.

[7] As is its effectiveness in terms of changing negotiations' outcomes given the limited operational meaning (Sengupta 2020, 189) of terms such as 'climate justice', the Gandhian notion of sustainable living, or quotes from the *Yajur Veda*, which were included in India's submission of its Intended National Determined Contribution ahead of COP-21 (Narlikar 2017, 103).

much in line with what Modi himself sought to communicate: a novel combination of nativism and modernity, of science and mythology. In this view, 'environmental degradation essentially [was] a result of the imposition of a Western, colonial civilization over a rooted, indigenous, Indian culture' (M. Sharma 2023, 106). The overlaps with climate change mitigation are obvious.

Ultimately, 'India's engagement with climate change [under Modi] was material to its aspirations as a rising power, and it was important for it to not just be part of the solution, but *be seen* to be part of the solution' (Dubash 2019, 3, emphasis added). At the same time, the increasing prominence of climate change in global politics, exemplified by the presence of world leaders at COP meetings, made it easier for Modi to use this issue to display global leadership both domestically and externally (Sengupta 2020, 184). For instance, Modi in his monthly radio speeches to the nation mentioned climate change usually in combination with India's global leadership, as in this quote from December 2018: 'The country secured a place of pride & glory in the entire world. The highest United Nations Environment Award "Champions of the Earth" was conferred upon India. The world duly took notice of India's efforts in the areas of Solar Energy and Climate Change' (Modi 2018). In his victory speech after the 2024 elections, Modi claimed 'India's next era will be a "Green era"' (Dasgupta 2024). Meanwhile, mobilization was also focused on the notion of using climate change mitigation to 'leapfrog development', and according to an interviewee '[this issue], it's everywhere!'[8] This framing, according to an Indian journalist, had much to do with the ultimately still low public interest in climate change mitigation, and its much bigger focus on economic growth.[9]

Strong Mobilization, Weak Personalization

Bolivia and Peace

A case illustrating the interplay of diverging degrees of mobilization and personalization is Bolivia's willingness to contribute to the global public good of peace, and particularly to UN peacekeeping missions under populist President Morales. Once elected, the new government initially continued the two main deployments agreed to by its predecessor government under Carlos

---

[8] Interview I01, expert on India's foreign policy, New Delhi, 20 February 2023.

[9] Interview I03, Indian journalist, New Delhi, 22 February 2023. Another interviewee argued that there was not much mobilization around climate change as compared to other topics, Interview I06. An interviewee at a think tank close to the BJP, by contrast, argued that there is 'tremendous awareness among the public today on climate', Interview I12, retired Indian diplomat at think tank, New Delhi, 2 March 2023.

Mesa (2003–2005). However, amid Morales's wider critique of UN peacekeeping efforts as 'imperial' (Agencia de Noticias Fides Bolivia 2016), Bolivia eventually withdrew its troops from the two main missions, MONUC in the Congo (in 2010), and MINUSTAH in Haiti (in 2015), without making any substantial new commitments. Thus, over time, we found a reduced readiness to contribute under Morales.

Designed as a Latin American mission with most troops from the region and initially commanded by a Brazilian general and a Chilean diplomat (Tripodi and Villar 2005), MINUSTAH in Haiti was widely regarded as an example of a new phase in UN peacekeeping. Bolivia's participation from the beginning in 2004 onwards was thus emblematic of the country's proactive involvement in regional affairs (also see Chapter 5). After nine years in which altogether 3,108 Bolivian soldiers were deployed to Haiti, Bolivia concluded its military participation in MINUSTAH in June 2015 (Hernández Bermúdez 2020). Bolivia's overall contributions peaked under Morales in 2007 at 452 peacekeeping staff deployed (United Nations Peacekeeping 2024) because of its parallel involvement in MONUC and MINUSTAH. To reflect a new phase of the mission in Congo, MONUC was renamed MONUSCO in 2010. Alongside this, Bolivia under Morales withdrew its troops. As La Paz did not commit to any new deployments, from 2015 onwards only a low two-digit number of peacekeepers remained (see Figure 4.3). As a result, in the overall ranking of troop-contributing countries, Bolivia over the course of the Morales presidency descended from rank 44 in 2006 to rank 88 in 2019 (United Nations Peacekeeping 2006a; 2019).

Thus, unlike Morales's populist patron Hugo Chávez in Venezuela (Jenne 2019, 334), Bolivia did not end its involvement in UN peacekeeping upon his election. Instead, with about 450 troops and military observers between 2006 and 2009 and about 220 between 2010 and 2014, Morales presided over Bolivia's most substantial contributions to UN Peacekeeping missions in history. We found reasons for this in the way security policy was made in Bolivia at that time. According to our interview with Bolivian security analyst Nataly Reguerin,[10] the Bolivian military was keen to continue their ongoing peacekeeping missions. Morales, in turn, needed to maintain the military's support for his revolutionary government and he did so, among others, by way of redirecting funds from the nationalization of Bolivia's hydrocarbon sector to the military (Rochlin 2007, 1339). The armed forces

---

[10] Interview B27, Nataly Reguerin, Bolivian foreign relation analyst and former diplomat, La Paz, 9 March 2023.

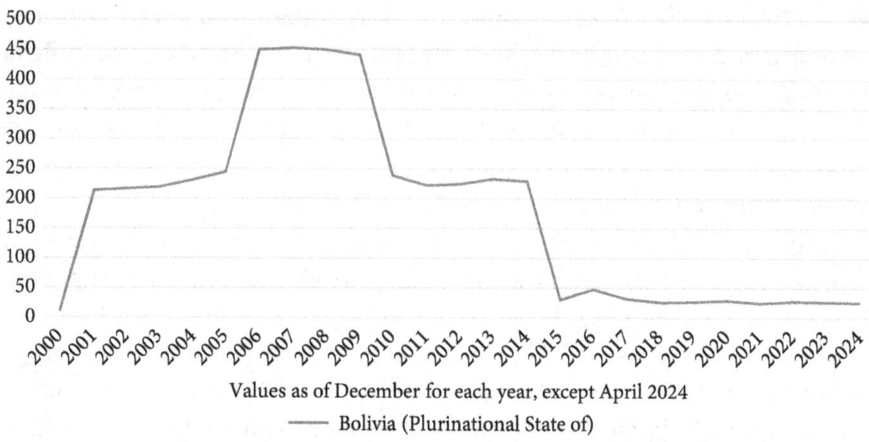

Figure 4.3 Bolivia's total peacekeeping staff contributions

Source: United Nations Peacekeeping, https://peacekeeping.un.org/en/troop-and-police-contributors (last accessed 1 July 2024).

also maintained a certain autonomy under Morales.[11] As for other small countries sending peacekeepers, UN coverage of operational costs, equipment, and other payments was a major factor inducing the military to hold on to existing commitments. By contrast, the more ideologically aligned Foreign Ministry was more sceptical of peacekeeping operations. According to Reguerin, Bolivia under Morales even refused to pay its shares to UN peacekeeping components—a refusal that had severe diplomatic repercussions when Bolivia assumed a non-permanent seat in the UNSC in 2017/2018 and that was eventually resolved when La Paz resumed its payments. Presumably, what influenced Morales towards eventually withdrawing troops from UN peacekeeping operations was his thick ideology, and its mobilization potential. Relatedly, an important factor may have been the influence of Hugo Chávez, often described as a key foreign policy advisor to the president (see Chapter 6). In fact, Morales in March 2006 joined the Chávez-led Bolivarian Alliance for the Peoples of Our America–Peoples' Trade Agreement (Alianza Bolivariana para los Pueblos de Nuestra América–Tratado de Comercio de los Pueblos, ALBA-TCP) and its Permanent Committee for Sovereignty and Defence, including ideologically aligned countries from Cuba to Ecuador. Venezuela within the ALBA-TCP spearheaded the International Civic–Military Rescue and Humanitarian Assistance Brigade 'Simón Bolívar' and the Humanitarian Task Force 'Simón Bolívar', which were

---

[11] Interview B27.

portrayed as alternatives to UN peacekeeping missions with their suppos-edly neo-imperialist major power patrons (Muhr 2012). Bolivia's decreased engagement in UN peacekeeping was thus related to the country's broader reorientation of partnerships towards fellow leftist Latin American countries (see Chapter 6). Morales at several occasions criticized UN interventions, condemning external interferences driven by UN missions[12] and the limited achievements of the UN in matters of peace, as in these quotes from 2014 and 2015, respectively:

> We must make use of the culture of peace to eradicate extremist fanaticism, but also the imperial warmongering promoted by the United States, which, faced with war, threatens more war. The United Nations was created to build and promote peace, not to justify wars and invasions. Using war against war is not the same as peace. That is a perverse formula—the formula for death and endless confronta-tion. (United Nations General Assembly 2014, 3)

> The Organization was founded to seek peace after the two World Wars. I feel it is important to make an in-depth economic, political, social, cultural and environ-mental assessment following 70 years of the existence of the United Nations. What has it achieved? In the eyes of the people, wars and invasions continue even after 70 years of the United Nations. (United Nations General Assembly 2015, 26)

Ultimately, we consider Morales's belated shift away from UN peacekeeping missions and the new (albeit limited) engagement in ALBA-initiated mis-sions, as well as the self-description of Bolivia as a 'pacifist' country in the new constitution adopted under the MAS government, as signs of an only some-what reduced readiness to contribute to the global public good of peace. This was driven by a mix of relatively low personalization, given the military's abil-ity to keep Bolivia engaged in UN missions for several years after Morales's election, combined with mobilization in line with his thick ideology.

Weak Mobilization, Strong Personalization

The Philippines and Climate

Under the populist presidency of Duterte, we observed a somewhat reduced readiness to contribute to climate change mitigation on the part of the Philip-pines, as compared to the non-populist presidency of Benigno Aquino III,

[12] Interview B27.

an assessment best illustrated by Duterte's initial refusal to adopt the Paris Agreement his predecessor had agreed to. However, Duterte did not use climate change to mobilize public support in any consistent manner; at the same time, despite not explicitly personalizing climate policy, this issue area became highly centralized and we argue that this centralization contributed to the Philippines' somewhat reduced readiness to engage.

For Aquino initially, like his predecessors, climate change was not high on the political agenda. According to one of his former lead UNFCCC negotiators, this changed with the 'Super Typhoon Yolanda', one of the most devastating tropical cyclones on record, that hit the Philippines in 2013, killing more than 6,000 people.[13] In addition to this, the lead-up to the Paris Agreement 2015 had a lasting impact with numerous high-level foreign visitors trying to convince Aquino to become more active in climate change initiatives. As a former official told us, 'climate policy was used to mobilize foreign aid and became a tool to get help with the South China Sea dispute. If we participate in climate change initiatives, we can have good relationships with other countries that care a lot about [climate change].'[14] Another former negotiator under Aquino emphasized the president's reluctance to adopt the climate justice discourse, including the blaming of industrialized countries that usually comes along with it.[15] Thus, although the Aquino presidency raised issues of climate justice (Tupaz 2015), pointing to the historical responsibility of industrialized countries for change and calling for more equitable solutions (Smith 2022, 5), it did not question the need for climate change mitigation efforts beyond the industrialized world.

Unlike some populists in the West, once in power Duterte did not deny climate change or the usefulness of climate change mitigation. In his 2017, 2018, and 2019 state of the union addresses he referred to the impact of climate change usually in relation with natural disasters hitting the Philippines. In a televised address given after visiting the storm-hit location Surigao del Sur in 2021, he said: 'At first, I did not believe in climate change but now the rains coming from the heavens are heavy due to the warming of the planet. Even by a certain degree higher, we are in serious trouble due to the fast evaporation of water in the ocean' (Kabiling 2021). Duterte's anti-elitist rhetoric includes painting Filipinos as vulnerable victims on a global scale (Marquardt, Oliveira, and Lederer 2022, 785). Relatedly, unlike Aquino, Duterte was vocal in his criticism of existing approaches to climate change mitigation. He called UN climate conferences a 'waste of time and money' (Ranada

---

[13] Interview P23, Filipino environmentalist and former DENR official, Zoom, 23 September 2023.
[14] Interview P23.
[15] Interview P19, senior civil society activist, Zoom, 17 September 2023.

2019) and, in 2016, in drastic terms he refused the commitments made by Aquino on climate change mitigation under the Paris Agreement: 'You are trying to stifle us [. . .]. That's stupid, I will not honor that. [. . .]. That was not my signature' (King 2016). In his response to a foreign ambassador asking him about the Philippines' plans for carbon emissions reduction, Duterte said: 'I'm mad at this ambassador. I want to kick him'. Moreover, he stated that limitations on carbon emissions were 'nonsense' for the Philippines (King 2016). And yet, Duterte eventually reversed his decision in March 2017, signing the Paris Agreement after more than 100 countries had already done so, thus effectively ensuring the Senate's ratification (Reuters 2017). This shift may have been driven by Filipinos' generally positive view of international organizations and agreements (Dellmuth et al. 2022, 63). As one interviewee pointed out to us, opposition to the Paris Agreement was not what the public wanted.[16]

Our interviews with Filipino experts, officials, and former negotiators shed some light on the political context behind Duterte's rhetoric and climate policies. For one, climate issues have little political salience in the Philippines, and this was the case both under Aquino and Duterte. According to a survey carried out between 2017 and 2019, as many as 59.9% of respondents among citizens of the Philippines had not heard of and did not feel well informed about climate change (Bollettino et al. 2020). A journalist covering climate issues in an interview with us said: 'Reports about climate garner low views compared to other topics. There are more pressing issues that ordinary Filipinos prioritize. For them it's abstract'. Moreover, climate change was viewed primarily from a disaster lens. 'The public perceives climate change as a trivial matter. They know it is important but their concept of which is heavy rains or typhoon'.[17] At the same time, the absence of a clearly identifiable 'thick' ideology with implications for the environment did not provide Duterte with a consistent template for mobilization against climate change mitigation. According to some experts we interviewed, Duterte—like other Filipino politicians—used climate change primarily as an excuse: in the case of a landslide, a flood, or some other natural disaster, instead of talking about land use or disaster prevention, Duterte blamed climate change.[18] Yet, climate change clearly was not a priority under him.[19] Thus, unsurprisingly, a journalist we interviewed—like other informants from civil society[20]—did

---

[16] Interview P23.
[17] Interview P20, Filipino environmental affairs journalist, Zoom, 18 September 2023.
[18] Interviews P19 and P21, Filipino environmentalist, Zoom, 21 September 2023.
[19] Interview P20.
[20] Interview P22, Filipino climate activist, Zoom, 22 September 2023.

not recall a single instance when Duterte actively used climate change to mobilize domestic support.[21] One interviewee described the Duterte government's involvement in climate change issues as 'lukewarm' and as reduced compared to the Aquino presidency.[22] Yet another interviewee thought of Duterte's comments on climate change as 'not part of a strategy' and 'random': 'That's why he eventually signed the ratification of the Paris Agreement, because he did not understand what it was in the first place.'[23] Mirroring his approach to policy in other areas, Duterte's leadership in climate-related matters was described to us as 'flamboyant' and 'reactive', with the sole exception of his strong views on climate justice and assigning responsibility for climate issues to industrialized countries, as visible in some of his yearly state of the union addresses.[24]

Instead of personalization, in the case of the Philippines' approach to climate change mitigation, we find a high degree of centralization. On the one hand, Duterte made the above-mentioned critical statements, but he did not make climate change mitigation a major issue in his own agenda, nor was it a personal issue to him.[25] Unlike Aquino, he was not personally involved in climate negotiations on the international level. Whereas Aquino had a presidential advisor on climate change, Duterte did not. Instead, he delegated climate policy matters to the heads of the Climate Change Commission (CCC), Senator Legarda, and, especially from 2021 onwards, Duterte's childhood friend and finance secretary Carlos Dominguez III (Ranada 2021; Algo 2021). As all our interviews confirmed, on climate matters Dominguez, 'called the shots'.[26] Thus, compared to the Aquino presidency, the number of relevant actors in climate policy making and negotiations was much smaller under Duterte, who almost exclusively relied on the Ministry of Finance and its secretary.[27] The result was a high degree of centralization in decision making, less transparency,[28] less input by the Department of Environment and Natural Resources (DENR), and significantly less space for civil society to get involved.[29] For instance, according to a former climate negotiator under Aquino, the Philippines' delegations to the UNFCCC under Duterte were

---

[21] Interview P20.

[22] Interview P21.

[23] Interview P23.

[24] Interview P19.

[25] E.g., Interview P23.

[26] Interview P22.

[27] Interview P23.

[28] According to a journalist we interviewed, one notable difference was how the Aquino and Duterte governments dealt with the press. Whereas the former was forthcoming and relatively open, the latter refused to even respond questions. Interview P20.

[29] Interview P19.

much smaller and included fewer experts from civil society.[30] Another activist and negotiator under Aquino concurred:

> Dominguez was telling us not to meddle as climate change is their own affairs. Because of this, the Philippines was seen as a non-player. But during Aquino, COP attendance was seen as very good. [. . .] That was a genuine all-of-government approach from negotiators to diplomats, to CSO representatives.[31]

In fact, all our interviewees underlined the significance of appointing Finance Secretary Dominguez as chair of the Climate Change Commission. As Dominguez was perceived to be close to Duterte, this gave the position additional weight.[32] Meanwhile, it also underlined the Philippines' focus on securing financial aid from abroad.[33]

Ultimately, this combination of low mobilization and high centralization (albeit not necessarily personalization) led to policies that displayed an only somewhat reduced readiness to contribute to the global public good of climate change mitigation as compared to the policies of the previous government. This was confirmed by both the activists and the journalists we interviewed, who regarded the Duterte government as less climate-conscious than the previous government under Aquino. Duterte's initial harsh rhetorical criticism was accompanied by ambivalent policies, but climate issues overall were not used for mobilization by Duterte.

Weak Mobilization, Weak Personalization

In several of our case studies and policy fields, we did not observe a declining readiness to contribute to the provision of global public goods. Instead, continuity as compared to the previous non-populist government prevailed.

Turkey and Climate

In the case of Turkey, there was a high degree of continuity in the government's approach to climate change mitigation before and after 2011. Turkey had been among the first signatories of the UNFCCC in 1992; in 2009, it signed the Kyoto Protocol, but without making any concrete commitments to

---

[30] Interview P21.
[31] Interview P23.
[32] Interview P18.
[33] Interview P20.

climate change mitigation (Baykal 2022, 36). Overall, during the entire period we analysed, Turkey's approach was marked by a recognition of the dangers posed by climate change, combined with a discourse focused on the need for climate justice, financial assistance to developing countries like Turkey, and resistance to the adoption of ambitious mitigation goals that would hamper national development. Ultimately, Turkey submitted its Intended Nationally Determined Contribution (INDC) in October 2015 and ratified the Paris Climate Agreement in 2021, after much hesitation and criticism about lacking financial support from industrialized countries (MENA Research Center 2021). Subsequent policies continued to be hesitant and contradictory. In 2021, a Directorate of Climate Change was established by presidential decree as an affiliated body of what was later called the Ministry of Environment, Urbanization, and Climate Change (Directorate of Climate Change 2024). In 2022, Erdoğan proudly announced the 'green development revolution' of Turkey at the Major Economies Forum that was held in the US (Erdoğan 2022), but in the same year a new coal-fired power plant began operating (Enerji ve Tabi Kaynaklar Bakanlığı 2022).

Such continuity in Turkey's approach to climate change mitigation before and after 2011 can be traced back to low levels of both mobilization and personalization. In fact, the issue of climate change mitigation was never used by the AKP government or Erdoğan personally for domestic political mobilization. Across both non-populist and populist governments we looked at, Ankara sought to present Turkey as a reasonable actor having no historical responsibility for climate change and 'contributing to the global climate action on equal terms with countries of similar economic levels' (Cumhurbaşkanlığı 2021). After 2011, Erdoğan increasingly embedded references to climate justice in a broader claim of representing the oppressed of the world and the poorest countries affected by the climate crisis,[34] as in this statement: 'Climate change is not only affecting certain states that are most polluting the world but actually affecting all humanity starting with the countries in the African continent' (Bir 2021). While this framing resonated with his more general foreign policy discourse, it was not employed prominently in his domestic discourse. Similarly, personalization was limited. To a large extent, Turkey's approach to climate issues was shaped by the Ministry of Energy, which had always been more assertive than the Ministry of Environment, Urbanization, and Climate Change, and was in fact long able to block the ratification of the Paris Agreement.[35] Erdoğan refrained from

---

[34] Interview T07, Muhammed Kafadar, Turkish journalist with *Hürriyet*, Istanbul, 30 March 2023.
[35] Interviews T14, climate activist and scholar, Istanbul, 27 April 2023, and T12, Mithat Rende, retired senior Turkish diplomat and former Chief Climate Negotiator, Istanbul, 18 April 2023.

making climate change mitigation a personal priority. The combination of this absence of both personalization and mobilization contributes to explain the high degree of continuity in Turkey's approach.

India and Peace

Another instance in which we did not observe a clear shift in the readiness to contribute to global public goods was that of India's approach to the promotion of peace. The provision of troops to UN peacekeeping missions has long been a key element in India's engagement in the United Nations (see Chapter 5), with India consistently being among the top troop contributors. In line with this tradition, the non-populist UPA-I and UPA-II governments (2004–2014) even strongly increased the number of troops sent to such missions in 2005 and 2006. This rise was driven mainly by the two missions to Congo (MONUC) and South Sudan (UNMISS) (United Nations Peacekeeping 2003; 2004; 2005; 2006b). When it comes to diplomatic engagement or mediation efforts, during the UPA-I and UPA-II years, India was confronted with a number of intra-state armed conflicts in in South Asia, which more or less directly impacted its own security via spillover effects. Here, the Indian government's reactions were mixed. On the one hand, New Delhi played a constructive role in ending the civil war in Nepal, where Maoist rebels under the leadership of Pushpa Kamal Dahal (alias Prachanda) had been fighting against the monarchic government since 1996. After several twists and turns and a number of highly ambivalent and unsuccessful efforts to save the ruling monarchy, New Delhi ultimately supported a broad protest movement that was calling for the establishment of a republic (Destradi 2012b). More important, India played a crucial role in facilitating an agreement between the Nepalese political parties and the Maoist rebels in 2005, which put an end to the country's civil war and paved the way for the abolition of monarchy and other far-reaching reforms (P. Jha 2008). Yet, this mediation was carried out with little publicity. For various reasons, Indian officials even refused to call it mediation. For one, India did not want to appear meddling excessively with Nepal's domestic affairs and was trying to shed its image of a 'big brother' (Destradi 2012b); even more important, India does not tolerate mediation in its own conflict with Pakistan and thus traditionally avoids to be called a mediator itself. As Joshi (2015, 259) puts it with reference to conflicts in the Middle East, 'Whereas Turkey revels in the pomp of mediation, India sees advantage in obscurity: why invite global scrutiny of India's position on a sectarian civil war, when success is improbable and India's stakes so low?'

The UPA-I years were further characterized by an escalation of the civil war between the Liberation Tigers of Tamil Eelam (LTTE) and the Sri Lankan state. The conflict ended in May 2009 with the military defeat and de facto annihilation of the LTTE, accompanied by massive human rights violations and war crimes. India's policies were highly ambivalent: as New Delhi continued to call for a peaceful resolution of the conflict, from 2007 onwards it started quietly supporting the ruthless military offensive of the government (Destradi 2012a). The UPA-II government did not consistently call for investigations into the war crimes by the Sri Lankan government, thus privileging its strategic interest in the maintenance of influence on Sri Lanka over the pledges to Sri Lankan Tamils (and their ethnic peers in the Indian state of Tamil Nadu). In Afghanistan, the other major conflict-affected country in India's region, the UPA-I and UPA-II governments equally were highly reluctant, refusing to support the Afghan government in security terms beyond a certain point, mainly out of fear of provoking Pakistan (Destradi 2014). Moreover, India consistently ruled out negotiations with the Taliban, based on the assumption that there were no 'good Taliban' one could talk to (Paliwal 2017).

With the shift to the populist government of Narendra Modi in 2014, the basic tenets of India's approach did not change much, with India becoming only slightly less willing to contribute to the global public good of peace. For one, India's engagement in UN peacekeeping did not change drastically as compared to previous years: the number of troops provided by India steadily declined after 2014, but this trend had started already in 2007, albeit at a slower rate; and in 2021–2022, there was a small increase (see Figure 4.4). According to a retired diplomat interviewed, India's fundamental commitment to UN peacekeeping 'has not gone down.'[36]

When it comes to mediation, the circumstances for the Modi government were different because both major armed conflicts in India's immediate neighbourhood, in Nepal and Sri Lanka, had just been terminated. In Afghanistan, India continued to pursue policies similar to those of the previous government, refusing extensive support to the Afghan government in its fight against the Taliban in the years before the Taliban took over the country in 2021. Over time, the Indian government gradually opened to the idea of negotiations with the Taliban, but it did not play any active role in, for instance, promoting the Doha talks. In Afghanistan, this was observed with scepticism: 'Afghan insiders [. . .], who have historically been well disposed toward India, argue that "New Delhi waited too long on the peace process"

---

[36] Interview I11, retired Indian diplomat, New Delhi, 2 March 2023.

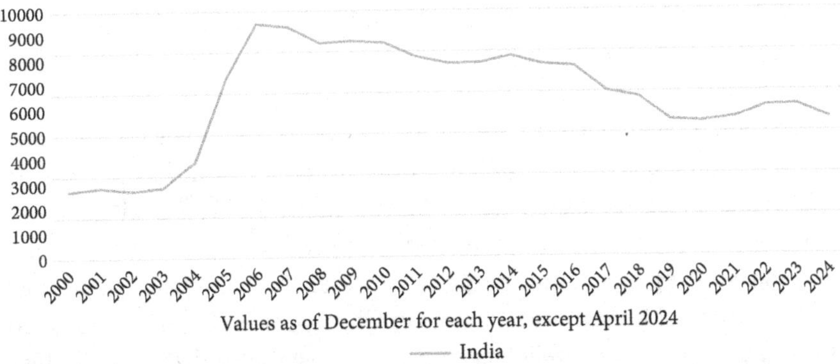

Figure 4.4 India's total peacekeeping staff contributions
Source: United Nations Peacekeeping, https://peacekeeping.un.org/en/troop-and-police-contributors (last accessed 1 July 2024).

and that despite its "enormous leverage and capital" in Kabul, it consciously pushed itself to "irrelevance"' (Chaudhuri and Shende 2020, 14).

Overall, India continued to adhere to its policy of keeping a low profile around the issue of international conflict mediation. All this was driven by a surprisingly low degree of personalization, with Prime Minister Modi not getting personally involved in peace-promoting activities. Following Russia's attack on Ukraine in 2022, there was a great deal of international interest in the position of India with its tradition of close relations with Russia. Not the least given India's self-stylization as a bridge builder between the West and the rest of the world, much international media attention was devoted to Modi addressing Putin at the Shanghai Cooperation Organization meeting in September 2022, where he declared: 'I know that today's era is not of war and we have talked to you many times over the phone on the subject that democracy and diplomacy and dialogue are all these things that touch the world [*sic*]' (Pratap and Chen 2022). Yet this much-publicized rebuke to Putin was not followed by any active form of engagement for peace on the part of Modi. In 2024, India's external affairs minister Jaishankar made some vague statements hinting at a potential readiness on the part of India to serve as a mediator and declared that India is 'deeply convinced and committed to bringing the Ukraine war to an end' (India Today 2024b). And yet, continuous Western calls for stronger Indian involvement notwithstanding, New Delhi only sent a mid-ranking diplomat to the Swiss Summit on Peace in Ukraine in June 2024—an indication of Modi's disinterest in being involved personally. Later in the same year, Modi visited both Moscow and, in August, Kyiv, where he stated: 'Personally, as a friend, if there is any role that I can play, I would very much like to play that role toward peace' (Arhirova 2024). However, again, there was no visible follow-up or engagement in structured negotiations.

The low degree of personalization in India's approach to peace was accompanied by some instances of mobilization in *support* of India's participation in UN peacekeeping missions. In Modi's monthly 'Mann ki baat' radio addresses, the prime minister repeatedly referred to India's contributions to UN peacekeeping as a source of national pride. For example, before remembering individual Indian commanders in UN peacekeeping missions, in 2017 Modi stated: 'You will surely feel proud to know that India's contribution is not limited to just peacekeeping operations but it is also providing training to peacekeepers from about eighty five countries. The brave peacekeepers from this land of Mahatma Gandhi and Gautam Budha have sent a message of peace and amity around the world' (Modi 2017a). Nonetheless, overall, personalization and mobilization in this case were low. According to a retired diplomat we interviewed, this was because 'the PM likes talking about things he initiated', but there was nothing new about peacekeeping.[37] In sum, when it comes to the readiness to contribute to the global public good of peace, India's engagement remained at levels comparable to those of the previous governments, with slightly decreased contributions to UN missions but continued rhetorical support for them, and a continuation of traditional low-key policies on matters of conflict mediation.

India and Development Aid

Also in the field of development aid, Modi's approach was one of continuity as compared to previous non-populist governments. Despite being a recipient country itself, providing development aid has been an integral part of India's foreign policy since the early 1950s (Fuchs and Vadlamannati 2013). In 1964 India launched the Indian Technical and Economic Cooperation Programme (ITEC) to share its expertise in areas like tropical medicine, irrigation, and railway infrastructure with Asian and African countries (Chaturvedi 2012). Especially from the late 1990s onwards, New Delhi ramped up its development cooperation activities, with expenditures increasing tenfold between the fiscal years 1998/99 and 2017/18 (Destradi and Gurol 2022, 166). Like other 'new donors' from the Global South, India refuses to coordinate its development activities with DAC donor countries. In fact, New Delhi traditionally

---

[37] Interview I18, retired Indian diplomat, New Delhi, 7 March 2023.

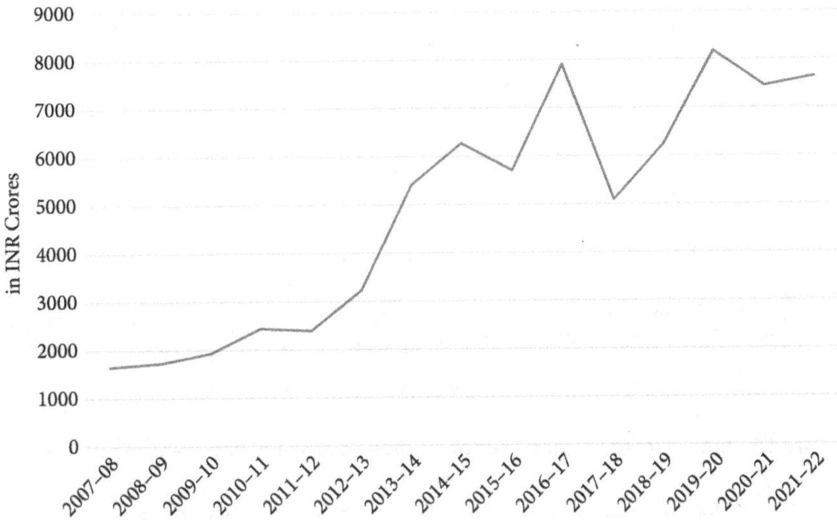

Figure 4.5 India's Technical and Economic Cooperation

Note that the government of India does not provide an exact definition of Technical and Economic Cooperation (TEC), thus making it impossible to identify the share of grants in TEC. *Source:* Ministry of External Affairs.

portrays its aid as unconditional and in line with the principle of non-interference, and as such different from Western aid (Chaturvedi 2016), and more recently also as friendlier and 'less exploitative' compared to that of China (Destradi and Gurol 2022, 167).

In absolute numbers, India's aid expenditures increased from the non-populist UPA-II government (2009–2014) throughout the populist government led by Modi and until 2022, albeit with some setbacks, as illustrated in Figure 4.5 (Ministry of External Affairs 2024a).

However, if we take into account development aid and loans (lines of credit) as a share of gross national income (GNI), we find no substantial increase over time, despite some peaks in the budgets for fiscal years 2005–2006, 2010–2011 (both during non-populist UPA governments), and 2016–2017 (during the populist NDA I government), as illustrated in Figure 4.6.

In terms of geographic priorities, data from the Ministry of External Affairs show that aid to the neighbourhood was selective, with the Maldives, Nepal, and Bhutan benefitting most. The latter two are located between India and its main rival, China. Both countries also have a long history of interdependence with (and dependence on) India. The Maldives, in turn, are strategically positioned in the Indian Ocean and thus of importance to India's maritime

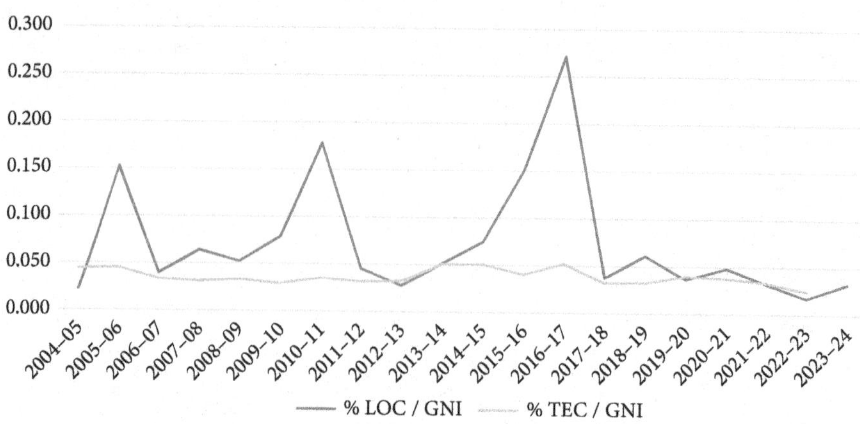

Figure 4.6 India's technical and economic cooperation and lines of credit as share of GNI

Source: own composition based on data from Ministry of External Affairs and World Bank

security. Beyond South Asia, India's aid was clearly driven by strategic considerations, with a prioritization of the Indian Ocean island countries Mauritius and the Seychelles. Aid to both countries increased substantially from 2017 onwards (see Ministry of External Affairs 2024a).

A geopolitical readjustment can also be seen in Indian development financing via credits. The systematic issuing of lines of credit (LOCs) to foreign countries, mostly for infrastructure, began with the creation of the Indian Development Initiative under the BJP-led NDA government in 2003 via the state bank EXIM. Although habitually portrayed as development assistance by the Indian government, LOCs at least in part are also meant to promote Indian business interests (Mukherjee 2015). Loan conditions vary from case to case and LOCs may have substantial grant components. It is thus legitimate to consider them as a 'special category' of Indian aid (Mukherjee 2015, 177). The Modi government brought a significant change to India's LOC pattern. Whereas in the ten years preceding 2014 almost two thirds of LOCs went to Africa and only the remaining third to Asia, from 2014 to 2022 this relationship was inverse (India Exim Bank 2024): the BJP-led government focused its LOCs on Asian countries, including South Asia, with Bangladesh by far the greatest beneficiary. Also, the Maldives under the pro-Indian President Ibrahim Mohamed Solih benefitted: his election in 2018 may explain much of the rise in Indian LOCs (and aid) to the Maldives post-2018. This all took place against the backdrop of intensifying Sino-Indian rivalry, and the appearance of Chinese naval forces in the Indian Ocean, which led Indian strategists to focus their attention on maritime issues (Plagemann and Prys-Hansen 2020).

The case of Bangladesh illustrates the interrelation of India's strategic interests with foreign assistance. For one, Bangladesh continued to receive a small but consistent share of aid in grants. More important, with four LOCs over the years 2016–2024 (that is, until the ouster of India-friendly prime minister Sheikh Hasina in August 2024) amounting to around $8 billion, Indian official sources habitually referred to Bangladesh as its 'largest development partner' (Ministry of External Affairs 2024b). Indeed, under Modi, India, along with China, emerged as Bangladesh's main funder in infrastructure, from ports to bridges and roads (Plagemann 2021, 747). Together with Russia, India constructed Bangladesh's first nuclear power plant. Further, Dhaka benefited from special initiatives like India's vaccine diplomacy, or #VaccineMaitri (Vaccine Friendship, see below). Again, both the domestic and international context mattered. Almost completely surrounded by India and a key pathway to Southeast Asia as well as India's northeastern states, Bangladesh is of vital geopolitical importance to India. Consequently, growing Chinese investments and arms supplies to Bangladesh irk Indian strategists fearful of Chinese intrusion into South Asia (Plagemann 2021). Moreover, Bangladesh throughout Modi's first and second mandates as prime minister was led by the relatively India-friendly prime minister Sheikh Hasina of the Awami League. India's aid and loans to the country thus were an expression of New Delhi's geopolitical desire to keep a key neighbour close.

In sum, then, we find a readjustment of Indian aid and LOCs in line with India's geopolitical interests under Modi's populist government. Moreover, we see a greater emphasis on loans over grants (Mullen in Gupta et al. 2019), even though this was mostly articulated at the rhetorical level and not necessarily reflected in expenditure shares (see Figure 4.6). The populist government's discourse on aid reflected an understanding that development cooperation 'should not be charity', as pointed out by one of our interviewees.[38] Similarly, at a think tank close to the BJP, an interviewee pointed out: 'Today, India is looking not to waste its money. The professionalism is bigger'.[39] In line with Modi's carefully crafted image as an apt economic manager, India's growing focus on LOCs over grants allowed it to have it both ways: engaging in geo-economic competition with China while also claiming to have Indian business interests in mind. Moreover, as it is the case with China's Belt and Road Initiative (BRI), Indian LOCs primarily fund major infrastructures in the near abroad, that is, visible manifestations of

---

[38] Interview I11.
[39] Interview I12.

Indian strength, that Modi also prioritizes in his domestic economic agenda (The Economist 2023). All this has led to an interpretation of India's aid becoming more 'mercantilist' under Modi (Mullen in Gupta et al. 2019, 6). Populism and mercantilism go hand in hand easily. Nonetheless, context matters too. In fact, the shift towards a somewhat less public goods–oriented approach under Modi was at least partially driven by the changed geopolitical context in which the populist government was operating. It was after 2014 that the very impact of the BRI became impossible for India to overlook: the single largest BRI project, the China Pakistan Economic Corridor (CPEC) launched in 2015, runs through Pakistani territory claimed by India; Chinese infrastructure funding to Sri Lanka was the very founding myth of China's 'debt trap diplomacy', that India took a big part in promoting (Brautigam 2020). And Bangladesh had started sourcing the majority of its arms from Beijing, fuelling fears in New Delhi around a deepening of security cooperation between Dhaka and Beijing, and prompting India to repeatedly provide for new loans and other aid after the announcement of new Chinese investments (Plagemann 2021). In many ways, thus, the more mercantilist approach adopted by Modi was the result of competition with China. Importantly, Modi did not explicitly personalize decision making in this field, nor was development aid a subject of public debate, or political mobilization, beyond India's exclusive strategic community. Against this backdrop, and because we did not observe remarkable changes in aid overall in term of shares in India's GNI or Union Budget, we consider this to be a case of continuity.

However, we found an exception to the overall picture of continuity: India's vaccine diplomacy during the Covid-19 crisis. Like Modi's endorsement of climate action, India's 'Vaccine Maitri' (maitri is Hindi for friendship) initiative (J. Sharma and Varshney 2021) was a major instrument for his government to display its benign nature and advanced capabilities both domestically and externally. For instance, in an online address to the World Economic Forum in Davos in January 2021, Modi self-confidently (and prematurely) declared the pandemic to be effectively over in India and underlined his country's capabilities in fighting the pandemic elsewhere: 'In these tough times, India has been undertaking its global responsibility from the beginning. When airspace was closed in many countries, India took more than 1 lakh [100.000] citizens to their countries and delivered essential medicines to more than 150 countries' (Aggarwal 2021). A second pandemic wave hit India throughout the first half of 2021. As vaccines and medical supplies were scarce, the Modi government suspended much of its vaccine shipments (Mazumdar 2021) and refrained from further highlighting its vaccine diplomacy. In any case, India's vaccine diplomacy was framed as a contribution to a global public good—albeit still primarily focused on those states that also benefit from Indian aid and LOCs, namely, India's neighbours in South Asia and the Indian Ocean Region.

The Philippines and Peace

Another instance in which the transition to a populist government did not lead to substantial foreign policy change was the Philippines' approach to peacekeeping and the promotion of peace more generally. Under the non-populist government of Aquino, the Philippines regularly contributed troops and other personnel to several UN missions, but a remarkable drop in contributions took place during his presidency (2010–2016). As revealed by Figure 4.7, under Duterte engagement in UN peacekeeping did not regain traction.

At least partially, the remaining decline in troop contributions under Duterte was due to the expiry of some of the missions in which personnel from the Philippines had been deployed. For example, the United Nations Stabilization Mission in Haiti (MINUSTAH) was discontinued in October 2017 (United Nations Peacekeeping 2023), United Nations Operation in Côte d'Ivoire (UNOCI) in June 2017, and the United Nations Mission in Liberia (UNMIL) in March 2018. At the same time, Duterte did not engage in new missions. According to a former government official we interviewed in Manila, 'that wasn't really a conscious policy decision, not being involved in UN peacekeeping operations [...]. The decision on that was at the

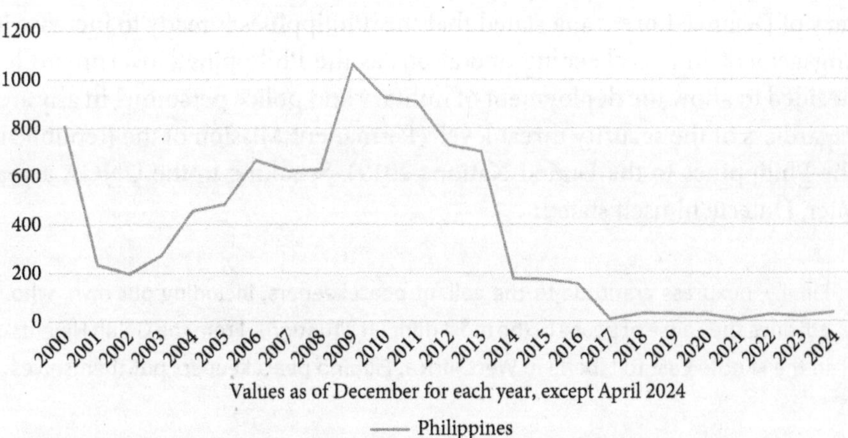

Figure 4.7 The Philippines' total peacekeeping staff contributions
Source: United Nations Peacekeeping, https://peacekeeping.un.org/en/troop-and-police-contributors (last accessed 1 July 2024).

cabinet level, not for the president. It was not a presidential decision'.[40] Also according to our e-mail communication with a Filipino scholar, the slight decline in troop contributions should not be understood as part of Duterte's 'populist anti-West, anti-UN rhetoric'.[41] The same expert also pointed out that Duterte had said repeatedly that he did not want Filipino peacekeepers to die in battle. Of course, with this he was not alone. In 2014 a contingent of the UN Disengagement Observer Force (UNDOF), including seventy-five Filipino soldiers, came under fire from Islamist rebels in the Golan Heights. The incident was widely reported in the Philippines as the outnumbered peacekeepers managed to escape at night in a dramatic rescue operation. The Department of Defense under the non-populist President Aquino shortly afterwards declared that as a result of the worsening security situation it was pulling out all 331 Filipino soldiers from the mission (Agence France-Presse 2014). Thus, both Aquino and Duterte shared a sensitivity towards the loss of Filipino lives in peacekeeping missions, and this might contribute to explaining the continuity in the two presidents' approaches. Another interviewee confirmed this continuity, pointing out that 'even during the Aquino administration we didn't show real interest in increasing [contributions to peacekeeping]'.[42]

Also, it is difficult to argue that the decline and subsequent stagnation in the Philippines' troop contributions under Duterte was related to his very personal aversion vis-à-vis the U N (see Chapter 5) as we did not find any instances of mobilization against participation in its missions on the part of Duterte or his government. To the contrary, speaking before the UN General Assembly at a UN Peacekeeping Defence Ministerial in March 2019, Secretary of Defence Lorenzana stated that the 'Philippines is ready to increase its engagement in peacekeeping operations as the Philippine Government has decided to allow the deployment of military and police personnel in any area regardless of the security threat level' (Permanent Mission of the Republic of the Philippines to the United Nations 2019). Speaking to the UNGA a year later, Duterte himself stated:

Finally, I express gratitude to the gallant peacekeepers, including our own, who advance the cause of peace in the most difficult situations. From the Golan Heights in the Middle East to Liberia in West Africa, Filipino peacekeepers put themselves

---

[40] Interview P29, former government official during the Duterte administration, Manila, 23 November 2024.

[41] P24, e-mail communication with Filipino scholar, 22 June 2024.

[42] Interview P27, Prof. Herman Joseph S. Kraft, University of the Philippines Diliman, 22 November 2024.

in the frontlines between the vulnerable and those who seek harm. We are committed to increasing the Philippine footprint in UN peacekeeping operations with
increased participation of women. (Duterte 2020)

In sum, then, we observe overall continuity in the readiness to contribute
to UN peacekeeping under Duterte alongside comparably weak personalization and the absence of mobilization. Whereas we may safely presume that
Duterte's personal agreement would have been a prerequisite for new troop
contributions,[43] he did not question UN peacekeeping in his efforts to mobilize the public, nor did he seek a mediating role for him or his government in
any other conflict abroad.

Bolivia and Climate

Finally, Bolivia under Morales did not exhibit a willingness to contribute to
climate change mitigation as a global public good that diverged much from
his predecessor government—despite the MAS government's new rhetoric.
Bolivia since the beginnings of the UNFCC has been a reliable supporter
and active participant in global climate negotiations (Bojanic 2001, 17) at
the same time that the economic exploitation of environmentally harmful extractive resources and deforestation continued (Krommes-Ravnsmed
2019). Morales did not personalize climate change issues nor did his government use it very much for *domestic* mobilization, thus conforming to our
expectations of continuity. However, this case is interesting as Morales visibly
used the protection of the environment, including the climate, for mobilization vis-à-vis an *international* audience (see in particular Aguirre and
Cooper [2010]). While strongly criticizing and, at times, boycotting the very
process of multilateral climate negotiations as insufficient, Morales domestically pursued extractivist policies (Krommes-Ravnsmed 2019; McNeish
2013).

Prior to Morales's first election as president in December 2005, his MAS
had belonged to a wider array of social movements emphasizing indigenous peoples' rights, the protection of their traditions, and the environment.
Not surprisingly, Morales's government initially raised hopes among environmental activists.[44] In his first appearances at the UNGA and at the

---

[43] According to one academic expert we spoke with, Secretary of Defence Lorenzana was 'only expected
to manage [his] department and to wait for orders'. Interview P05, Filipino scholar, Manila, 30 September
2022.

[44] Interview B07, Carmen Capriles, civil society expert in climate change, La Paz, 20 January 2023.

global climate summits, Morales emphasized the need for respect of 'Mother Earth' (*Madre Tierra* or *Pachamama*), a trope that emanated from Bolivia's indigenous rights and environmentalist groups and which was prominently included in the preamble to Bolivia's new constitution from 2009. Being the country's first indigenous president, Morales's international appearances created the impression of a new Bolivia dedicated to environmental protection domestically and willing to stand up for it internationally. Once in power, Morales substituted existing institutions that were in charge of climate policies with the 'Plurinational Authority of Mother Earth', tasked with formulating and implementing climate change mitigation policies 'with a horizontal and intersectional approach' (Ministerio de Medio Ambiente y Agua—Autoridad Plurinacional de la Madre Tierra, 35). Moreover, claiming leadership on alternative approaches to climate change mitigation, Morales's populist government in 2010 hosted the World Peoples Conference on Climate Change and the Rights of Mother Earth (Cevallos 2013, 12). Announced as a response to the eviction of NGOs from the 2009 Copenhagen summit, the conference gathered thousands of representatives from more than 100 countries. In 2015, Bolivia carried out another Peoples World Conference in Tiquipaya. Among the attendees was UN Secretary General Ban Ki-moon. Presidents Morales, Rafael Correa (Ecuador), Nicolás Maduro (Venezuela), and Cuban foreign minister Bruno Rodríguez took part in the closing event, calling for differentiated responsibilities in climate change and pointing to the links between environmental problems and capitalism (Corz 2015). Some mobilization along the lines of the MAS's thick ideology occurred as, here and elsewhere, Morales explicitly linked climate change to the MAS's thick ideology of socialism. According to him, the climate crisis originated in capitalist development and colonialism, thus leading to a 'historical ecological debt' of developed countries (Morales 2008b). In international fora, Bolivia under Morales was more vocal than under the predecessor government[45] making a series of demands, including international compensation, the involvement of local communities and social movements in mitigation activities, and the respect for national sovereignty in managing mitigation and adaptation funds.

However, our interviews also reveal a stark contrast between Bolivia's international discourse and its domestic actions.[46] In fact, the MAS government intensified Bolivia's reliance on hydrocarbons and commodity exports domestically (Poupeau 2013, 110–11).[47] An apt illustration is the significant

---

[45] Interview B26, former career diplomat, La Paz, 8 March 2023.
[46] Interview B23, academic and former senior diplomat, La Paz, 6 March 2023.
[47] Interview B07.

loss of forests due to agricultural expansion, mining, and uncontrolled wild-fires over the course of Morales's presidency (Redo, Millington, and Hindery 2011).[48] Another expert concurred that despite Morales's discourse around the protection of the environment, his government did not respect even those policies or legal frameworks that already were in the Constitution, instead intensifying mining through its state companies and expanding the agricultural frontier into protected forests. In that sense, the law of Mother Earth was a 'poetic law that talks about being in harmony with Mother Earth', but it was never complemented by more concrete procedural rules that would have effectively contributed to the reductions of emissions.[49] Likewise, the Mother Earth summits never went beyond issuing declarations,[50] and they visibly failed to hold the host country accountable regarding its own climate record.

A closer look at the foreign policy process under Morales helps explain this disconnect between words and action as well as between the domestic and the international. A diplomat and lead negotiator under Morales in an interview with us underlined how Bolivia's stance on climate issues originated in the MAS's involvement with social movements prior to Morales's election. According to her, the new government sought to give space to social movements in Bolivia's multilateral negotiations over climate and other environmental issues. While emphasizing Morales's personal ability to better position Bolivia in such negotiations,[51] none of our interviewees stated that Morales had been personally involved in Bolivia's climate policies. Instead, the activist-turned-diplomat Pablo Solón, Bolivia's ambassador to the UN from 2009 to 2011, was the key figure in the Morales's government's climate change policies during its first years. As one Bolivian expert noted:[52]

> There was a relatively small group within MAS that really believed in the issue of *Pachamama* and Living Well [. . .]. Evo would have learned, to a certain extent, to repeat this in international forums, he liked the limelight, but he never took it on as a personal philosophy.[53]

While overseeing negotiations on behalf of Bolivia at the COP in Copenhagen (2009) and Cancún (2010), Solón strongly criticized both agreements

---

[48] Interview B25, Daniel Robison, Bolivian academic and environmentalist, Zoom, 8 March 2023
[49] Interview B12, Soledad Enríquez, Bolivian expert in agroforestry and natural resource management, Zoom, 1 February 2023.
[50] Interview B07.
[51] Interviews B26 and B22, former senior diplomat, Zoom, 3 March 2023.
[52] Interview B24, journalist and former senior diplomat, Zoom, 8 March 2023.
[53] Interview B25.

as vastly insufficient to deal with the severity of climate change (see Solón in *The Guardian* 2010a; 2010b). Internationally, Bolivia at that time radically rejected the 'commodification of the environment' supposedly put forward in UNFCCC negotiations and strongly called for binding and stringent emission targets for industrialized countries.[54] Whereas Bolivia along with Tuvalu, Venezuela, Cuba, and Nicaragua, among others, prevented the Copenhagen Accord from being a formal UNFCCC agreement, Solón stood isolated at the COP in Cancún in the following year. However, as Morales was eager to shine abroad, he also needed the support of other leftist governments. As one former Bolivian diplomat told us: 'We had a big problem with the Climate Change Summit, COP in Cancún, when we were left absolutely alone with [. . .] the proposal made by Pablo Solón.'[55]

Thus, Cancún was the 'perfect opportunity' for Morales to remove a by then disillusioned[56] Solón from government, as happened in 2011. Solón's swift departure occurred against the background of a wider lack of public support for his climate agenda. His initial proximity to power notwithstanding, he had few followers within the MAS and its wider support base. As one interviewee put it:

> [The discourse around Mother Earth and its implications for Bolivia's climate policies] were an elitist line of thinking that never interested the coca growers, the miners, and I can't think of one of the main supporters of MAS who really thinks it is important to make sacrifices to protect Mother Earth. It was sincere at the time as an external position, but it did not reflect any critical mass, there is no significant percentage of Bolivians who believe that way and for me the proof is that when election time comes, it is not an electoral issue. There is no one who talks about *Pachamama* and Living Well in the different elections.[57]

With a key figure in the climate agenda gone, Bolivia's international climate policies lost much of their diplomatic momentum. Meanwhile, habitual claims that the solution to the problem of climate change was the destruction of capitalism (Alvarez, n.d.; Plurinational State of Bolivia, n.d.), coupled with an ongoing unwillingness to communicate verifiable national contributions, diminished Bolivia's reputation as a constructive negotiator. Thus, an environmentalist interviewed by us concluded: '[Morales] has been given much

---

[54] Interview B12.
[55] Interview B15, former senior diplomat, La Paz, 6 February 2023.
[56] Interview B15.
[57] Interview B25.

more [international] coverage than he really deserved'.[58] Far from adopting Solón's green agenda, influential political figures more in line with the MAS's leftist orthodoxy, such as Vice President García Linera, regarded environmentalism as a 'gringo idea' that did not matter to Bolivia's circumstances.[59] As a result, whereas internationally the mediatic president managed to portray himself as a staunch environmentalist, climate protection never was a matter of political salience domestically. At the same time, Morales did not question the reality of climate change and the science accompanying it. Instead, in tandem with his ideological Latin American allies, he made use of existing international platforms and created new ones to denounce capitalism and the developed world's implications in environmental and economic crises in the Global South. To some this amounted to bravely standing up to Western hegemony, whilst others regard it as rather inconsequential. In the meantime, Bolivia's forests—presumably the country's most important contribution to mitigation—shrank further.

Conclusion

While we expected populist governments to be less likely than non-populist ones to contribute to the provision of global public goods, the empirical analysis disconfirmed our expectations. In none of the countries analysed did the shift to a populist government lead to a clearly reduced readiness to contribute to the global public goods considered here. In fact, in several sub-cases—India on climate, Turkey on development and peace—it even led to the opposite: to a greater engagement in global governance. Remarkably, both right-wing populist leaders Erdoğan and Modi used some fields of global governance to display personal leadership. This allowed them to project an image of themselves and of their countries as responsible actors in world politics, and thereby to increase their international prestige and status, while at the same time using these issues to mobilize support at home (Wajner 2022; Destradi 2023). In Bolivia, populist leader Morales initially displayed considerable diplomatic activism around climate change mitigation and used this field to project himself as an innovative leader internationally, but when it came to actual policies at the domestic level, he was not more willing than his predecessors to contribute to climate change mitigation. Also in some other cases, populist governments ultimately did not bring

---

[58] Interview B12.
[59] Interview B25.

about significant change, notably when it came to Turkey's approach to climate, to India's readiness to contribute to development and peace, and to the Philippines' engagement for peace. In the case of the Philippines' approach to climate change mitigation and Bolivia's contributions to peace, different combination of weak/strong personalization and mobilization led to a somewhat lower readiness to contribute to global public goods, as we had expected.

In our conclusion (Chapter 8), we discuss at length some explanations for these surprising results. One of them is that global governance issues and the provision of global public goods tend to be detached from ordinary peoples' lives. On the one hand, this makes them the 'elitist' projects that populists often criticize and politicize. On the other hand, these issues are also less interesting for a populist's audience. This is especially so in countries of the Global South, where costly contributions to each of these issues are much rarer than in the West. The deployment of soldiers to UN peacekeeping operations does not affect the masses but may have tangible benefits for the respective militaries to hold on; non-binding climate change mitigation targets are abstract commitments that will not be felt by ordinary citizens in the same way that Western funding for mitigation efforts and the energy transition can have tangible effects. Using these topics to mobilize support in domestic politics is therefore much more difficult as compared to mobilization focused on, for instance, some external enemy. Thus, our selection of cases from the Global South matters for our assessment, given the relatively limited expectations, for example on climate change mitigation, articulated vis-à-vis those countries by the international community during the years analysed. We return to this in our comparison with European populist governments (see Chapter 7).

This all points to the fact that populism will be particularly consequential for foreign policy change only where there are clear electoral gains to be made via mobilization on specific issues. Moreover, status seeking can offset the expected negative consequences of populism, leading populist governments to even become particularly active in providing global public goods. Especially where there are gains to be made by the populist leader personally—as in conflict mediation—populism may lead to greater engagement.

5

Engagement in International Institutions

Over the past decade, one of the most debated issues in International Relations has been the demise of the so-called 'liberal' or 'rules-based international order', and populism has often been mentioned as one of the main drivers of this dynamic (Adler-Nissen and Zarakol 2021; Börzel and Zürn 2021; Colgan and Keohane 2017; Jahn 2018; Lake, Martin, and Risse 2021). What has particularly puzzled analysts is that populism has challenged this order 'from within', unfolding alongside other challenges from the rise of China to the intensification of great power rivalries. The challenge on the part of populists especially revolves around their apparent rejection of multilateralism per se, one of the key components of the 'liberal international order' (Ikenberry 2018; Stephen and Skidmore 2019). The assessment that populists are at the forefront of a backlash against international institutions was driven by prominent episodes like Brexit, but also policies of the Trump administration such as the US withdrawal from UNESCO in 2017 and from the UN Human Rights Council in 2018, Trump's repeated threats to leave NATO, and his administration's sanctioning of the International Criminal Court in 2025. As a result, several authors have drawn a connection between the rise of populist parties and politicians and a general crisis of multilateralism (Liang 2007b, 9; Wright 2021). However, a brief consideration of empirical cases beyond Trump and European right-wing populists points to the need for a more nuanced assessment. For one, despite extremely widespread Euroscepticism among both right- and left-wing populists in Europe, Brexit has so far remained an isolated phenomenon as no other populist government has exited the EU so far. Moreover, there are several instances of populists engaging in regional and international organizations, and even creating new ones, from Hugo Chávez's initiatives for the creation of ALBA, the Bolivarian Alliance for the Peoples of Our America, to Viktor Orbán's promotion of the Visegrad Group (V4) of Central and Eastern European countries.

The observation that populists do not always or automatically reject cooperation in international organizations has led to differentiated analyses of

Populism and Foreign Policy. Sandra Destradi and Johannes Plagemann, Oxford University Press.
© Oxford University Press (2025). DOI: 10.1093/9780197695012.003.0005

populists' approaches to international institutions. Copelovitch and Pevehouse (2019) argue that the combination of populism and nationalism should lead us to expect a withdrawal from international organizations. But since nationalist populists have often remained active members in international institutions, subsequent analyses developed more nuanced assessments. In his analysis of populists' approaches to international courts, Voeten (2020) concludes that populist backlashes against courts are not always successful either because populists do not follow up on their threats to leave or because they are unable to form coalitions with other populists due to the 'thin' character of populist ideology. Söderbaum et al. (2021, 3) argue that 'populist leaders are not anti-internationalist but in fact ascribe a positive value to certain forms of international cooperation, especially regional mechanisms that are malleable to populist ideas and preferences'. They point out that it is necessary to analyse individual populists' preferences concerning international cooperation, highlighting that populist framings of regional cooperation emphasize 'anti-liberalism, multilayered and threatened identity, and popular sovereignty' (Söderbaum, Spandler, and Pacciardi 2021, 3). Thus, populists prefer 'leader-driven formats, political symbolism, and à la carte cooperation' in multilateral settings (Söderbaum, Spandler, and Pacciardi 2021, 3). Spandler and Söderbaum (2023) delve into the ways in which populists delegitimize or legitimize international organizations, and they argue that populists often apply peculiar legitimacy standards to international organizations: For populists, the legitimacy of international organizations derives from their ability to represent the 'people' (popular identity) and to protect popular sovereignty. According to Spandler and Söderbaum (2023, 1025), '[f]rom a populist vantage point, what is primarily wrong with many established [International Organizations, IOs] is not that they lack transparency or are ineffective, but that their procedures and functions reflect a liberal, elitist order and fail to represent "the people"'. According to this logic, populist leaders will challenge IOs that are not considered representative in a populist sense. In another contribution, Spandler and Söderbaum (2025) propose a classification of various forms of disengagement of populist governments from international organizations, highlighting that there are many ways in which populist scepticism of international organizations can manifest itself. While exit is the most radical option, the authors also point out that extortion (the threat to leave the organization or to stop cooperating if certain conditions are not met), obstruction, and criticism are other possible—and empirically prevalent—forms of disengagement.

In this chapter, we build upon the literature on populists' approaches to international organizations, and we relate it to our broader theoretical framework. Generally, there are a number of reasons to expect populism—understood as a thin-centred ideology—to have a negative impact on governments' engagement in international institutions. First, the anti-elitist dimension of populism might lead to a high degree of scepticism vis-à-vis international institutions because these are by definition managed by an international or even cosmopolitan elite. In fact, according to Chryssogelos (2020), one of the main driving forces of the electoral success of populist parties over the past years has been the growing influence of supranational institutions and trans-governmental policy networks on peoples' lives and on the basic functions of their states. These deep processes of state restructuring led to the emergence of the 'internationalized state' and, in turn, to a shift in 'the reference point of state legitimacy from state elites' vertical relationship with the political community to their horizontal cosmopolitan relationship with equivalent elites from other states' (Chryssogelos 2020). It is not surprising that populists have seen these developments with great scepticism. Indeed, in several cases, the success of populists has been driven by fears of challenges to popular sovereignty in the face of a perceived growing intrusiveness of international bodies. This can best be observed in European populists' denunciation of 'Brussels' as the epicentre of dangerous elites detached from the people, which nonetheless are able to impinge on people's daily lives via regulations that are frequently portrayed as absurd.

Besides being perceived as 'elitist' institutions, international organizations are typically highly technocratic, managed by unelected bureaucrats or experts whom populists consider to be detached from commonsense reasoning and the needs of the people. Indeed, technocracy can be understood as a form of representation that 'stresses responsibility and requires voters to entrust authority to experts who identify the general interest from rational speculation' (Caramani 2017, 54). This stands in contrast to populism, which 'stresses responsiveness and requires voters to delegate authority to leaders who equate the general interest with a putative will of the people' (Caramani 2017, 54). The anti-elitist and the people-centric dimensions of populism are thus intertwined in what we expect to be a clear rejection of international organizations. This interrelation is best illustrated in populists' characteristic insistence on sovereignty. The idea of 'taking back control' for the people is one important component of contemporary populism, both in its right-wing and in its left-wing variants. As pointed out by Chryssogelos (2017), 'sovereignty' is probably the term that most accurately captures the populist logic of international affairs'. Indeed, some authors point towards a preference on the part of populists for 'a defensive re-territorialisation of power along existing fault lines of nation-statism' (Kallis 2018, 285). According to

Basile and Mazzoleni (2020, 157), 'sovereignism' can take different forms. At least two of these are particularly relevant in this context. Following the thin ideology of populism, popular sovereignism entails the notion that the ultimate source of political legitimacy should be the will of the 'true' people; and national sovereignism emphasizes the territorial dimension of the nation state as opposed to supranational forms of political authority such as that of the European Union. Based on both, we should expect populists to be more sceptical of, and probably also less willing to engage in, international organizations.

Finally, there is one more reason to expect populists to dislike multilateralism: their more general aversion towards all kinds of intermediating institutions. According to the ideational understanding of populism (Mudde 2004b), the representation of a presumed 'general will' of the people is the central element in populists' understanding of democracy. As we have discussed in Chapter 2, populist notions of democratic representation are often focused on the idea of an 'embodiment' of the popular will, and therefore on a direct connection between populist leaders and their 'people'. Acclamation is preferred over deliberation as the way to express the will of this supposedly unified people: 'the public manifestation of the consent of the people in the form of identification with and acclamation of its leader is the only valid accountability because it is the truly political one, not procedural and formal, not mediated but immediate' (Urbinati 2019b, 122). This explains why populists, once they come to power, end up weakening all sorts of democratic institutions that stand between them and the 'people': courts, parliament, or the traditional media in many cases are targeted by populists in power (Pappas 2019). Democratic backsliding is a consequence of this weakening of domestic intermediary institutions (Bermeo 2016), and recent empirical research has shown that it directly flows from the thin-centred ideology of populism (Benasaglio Berlucchi and Kellam 2023). Correspondingly, the main cases analysed in this book, Bolivia, India, the Philippines, and Turkey, have all been defined as cases of 'extreme' democratic backsliding (Benasaglio Berlucchi and Kellam 2023, 818). Thus, as populists weaken domestic institutions, we expect them to also work against international institutions that would seem to impinge on their direct connection with the people.

In sum, there are a number of theoretical reasons to expect the formation of populist governments to have a detrimental impact on countries' engagement in multilateral institutions. At the same time, we know that not all populists undermine all international organizations all the time (Destradi and Plagemann 2019; Söderbaum, Spandler, and Pacciardi 2021; Spandler and Söderbaum 2023; 2025). To make sense of variations in changing degrees of engagement in international organization after populist government formation, we again resort to our theoretical framework based on combinations of various degrees of personalization and mobilization.

We argue that a combination of strong mobilization and strong personalization allows populists' aversion to international organizations to play out most forcefully, leading to a clearly reduced readiness to engage in them. For one, as we have seen in Chapters 3 and 4, a strong personalization of power will give populists greater leeway to transform their distaste for international organizations into actual policies. If traditional foreign policy elites are marginalized, foreign ministries are weakened, and advisors inclined to see the benefits of multilateral cooperation are sidelined, populists will be less constrained in their approach to international institutions. At the same time, mobilization is a key factor here. In fact, we expect foreign policy change to be particularly strong where populists have seen an opportunity for mobilization against international institutions. Yet, the potential for mobilization will vary dramatically depending on how directly such institutions impinge on peoples' daily lives, that is, depending on the degree of authority exercised by such institutions and, by extension, on their salience to the public. To illustrate this, there is little point in mobilizing against the Universal Postal Union (UPU) or the Intergovernmental Organization for International Carriage by Rail (OTIF), which hardly any common citizen would have ever heard of. By contrast, the EU has been an obvious target of European populists. Similarly, mobilization against austerity measures directly impinging on peoples' lives imposed by the International Monetary Fund (IMF) was deeply connected to the strengthening of populism in Greece (Chryssogelos 2021; Vasilopoulou, Halikiopoulou, and Exadaktylos 2014). If international organizations are known to the people and their policies have implications for their lives, mobilization against them, along the lines of thin and thick ideology, will thus pay off for populists. All this will ultimately compel populists to then also live up to their domestic audience's expectations and to engage significantly less and express much harsher critiques of such organizations as compared to their non-populist predecessors.

If only either mobilization or personalization is strong while the other dimension is weak, we expect populists to be only somewhat less willing to engage in an international organization. This is the case either because the bureaucracy continues to keep at least a certain degree of engagement in the organization (low personalization), or because mobilization against an international organization does not work well, thus creating less incentives for rupture with past policies. Finally, as in previous chapters, we argue that a low degree of both personalization and mobilization will result in policies

Table 5.1 Populism and the readiness to engage in international institutions

		Personalization	
		Strong	**Weak**
Mobilization	**Strong**	*Clearly reduced readiness to engage in international institutions*	*Somewhat reduced readiness to engage in international institutions*
	Weak	*Somewhat reduced readiness to engage in international institutions*	*Continuity: no reduced readiness to engage in international institutions*

that display continuity with those of a previous non-populist government. These expectations are summarized in Table 5.1.

We focus on the 'readiness' to engage in international institutions (as we did for the readiness to contribute to global public goods) since this allows us to capture not just forms of disengagement like cuts to contributions to an international organization's budget, but also the dimension of rhetoric. In fact, we find a decreased readiness to engage also if a populist leader heavily criticizes an international institution, calling into question its legitimacy in various ways. This can be distinguished from mobilization if the criticism is largely unconnected to domestic political debates, that is, if there are no evident efforts at politicizing the issue by criticizing the policies of previous non-populist governments or by making the approach to an international institution an issue in domestic political contests (Cadier 2024). We thus operationalize a 'clearly reduced readiness to engage in international institutions' as a combination of increased criticism and the introduction of cuts to contributions to the institution. The latter can involve material contributions, such as those to the budget of the organization. Moreover, 'engagement' also entails a more ideational component, that is an active participation in the organization, for example via developing proposals for resolutions, taking new initiatives, or sending high-ranking political representatives, rather than mere bureaucrats. A reduction in these contributions, paired with criticism, helps us in identifying a clearly reduced readiness to engage. We operationalize a 'somewhat reduced readiness to engage' as either criticism or a reduction in contributions, but not a combination of both. Finally, we consider populists' approaches towards international institutions to display continuity with those of previous non-populist governments if we see neither an increase in criticism nor a reduction in material and ideational contributions.

In our empirical analysis, we focus again on changes in the policies of Bolivia, India, the Philippines, and Turkey after the formation of populist governments. Since there is a high number of international institutions these countries are members of, we need to narrow down our analysis. For all cases, we focus on their approach to the United Nations since this is the most important international organization with a global reach and a key pillar of the post–Second World War international order. Moreover, for each country case, we analyse the government's approach to one or several important regional organizations: the OAS, ALBA, Mercosur, and UNASUR for Bolivia, SAARC for India, ASEAN for the Philippines, and the EU for Turkey. Empirical data include contributions to the UN and regional organizations' budgets; contributions to UN peacekeeping missions; ideational engagement in these organizations via sponsorship of resolutions or development of other initiatives; for the UN, a qualitative content analysis of all non-populist and populist governments' representatives' speeches at the UN General Assembly in order to identify possible shifts in rhetoric at the UN;[1] and an analysis of the governments' discourse about the respective regional organizations. Finally, beyond the systematic assessment of engagement in the UN and regional organizations, we also look at the four countries' governments' approaches to multilateralism in general, trying to identify their broader preferences on multilateralism and thus inductively complementing our findings.

Finally, we also take into account context factors that might mitigate the impact of populism on the engagement in international institutions. Again, countries' varying capabilities but also the degree of authority they have ceded to international organizations co-determine populists' engagement with them. Here, analysing countries from the Global South located in regions that display a relatively low degree of integration as compared to Europe makes a significant difference: it will make much less sense for populists in these countries to mobilize against regional organizations as compared to populists in Europe. At the same time, the literature on small or weak states in international politics tells us that they tend to appreciate IOs as these may entail numerous benefits, from the reduction of transaction costs to coalition-building and other constraints on more powerful countries (Thorhallsson and Steinsson 2017). We return to these observations in the Conclusion.

---

[1] The text corpus comprised all speeches given by government representatives of the non-populist and populist governments analysed (see Table 1.1). In total, the corpus comprised 74 speeches and 171,075 words. Coding was performed manually with the help of the software MaxQDA. The unit of coding was the paragraph. The codes used for this analysis were the following: support for UN; criticism of UN structure/procedures; criticism of the role of the West in the UN; criticism of double standards within the UN; proposal of reform of the UN.

Table 5.2 Summary of findings

| | | Personalization | |
		Strong	Weak
Mobilization	Strong	*Clearly reduced readiness to engage in international institutions* Turkey-EU *Increased readiness to engage, against our expectations:* Bolivia UN and regional organizations India-G-20	*Somewhat reduced readiness to engage in international institutions*
	Weak	*Somewhat reduced readiness to engage in international institutions* Philippines-UN	*Continuity: no reduced readiness to engage in international institutions* India-UN India-SAARC Turkey-UN Philippines-ASEAN

Our Findings

In Table 5.2, we summarize the findings of our analyses of the engagement of Bolivia, India, the Philippines and Turkey in the UN, in regional organizations, and in multilateralism more generally.

Strong Personalization, Strong Mobilization

Turkey and the EU

The only case that confirmed our expectations is the shift in Turkey's approach towards the European Union after 2011. Under the populist government of Erdoğan, Turkey displayed a clearly reduced readiness to engage, driven by a combination of strong personalization and mobilization.

Turkey had long been negotiating the accession to the European Union. It was under the non-populist ANASOL-M government led by Bülent Ecevit, in December 1999, that the EU formally recognized Turkey as a candidate country for membership. In fact, pursuing EU membership had been the most important item on Turkey's foreign policy agenda under that government (Cem 1999). During those years and in line with EU membership criteria, economic reforms were a priority, and the government appointed Kemal Derviş, an economist and former head of the UN Development Programme, to the position of minister of state for economic affairs. Under his leadership, Turkey underwent painful economic reforms via an IMF recovery programme (Öniş 2003). Notably, the government deliberately presented those reforms not as something that was imposed by outsiders, as illustrated in the following quote from Derviş: 'This is Turkey's program, the program of the Turkish government, the program of Turkish bureaucracy. We have presented this to the IMF, the World Bank, and other international financial institutions. We also saw these in today's discussions. It is a program that deserves support' (Hürriyet 2001). Moreover, in order to meet EU standards, the parliament approved a range of 'harmonization' packages that gave more rights to ethnic and religious minorities and reduced the political influence of the military (Balta 2018). Ultimately, the government fell in 2002, and the AKP won the elections and subsequently reaped the fruits of the previous government's reforms.

The AKP during its first two terms (2003–2007, 2007–2011), which we consider non-populist, essentially pursued a policy of continuity with the previous government.[2] According to Alpan (2016, 16), Turkey in those years promoted a '*cosmopolitanism* narrative, which meant integrating with the rest of the world and Europe, both culturally and economically', and it also depicted Europe as a 'promised land' to its domestic audience. Meanwhile, Turkey diversified its trade relations and became more engaged in a number of regions, expanding its activities beyond the Middle East and the Balkans to regions such as Africa and Latin America (Kösebalaban 2011, 3–4). Vis-à-vis the EU, '[t]he AKP initially followed a liberal internationalist path, seeking European Union (EU) membership and adopting reforms aiming to democratize Turkey's political system in conjunction with the EU's "harmonization packages"' (Balta 2018). In a 2003 speech directed at a domestic audience, Erdoğan took care to present the necessary reforms as something his government was happy to promote, thus following a pattern similar to that of the ANASOL-M government:

> With the experience of a civilization that has built history, Turkey has come closer than ever to the goal of the European Union, which has gained great consensus over the state and society. The legal regulations we have made domestically are not

---

[2] Interview T15, Turkish academic, Istanbul, 5 May 2023.

> because the European Union forced us, but to ensure that our citizens can exercise their rights at the highest level. Our goal is far beyond meeting the Copenhagen political criteria. It is clear that our nation deserves the most advanced democratic rights, and democratic rights cannot be withheld from any of our citizens. I have personally witnessed the enthusiastic reception of Turkey's determined march in this direction in all European centres I visited. (Erdoğan 2019a, 203–4)

At that time, EU membership seemed within reach for Turkey, and formal accession negotiations started in October 2005 (Öniş 2010). Erdoğan himself in the early 2000s was an enthusiastic supporter of EU membership, as is visible in this quote from 2005: 'Membership in the European Union is a natural extension of Turkey's historical journey. EU membership is a manifestation of Turkey's claim to be a democratic, free, just, and prosperous society. EU membership is a necessity for Turkey's interests' (Erdoğan 2019f, 307). Yet the pace of reforms in Turkey slowed down from 2005 onwards, thus putting an end to the 'golden age' of Europeanization (Öniş 2010). Towards the end of the second AKP term, we see a growing disillusionment on the part of Erdoğan vis-à-vis the EU, paired with first instances of blaming the EU:

> Full membership in the European Union is Turkey's strategic goal and a state policy. [. . .] It is true that the initial enthusiasm for EU membership has sometimes waned in our society. However, I must emphasize that this occasional loss of enthusiasm in society is not due to a decrease in the government's determination but rather stems from the attitudes of the European Union towards Turkey. (Erdoğan 2019c, 114)

After the electoral victory for the AKP in 2011, which left Erdoğan virtually without a parliamentary opposition (Ülgül 2024) and marked the beginning of the populist era, his government dramatically reduced its readiness to engage with the EU. This manifested in ever harsher criticism of the EU as well as in a decreased engagement in accession negotiations on the part of Turkey.[3] A look at the AKP election manifesto of 2011 already reveals the extent of change: Whereas accession to the European Union had been Turkey's main foreign policy objective for years, now the EU was mentioned only twice on 160 pages (Alpan 2016, 21). In his much-cited victory speech of 2011, moreover, Erdoğan clearly articulated Turkey's ambition to be seen as a leader of the Muslim world and thus spelled out the country's new foreign policy priorities, in line with the AKP's thick ideology but also

---

[3] As Turkey was not an EU member yet, we cannot assess changes in material contributions to the organization.

with an understanding of the 'people' reaching beyond Turkey's national borders:

In all friendly and brotherly nations from Baghdad, Damascus, Beirut, Cairo, Sarajevo, Baku and Nicosia . . . [t]he hopes of the victims and the oppressed have won . . . Beirut has won as much as İzmir. The West Bank, Gaza, Ramallah, Jerusalem have won as much as Diyarbakır. The Middle East, the Caucasus and the Balkans have won, just as Turkey has won. (quoted in Alpan 2016, 21)

Erdoğan contributed to the deterioration of relations with the EU by deliberately challenging European standards on democracy and human rights. This was a highly personalized policy, reflecting both the more general personalization of decision making during the populist phase and his autocratic tendencies. According to a former Turkish diplomat we spoke with, 2011 also marked the beginning of the extensive use of foreign policy as a mobilizing device domestically,[4] including around EU issues.

The Gezi protests from May to August 2013 greatly reinforced anti-EU mobilization on the part of Erdoğan, and the turn away from Europe.[5] To Erdoğan, the protests were a direct threat to his personal political survival, especially since in Egypt, exactly at the same time, Mohamed Morsi was deposed following the June 2013 protests and the subsequent coup on 3 July. Thus, according to Taş, 'Since Gezi, Erdoğan has directed his anti-elite discourse against the "Western imperialists", "interest lobbies", and "Crusaders"—all combined under the umbrella term *üst akıl* (mastermind), which is determined to hinder Turkey's unbridled rise' (Taş 2020, 567). The European Union was subsumed under this discourse. In the following years, in Turkish pro-government media, political and diplomatic tensions with the EU were increasingly framed as driven by Europeans' fear of the rise of a 'New Turkey' and their apprehension towards a strong leader like Erdoğan. For instance, a pro-government newspaper proclaimed: 'Europe is afraid of Erdoğan' (Yeni Akit 2016; 2022). In parallel to these developments, and despite agreeing to a migration deal with the EU in 2016 (see Chapter 3), Erdoğan dramatically changed his own rhetoric in referring to the EU. Among other things, he accused the EU of being Islamophobic (Presidency of the Republic of Türkiye 2016), of pursuing double standards in its policies on new members (Presidency of the Republic of Türkiye 2017a), and of discriminating against Turkey (Presidency of the Republic of Türkiye 2018).

---

[4] Interview T04, retired Turkish diplomat, Istanbul, 23 March 2023.
[5] Interview T04.

We observed an especially harsh tone in Turkey's language on the EU in 2017, as Erdoğan was campaigning for the constitutional referendum of 16 April that would transform Turkey into a presidential system. In that context, he resorted to mobilization against the EU, capitalizing on the high salience of a potential EU membership for Turkish voters. He often linked his heavy criticism of the EU to domestic conflicts by arguing that the EU was allowing its members to harbour organizations classified as terrorist by Turkey such as the PKK and FETO, the Gülenist movement (Presidency of the Republic of Türkiye 2017a), while countries like Germany were not allowing the AKP to campaign among the Turkish diaspora: 'These terrorists are roaming freely across Europe, aren't they? Pay attention, the doors are open to them. But the doors are closed to yea-sayers. Their ministers and deputies are freely conducting propaganda in favor of "no". We will talk to you after April 16' (Presidency of the Republic of Türkiye 2017c). Moreover, Erdoğan repeatedly referred to a supposed conflict between Islam and Christianity, thus leveraging elements of his thick ideology to mobilize against the EU. Here, the main claim was that Turkey had been denied accession to the EU primarily because an organization of predominantly Christian countries would not tolerate a Muslim-majority state as a member. Also on the campaign trail, after EU leaders visited the Vatican, Erdoğan stated:

> What are you doing in the Vatican? Is the Vatican an EU member? No. There are Protestant, Orthodox, atheist, Catholic ones among them and they all went to the Vatican. Why? They all lined up and took advice. The Pope gave them advice and then they left submissively. Because they are one nation. No one should tell us excuses. They have stalled this country for 54 years. You should know that the 16th of April will be a turning point for that. They say 'Erdoğan is very harsh'. We know to whom to be harsh or soft, but we never succumb. They are disturbed because we tell the truth. (Presidency of the Republic of Türkiye 2017b)

The constitutional referendum on the introduction of presidentialism further strained Turkey's relations with the West and especially the continuation of EU accession talks, which had already been stalled since 2016.[6] After the referendum, which was widely criticized in the Western media as an instance of democratic backsliding, Erdoğan stated:

> We cannot allow certain organizations, the EU first and foremost, and states to question our democracy over the results of the April 16 referendum. The Turkish

---

[6] Interviews T04; T06, Ambassador (retired) Fatih Ceylan, former Permanent Representative to NATO, Istanbul, 28 March 2023; T11, senior Turkish journalist, Istanbul, 13 April 2023.

nation made a choice based on its own will and all must respect this choice. (Presidency of the Republic of Türkiye 2017d)

In February 2019, an EU parliamentary committee voted for the suspension of accession talks, which sparked renewed criticism from Erdoğan. Interestingly, however, he did not completely turn his back to the EU but emphasized that the EU needed Turkey:

> Without Turkey, it is impossible for the EU to successfully deal with such existential threats as Islamophobia, cultural racism, discrimination and anti-immigrant stance, which dynamite the European Union's founding values [. . .]. The European Union's claim to be living up to its founding values is doomed to remain unfulfilled without Turkey's full membership. (Presidency of the Republic of Türkiye 2019)

Yet, with the transformation of Turkey into a presidential system complete, and a subsequently growing personalization of foreign affairs under Erdoğan, over time the tone became harsher again. For instance, following foreign criticism of the conversion of the Hagia Sophia in Istanbul into a mosque, Erdoğan stated: 'We are Muslims and they are enemies of Islam' (SCF 2019). Erdoğan moreover used criticism of Israel's war against Hamas in response to the terrorist attack of 7 October 2023 for domestic mobilization against the West, accusing the EU of complicity:

> As we condemn the Israeli administration, we don't forget those who overtly support or who make all sorts of excuses to legitimize these massacres, either [. . .]. The blood of the kids killed in Gaza sticks as a stain of shame to the foreheads of those who provide weaponry, ammunition and intelligence support to the Israeli administration. Can you imagine it? Hundreds of children die under the bombs on a daily basis; yet, none of those from the European Union or the US, who always talk about human rights and freedoms, can come forward and utter one single word. (Presidency of the Republic of Türkiye 2023c)

Overall, therefore, during the populist phase starting in 2011, Turkey's approach towards the EU became increasingly confrontational, thus revealing a clearly reduced readiness to engage with the organization. However, full membership had become less realistic also due to growing political opposition to it in key EU member states (Scazzieri 2024), a development Turkey was clearly aware of. In any case, while Ankara did not turn its back to the EU completely, the aggressive tone adopted by Erdoğan is remarkable. Mobilization was particularly evident ahead of the constitutional referendum in 2017 but it also remained an important component across the years after 2011. Moreover, the antagonistic approach towards the EU was driven by high personalization, as Erdoğan centralized decision making within Turkey's new presidential system and further marginalized traditional foreign policy elites.

Bolivia and Latin American Regionalism

Other than in the case of Turkey's approach to the EU, there were also instances in which a combination of high personalization and high mobilization led to the opposite result than the one we had expected, namely to an *increased* readiness to engage. Bolivia's active participation in institution-building in Latin America stands out. To be sure, Bolivia has always been a proponent of multilateralism regionally and, typically for a small state, globally (Bertelsmann Stiftung 2006). Thus, Bolivia was a founding member of the Organization of American States (OAS) in 1948 and the Andean Pact in 1969 (renamed into Andean Community, CAN, in 1996), comprising neighbouring Chile, Colombia, Ecuador, and Peru. Morales's immediate predecessor as president, Carlos Mesa, at the Third South American Summit in 2004 signed the Cusco Declaration promising the establishment of a new South American regional organization, UNASUR. Spearheaded by Hugo Chávez and supported by leftist leaders from Brazilian president Lula to Néstor Kirchner in Argentina, this was supposed to become a strong regional organization bypassing US influence in the Washington-based OAS. With plans for an international parliament, a central bank, a unified passport, a single currency, and cooperation in matters of security and defence, UNASUR arguably was the most ambitious regional integration project in Latin American history (Briceño-Ruiz and Ribeiro Hoffmann 2015), and Bolivia prior to the Morales presidency supported it.

Morales from his first year in office onwards intensified his predecessor's support for UNASUR, convening the second meeting of UNASUR presidents in Cochabamba in December 2006 and offering to host a planned South American Parliament in the same city. Under him, Bolivia was the first country to ratify UNASUR's Constitutive Treaty in March 2009. A year earlier, UNASUR then led by Chilean president Bachelet on an interim basis, had played a key role in resolving a political and constitutional crisis following demands for autonomy by a series of Bolivian regions that threatened the country's territorial integrity as well as the central government (Wehner 2020, 261).

Moreover, once in power, Morales co-founded or entered a series of new and old regional organizations, thus greatly contributing to the intensification of multilateralism regionally. In 2006, Bolivia joined the Bolivarian Alliance for the Peoples of Our America (ALBA) and concluded several trilateral assistance treaties ('Peoples' Trade Treaty', ALBA-TCP in short) with Venezuela and Cuba thus benefitting from Venezuela's oil riches in the form of scholarships, Cuban doctors paid by Caracas, and local development programmes targeting areas where support for the MAS was strongest (Bertelsmann Stiftung 2010, 38). One indication of the importance that the Morales government attributed to ALBA and its major members is that he destined important political cadres to diplomatic missions there. For instance, the former foreign minister and later vice president David Choquehuanca was appointed ALBA's secretary general between 2017 and 2019. Morales together with leaders from Uruguay and Paraguay in 2006 also reactivated URUPABOL, a trilateral integration accord founded in 1963 that had been dormant for the most time since then (Souza, Cunha Filho, and Santos 2020, 9; Muhr 2011, 111). In addition to this, Bolivia in 2010 was a founding member of the Community of Latin American and Caribbean States (CELAC), a regional forum bringing together Latin American and Caribbean countries (Souza, Cunha Filho, and Santos 2020, 9). CELAC, according to a senior Bolivian diplomat, was 'a political space that generated important inter-regional relations through high-level meetings with the European Union, China, Turkey and Russia, among others'.[7] Moreover, Morales sought membership to Mercosur, a South American trade bloc, whose presidents at their 2015 summit invited Bolivia to join. Interestingly, given the economic context at that time, membership in Mercosur was important more for political than for commercial reasons, a Bolivian expert told us: 'with Evo, we insisted on being part of Mercosur as a full member because that's where our friends were, not because that's where the trade was'.[8] Bolivia also continued to be an active member of the Andean Community, albeit rejecting proposals for trade agreements with the US and the EU (Bertelsmann Stiftung 2010). A commonality of all these initiatives was their exclusively Latin American character, thus deliberately excluding the US.

Nonetheless, an account of Bolivia's regional institution-building under Morales must also mention the difficulties in maintaining the initial political and diplomatic impetus and in establishing regional schemes capable of outlasting changes in the presidencies of key Latin American states (Nolte 2021). A prime example is UNASUR, which in the words of a senior Bolivian diplomat we interviewed in 2023 by then was 'practically extinct'.[9] Neither was

---

[7] Interview B19, acting senior diplomat, La Paz, 20 February 2023.
[8] Interview B23, academic and former senior diplomat, La Paz, 6 March 2023.
[9] Interview B16, acting senior diplomat, La Paz, 9 February 2023.

the planned South American parliament built in Bolivia nor did UNASUR hold any summit between 2014 and 2023. Likewise, CAN due to internal divisions in its Presidential Council did not convene a single time between 2011 and 2019 (Garcés 2020, 75). CELAC paralyzed to the extent that it failed to hold presidential summits from 2018 to 2020. Concrete infrastructural developments, such as a gas pipeline through URUPABOL, never went beyond the planning stage (CAF 2010) and ALBA remained dependent on leadership support from Chávez in Venezuela and Castro in Cuba, both of whom were succeeded (in 2013 and 2011, respectively) by leaders with less enthusiasm for it. In any case, leftist leaders' insistence on national sovereignty and, thus, intergovernmentalism—a hallmark of regionalism in Latin America anyways—put limits to the prospects for deeper regional integration once key leaders had left.

Having said that, Morales pursued an active regional diplomacy with the personal involvement necessary to reach agreements in Latin American regionalism. As a senior diplomat serving under him reiterated, in regional affairs Bolivia 'played a really important role with innovative proposals, in contrast to previous administrations where no concrete proposals were presented'.[10] Morales did so in line with his thick ideology. Thus, his views on domestic and international politics led to a shift of the Bolivian foreign agenda: away from 'neoliberal capitalism' and the liberalization of trade, away from the US, and towards another type of regionalism with countries like Venezuela and Cuba (Quitral Rojas 2014, 181). Consequently, Bolivia opposed plans for a Free Trade Area of the Americas (FTAA or ALCA by its Spanish acronym), a decade-long initiative led by the US, at the same time that it 'played a fundamental role in the construction of UNASUR'[11] and enthusiastically joined ALBA-TCP. Both personalization and mobilization contributed to this. On the former, our interviews with senior Bolivian diplomats as well as other experts underline the importance of personal relations in regional affairs in the 2000s and 2010s. According to one interviewee from within Morales's government, the president's advisors 'were the governments and heads of state of Cuba, Venezuela, Argentina, Brazil, Ecuador, in the regional space'.[12] Likewise, a Bolivian journalist and academic stated that Bolivia 'totally' adhered 'to the postulates of the Chávez and Maduro governments in Venezuela and the other allies, especially the Cuban government, and Bolivia was totally aligned with these proposals'.[13] As a result of Bolivia's

---

[10] Interview B19.

[11] Interview B09, senior career diplomat, Zoom, 27 January 2023.

[12] Interview B04, senior career diplomat under Veltzé and Morales, La Paz, 16 January 2023.

[13] Interview B24, journalist and former senior diplomat, Zoom, 8 March 2023.

own limited foreign policy capabilities and of such personal and ideological alignments, 'Morales adopted the role of a faithful ally and follower of Venezuela' (Wehner 2020, 261). Ideological alignment with Bolivia's neighbours and the regional schemes supported by them greatly facilitated the mobilization of public support with reference to ALBA, UNASUR, and other initiatives. As a senior acting Bolivian diplomat told us, 'ALBA [was] the last refuge and resource of its founders to express mutual solidarity'[14] and Morales used its summits, public outreach, and policies for this. For example, Bolivia's foreign ministry reported about an ALBA meeting in 2018 in the following way:

> The President of the State, Evo Morales Ayma, during his speech referred to the imperialist voracity to override the sovereignty of the Latin American peoples and organizations. 'There are other kinds of coups, judicial coup or congressional coup; these are other instruments of the empire so that the ALBA countries or progressive countries do not continue to grow in Latin America', Morales warned. (Ministerio de Relaciones Exteriores del Estado Plurinacional de Bolivia 2018)

Very frequently, in his public pronouncements Morales also decried US attempts to undermine Bolivia's sovereignty through the OAS (San Diego Union-Tribune 2016; Serna Duque 2018)—in contrast to ALBA and other regional schemes' quality as defenders of Bolivia's sovereignty. However, ideological commitment and personal relations did not entirely override pragmatism in Bolivia's regional relations. In fact, the international context and Bolivia's character as a small state mattered greatly under Morales (Wehner 2020). This meant, for instance, that Morales—unlike Chávez—did not leave CAN, which continued to be valuable economically, despite some of its members' differences in ideological terms. Likewise, despite Venezuela's suspension from Mercosur in 2016 over human rights and trade rules, Bolivia did not end its quest for membership. Neither did Morales leave the OAS.

Bolivia and the UN

Under the populist government of Morales, several, at times contradictory, shifts took place in Bolivia's approach to the United Nations. Yet, overall, the populist government of Morales displayed a greater readiness to engage in the UN as compared to previous non-populist governments.

---

[14] Interview B16.

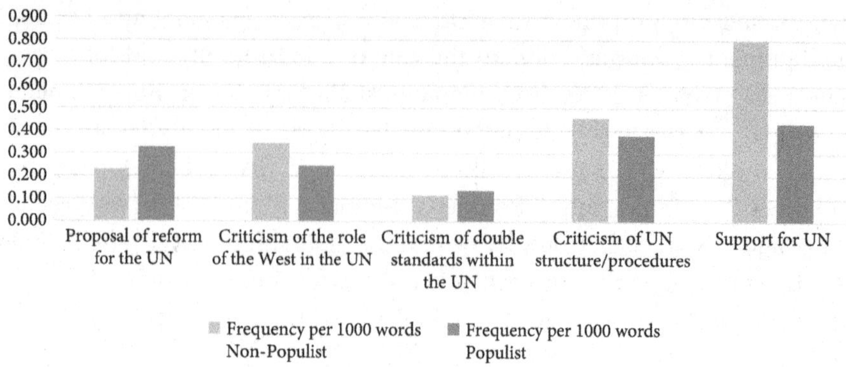

Figure 5.1 Results of qualitative content analysis of UNGA speeches (2002–2006; 2006–2019), Bolivia
Source: own composition.

Bolivia had always been a supporter of the United Nations. However, Morales's non-populist predecessors had also been quite critical of UN structures and procedures as well as of the role of the West in the UN, as revealed by our qualitative content analysis of non-populist and populist government representatives' speeches at the UNGA (see Figure 5.1). After Morales came to power, eager to shine internationally as the country's first Indigenous president, he sought to amplify Bolivia's voice within the UN through his appearances in the UNGA, Bolivia's membership of the UNSC in 2017/18, and through participating in numerous subgroups such as the Landlocked Developing Countries group and the G-77 + China. In his rhetoric at the UNGA, Morales frequently spoke about his country's commitment to the UN, juxtaposing it to the United States' alleged 'contempt' for multilateralism (United Nations Security Council 2018). In 2019, for example, he stated:

> our generation's responsibility is to pass on to the next generation a fairer and more humane world. That will be achieved only if we work together to build a multipolar world with rules common to all, while defending multilateralism, the purposes and principles of the Charter of the United Nations and international law. (United Nations General Assembly 2019, 37)

Whereas the frequency of statements in *support* of the UN was much smaller under Morales than among his predecessors, the share of statements critical of UN structures and procedures (and surprisingly also the share of statements criticizing the role of the West in the UN) declined (see 1).

Most criticism of practices in the UN system came in the form of Morales's trademark anti-imperialist and anti-capitalist rhetoric. For instance, in 2011 he stated:

> When Israel bombs, attacks, kills and takes Palestinian land, there is no Security Council for that [. . .]. When there was a coup d'état in Honduras, where [. . .] was the Security Council or the Inter-American Commission on Human Rights to defend democracy in Honduras? It is time for us to think deeply about this. When there are anti-imperialist Presidents with anti-capitalist Governments, the empire tries to create internal conflicts with what appear to be major confrontations, making it appear in the media that a certain President should fall, or it tries to divide a country to justify intervention. When there was a coup d'état in Honduras and there were killings in Palestine, where was NATO? Where was the Security Council? They were nowhere to be found. (United Nations General Assembly 2011, 11–12)

While decrying the UNSC's inaction, Morales also often critiqued UN-backed interventions and the supposedly 'neo-imperial' interests behind it (see Chapter 4). For instance, he vocally opposed the UNSC-backed NATO intervention in Libya in 2011, portraying the UNSC as an 'organization of invading nations' (MercoPress 2011). Morales thus used the UNGA as a stage to address both domestic and international audiences.

Bolivia's voluntary financial contributions to the UN had seen a peak in 2006, Morales's first year in office, but they sharply declined immediately after that, soon reaching levels comparable to those of the times before Morales (UNGA 2010). However, we observed a major difference in the manifold initiatives that Morales took at the UN, which led us to classify the case of Bolivia as one of *increased* readiness to engage, despite Morales's sometimes critical rhetoric. Several of such initiatives were rather successful and they came along with a high potential for domestic mobilization. The UNGA's recognition of the human right to water in 2010, its declaration of 22 April as 'International Mother Earth Day' in 2009, as well as 2013 as the 'International Year of Quinoa' (Food and Agriculture Organization of the United Nations 2024) were all highlighted to us as significant manifestations of Bolivia's engagement in the UN by a former senior government official, and as a novelty compared to previous Bolivian governments' involvement in the UN.[15] An even more important indicator of Morales's engagement with the UN system was his government's referral of Bolivia's dispute over access to the sea with Chile to the UN-backed International Court of Justice in The Hague

---

[15] Interview B17, senior political appointee under Morales, La Paz, 13 February 2023.

(see Chapter 3), a step not much in line with our expectations about populists and multilateralism outlined above. Within the UN, another focus of the Morales government was the group of landlocked countries. Although not a novelty in itself—Bolivia in 1965 participated in the Conference on Transit Trade of Landlocked Countries, sponsored by the UN Conference on Trade and Development (UNCTAD)—Bolivia under Morales increased its engagements, for instance via hosting the High-Level Meeting on Sustainable Transportation for Landlocked Developing Countries in Santa Cruz (Bolivia) in October 2016 (Corz 2016). Similarly, Morales assumed the pro tempore presidency of the G-77 + China in 2014 and convoked a summit in Santa Cruz (Brazil), to commemorate fifty years of the founding of that group. Clearly, this large grouping of developing countries suited both Morales's global activism and his domestic agenda. In a show of his activist diplomacy, the Bolivian government used the occasion to distribute 'The Book of the Sea' (americaeconomia.com 2015) among the representatives of foreign governments, a collection of the main arguments in favour of its maritime demand vis-à-vis Chile. The summit's 'Declaration of Santa Cruz' included numerous other topics close to the Morales government's agenda, from sovereignty to natural resources, industrialization and infrastructure development, Indigenous peoples' rights, and South-South cooperation (Cumbre de Jefas y Jefes de Estado y de Gobierno del Grupo de los 77 2014).

The most remarkable and visible initiative, however, was Morales's elevation of his coca policy, and thus of one of his most important domestic agenda items, to the UN level (Barbier 2015; CND Blog 2013). From Morales's first election onwards, his government sustained an intense diplomatic campaign for the legalization of coca leaf cropping and traditional consumption while also respecting international agreements over fighting narcotrafficking. To do so, Bolivia first tried to change the UN 1961 Single Convention on Narcotic Drugs provisions on coca leaf by consensus. When it became clear that this would not be successful, Morales abandoned the Single Convention in December 2011 (a practice known as denunciation) to immediately re-enter with a reservation on coca leaf, a common practice allowed by international law (Room 2012). Bolivia's re-accession to the Single Convention after a waiting time of one year was possible for as long as fewer than one third of the signatory members objected to its reservation. As it turned out, only fifteen countries, including the US, did so, far from the sixty-two required for blockage (Kim 2014, 572–73), thus turning Bolivia's manoeuvre into a major diplomatic success. Illustrating the interconnection between the MAS's domestic agenda and its international engagement, a key argument for the Bolivian reservation was that the prohibition of coca leaf consumption conflicted with its 2009 Constitution and the 2007 UN Declaration on the Rights of Indigenous Peoples, both of which recognized cultural rights to follow traditional customs and the use of traditional medicines and health practices (Kim 2014, 567–68).

In sum, despite at times criticizing the UN and not increasing his country's material contributions to it, Morales chose to engage more actively in this organization as compared to his predecessors, making the UN a key vehicle for his international engagement. As an acting senior diplomat told us, 'the main foreign policy changes under the Morales government were the visualization of our country on the international scene, having our own proposals with sovereign action and active participation.'[16] A former diplomat under Morales concurred that Bolivia's diplomats in multilateral fora fought hard to establish the 'figure of Evo' so that Bolivia did not have to merely follow the currents of international politics.[17] Moreover, its main theatres were, in fact, the United Nations and, as described above, regional integration mechanisms.[18] In both areas, Morales's personality—his relationships with foreign leaders as well as his desire for international visibility—and the mobilization of public support—through the adoption of indigenous themes internationally[19]—reinforced Bolivia's engagement with multilateral institutions. Thus, contrary to our expectation, in the case of Bolivia strong mobilization and strong personalization on the part of the populist leader resulted in a remarkable increase in engagement in international institutions.

India and the G-20

The case of India's approach to the G-20 is another exemplary case of increased multilateral engagement, albeit in a less institutionalized forum, driven by strong mobilization and personalization. On 1 December 2022, India took over the one-year rotating presidency of the G-20 for the first time. This otherwise routine affair concerning a summit that by then had lost much of its previous glory (Chu et al. 2024) was used by populist prime minister Modi for domestic political mobilization to an extent previously unseen. In the lead-up to the 2024 general elections, Modi and his BJP devised a campaign that focused, on the one hand, on Modi's personal 'guarantees' to India's citizens, emphasizing the government's achievements; on the other

---

¹⁶ Interview B19.
¹⁷ Interview B15, former senior diplomat, La Paz, 6 February 2023.
¹⁸ Interview B19.
¹⁹ Interview B06, senior career diplomat, La Paz, 18 January 2023.

hand, the campaign sought to instill a sense of pride into the population, conveying the message that Prime Minister Modi finally realized India's long-standing foreign policy goal of great power status. It is against this backdrop that the Indian government asked the Italian government, which should have taken over the rotating presidency at the end of 2022, to switch places—thus allowing the BJP to resort to this issue for campaigning throughout the year preceding national elections in May 2024.[20] The logo of India's G-20 presidency—a globe embedded in a lotus flower—entailed a clear allusion to the logo of the BJP, a saffron lotus flower. The presidency's motto *Vasudhaiva Kutumbakam* ('One earth—one family—one future') was taken from a Sanskrit text, much in Modi's tradition of embedding his political projects in the language of ancient scriptures. Indeed, mobilization around the G-20 presidency was massive. During field research in India in February–March 2023, we observed the G-20 logo everywhere: on huge billboards at petrol stations and bus stops in Delhi, on stickers on all railway carriages of passenger trains in Haryana, on packages of tea sold at a governmental handicraft emporium, on rikshaws in Old Delhi's Chandni Chowk, as sculpture-fountains at the centre of roundabouts in the city of Agra in Uttar Pradesh, or as murals on public toilets in the upper-middle-class Delhi neighbourhood of Greater Kailash. Anecdotal evidence from conversations with ordinary Indians reflects that the message of this massive advertising of the G-20 presidency was the following: the world's twenty most important leaders would come to India for the summit in September 2023 and pay respect to Prime Minister Modi, who had finally turned India into a great power. Ultimately, this mobilization amounted to almost physically 'bringing foreign policy to the people', thus vastly increasing the public salience of an otherwise mundane foreign policy event. Our interviewees confirmed this assessment: 'G-20 has been sold as something special happening'.[21] All this was underscored by the fact that numerous G-20-related events were deliberately scheduled to take place in a total of sixty cities all over the country (g20.in 2023), in order to involve the largest possible number of citizens in experiencing India's great-power status first-hand. In this sense, the Modi government was trying to make the G-20 'a mass movement',[22] or, as an Indian journalist put it in an interview with us, a '*mela*', that is, a big festival.[23] All this was explicitly framed in people-centric populist terms, with mobilization and politicization thus being mainly

---

[20] Interviews I02, Indian journalist, New Delhi, 21 February 2023.
[21] Interview I03, Indian journalist.
[22] Interviews I08, retired Indian diplomat, New Delhi, 1 March 2023; I15, retired Indian diplomat at think tank, New Delhi, 6 March 2023.
[23] Interview I16, Indian journalist, New Delhi, 7 March 2023.

driven by the people-centric dimension of populism (Destradi, Plagemann, and Taş 2022). As the G-20 website reports, '[m]any [. . .] activities were also simultaneously held with active public participation in a whole-of-nation and whole-of-society approach, making India's G20 Presidency a "People's G20"' (g20.in 2023). Also, personalization around the G-20 presidency was high, with the figure of the prime minister playing a central role in the above-mentioned advertising campaign, thus conveying the message to the public that 'it's because of the Prime Minister that we got the G-20'.[24] As another interviewee put it, the 'G-20 is entirely a PMO-driven thing. The Sherpa is not a person from the MEA: Amitabh Kant. He is very close to the PM. He has a background in tourism, the planning commission, but he has never been a foreign policy person. The government sought someone who would carry the PM's narrative. Every point on the G-20 agenda refers to something that the PM said before'.[25]

In the case of India's approach to the G-20, we thus saw a combination of strong mobilization and personalization, but this did not lead to a reduced readiness to engage in this specific international institution (similar to India's approaches to climate change mitigation, and Turkey's approach to development aid and peace discussed in Chapter 4). At the same time, we should not over-emphasize the importance of the G-20 Delhi summit. In the run-up to the event, it was unclear whether G-20 members would adopt a final declaration given their differences over the Russian war on Ukraine. In the end, the declaration's preamble mentioned 'human suffering and negative added impacts of the war in Ukraine with regard to global food and energy security, supply chains, macro-financial stability, inflation and growth' (G20 India 2023, 2)—an outcome that was hailed by some as an achievement of India's negotiating team navigating contradicting demands from Western governments, countries in the Global South, and its traditional Russian partner (P. Jha 2023). Moreover, India used the G-20 to show its leadership ambitions in the Global South by formalizing the invitation of the African Union (AU) to become a permanent member of the G-20, a process that had been started prior to India's presidency, however. In any case, strong mobilization and personalization did not lead to the anticipated decrease in readiness to engage in a multilateral institution, but rather to the opposite effect. Nonetheless, India's much-publicized presidency did not differ much from other summits in terms of concrete outcomes and it was also diminished by the notable absence of both Vladimir Putin and Xi Jinping.

---

[24] Interview I08.
[25] Interview I02.

Strong Personalization, Weak Mobilization

The Philippines and the UN

In the case of the Philippines' approach to the UN, the transition to a populist government led to a somewhat decreased readiness to engage, which was driven by a combination of strong personalization and weak mobilization.

Under the previous Aquino presidency, the Philippines had been engaged in the UN, emphasizing especially developmental aspects (United Nations General Assembly 2010). In 2011, the Philippines ratified the Rome Statute, thus joining the International Criminal Court (ICC). This was much in line with the country's historical approach to multilateralism. As one expert we interviewed put it, 'the Philippines has always seen the UN, international organizations, international law as one important pillar of [its] foreign policy; after all, we are a founding member [of the UN]'.[26]

After Duterte was elected, a number of highly visible incidents in response to the UN's condemnation of his brutal war on drugs took place. Already during his election campaign, and later shortly after taking office, Duterte had publicly called for law enforcement agencies and even private persons to kill suspected drug dealers as well as drug users (Agence France-Presse 2016a). After over 850 people were killed in Duterte's first three months in office in 2016, Special Procedures experts from the UN Human Rights Council strongly condemned Duterte's policies. The UN Special Rapporteur on summary executions called on the authorities of the Philippines 'to adopt with immediate effect the necessary measures to protect all persons from targeted killings and extrajudicial executions' (OHCHR 2016). Further, together with the UN Special Rapporteur on the right to health, she called for investigations into all reports of killings and extrajudicial executions (OHCHR 2016). Already two months earlier, in June 2016, UN Secretary General Ban Ki-moon had condemned Duterte's 'apparent endorsement of extrajudicial killings' (Agence France-Presse 2016b). Duterte reacted sharply to these statements, in what was one of the most extreme displays of his populist-style 'bad manners' (Moffitt and Tormey 2014): He stated, 'You're a son of a bitch, UN. You can't even solve the killings there in the Middle East. [...] They're killing people. You cannot even lift a finger in Africa. They're butchering the black people there' (Esmaquel II 2016a). And in August, after the criticism by the Special Procedures experts, he stated:

---

[26] Interview P35, Filipino academic, Manila, 28 November 2024.

I do not want to insult you. But maybe we'll just have to decide to separate from the United Nations. [. . .] So take us out of your organisation. You have done nothing. Where were you here the last time? Never. Except to criticise [. . .]. You now, United Nations, if you can say one bad thing about me, I can give 10 [about you]. I tell you, you are [useless]. Because if you are really true to your mandate, you could have stopped all these wars and killings. (BBC News 2016)

A few months later, after UN High Commissioner for Human Rights Zeid Ra'ad Al Hussein called for an investigation into Duterte's admission that he had killed three persons when he was the mayor of Davao City, Duterte reacted similarly. At a gathering of around 9,000 women volunteers for a local drug watch programme, he stated:

The problem with the United Nations, you guys, you are employed by an organization composed of nations whose officials are elected by the people. You officials sitting there on your asses, we pay you your salaries. You idiot. You do not tell me what to do. I am your employer. Who gave you the right? You lack knowledge of international law. We are the ones who contribute to the United Nations. You shameless sons of a whore. I pay your salaries. (Malig 2016)

In 2019, the Philippine government declared its refusal of financial assistance from the eighteen countries that voted to approve a UNHRC resolution calling for an investigation of summary killings linked to Duterte's drug war (Ranada 2019). As the UN-backed International Criminal Court started investigating Duterte's war on drugs (Amnesty International Philippines 2024), as remembered by a senior Philippine representative to the UN, Duterte's initial reactions to the investigation were 'confusing; waxing hot and cold; belligerent and pitiful'.[27] Ultimately, reacting to the investigations, in March 2018 Duterte declared the Philippines' withdrawal from the ICC's founding treaty, given its 'baseless, unprecedented and outrageous attacks', which he claimed were 'in violation of due process and the presumption of innocence expressly guaranteed by the Philippine Constitution' (Guzman 2023). Formally, the Philippines' membership of the court ended a year later.

Despite criticizing the UN and leaving the ICC, and despite also having threatened to leave the UN, the Duterte government ultimately did not do so. Meanwhile, the Philippines' financial contributions to the United Nations—most notably the voluntary non-core (earmarked) contributions, which can be changed more easily by governments as compared to the

---

[27] Interview P01, former high-ranking government official, Manila, 26 September 2022.

assessed contributions—declined dramatically after Duterte came to power. However, this shift ultimately implied a return to pre-Duterte levels and thus was not a dramatic break with past commitments (see Figure 5.2).

When it comes to Duterte's rhetoric, in his speeches at the UNGA, the president of the Philippines was critical of the United Nations (as opposed to his predecessor, who did not criticize the UN in his UNGA addresses). Mostly, such criticism referred to UN structures and procedures. Yet, it was articulated in a more moderate tone as compared to the above-mentioned statements. In 2021, for example, Duterte pointed out that the United Nations was 'inadequate' and anachronistic:

> The UN is a product of an era long past. It no longer reflects the political and economic realities of today. Democracy and transparency are concepts that reverberate in the halls of the UN. But ironically, the Security Council—the pinnacle of the UN structure—violates every tenet of these values. It is neither democratic nor transparent in its representation and processes. (Duterte 2021)

However, in the same speech, Duterte also emphasized the Philippines' commitment to 'inclusive' multilateralism (UN News 2021), and more generally, in our content analysis we found that his share of statements in support of the UN was not much smaller than that of the preceding non-populist presidency. The experts we interviewed confirmed that Duterte's criticism of the UN was primarily driven by the perception that he was being personally attacked due to his war on drugs: 'His distaste for multilateralism is more personal, [it is] about the ICC [. . .]. His distaste regards human

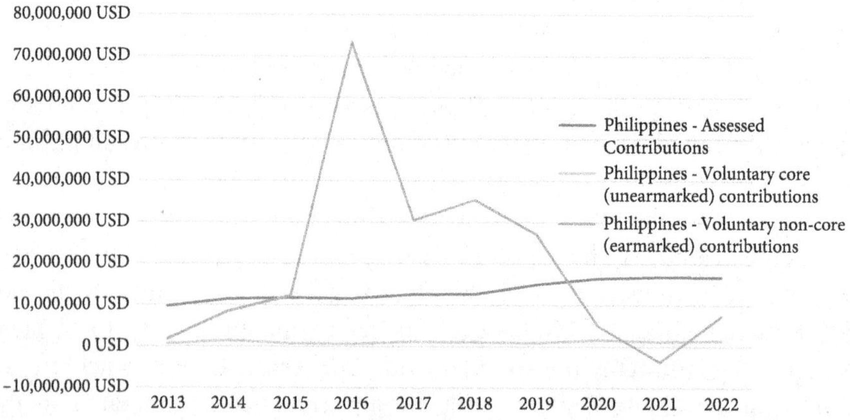

Figure 5.2 The Philippines' contributions to the UN budget

Source: own composition based on https://unsceb.org/fs-revenue-government-donor (last accessed 30 June 2024).

rights but not multilateralism in general'.[28] A former government official who had served in the Duterte administration confirmed that 'he was ambivalent on the UN'.[29] Ultimately, Duterte's emotional busts were short-lived. For example on 23 August 2016, shortly after Duterte had threatened to leave the UN, his foreign secretary Perfecto Yasay Jr. issued an assurance stating that the president remained committed to the United Nations, its objectives, and purposes (Official Gazette 2016).

Against this backdrop, we consider the shift in the Philippines' approach to the UN to amount to a somewhat reduced readiness to engage as compared to the Aquino administration. This was driven primarily by personalization and Duterte's sensitivity to criticism of his trademark war on drugs. As a senior foreign affairs journalist recounted in an interview with us, Duterte 'would blow up on any criticism coming from the US and the UN'.[30] At the same time, Duterte did not mobilize against the UN by connecting it to his domestic enemies. This most likely was due to Filipinos' generally positive views of the UN as an institution (Dellmuth et al. 2022). Indeed, support for the UN at the end of Duterte's presidency in 2022 was as high as it had been in the early 2000s, with no significant shifts during those two decades (Integrated Values Surveys and Our World in Data 2022).

Weak Mobilization, Weak Personalization

Several cases in our analysis displayed continuity in populists' vs. non-populists' readiness to engage in multilateral institutions, driven by relatively weak levels of both mobilization and personalization.

India and the UN

India's approach to the United Nations did not change much under populist prime minister Modi as compared to the previous non-populist UPA-I and UPA-II governments. India had traditionally been an active supporter of the United Nations, both in rhetorical terms as well as in terms of contributions to peacekeeping operations. Pre-independence India was one of the founding members of the UN, as it signed the Washington Declaration of 1942 and participated in the San Francisco Conference in 1945 (Mukherjee 2017). It

---

[28] Interview P27, Prof. Herman Joseph S. Kraft, University of the Philippines Diliman, 22 November 2024.

[29] Interview P29, former government official during the Duterte administration, Manila, 23 November 2024.

[30] Interview P16, foreign affairs journalist, Manila, 13 October 2022.

also played an active role in drafting the Universal Declaration of Human Rights (Bhagavan 2010). Over the decades, India has been one of the most frequently selected non-permanent members in the UN Security Council (UNSC) (Mukherjee 2017), and it has actively contributed to the agenda of the United Nations. Among the topics pursued by India were the establishment of the New International Economic Order, the Indian Ocean as a zone of peace, and the issue of nuclear disarmament (Murthy 2010). India has regularly figured among the top contributors of troops to UN peacekeeping missions, albeit with absolute numbers of peacekeeping staff deployed steadily decreasing from 2006 onwards (see Chapter 4). At the same time, despite their support for the UN, since the late 1970s successive Indian governments have called for reforms of the organization, and particularly for India to become a permanent member to the UNSC (Binder and Heupel 2020; Stuenkel 2010).

Perhaps because of India's long history of support for the UN, during fieldwork in India in 2023, we encountered some remarkable disillusionment about the organization. As an interviewee at a think tank close to the BJP-led government summarized it, 'we want the G-20 to succeed because the UN is not working.'[31] This more critical attitude was also reflected in the speeches given by representatives of non-populist vs. populist Indian governments at the UNGA, with criticism of UN structures and procedures as well as of the role of the West in the UN becoming slightly more frequent after 2014, while statements in support of the UN or constructive proposals for reform became more rare.

Despite such disillusionment, between the non-populist UPA-I and UPA-II governments and the populist NDA-I and NDA-II governments led by Modi, there were no dramatic shifts in India's approach to the United Nations. India's assessed contributions to the UN budget increased over the years reflecting India's economic development (see Figure 5.3). Also, voluntary contributions grew quite remarkably under Modi's populist government, at least until 2022. Perhaps as a reflection of the disillusionment with the UN towards the end of Modi's second term, however, in the Indian government's budget estimates for 2024–2025, contributions to the UN saw a sharp decrease of as much as 54% from the 2023–2024 revised estimates (Padmanabhan 2024)—an information not yet reflected in Figure 5.3, which builds on UN official statistics. Still, as we discussed in Chapter 4, India's readiness to contribute to the global public good of peace in the UN context did not decrease.

---

[31] Interview I15.

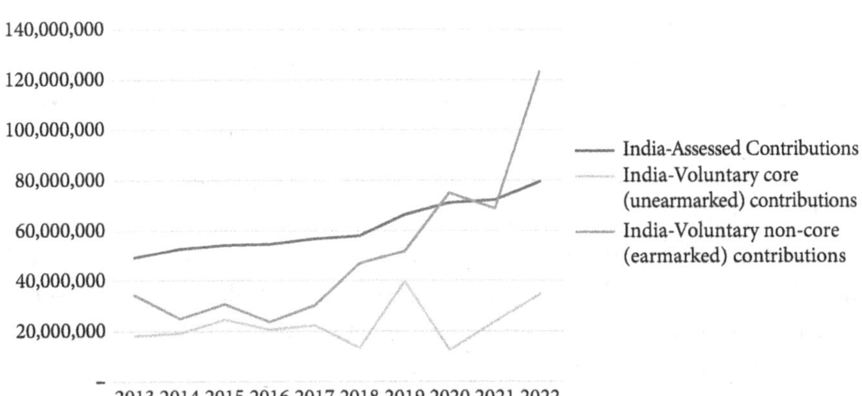

Figure 5.3 India's contributions to the UN budget, USD

Source: own composition based on https://unsceb.org/fs-revenue-government-donor (last accessed 30 June 2024).

The overall continuity in India's approach to the United Nations between non-populist and populist governments can be explained with the low degree of personalization and mobilization around this issue. Prime Minister Modi of course gave speeches at the UNGA but he did not particularly emphasize his personal engagement in the organization—something that is related to the very institutional structure of the UN, which lends itself less well to personalization than, for example, G-20 summits centred on individual leaders. Moreover, there were no attempts at mobilization around UN-related themes by connecting them to criticism of the opposition. Instead, references to the UN mainly served the purpose of highlighting the greatness of India under Modi's leadership. Modi repeatedly mentioned India's contributions to UN peacekeeping in his monthly radio addresses, and at the 100th edition of his 'Mann ki baat' radio address in April 2023, an intervention by the Director General of UNESCO was aired (PM India 2023). The fact that India managed to institutionalize the International Day of Yoga in the UN context was also frequently mentioned in Modi's addresses to the people, mostly to emphasize the greatness of India's culture and Hindu tradition, in line with Modi's thick ideology. For example, on 14 December 2014, Modi (2014) stated:

Two days back, the United Nations has decided to celebrate June 21st as International Yoga Day. It is a matter of great pride and honour for India. Our ancestors developed a beautiful tradition and today the entire world is associated with it. It does not merely benefit one personally but it has the potential to bring all the people together globally. The entire world came together on the issue of Yoga in the UN and a unanimous resolution was passed just two days back. 177 countries became

> the co-sponsors [. . .]. I am thankful to all the countries that have come out in sup-
> port and have honored the sentiments of the Indians and decided to observe World
> Yoga Day. It is now our duty that Yoga reaches out to the masses in its true essence.

In the following years, the prime minister repeatedly performed yoga on the International Day of Yoga with thousands of participants. For example, an event in 2015 at Rajpath in New Delhi—with Modi and 18,537 other participants—earned the Guinness world record for the largest yoga class ever held and set a precedent for subsequent, even larger events (Guinness World Records 2017).

But overall not much changed in India's approach to the UN: New Delhi remained engaged both under the non-populist and the populist governments. Whereas disillusionment about the functioning of the UN system and its prospects for reform may have deepened under Modi—not exactly surprising given its visible sclerosis in the face of major power rivalries throughout the 2010s—New Delhi did not call into question the UN's wider legitimacy and it continued to contribute to its peacekeeping missions.

India and SAARC

India's approach to the South Asian Association for Regional Cooperation (SAARC) also displayed a high degree of continuity between the non-populist UPA-I and UPA-II governments and the populist NDA governments after 2014. SAARC, established in 1986, is the sole regional organization encompassing all nations commonly identified as part of South Asia: Afghanistan, Bangladesh, Bhutan, India, the Maldives, Nepal, Pakistan, and Sri Lanka. According to its charter, SAARC is dedicated to advancing regional welfare and development as well as the nurturing of mutual trust through cooperation across economic, social, cultural, technical, and scientific domains. However, the organization has been largely unable to achieve any meaningful objective—and this also because India always deliberately avoided engaging in it (Destradi 2025b). In fact, SAARC was created at the initiative of Bangladesh and other smaller South Asian countries, and in 1983 the Indian government conditioned its participation on the inclusion of two clauses in the SAARC Charter: that 'bilateral and contentious issues' would be excluded from SAARC deliberations, and that decisions would be unanimous (Khan 2021, 150; Michael 2013, 65). Over the decades, successive Indian governments kept alive such latent scepticism of SAARC, fearing that it would be used by smaller South Asian states to curtail India's influence on the region.

As a result, New Delhi failed to develop a vision for more meaningful regional cooperation (Destradi 2012c). Thus, in a region marred by the long-standing bilateral conflict between India and Pakistan (see Chapter 3) and numerous border disputes and rivalries, SAARC remained largely dysfunctional.

Nonetheless, the UPA-I government had invested some political capital in SAARC. For example, in 2005 the UPA-I government proposed the foundation of the South Asian University (SAU) in New Delhi (Mattoo 2024), arguably one of the few concrete achievements of SAARC (Destradi 2025b). Moreover, India in 2007 pushed for the inclusion of Afghanistan as a new member state—a decision driven by a desire to strengthen the region's common identity, but also by India's strategic interest in friendly relations with Afghanistan (and conflictive relations between Afghanistan and Pakistan) (Paliwal 2017).

Under the populist government of Narendra Modi and against the backdrop of worsening relations with Pakistan, India's engagement in SAARC saw a further slight decline as compared to previous years. No SAARC summits took place between 2014 until the time of this writing (March 2025)—a much longer break as compared to the sporadic (but frequent) cancellations of summits in 1992, 1994, 1996, 1999, 2000, 2001, 2003, 2006, and 2009 (SAARC 2020). In March 2020, at the outset of the Covid-19 pandemic, Prime Minister Modi organized a virtual meeting with his SAARC counterparts, proposing to introduce visa exemptions for medical personnel and regional air ambulances to cooperate in fighting the pandemic—but ultimately nothing of this was implemented (Bhattarai 2022). Yet, India's disengagement under Modi was neither driven by personalization nor by mobilization. Given the extremely shallow institutionalization of SAARC (Hooghe et al. 2017, 463) and the low degree of authority India had ceded to the organization in the first place, there was little to gain for the populist government by mobilizing against it. The much-publicized introduction of the slogan 'Neighbourhood First' under Prime Minister Modi (Kaura and Rani 2020)—if it had any practical implications at all—was not conceived as a multilateral strategy for approaching the region. Instead, it remained in the tradition of India seeking close bilateral relations with each of its smaller South Asian neighbours separately (Sidhu and Godbole 2015). If we broaden the scope of the analysis to regional multilateral organizations in general, we see that India's slight disengagement from SAARC under Modi was paralleled by an increased engagement in a number of other organizations, most notably the Indian Ocean Rim Association (IORA), Bangladesh, Bhutan, India, Nepal (BBIN), and the Bay of Bengal Initiative for Multi-Sectoral Technical and Economic Cooperation (BIMSTEC) (Destradi 2025b). In a way, this greater engagement compensated for the disengagement from SAARC, but it was mainly driven by the fact that neither of these organizations included Pakistan as a member. Thus, it was more reflective of India's conflictive approach to Pakistan and of efforts to exclude Islamabad from the region, than of a genuine interest in regionalism. Ultimately, under Modi, India kept following its' 'traditional approach' to the region, one focused on bilateral relations,[32] as it had been in the previous decades (Sidhu and Godbole 2015).

Turkey and the UN

Another case of continuity after the transition to populism is that of Turkey's approach to the United Nations. Turkey had long been actively engaged in the UN, among other things by participating in a number of UN operations in the Balkans in the 1990s (Oğuzlu and Güngör 2006, 476) (see Chapter 4). At the same time, under the non-populist but nationalist ANASOL-M government there were also points of contention, especially around the United Nations' proposals for a settlement of the conflict in Cyprus (Republic of Türkiye Ministry of Foreign Affairs 1999b) (see Chapter 3).

After Erdoğan's rise to power in 2003, during the non-populist phase, Turkey's approach to the UN became more cooperative. In a remarkable change of course, Erdoğan agreed to the Annan Plan for Cyprus:

> Our common goal is to achieve a lasting and just peace within the framework of the United Nations Secretary-General's good offices mission and based on the realities on the island. In this regard, we will continue to make an effective contribution to the United Nations negotiation process in close consultation and cooperation with Mr. Denktaş and the new government expected to be established in the Turkish Republic of Northern Cyprus. (Erdoğan 2019e, 272)

Ultimately, the Greek Cypriot population rejected the unification proposal in a referendum in 2004 (Tocci 2012), but Erdoğan's willingness to cooperate in the UN framework remained significant and even increased during this period (see Chapter 3).[33] Turkey continued to engage in a number of UN peacekeeping missions (see Chapter 4) and it also took initiatives in the UN framework, among them co-sponsoring with Spain the Alliance of Civilizations in 2005, a UN body aiming to counter polarization and narratives about a clash of civilizations (United Nations Alliance

---

[32] Interview I04, Indian academic, New Delhi, 22 February 2023.
[33] Interview T15, Turkish academic, Istanbul, 5 May 2023.

of Civilizations 2023), and promoting the Mediation for Peace Initiative together with Finland in 2010 (see Chapter 4). Moreover, Turkey served as a non-permanent UNSC member in 2009–2010. In this context, Erdoğan emphasized Turkey's position as a well-connected emerging power, thus underlining the usefulness of multilateral engagements for his government:

> We made Turkey a non-permanent member of the United Nations Security Council for the 2009–2010 term. We have become a country that takes an active role in regional and global issues, not just a spectator. We are now successfully hosting major international events, meetings, and congresses. We are implementing the Alliance of Civilizations project together with Spain. We are hosting the IMF-World Bank Annual Meeting, the 2011 World University Winter Games in Erzurum, and the European Youth Olympics in Trabzon. The list goes on. We have elevated Turkey to a new league. (Erdoğan 2019d, 154)

At the same time, already during that phase, this engagement was presented in 2009 as a way of giving a voice to the oppressed and the underdogs: 'Wherever it is in the world, Turkey is alongside the oppressed and those who have been wronged, with diplomacy, the Red Crescent, and peacekeeping soldiers' (Erdoğan 2019b, 146).

After 2011, as Turkey entered the populist phase, the frequency of statements in support of the UN made by Turkish government representatives at the UNGA declined, and the number of critical statements increased. According to an interviewee, a more critical discourse was related to Turkey's unsuccessful bid for non-permanent membership for the years 2014–2015.[34] Yet, Turkey's criticism of the UN as voiced in the UNGA was not phrased in terms of a radical questioning of the usefulness of the UN as such. To the contrary, it was paired with calls for reform of the UNSC. Under the motto 'The world is bigger than five', Erdoğan throughout this phase advocated for the inclusion of a more diverse set of countries in the UNSC, and for an increase in the number of permanent members from five to twenty (Presidency of the Republic of Türkiye 2023b). For a domestic audience, such criticism was also framed more explicitly in anti-Western terms and thus used to mobilize support:

> Those, who cannot explain the shame of imperialism and genocides in their pasts, also avoid making a sincere review of the heavy casualties caused by the two great

---

[34] Interview T15.

world wars started by themselves in the past century and of their failure against terrorist organizations. (Presidency of the Republic of Türkiye 2021)

Especially during the war in Gaza from 2023, Erdoğan adopted ever more scathing criticism of the UNSC and of Western countries' policies:

We observe that the United Nations Security Council has deepened the crisis with its one-sided attitude, instead of stopping the bloodshed, ensuring a ceasefire as soon as possible, and taking steps to prevent civilian casualties. It is of course impossible for a structure that can only look on the total punishment of the people of Gaza, to offer hope for humanity and to ensure global peace and stability. UN agencies, in particular the United Nations Relief and Works Agency for Palestine Refugees in the Near East (UNRWA), are being rendered dysfunctional by the UN Security Council itself. The biggest damage to UN's reputation is done yet again by one of the main bodies of the UN. (Presidency of the Republic of Türkiye 2023a)

Yet, while Turkey became more critical of the UN from 2011 onwards, such criticism was mostly an extension of Erdoğan's anti-Western attitude (see Chapter 6). It ultimately was about the unfair structures in the UN and the predominance of the West in the UNSC, and less about the existence or the fundamental principles of the organization as such. To the contrary, the Turkish government called for a 'strong, efficient, and credible United Nations', not its dispensation (United Nations General Assembly 2012). In particular, criticism was more explicit when Erdoğan addressed domestic audiences, while at the UNGA he kept a constructive tone, as in the UNGA speech of 2021:

we continue to view the United Nations as the unique platform for solving issues that concern the entire human race. Located straight across from this building, our new Turkish House building, which we inaugurated yesterday, is a testament to our trust and confidence in the United Nations system. (United Nations General Assembly 2021)

Correspondingly, according to UN budget data for 2013–2022, there were no significant shifts in Turkey's financial contributions to the UN as Erdoğan became increasingly populist. In a highly visible instance of foreign policy activism, Turkey cooperated closely with the UN over the Ukrainian grain deal with Russia in 2022, including the establishment of a Joint Coordination Centre in Istanbul for monitoring its implementation (see Chapter 4). This dovetailed with a more general support of multilateral institutions, which also during the populist period were seen by Erdoğan as vehicles to expand Turkey's international influence. For example, in 2020, Erdoğan stated:

> The fact that our brother Ambassador Volkan Bozkır has been elected as the President of the 75th UN General Assembly with the support of the vast majority of the member countries shows that the confidence put in Turkey and the Turkish diplomacy has reached the highest level. Our diplomats assume high-level posts not only in the UN but also in NATO, OSCE, UNESCO and the OIC. Thanks be to Allah, we have assumed the term presidency of seven international organizations this year alone. (Presidency of the Republic of Türkiye 2020b)

Thus, despite some instances of mobilization, Erdoğan during the populist phase mostly referred to Turkey's role in international organizations by highlighting the achievements and strengths of his country. This was much in line with some of his patterns of mobilization in other issue areas, for example during the Covid-19 pandemic, when he regularly claimed that Turkey was performing better than the West (Belder et al. 2023). At the same time, it was a more moderate complement to his conspiratorial discourse about an obscure Western-driven 'mastermind' (*üst akıl*) trying to divide and conquer Turkey (Destradi, Plagemann, and Taş 2022). Finally, according to a Turkish scholar we interviewed, activism in international institutions was also a way for Erdoğan to display his personal engagement as a 'world leader'.[35]

The Philippines and ASEAN

Also in the case of the Philippines' approach towards the Association of Southeast Asian Nation (ASEAN), the formation of a populist government did not lead to any substantial foreign policy change. The ASEAN is the most important regional organization in Southeast Asia. Founded in 1967, it comprises Indonesia, Malaysia, Philippines, Singapore, and Thailand as well as Brunei Darussalam (since 1984), Vietnam (since 1995), Laos (since 1997), Myanmar (since 1997), and Cambodia (since 1999). ASEAN's core principles are the norms of sovereignty, non-intervention, and consensus decision making—that is, decisions based on unanimity. All this has been summarized under the label 'ASEAN Way' (Acharya 1997). The non-populist government of Aquino had generally supported ASEAN. However, the Aquino government was also disillusioned about ASEAN as it repeatedly sought the regional organization's support against China's expansionism in the South China Sea

---

[35] Interview T15.

(De Castro 2020), with little success. According to one of the experts we interviewed, 'the Philippines were always kept at arm's length [by ASEAN]'[36] due to their alliance with the United States.

Once in power, Duterte did not significantly change the Philippines' engagement in the organization. Whereas past presidents had traditionally visited an ASEAN member state in their first trip abroad, Duterte chose to travel to China instead, thus reflecting his veering away from the US and towards China.[37] Against the security establishment's will, Duterte supported joint ASEAN-China naval exercises in China (see below).[38] At the same time, Duterte's 'Independent Foreign Policy' not only meant a rapprochement with China but also an ongoing reliance on ASEAN (as well as other Asian countries, see Chapter 6).[39] In fact, a senior military official under Duterte told us that the president was keen to develop 'personal relationships with his fellow dictators' in ASEAN.[40] At the same time, we did not find any mobilization against ASEAN, which also had a low salience to Filipinos.[41] This is not surprising given the comparably shallow nature of institutionalization in ASEAN and the low degree of authority exercised by it.

In terms of contributions to ASEAN, not much changed under Duterte. While the finances of the organization are rather opaque, ASEAN works based on equal contributions by all member states in order to avoid the formation of hierarchies of spenders that would enable single countries to play a disproportionate role in shaping the agenda of the organization (Destradi 2019). This is much in line with ASEAN's overall emphasis on the equality among member states entailed in the 'ASEAN Way'. We did not find any reports about the Philippines curtailing its contributions to ASEAN under the populist government of Duterte.[42] When it comes to policy initiatives and engagement in the organization, under Duterte we observed a shift to a more narrowly understood agenda that followed the policy priorities personally set by him—fighting drugs and rapprochement with China. This was most clearly reflected in Duterte's approach when the Philippines took over the rotating chair of ASEAN in 2017.

---

[36] Interview P35.

[37] Interview P02, former senior diplomat, Manila, 28 September 2022.

[38] P12, former senior navy official, Manila, 11 October 2022.

[39] Interview P10, former high-ranking government official, Manila, 10 October 2022.

[40] Interview P06, senior military official, Manila, 4 October 2022.

[41] According to a poll conducted in 2019, when asked what their 'top concerns about ASEAN' were, 79.3% of respondents in the Philippines mentioned that 'the tangible benefits of ASEAN are not felt', thus hinting at the low salience of the organization to people's daily lives (with only Brunei Darussalam having a higher share of respondents, 80.0%, sharing this assessment) (ISEAS-Yusof Ishak Institute 2019, 12).

[42] ASEAN 'lacks a proper feedback mechanism, a way to track compliance of members' agreements, and applying sanctions when commitments are not honored' (ADB Institute 2015, 186). Moreover, there are no rules on budgetary non-compliance in the ASEAN Charter.

The war on drugs, Duterte's domestic political signature project, was the topic that the Philippines promoted most explicitly within ASEAN under its chairmanship, as illustrated by Duterte's inaugural speech of the ASEAN Summit in Manila in April 2016:

> We must also be resolute in realizing a drug-free ASEAN. The scourge of illegal drugs threatens our gains in community-building. I have seen how illegal drugs have ended the hopes, dreams, future and even lives of countless people, especially the youth. The illegal drug trade apparatus is massive. But it is not impregnable. With political will and cooperation, it can be dismantled, it can be destroyed before it destroys our societies. (Duterte 2017)

Also in the following years, Duterte repeatedly called on ASEAN members to 'redouble our collective efforts to counter these threats effectively and with finality', referring primarily to drugs, but also to terrorism and transnational crime (FORUM 2019). While Duterte's personal interest in fighting drugs led to a greater emphasis on this issue, it was not a new topic to ASEAN: a 'drug-free ASEAN' had already been called for in a declaration of leaders in 2012 (ASEAN Secretariat 2017). In terms of policies, the organization in 2017 adopted a novel ASEAN Plan of Action in Combatting Transnational Crime, which among many other things, encouraged member states to improve information sharing and cooperation between law enforcement agencies (ASEAN Ministerial Meeting on Transnational Crime [AMMTC] 2017). Overall, instead of disengaging from regional cooperation, Duterte used the regional organization ASEAN to elevate his own domestic agenda to the regional level (Söderbaum, Spandler, and Pacciardi 2021).

More important, Duterte's policy of rapprochement with China (see Chapters 3 and 6) dovetailed with the preferences of several ASEAN countries. As a Filipino academic pointed out to us, 'Duterte was the closest [Filipino president] to the ASEAN consensus in terms of being critical of America's role in this region'.[43] In fact, under the Aquino presidency, the Philippines had sought the support of ASEAN for their resort to the Permanent Court of Arbitration (PCA) in The Hague over the issue of territorial disputes with China in the South China Sea (Krejsa 2016). However, Cambodia, which was close to Beijing, had opposed making this an ASEAN issue (Esmaquel II 2016b). By contrast, already during his election campaign, Duterte had expressed a desire for the Philippines to move

---

[43] Interview P36, Filipino academic, Manila, 28 November 2024.

closer to China, as well as his preference for bilateral negotiations with China over the South China Sea dispute (South China Morning Post 2016). After the ruling of the PCA on 12 July 2016, less than two weeks after being sworn in as president, Duterte used markedly ambivalent language vis-à-vis China and the PCA ruling (Krejsa 2016). The government of the Philippines only stated that it welcomed the ruling, and advised citizens 'to exercise restraint and sobriety' (De Castro 2022, 40), while even refraining from asking China to abide by the PCA ruling. Within ASEAN, the Philippines' foreign secretary Yasay ultimately withdrew his previous motion to include the PCA's decision in the ASEAN Joint Communiqué. Also, ahead of the September 2016 ASEAN Summit in Laos, Duterte stated that the PCA's ruling was a bilateral issue between the Philippines and China, and nothing ASEAN should be involved in (De Castro 2016). In line with this position, the PCA ruling was never mentioned during the Philippines' chairmanship of ASEAN in 2017 (Esmaquel II 2017). As part of Duterte's friendly China policy, he also urged fellow ASEAN governments to reach a conclusion of the Regional Comprehensive Economic Partnership (RCEP), a trade agreement involving China, while criticizing the US-led Trans-Pacific Partnership (TPP) (Department of Trade and Industry 2017; Katigbak 2017). Interestingly, however, as over the years Duterte's approach to China returned to be more cautious (see Chapters 3 and 6), this was also reflected in Duterte's preferences for ASEAN's interactions with Beijing. In 2019, Duterte vigorously pushed for 'the immediate passage of the Association of Southeast Asian Nations (ASEAN)-China Code of Conduct (CoC) of Parties of South China Sea' in an effort of 'soft balancing' against China (De Castro 2022, 39). At the 2019 ASEAN Summit Retreat, Duterte 'expressed concern and disappointment' regarding delays in the negotiation of the CoC, stating that the Philippines, '[a]s country coordinator for ASEAN-China Dialogue Relations, together with fellow ASEAN member-states, [. . .] will continue to push for the full and effective implementation of the 2002 Declaration on the Conduct of Parties in the South China Sea' (Mendez 2019).

In sum, Duterte did not disengage from ASEAN. To some extent, his more China-friendly approach even led to an improvement of the Philippines' position in the organization. But overall, according to a former government official, 'nothing changed in the process, nor in the substance'.[44]

---

[44] Interview P29.

Conclusion

Populists do not reject multilateralism in a wholesale manner. Instead, what we have learned from the four cases of Bolivia, India, the Philippines, and Turkey is that the readiness to engage in international institutions decreases only where the leader has a personal aversion for them. Disengagement is particularly strong if there are also opportunities for populists to mobilize against such institutions. In turn, such mobilization can only work if those institutions are highly salient to the public, as in the case of the EU for the Turkish population. For a country like India, which has only ceded an extremely low degree of authority to international organizations, and which is placed in the least integrated region in the world (South Asia), there are hardly any opportunities for mobilization against multilateral institutions. This helps explain why India under the populist government of Modi did not display a reduced readiness to engage in international institutions.

At the same time, populists may also increase their engagement in multilateral institutions, as seen in the case of Bolivia under Morales. His regional integration initiatives helped him domestically, through funding of social programs, among others, and internationally, by compensating for the breaking down of relations with the US (see Chapters 3 and 6). Meanwhile, the UN provided a forum for Morales to pursue elements of his domestic agenda (a new coca policy, access to the sea) and, crucially, gave him a stage for his persona to radiate far beyond what Bolivian presidents had achieved in the past. Bolivia, the weakest state in our sample, also shows that small state pragmatism prevails in populist-run countries: Rather than exclusively relying on Chávez's Bolivarian agenda, Morales retained membership in other regional groupings and sought access to new ones excluding Chávez, Mercosur in particular (also see Chapter 6).

Beyond this assessment, a more detailed look into populist leaders' discourse on the United Nations was helpful. As we have seen, one element that all four populist governments had in common was the criticism of the inequalities within the United Nations, and particularly of the disproportionate role of the five permanent members of the UNSC. Such criticism is obviously not exclusive to populist governments, and in fact in several cases populist governments took over similarly critical stances from previous non-populist governments. At the same time, recent research has shown that populism does not make governments less likely to participate in UNGA voting (Destradi and Vüllers 2024).

Thus, our findings point to the importance of distinguishing the specific types of international institutions under discussion. For one, populists will mobilize more against institutions to which their countries have ceded (or are about to cede, as in the case of Turkey's accession negotiations with the EU) a high amount of authority. This relates to populists' preference for sovereignty, much in line with the notion of people-centrism. Looking beyond Global South cases in Chapter 7 will allow us to explore whether this finding also applies to Hungary and Italy as member states of the European Union. People-centrism is also a driving force in populists' criticism of institutions that strongly espouse norms of the 'liberal international order' such as the promotion of democracy and human rights abroad. Finally, populists' anti-elitist discourse dovetails well with their criticism of hierarchical institutions shaped by hegemonic powers, but it does not induce them to oppose international institutions that are neither hierarchical nor significantly impinging on national sovereignty (Cooper 2010). To the contrary, Morales celebrated ALBA as a defence of Bolivia's autonomy against US imperialism and Modi turned India's G-20 presidency into a mobilizing exercise domestically, while at the same time showcasing his country's aspiration for global power status.

6

Reorientation of International Partnerships

Over the past years, numerous episodes of populists cooperating with each other have fuelled debates around a new 'populist international'. Think of Brazil's right-wing populist President Bolsonaro visiting the United States in 2019 and expressing his 'admiration' for US President Trump (Watson 2019), of Trump hailing Boris Johnson as 'Britain Trump' (Smith 2019), or of Netanyahu moving out of his house to stay at the hotel with Modi during the latter's visit to Jerusalem.[1] Apart from personal leader-level relationships, the past years have also seen an increase in connections between populist parties across borders. In Europe, this is most visible in the formation of right-wing populist parliamentary groups in the European Parliament such as Identity and Democracy in 2019, but also in bilateral connections such as those between right-wing populist FPÖ in Austria and AfD in Germany (ORF 2023). On the left side of the political spectrum, populist movements, leaders, and governments in Latin America learned from Venezuela's Hugo Chávez, and from each other, among other things in the context of the regional organization ALBA (De la Torre 2017). The Democracy in Europe Movement 2025 (DiEM25), created by former Greek finance minister Yanis Varoufakis, tried to discursively construct a transnational populism, with a 'European people' opposed to an international elite (De Cleen et al. 2020). At the same time, over the past years, various populist actors have emphasized relations with authoritarian leaders and governments. Populist leaders and parties supported Vladimir Putin's Russia (Wesslau 2016), including after Russia's invasion of Ukraine in 2022.[2] From Germany's right-wing AfD to Spain's left-wing populist Podemos, several populist parties in Europe have blamed NATO expansion for Russia's war of aggression and called for a softer

---

[1] Interview I01, expert on India's foreign policy, New Delhi, 20 February 2023.

[2] Some authors consider Russian president Vladimir Putin to be a populist leader (e.g., Eksi and Wood 2019; Robinson and Milne 2017). We do not follow this approach and consider him an authoritarian leader, based on the understanding that populism is a phenomenon taking place in democracies. For various arguments against considering Putin a populist, see Moffitt (2020, 36); Lassila (2018); March (2023).

Populism and Foreign Policy. Sandra Destradi and Johannes Plagemann, Oxford University Press.
© Oxford University Press (2025). DOI: 10.1093/9780197695012.003.0006

foreign policy stance vis-à-vis Russia (Podemos 2022; Arzheimer 2023). In February 2024, Trump infamously stated that, if re-elected, he would allow Putin to 'do whatever the hell he wants' to those NATO members not paying their contributions to the alliance (Sullivan 2024). Once in power, he repeatedly displayed his appreciation of Putin (and disregard for the democratically elected Ukrainian President Zelensky), suggesting the easing of sanctions and other fundamental foreign policy changes benefitting Russia early on.

Populists thus seem to be attracted towards other populists as well as towards authoritarian regimes, and this often goes hand in hand with a questioning of traditional alliances and partnerships. At the same time, not all populist governments have subverted the basic tenets of their countries' international alignments. For example, with President Joe Biden still in the White House, Italy's post-fascist populist leader Giorgia Meloni[3] invested a huge amount of political capital to show her allegiance to the traditional transatlantic tenets of Italy's foreign policy (Fasola and Lucarelli 2024).

This chapter addresses the issue of populist governments' reorientation of international partnerships by asking if and under what conditions populist government formation leads to a shift in states' foreign policies towards populist and authoritarian governments. While the previous chapters focused on issue areas or fields of international engagement and thus were mostly interested in what Hermann (1990, 5) called 'program changes' (with a particular emphasis on different intensities of change), here we are interested in the broader shifts in a country's orientation towards its traditional vs. new partners. This means that we are closer to the category of 'international orientation change' (Hermann 1990, 5–6), albeit with a focus on different intensities of change.[4] Based on the ideational understanding of populism as a thin-centred ideology entailing anti-elitism, people-centrism, and the notion that politics should be an expression of a presumed general will of the people (Mudde 2004a), we argue that there are several reasons to expect populists to be more likely than non-populist governments to move away from traditional international partners, and to expect them to reorient their partnerships towards populist and authoritarian regimes. First and foremost, this has to do with populists' anti-elitism. In fact, representatives of foreign allies or partners usually display their countries' proximity by mingling with political, diplomatic, economic, and cultural elites. Since populists claim that they are different from the 'establishment', they are

---

[3] On the classification of Meloni as a populist, see Baldini et al. (2022).

[4] Again, we do not consider a successful outcome of an attempted reorientation of international partnerships to be a precondition for change. Instead, the very attempt to reorient a country's partnerships towards fellow populist or authoritarian regimes already amounts to foreign policy change (see Chapter 2).

prone to break with past policies and conventions in foreign relations. Populists promise change as they want to underscore that they differ from the 'establishment'. Calling into question traditional alliances and partnerships is one of the most immediately visible policy changes a populist government can make.

The impact of the people-centric dimension of populism on possible foreign policy reorientations is potentially more ambiguous. On the one hand, there are grounds to challenge assumptions regarding populist foreign policy being inherently more aligned with that of other populists and/or autocrats. In particular, being just a thin-centred ideology, populism offers limited guidance for international partnerships. Quite to the contrary, people-centrism may induce populists to focus exclusively on their own 'people', leading to isolationism rather than the close collaboration with any other peoples, even if run by fellow populists. Moreover, even shared thick ideologies among populist governments do not always translate into agreements over key foreign policy issues, as demonstrated by vastly diverging views of Russia in Poland under the right-wing populist PiS party and Hungary under Viktor Orbán. Where thick ideologies differ substantially, populism as a thin ideology is very unlikely to overcome substantial differences, as for instance between Narendra Modi's Hindu nationalism and Recep Erdoğan's Muslim nationalism. Meanwhile, in specific regional contexts like South America, thick-ideological similarities often superseded the populist/non-populist divide (Cason and Power 2009, 127). On the other hand, the notion of embodying the popular will and the personalization of politics are elements that induce us to expect populists to gravitate towards other personalistic or strongmen regimes that pursue a similar approach. For one, populists' propensity to use foreign relations for mobilization may lead them to appreciate spectacular state visits and crowds arranged by fellow populists, thus increasing mutual sympathy. More important, populists tend to view such personalistic leaders as actors more legitimately representing their respective peoples as compared, for example, to some coalition government. This is in line with theoretical approaches on 'regime affinity', which argue that states with similar political systems find it easier to understand each other's motivations, goals, and decision-making processes, thus facilitating cooperation. This is one of the arguments at the core of the democratic peace theory (Doyle 1983; Russett 1994), but also the literature on authoritarian cooperation refers to shared regime type characteristics as a possible driver of collaboration among authoritarian states (Leeds 1999; Mattes and Rodríguez 2014).

We thus expect populist governments to be, overall, more likely than non-populist ones to re-align their countries' international partnerships towards collaboration with populist and autocratic governments, to break with the conventional alignments established and cherished by the foreign policy 'establishment'. But again, we also expect variations in the intensity of these re-alignments, depending on how strong mobilization and personalization are.

As in the other chapters, we expect change to be strong—that is, a reorientation of international partnerships to be radical—if both mobilization with reference to and personalization of foreign policy are strong. Mobilization plays an important role in this dynamic mainly because changing whom you partner with in international politics can be very easily conveyed to a domestic audience, even to one that might not be well informed about specific foreign policy issues. Already during election campaigns, in which foreign policy issues rarely play a central role, populist politicians often promise to subvert the foreign policy of the establishment—think of left-wing populists in Latin America promising to sever ties with the US, as in the case of Evo Morales discussed in Chapter 3. These desired drastic foreign policy reorientations are easy to communicate publicly in the Manichean and moralistic terms that are typical of populist discourse. The celebration of fellow populist or admired authoritarian leaders and regimes may also play a part in mobilization. For example, in 2017 the Italian right-wing populist party Lega signed an agreement with Putin's United Russia party, and Matteo Salvini frequently referred to his admiration for Putin during the 2018 election campaign (see Chapter 7). An 'opening' to Russia was a prominent point mentioned in the Lega's 2018 electoral programme—and the mobilization aspect was very visible as this, together with support for the Trump administration, was presented as a call for change vis-à-vis the policies of the previous governments: 'We should reverse the foreign policy of Renzi and Gentiloni, who chose to cultivate relations more with the United States and its liberal political wing [. . .] by aligning with the internal opposition against the presidency of Donald Trump' (Lega 2018). As for the other policy areas discussed in previous chapters, a high degree of mobilization in favour of a reorientation of international partnerships is likely to force populists to live upon the expectations generated among the public and to pursue such a policy course. Meanwhile, a high degree of personalization promotes foreign policy change, as the leader will be less constrained by bureaucracies and advisors oriented towards continuity and the preservation of foreign policy traditions. For the specific issue of key international partnerships, this is all the more relevant: Here, we are talking about the fundamental tenets of a country's foreign policy, around which we will likely find friction among populist governments' desire for change and bureaucracies' quest for continuity.

As outlined in previous chapters, we expect change to take place, but in a milder form, if only one of the two dimensions (mobilization or personalization) is strong, while the other is weak. In those cases, we expect a partial reorientation of international partnerships. Finally, we do not expect a reorientation of international partnerships if both personalization of and mobilization around foreign policy are weak.

We consider a radical reorientation of international partnerships to take place if a government both weakens existing international commitments and builds up new ones, that is, if it essentially replaces the country's main international partners with new ones. In its most extreme form, this involves quitting an existing alliance and forming or joining a new one. If no formal alliances are in place, it may involve severing or radically diminishing diplomatic ties and important forms of military or economic cooperation with established partners and setting up new avenues for cooperation with populist or authoritarian partners. Such cooperation can be formalized via new 'strategic partnerships' or other agreements, or it can take place in less formalized ways.

A partial reorientation of international partnerships would take place if new, populist or authoritarian, partners are taken on board via new agreements and collaborations, while ties with previous partners are criticized and diminished rhetorically, but not substantially diminished in practice. This would mean that a populist government might criticize conventional partners without leaving existing alliances or international organizations. In other words, a partial reorientation would equal the diversification of a country's international partnerships. The 'no-reorientation' field at the bottom right in Table 6.1 would entail cases in which the populist government by and large sticks to previous commitments, alliances, institutions, and partnerships even if it might criticize them; and at the same time, the populist government does not build meaningful collaborations with alternative partners.

Table 6.1 Populism and the reorientation of international partnerships

		Personalization	
		Strong	**Weak**
Mobilization	**Strong**	*Radical reorientation*	*Partial reorientation*
	Weak	*Partial reorientation*	*No reorientation*

Our Findings

Instead of focusing on single instances of conflict (Chapter 3) or on specific policy fields (Chapter 4) or organizations (Chapter 5), in the following sections we address the overall set of alliances and partnerships of the populist governments as compared to those of their respective non-populist predecessors. This is why, for each country case, we have just one entry in Table 6.2, as we are interested in a more holistic view of their respective foreign policies. Note that some of those cases (especially the Philippines' approach to the US and China, and Bolivia's approach to the US) were already discussed in much detail in Chapter 3, which allows us to keep their analysis shorter here.

Strong Personalization, Strong Mobilization

Bolivia

A key element in Morales's agenda was the reorientation of his country's foreign policy away from the US and towards ideologically aligned Latin American countries as well as towards other states opposed to the US. Not only did this play a key role in his attempts to mobilize support ahead of elections, but Morales also was deeply involved personally in this radical foreign policy reorientation.

Bolivia, a country with little more than 10 million inhabitants when Morales took power in 2006, has often been described as a quintessential small country in international politics (Jesse 2016; Guimarães and Maitino 2019). Politically unstable and economically dependent on the export of natural resources, landlocked, and situated in a relatively poor world region,

Table 6.2 Summary of findings

		Personalization	
		Strong	**Weak**
Mobilization	**Strong**	*Radical reorientation* Bolivia Turkey	*Partial reorientation*
	Weak	*Partial reorientation* India Philippines	*No reorientation*

the Andean state for long profoundly depended on foreign support. Following the return to democracy in 1982, state finances relied heavily on foreign donors, the IMF, and the US in particular. In 1997, the IMF relieved Bolivia of much of its foreign debt. In 2006 the World Bank and the Inter-American Development Bank further reduced Bolivia's foreign debt substantially, thus contributing to economic stabilization (Kohl 2010, 118). However, the IMF's structural adjustment programme in particular also deepened Bolivians' disillusionment with their country's young democracy: 'Programmatic convergence in relation to neoliberal policies among all the significant [political] parties created growing discontent with the model, to the extent that the reforms were not only incapable of resolving the country's serious socio-economic problems, but were also perceived by the population as having aggravated them' (Souza, Cunha Filho, and Santos 2020). Like many small states elsewhere, Bolivia's self-understanding also included a narrative that favoured its integration with the region. Its self-description as the 'connection country' (*país de contactos*) at the heart of South America was 'ubiquitous from educational narratives to political speeches'; it stated that 'the country's future can only be secured by its political, economic and infrastructural insertion into the continent', thus making La Paz a strong proponent of regional integration (Bruslé 2015). This traditional regionalist foreign policy agenda was enthusiastically embraced by the MAS and by Morales personally, but it was complemented with 'granite-like'[5] anti-US views. Even before assuming office, and in contrast to his predecessors' focus on the traditional partner US, Morales paid visits to China, Spain, and South Africa (Kohl 2010, 117), thus illustrating his personal ambition to expand Bolivia's foreign relations. The result was both a continuation of Bolivia's engagement for regional integration and a clear foreign policy reorientation, away from the US (Souza, Cunha Filho, and Santos 2020) and towards Venezuela, Cuba, but also Brazil under President Lula. All of this was driven by Morales's personal involvement and was widely used for mobilizing support.

From its first term in office onwards and within the wider context of its striving for 'decolonization', the Morales government broke with past governments' coca policies, thus knowingly running counter to US foreign policy. Washington's 'war on drugs' at that time offered some benefits for crop substitution, but mostly relied on the militarized eradication of coca crops (Farthing and Grisaffi 2024). While unable to effectively curb the production of cocaine, the social effects of the US 'war on drugs' were devastating, frequently pitting poor subsistence farmers against heavily armed military

---

[5] Interview B24, journalist and former senior diplomat, Zoom, 8 March 2023.

forces. As pointed out in Chapter 3, the MAS emerged in this context from a variety of social movements with strong links to farmers' unions and coca growers. Opposition to the US in this sense was an integral ideological and policy component of the Morales government's agenda from the very beginning. Not only was a degree of confrontation with the US politically imperative for the MAS, Bolivia at that time could also afford to do without US support thanks to a commodity boom driven by the export of natural gas. Thus, once in office, Morales abandoned Bolivia's standby agreement with the IMF and terminated its participation in the World Bank's International Center for the Settlement of Investment Disputes (Kohl 2010, 118) while quickly enacting radical policy changes contrary to previous 'structural adjustments', including the enforced majority control of foreign-owned energy firms and increased taxes and royalties (Kaup 2010). Seeking to minimize dependence on private foreign hydrocarbon companies, Bolivia's state energy firm YPFB (Yacimientos Petrolíferos Fiscales Bolivianos) established partnerships with other non-Western state-run energy firms such as Gazprom from Russia, PDVSA from Venezuela, and Shengli from China (Kohl 2010, 117).

All this in the mid-2000s coincided with the political rise of leftist movements and leaders in neighbouring states. Among them, the most consequential for Bolivia's foreign relations was Hugo Chávez in Venezuela, in power from 1999 to his death in 2013. The boom in commodity prices of the 2000s allowed the Venezuelan populist leader to both heavily increase social spending domestically and to inject huge resources into foreign policy, for instance via the funding of development projects in Africa and Latin America (Sagarzazu and Thies 2019), including in Bolivia (Romero 2007). According to a senior Bolivian diplomat we spoke with, Morales and Chávez were in lockstep, both in style and substance. They 'intoned similar speeches, such as the "liberating role" of the great homeland and the "Bolivarian revolution", the anti-imperialist and revolutionary nature of their projects' and together 'resorted to UNASUR and ALBA to generate motions of mutual support in the face of the internal conflicts they were experiencing. [. . .] Both resorted to the massive mobilization of their supporters'.[6] However, their relationship was unequal (Wehner and Thies 2021, 334). Once Morales took power, Venezuela's state oil company PDVSA began exploring prospective hydrocarbon areas with Bolivia's YPFB; at the same time, Venezuelan capital entered the Bolivian agricultural sector and the media; and Venezuelan advisors to senior members of the Bolivian government quickly became visible emblems of a leader-follower relationship between the two countries.

---

[6] Interview B16, acting senior diplomat, La Paz, 9 February 2023.

Illustrating their proximity, Venezuela's ambassador to Bolivia frequently travelled with Morales on both domestic and foreign trips in an airplane and helicopter provided by PDVSA, according to the *New York Times* in 2007 (Romero 2007).

Given all of this, it is not surprising that Morales was an enthusiastic supporter of ALBA (see Chapter 5). Created by Venezuela and Cuba, the regional body according to Bolivia's government in 2008 invested more than $16 million in sixty-three projects, thus creating 33,000 jobs in the country (Kohl 2010, 118). Among the projects revealing the close connections to ideologically aligned Latin American governments was the establishment of an 'Anti-Imperialist School' meant to guarantee the 'sovereignty of the continent and of the entire world' through the training of Bolivian, Venezuelan, Nicaraguan, and Ecuadorian soldiers—thus counteracting decades of military training at the US-based School of the Americas (since 2001 the Western Hemisphere Institute for Security Cooperation).[7] Rooted in the idea of a 'Bolivarian project of the peoples',[8] ALBA heavily relied on the ideological affinity of its member states' governments. As we outlined in Chapter 5, Morales further revived existing regional integration schemes and created new ones in line with Bolivia's traditional narrative as a 'connection country'. Some of these also allowed the Morales government to reach beyond Latin America. CELAC, for instance, facilitated high-level meetings with the EU, China, Turkey, and Russia.[9]

Another key partner for Morales was Brazilian President Lula, a former union activist in power from 2003 to 2010. The two leaders, according to our interviews, maintained a personal relationship that went far beyond the necessities of pragmatic cooperation between Bolivia and its primary export destination for natural gas.[10] As one interviewee from within the Morales foreign policy establishment told us, Lula, alongside leaders from other leftist governments at that time, was a key foreign policy advisor for Morales.[11] Notably, relations remained close despite the 'nationalization' of Bolivia's gas production, from which Brazil's state energy giant Petrobrás suffered most. Having promised to end 'the permanent theft of Bolivian natural resources' (Guimarães and Maitino 2019, 10), Morales and his aggressive minister of hydrocarbons, Solíz Rada, ordered the military occupation of Petrobrás

---

[7] Interview B16. Also see BBC 2016.

[8] Interview B16.

[9] Interview B19, acting senior diplomat, La Paz, 20 February 2023.

[10] Interviews B18, David Agramont, Research Associate at the Peace Research Institute Frankfurt, Zoom, 15 February 2023; B03, international affairs expert and foreign policy advisor under Morales, La Paz, 16 January 2023.

[11] Interview B04, senior career diplomat under Veltzé and Morales, La Paz, 16 January 2023

refineries on 1 May, Labor Day, 2006, and declared their nationalization alongside those owned by other foreign companies. Despite fierce domestic critiques from the Brazilian media as well as from within Petrobrás and other state agencies, Lula and his foreign minister Celso Amorim at numerous occasions expressed sympathy with their small neighbour and refrained from breaking ties with Morales. Instead investing in behind-closed-doors negotiations, their efforts eventually led to a negotiated agreement, which however still accrued considerable financial losses to Petrobrás (Guimarães and Maitino 2019, 9–15). Under Morales, relations with Brazil deepened in other sectors. Alongside the boom in soy exports, the Brazilian agricultural sector became deeply immersed into Bolivia's soy industry in the province of Santa Cruz so that 'today [...] there is a consolidated agro-industrial Brazilian elite that holds a significant amount of power within governmental structures at the local, regional, and even national levels' (Fabricant and Gustafson 2020, 51). Diplomatically, governments of the two countries cooperated closely on matters related to UNASUR, an initiative both Lula and Morales prioritized.[12] With the departure of Lula in 2010 and shifting priorities under Brazilian President Dilma Rousseff, relations cooled: whereas Lula as president visited Bolivia nine times, Rousseff, in power from 2011 to 2016, visited La Paz only once (in 2015).

Beyond leftist governments in Latin America, the Morales government was keen to strengthen ties with countries seen as opposed to 'US-imperialism' globally—China, Russia, and Iran especially. According to former foreign minister and permanent representative to the UN Javier Murillo in an interview with us, rather than seeking ties with all countries of the world, as was the case under previous governments, the Morales government prioritized ideological affinities and singled out potential partners that would speak out against neoliberalism. As a result, Bolivia 'moved closer to China, Russia, Syria, Iran.'[13] Other Bolivian diplomats we spoke with confirmed that, under Morales, relations with China were a priority given that it offered an 'alternative space for development and trade to those with the West'[14] and that the Morales government regarded China as a 'great partner.'[15] Moreover, Russia and China 'exerted a lot of pressure and at times had a lot of influence on Bolivian decisions.'[16]

---

[12] Interview B09, senior career diplomat, Zoom, 27 January 2023.

[13] Interview B30, Javier Murillo de la Rocha, former foreign minister (1997–2001), La Paz, 14 February 2023.

[14] Interview B16.

[15] Interview B10, diplomat under Morales, La Paz, 30 January 2023.

[16] Interview B27, Nataly Reguerin, Bolivian foreign relation analyst and former diplomat, La Paz, 9 March 2023.

Speaking to members of the Politburo during his 2006 trip to China as president-elect, Morales declared his admiration for Mao Zedong. However, relations intensified only a few years into his presidency (Berg and Ziemer 2024, 31). With the constitutional crisis of 2009 over and Morales's political position more secure, Chinese companies began investing heavily in extractive industries and infrastructure projects, thus over time turning China into one of Bolivia's most important investors as well as creditors. As president, Morales visited China twice, in 2011 and 2013. During the latter visit, he was present at the launch of the *Tupac Katari* satellite built by China for Bolivia (Ellis 2016, 5). According to a diplomat who had served under Morales, China cancelled some of Bolivia's debt following a similar agreement with Japan.[17] Leaders from both countries since 2010 meet regularly in the China-CELAC Forum aimed at strengthening ties between China and Central and Latin American countries. At the height of Chinese investment abroad via the Belt and Road Initiative (BRI), Morales in 2015 announced an agreement with China that would provide Bolivia with $7.5 billion in loans, funding eleven strategic projects from Bolivia's 2016–2020 National Economic and Social Development Plan (Ellis 2016, 1). Cooperation with China notably included arms procurement. Bolivia bought fighter jets, helicopters, and armoured vehicles in addition to several Chinese donations of military equipment. As a result, under Morales China turned into Bolivia's most important provider of arms and military equipment (Berg and Ziemer 2023, 21), thus replacing the US. Chinese exports also included material for domestic surveillance. In 2016, Bolivia purchased cameras including face recognition, telecommunications equipment, and a command centre for Bolivia's newly established citizen security system (Berg and Ziemer 2024, 33).

The Morales government also turned towards Russia, another global power in competition with the US. As one Bolivian scholar told us: 'Based on the policy of anti-imperialism, many partners have been made, with whom there is not necessarily an ideological affinity. Russia is an imperialist capitalist country, but as opposed to the United States, because Evo Morales's anti-imperialism is only against the United States.'[18] At the same time, Morales mobilized around Bolivia's rapprochement with Russia, as in this speech he gave on the *Kausachum Coca* (Long Live Coca, in Quechua) radio channel, run by the coca growers' union in Cochabamba: 'Latin America will no longer be the empire's backyard; that's over, and with Russia's return to Latin America, the history of this new millennium will completely change'

---

[17] Interview B02, former diplomat and academic, La Paz, 15 January 2023.
[18] Interview B08, Bolivian foreign relations scholar, Zoom, 25 January 2023.

(El Espectador, 2009). Although (unlike in Venezuela) Russian arms supplies to Bolivia remained negligible, Morales was the first Bolivian president to visit Moscow in 2009. He returned to Russia in 2013, for the world football championship in 2018 and, again, in 2019. Indeed, Morales praised his 'friend' Putin for protecting the 'international order, for opposing the use of force in international affairs, and for the prevention of interferences in other nations' internal affairs' (AP 2019). Russia's energy giant Gazprom from 2007 onwards signed a series of agreements with Bolivia's YPFB but did not actually begin drilling oil or extracting gas (Ziemer, Dolbaia, and Droin 2024; Gazprom International 2024). More consequential has been Russia's atomic energy firm Rosatom. In 2016 it signed an agreement for the construction of a nuclear complex near La Paz, including a research reactor, thus helping Morales realize his ambition for a Bolivian nuclear programme for scientific and energy purposes (Reuters 2016). Alongside Chinese companies, the Morales government invited Rosatom's Uranium One Group for the exploitation of the world's largest and strategically relevant lithium deposits.[19] Shortly after Morales's resignation as president, Russia's foreign propaganda channel RT offered him to moderate a show in its Spanish-language program (Schmidt 2019).

Another country the Morales government turned to was Iran under President Mahmud Ahmadinejad (2005–2013), who visited Morales three times.[20] At the first state visit of any Iranian president to Bolivia in 2007, he pledged to invest $1.1 billion in agriculture and energy, among others (MercoPress 2009). Morales visited Teheran several times, also a novelty for Bolivia's diplomacy. In 2008 Iran set up a Spanish-language TV channel in Bolivia and, in line with its courting of other ALBA countries, relations were 'very close'.[21] Over the years, Iran increased its diplomatic presence and the two countries supported each other at the UN level. For instance, speaking at the UNGA, Morales accused the US of 'meddling in Iran' in 2018 (Al Jazeera 2018). Foreign observers speculate that bilateral defence and security agreements may have included access to Bolivian passports for Iranian citizens, 'a strategy Teheran has already used in Venezuela to infiltrate the region' (Ziemer, Dolbaia, and Droin 2024, 5).

Whereas the MAS's thick ideology played a prominent role in Bolivia's intensification of relations with ALBA members and with Brazil, Morales's

---

[19] Interview B03. China and Russia in 2023 signed agreements for the large-scale extraction of lithium in Bolivia (D. Ramos 2023).

[20] Interviews B24; B16.

[21] Interview B24.

turn to Russia and Iran was motivated more by their offering an alternative pole in international politics.[22] In fact, Bolivia under Morales was 'uniquely divorced from its traditional Washington-friendly orientation' pursuing the 'central objective [. . .] to break from the past and move toward an uncharted, left-leaning future, with primary attention being directed toward domestic affairs, rather than foreign policy'(Birns and Sanchez 2011, 103). As outlined in Chapters 3 and 5, Morales publicly displayed his personal proximity to the (at that time) hugely popular Chávez. Moreover, according to our interviews, Chávez quickly became one of his—if not the—most important foreign policy advisors to Bolivia's president. It was he and Castro who recommended to turn to Iran, China, and Russia.[23] Besides personalization of decision making, also mobilization played a role in driving the radical reorientation of Bolivia's foreign policy under the populist presidency of Morales. As we discussed in previous chapters, being against the US was a foundational element of Morales's thick ideology, which was further reinforced by an anti-elitist component (with the US being depicted as the leading actor in a global capitalist and imperialist elite system). Turning to alternative partners was a logical conclusion for a small country like Bolivia at the same time that Morales's anti-imperialist discourse mirrored elements of Chinese and Russian anti-Western propaganda. As put by a former diplomat under Morales: 'There was a strong ideological affinity with China.'[24] However, Morales in his first term in office in particular instrumentalized his opposition to the US to publicly 'justify his rapprochement with what later came to be called 21st century socialism.'[25] Moreover, as detailed in Plagemann et al. (2022), the most drastic measures vis-à-vis the US occurred at times in which Morales's political leadership was challenged domestically.

At the same time, the deepening of relations with China, Russia, and other countries opposed to the US remained a more permanent policy guideline, motivated both by ideological factors and by substantive interests from infrastructure funding to extractive industries. All this, together with Morales's personal involvement and 'friendship' with leaders from Putin to Ahmadinejad and Xi,[26] contributed to the most drastic case of foreign policy reorientation among those analysed in this book.

---

[22] Interview B24.
[23] Interview B16.
[24] Interview B02.
[25] Interview B29, Bolivian foreign relations analyst and former senior diplomat, La Paz, 22 March 2023.
[26] Interview B03.

Turkey

Turkey during the populist phase under Erdoğan was the other case of a radical reorientation, albeit less complete than Morales's Bolivia. As mentioned above, we consider a reorientation to be radical if the country's main international partners are essentially replaced with new ones—and in the case of Turkey, indeed, Erdoğan quite substantially distanced himself from Western partners over time and built a range of new partnerships.

As we discussed in detail in Chapter 5, the process of EU accession was shattered and Erdoğan in his rhetoric began attacking the 'West' from the early 2010s onwards. In fact, according to a journalist we interviewed, Erdoğan's turn away from the West started with the 'Davos crisis' of 2009, when he stormed out of a debate with Israel's Shimon Peres at the World Economic Forum following a clash over Israel's offensive in Gaza, and it further intensified with the Gezi Park protests in 2013:

> Western support for the protests made [Erdoğan] very angry. When does he get angry? Approximately six months before the elections. He used to escalate tensions and his main target was the opposition media [. . .]. He realized that the West abandoned him. At that time, Erdoğan had also intelligence about how Gezi Park protests were encouraged from outside. Erdoğan implicitly declared the European countries as his enemies. Some people who were working in NGOs were accused of espionage and arrested. These arrests increased the tension between Turkey and Europe.[27]

Among the many examples of Erdoğan's hostility towards Turkey's traditional partners in Europe and North America, and the use of this topic for domestic mobilization, was the discourse around the conversion of the iconic Hagia Sophia into a mosque. Formerly a Christian church and Turkey's most prominent tourist site, this was championed by Erdoğan personally and defended publicly as a 'victory against the Christian West' (Öztürk 2020). Other instances of open frictions with the West included the detention of US priest Andrew Brunson in Turkey and the refusal on the part of Washington to extradite Fethullah Gülen as well as the introduction of new tariffs by the US during President Trump's first administration (Martin 2019). Indeed, personal ties between Erdoğan and Trump could not offset the overall negative trend in Turkish-US relations during the first Trump administration (Ülgül 2019, 175–76)—ultimately revealing some of the limits of populist

---

[27] Interview T11, senior Turkish journalist, Istanbul, 13 April 2023.

leader-level bromances.[28] In distancing himself so clearly from the US and the West more generally, Erdoğan moved away from a longer-term consensus in Turkish foreign policy that had seen the country firmly embedded in NATO and cultivating close relations with the US and European partners. While this relationship had not been without frictions—think of Erdoğan's predecessor Ecevit accusing Western countries of not doing enough to suppress Kurdish activism (Republic of Türkiye Ministry of Foreign Affairs 1999a)—it had been a key pillar in Turkish foreign policy.

Erdoğan's approach to NATO mirrored his distancing from the US and the West as he became more populist over time. This entailed two main aspects: first, at the rhetorical level, Erdoğan became increasingly critical of NATO. While highlighting Turkish contributions to NATO and emphasizing his commitment to the organization, Erdoğan argued that NATO should be more engaged in Syria, supporting Turkish efforts in fighting DAESH (the so-called Islamic State), and that it should more generally live up to 'global challenges' (Presidency of the Republic of Türkiye 2020a; 2021a). The second dimension in Erdoğan's shifting approach to NATO entailed an increasingly transactional attitude and the adoption of policies that challenged the alliance's basic tenets. Most emblematic in this regard was Turkey's acquisition in 2019 of the Russian S-400 missile defence system. This led to a strong reaction on the part of the US, as Turkey was removed from the F-35 fighter jet consortium and the US Congress imposed sanctions on Turkey in 2020 (Danforth and Stein 2024). Moreover, Erdoğan blackmailed NATO by stalling the accession of Finland and Sweden after their application for membership in the wake of Russia's invasion of Ukraine in 2022. Erdoğan argued that the two Scandinavian countries were not doing enough to fight terrorism as they were harbouring PKK and FETO members. Ultimately, however, despite concessions being made to Turkey on counter-terrorism (NATO 2023), it was the United States agreeing to sell forty new F-16 fighter jets to Turkey that induced Erdoğan to greenlight these countries' NATO membership (Danforth and Stein 2024). In any case, Turkey did not leave NATO. Instead, Erdoğan outlined his approach as follows in a speech after the 2024 NATO summit:

> Türkiye is a country that cannot be confined to a single bloc due to its geographical, social, economic and historical ties. Strengthening our cooperation with other regions from Asia to Africa and Latin America is as important to us

---

[28] Interview T10, Gürkan Emre Melikoğlu, Turkish journalist, Istanbul, 10 April 2023. On the Trump-Erdoğan relationship also see the memoir by Trump's National Security Advisor H. R. McMaster (McMaster 2024)

as improving our relations with the Western world. We will never allow anyone to confine us to their own constricted patterns. (Presidency of the Republic of Türkiye 2024)

One key element in this reorientation of international partnerships was Turkey's closer cooperation with Putin's Russia. This seems surprising given the centuries-old legacy of wars and competition between the Ottoman and the Russian empires—entities which Erdoğan and Putin habitually referred to, underscoring the greatness of their respective nation. More than that, the rapprochement was surprising because the two countries pursued widely diverging interests in several violent conflicts. Turkey in 2016 militarily intervened in the Syrian civil war in support of the Syrian National Army, an armed opposition coalition, and occupied parts of northern Syria. Meanwhile, Russia's air force was of crucial importance for Bashar al-Assad's regime survival and the Syrian army. Moreover, Ankara armed its ally Azerbaijan in the Nagorno-Karabakh conflict with Armenia, in opposition to Russia's role as Armenia's treaty ally and de facto security patron. In 2015 Turkish-Russian relations reached their lowest point since the end of the Cold War, after Turkey shot down a Russian jet on the Turkish-Syrian border (Ülgül 2019). Personal leader-level diplomacy played a major role in the rapprochement between Turkey and Russia and the subsequent consolidations of relations, as confirmed by our interviews.[29] Reportedly, it was a phone call by Erdoğan to Putin that initially alleviated the crisis, and direct bilateral interactions between the two leaders intensified markedly in the following years: 'Erdoğan and Putin met with each other thirteen times and had eight phone conversations in 2018 alone, all of which played a significant role in the coordination of regional policies and the strengthening of relations' (Ülgül 2019). Erdoğan reportedly chose to buy the Russian S-400 air defence system, 'without full consultation with the Turkish foreign ministry' and possibly with the primary aim of securing the presidential palace (Toygür et al. 2022, 11). Driven by personal ties, bilateral relations with Russia strengthened over time. They also included cooperation in the field of intelligence, as revealed by Turkey allowing a Russian special forces team to destroy a Russian intelligence ship that had sunk in the Black Sea in 2018.[30] After Russia's invasion of Ukraine in February 2022, Erdoğan sought to maintain ties with Moscow while also showing support for Ukraine, and serving as a mediator between the conflict parties (see Chapter 4). Turkey did not join the West in imposing sanctions

---

[29] Interviews T10; T04, retired Turkish diplomat, Istanbul, 23 March 2023.
[30] Interview T11.

on Russia (while still observing some secondary sanctions, for example by having Turkish banks cut their ties to Russian ones), and it benefitted from cheap oil imports from Russia as well as from selling re-labelled fuel products from Russia to European countries, thus helping Russia circumvent sanctions (Bechev 2024; Jack 2024). All this temporarily made Russia (instead of China) the biggest source of imports for Turkey in late 2022 and early 2023 (TÜİK Turkish Statistical Institute 2023; 2022). Moreover, despite differences over a number of issues such as the war in Syria, Turkey and Russia increasingly found themselves on the same anti-Western front in the context of Israel's war against Hamas in Gaza following the terrorist attack of 7 October 2023 (Suleymanov 2023).

China was another player in Erdoğan's reorientation of Turkey's international partnerships away from the West. While he had been critical of China during the non-populist phase, up to the point of openly accusing China of committing a genocide in the Muslim-majority region of Xinjiang in 2009 (Reuters 2009), Erdoğan gradually moved closer to China. From 2015 onwards, the Turkish government stopped its public condemnations of China's oppression of Uyghurs in Xinjiang, while Uyghur activists were increasingly prevented from operating in Turkey (Yıldırım 2024). Economic cooperation intensified as Turkey and China signed a Strategic Partnership Agreement in 2010 and Turkey joined the Belt and Road Initiative (BRI) in 2015 (Öniş and Yalikun 2021). In that context, Chinese foreign direct investment (FDI) to Turkey grew tremendously, from $82 million before Turkey joined the BRI to $1.7 billion in 2022 (TCMB 2024). The new proximity to Russia and China did not just have economic implications but was increasingly framed by Erdoğan as an alternative to Turkey's relationships with Western countries. Erdoğan during his populist phase expressed his desire for Turkey to join the Shanghai Cooperation Organization (SCO) as a full member, explicitly presenting this as an alternative to EU membership: '"Take us to Shanghai and relieve us from this pain", Erdoğan told the Russian President Vladimir Putin in a joint press conference. He also added that Turkey is "ready to ink free trade agreements with countries in Eurasia". Erdoğan further stressed that Turkey has more values in common with the Shanghai Five, which, he thinks, is better and more powerful than the EU in both political and economic terms' (Taş 2014).

In the Middle East, after the Arab Spring uprisings, Erdoğan supported Islamist actors, first and foremost the Muslim Brotherhood (MB-Ikhwan and its various offshoots), along with Qatar. This put Turkey at odds with countries such as Saudi Arabia, the United Arab Emirates (UAE), Bahrain, and Egypt, which designated Ikhwan as a terrorist organization and perceived the

MB as a threat. Among the episodes that marked a deterioration in Turkey's relations with these Arab states were the 2017 Gulf Cooperation Council (GCC) crisis, which saw Saudi Arabia, the UAE, Egypt, and Bahrain cutting their diplomatic ties with Qatar, and Turkey supporting Qatar with troops and supplies. Moreover, the murder of Jamal Khashoggi, a Saudi dissident and journalist, at the Saudi consulate in Istanbul in 2018 further contributed to a worsening of Saudi-Turkish relations (Taş 2022b, 730–31). Domestic mobilization was a key driver in Turkey's support for the MB, as foreign policy issues were regularly politicized by the AKP, as described by Yesilyurt (2017):

> by supporting the MB and identifying closely with it, the AKP has sought to present itself as the guardian of the oppressed against the authoritarian regimes of the Arab world. The AKP has always claimed to be the representative of the oppressed in Turkey, but now it extends this vision by claiming to represent all oppressed peoples in the region. In this way, it seeks to fortify its domestic legitimacy. [. . .] it simultaneously equates its Turkish and Kurdish opponents with authoritarian regimes and the forces of counter-revolution in the region, and as major enemies of the MB. Thus, Turkish opposition parties and movements are continuously presented by the government as being 'Baathist', 'Assadist', or 'supporters of coups d'état'. In this way, the political cleavages within regional countries are systematically used and intentionally internalized by the AKP in order to reproduce and deepen the ongoing political cleavages and polarization within Turkey.

Ultimately, after 2020, relations with Arab states became less tense, also thanks to a more general détente in the region following the Abraham Accords between Israel and several Arab countries. Meanwhile, relations with Iran remained fraught after Turkey and Iran found themselves on opposing sides during the Syrian civil war. Still, Erdoğan and the Iranian President continued meeting (with the exception of the years 2019 and 2021) in the context of a yearly bilateral 'High-Level Cooperation Council' format.[31]

However, the region in which Erdoğan's efforts towards a diversification of partnerships and foreign policy activism are most evident is Africa. While an 'Africa Opening Action Plan' had already been developed in the pre-Erdoğan era in 1998, it was under the AKP that Turkey began pursuing its interests in Africa systematically. Erdoğan made this a personal priority, travelling to dozens of African countries and promoting the expansion of Turkish embassies (forty-four by 2022). By 2024, Turkish Airlines flew to sixty-one destinations in forty African countries (Heibach and Taş 2024a, 315).

---

[31] Interview T01, Turkish academic, Istanbul, 8 March 2023.

Moreover, between 2003 and 2020, bilateral trade grew from $5.4 billion to $25.3 billion, and Turkish FDI to the region jumped from $100 million to $6.5 billion (Heibach and Taş 2024b). Beyond the economic dimension, Turkey has sent troops to UN peacekeeping operations in Mali and other African countries, and it maintains an overseas military base in Somalia since 2017, where it engages in joint military training (Heibach and Taş 2024a, 315). Clearly, the deepening of relations with Africa were first and foremost a political project, driven by Erdoğan's vision of Turkey as a 'Afro-Eurasian state'—a vision that entails an even greater projection of power as compared to previous understandings of Turkey's sphere of influence reaching 'from the Adriatic Sea to the Great Wall of China' (Heibach and Taş 2024a, 315). This drive towards Africa dovetailed well with Erdoğan's anti-Western rhetoric, as he explicitly presented his country's initiatives as (better) alternatives to those of Western powers:

> Believing that Africa will have a determining role in the 21st century, we want to advance our relations with the continent on the basis of win-win and equal partnership. As I always say, we never approach our cooperation with African countries from a short-term and interest-oriented perspective. We are not one of those who seek to maintain their old colonial orders through new ways and methods. We desire to walk and win with our African brothers and sisters. (Presidency of the Republic of Türkiye 2021b)

All this was paralleled by Erdoğan reaching out to a number of other authoritarian or populist leaders, from Hungarian Prime Minister Viktor Orbán, from whom he got inspiration for his anti-LGBT campaign (SCF 2023), to President Maduro in Venezuela ('Maduro brother, stand tall, Turkey stands with you!', see Oner 2020), to Prime Minister Edi Rama in Albania (Madhi 2021). Overall, therefore, we consider Turkish foreign policy to clearly reorient away from the West and towards new, alternative partners, many of which autocratic.

Strong Personalization, Weak Mobilization

India

Under populist Prime Minister Modi, India's overall foreign policy orientation changed partially, with a rapprochement to the US and the West paired with a broader drive towards a diversification of international partnerships.

Both developments were a continuation of pre-existing trends, to which Prime Minister Modi gave a new impetus via his personal engagement in foreign policy.

Since independence, India has had a long tradition of pursuing what can be summarized as an 'independent' foreign policy. India's first prime minister (and minister of external affairs), Jawaharlal Nehru, shaped India's approach to the world right after independence by devising non-alignment as the most suitable strategy for a poor and weak young country like India to navigate world politics. At that time, non-alignment implied that India and other developing countries refused to join one of the two Cold War blocs led by the US and the Soviet Union, respectively. For Nehru, non-alignment was, on the one hand, a way to present India as a force for good, a 'moral' player in international politics, and as a leader of the 'Third World'. On the other, it was a policy used strategically by a weak country to punch above its weight while maximizing its autonomy vis-à-vis the two great powers. However, ultimately, India's non-alignment did not mean a policy of equidistance from the two blocs, as New Delhi over time moved closer to the Soviet Union, with which it signed a Treaty of Friendship in 1971 (Harshe 1990; Keenleyside 1980). Besides at times conflicting interests with the US, Nehru's leftist ideology, with its anti-imperialism, made him and Indian elites deeply sceptical of the United States (Ganguly and Pardesi 2009).

With the end of the Cold War, the notion of pursuing an independent foreign policy and of not binding India to one single great power remained the central tenet of India's approach to the world. After India liberalized its economy in 1991 and gradually benefitted from globalization and economic relations with the West, its traditional scepticism of the US became less visible. The Clinton administration sought to improve ties with India. However, India's nuclear weapons tests of 1998 complicated a rapprochement, since the US 'did not want to compromise on its goal of non-proliferation' (Pant 2007) and imposed sanctions on India. It was under the UPA I government that a remarkable shift took place, with India and the US signing the Civil Nuclear Agreement in 2005—an agreement that de facto recognized India as a nuclear weapons state despite India's not having signed the Nuclear Non-Proliferation Treaty. Among other things, it obligated India to separate civil and military nuclear facilities and to put the civil ones under the safeguard of the International Atomic Energy Agency (IAEA) (The White House 2005); the US, in turn, asked the Nuclear Suppliers Group (NSG) to give India access to civilian nuclear fuel and technology, something that was ultimately allowed in 2008 (Varadarajan 2008). Within India and beyond, the so-called nuclear deal was widely perceived as a game changer for India's rise to great power status, finally putting an end to what had been decried by previous Indian governments as 'nuclear apartheid' (J. Singh 1998), that is, India's exclusion from the club of nuclear powers. Beyond this rapprochement with the US, India's non-populist UPA I and UPA II governments carried on with the Nehruvian-inspired notion of an independent foreign policy, variously rebranded as 'non-alignment 2.0' (Khilnani et al. 2012) or 'strategic autonomy' (Raja Mohan 2008; Monsonis 2010). The key principles thus remained the same, with India refusing to bind itself to a single international partner or to enter any formal alliance. Therefore, despite the rapprochement with the US, India continued cultivating friendly ties with countries like Russia, which as the successor state to the Soviet Union remained its main supplier of weapons (see below). In parallel, it expanded its range of 'strategic partnerships' with countries ranging from Afghanistan to the UK and the European Union (I. Hall 2016, 277), and it joined minilateral groupings such as the BRICS, IBSA, and the G-20, thus further diversifying its international partnerships (I. Hall 2016).

Under populist Prime Minister Modi, all language reminiscent of Nehru's imprint on foreign policy was removed from India's foreign policy discourse (I. Hall 2017). The Indian government refrained from using the rhetoric of non-alignment, and Modi, for example, did not attend any of the in-person Non-Aligned Movement (NAM) summits that were held since 2014 (G. Singh 2024). However, the basic notion of pursuing a foreign policy that would not make India dependent on a single international partner remained very much in place (Basrur 2017). In fact, the 'multi-alignment' that had already been initiated under the UPA governments was pursued 'more energetically' (I. Hall 2016, 281) by India's populist government.

One important component of this shift was India's ever closer rapprochement with the US and other Western countries under Modi, mainly in an effort to balance against China—albeit paying attention not to be instrumentalized as a balancer by the US.[32] In fact, among the most substantive changes in Indian foreign policy in the years 2014–2024 was the development of extensive security cooperation with the United States, building upon what the UPA government had initiated. In 2016, the US elevated India to the status of a 'Major Defense Partner', thus allowing for levels of military technology-sharing comparable to those with the United States' main allies. In the following years, the two countries signed a number of important agreements, including the Logistics Exchange Memorandum of Agreement (LEMOA) (2016), which focused on military logistics; the Communications

---

[32] On India's approach to China, see Chapter 3.

Compatibility and Security Agreement (COMCASA) (2018); and the Basic Exchange and Cooperation Agreement (BECA) for Geospatial Intelligence (2020) (Joshua White 2021). These accords 'increas[ed] the synergy and interoperability between the two militaries' (Kumar and Bharadwaj 2024). Moreover, the US granted India Strategic Trade Authority-1 (STA-1) status, which allows entities from the US to give India license-free access to advanced dual-use technologies (Kumar and Bharadwaj 2024). In turn, India changed its regulation on defence acquisition so as to allow joint development and production with foreign partners. From 2023, the initiative on Critical and Emerging Technologies (iCET) promoted the co-development of military technologies including the private sector. To bring together defence companies, start-ups, investors, and universities, the India-US Defence Accelerator Ecosystem (INDUS-X) was created in 2023. According to observers, INDUS-X 'has finally institutionalized a process that meets India's decades-long demand for defense technology cooperation while advancing the Pentagon's concept of integrated deterrence by bolstering Indian defense capabilities, diversifying supply chains and building trust for deeper operational cooperation between [the] two militaries' (Lalwani and Singh 2024).

Besides defence cooperation, India under Modi intensified India's participation in the 'Quad', a minilateral grouping also involving the US, Australia, and Japan. While the Quadrilateral Security Initiative was initiated by Japanese Prime Minister Shinzo Abe in 2007, it re-emerged with new vigour after 2017 as a reaction to China's increasingly assertive policies (Roy-Chaudhury and Sullivan de Estrada 2018). Representatives of the Quad states, such as the foreign ministers at a roundtable at the Raisina Dialogue in 2023 (Observer Research Foundation 2023), have emphasized that the Quad does not focus on security issues but on a broad range of areas. For example, the Quad introduced a humanitarian assistance and disaster relief mechanism. However, its main strengths remain high-level as well as more technical consultations around issues of 'maritime security, technology, supply chains, cybersecurity, counterterrorism, countering disinformation, and space' (Madan 2022, 52). While Indian interlocutors emphasize that the Quad is not an alliance, it entails, among other things, 'some substantive intelligence sharing',[33] efforts to increase interoperability, and joint naval exercises.[34] Thus, according to one expert we interviewed, India's engagement in the Quad has been 'the most important strategic shift' of the past years.[35] Besides

---

[33] Interview I01, expert on India's foreign policy, New Delhi, 20 February 2023.
[34] Since 2020, the yearly Malabar exercises, which in the past involved India and the US, and later also Japan, have involved all four Quad members, even though they were not openly related to the Quad.
[35] Interview I01.

defence aspects, the Quad should be seen as 'a technology alliance, your way of saying "I'm going to write the rules". Among others, "open random access networks" will be established, which are an open access technology for communication that is software based. Huawei will be out'.[36] Still, much in the spirit of maintaining its independence in foreign policy, the Indian government in the context of the Quad has been careful to avoid common normative statements about a supposedly 'liberal' character of the Indo-Pacific (Sullivan de Estrada 2023).

India's engagement with the United States and other shifts towards Western partners were very much driven personally by Prime Minister Modi. This became clear as early as in January 2015, when President Obama was invited as the guest of honour to India's Republic Day celebrations. Modi visibly enjoyed the company of the US president, wearing a 1 million rupee suit displaying his name in small letters in the pinstripe design (BBC News 2015). Personalized politics became even more evident, however, during the first Trump administration, reinforced by public celebration of personal affinities between the two strongman leaders. Among the most remarkable episodes were two events during the second half of Trump's first administration. At the 'Howdy Modi' event, a large gathering of the Indian diaspora in Houston, Texas, in 2019, Modi and Trump praised each other in front of cheering crowds (BBC 2019). Trump's return visit to India took place in February 2020, the beginning of his campaign for re-election, where he spoke to a crowd of more than 100,000 at the world's largest cricket stadium (BBC 2020). Under the Biden administration, this intense inter-personal component between the two leaders was missing, but relations remained close, with Biden inviting Modi to a state visit to Washington, DC, in 2023 and stating that the 'friendship between the United States and India is among the most consequential in the world. And it's stronger, closer, and more dynamic than ever' (President Biden [@POTUS] 2023). The agreements signed on that occasion concerned defence-industrial cooperation and investments in the semiconductor sector (BBC 2023). According to Pant and Lall (2024, 9), for the Indian government, '[o]ne reason behind this growing strategic embrace lies in individual conviction. The US remains essential to Modi's vision of India's radical transformation. The success of his many ambitious plans for India's economic transformation, from "Make in India" to "Digital India", hinges upon greater cooperation with the US'.

In sum, while the seed for the India-US rapprochement was sown during the UPA era, the intensity with which Modi pursued bilateral ties was

---

[36] Interview I01.

new and certainly constituted a shift away from India's traditional deep scepticism of the US and the West more generally. As one interviewee put it, 'Modi['s government is the] most pro-Western government—pro-Western but anti-liberal'.[37] This focus on the US was strongly driven personally by Modi: according to another expert we interviewed in Delhi, '[t]he first country he [Modi] cleaned up relations with was the US. I was told the most pro-US person in your country is your PM'.[38] The other key actor driving relations with the US was External Affairs Minister Jaishankar, who had served as Indian ambassador to the US in 2013–2015, that is, during the transition from the UPA II to the first government under Prime Minister Modi. According to one of our interviewees, Jaishankar was selected for the post also due to his good connections to the US establishment: 'Pompeo in his book writes that he didn't like Sushma Swaraj. The Americans have been happiest with Jaishankar. He has good connections with the Americans. And he is "the US' man in India". Now he is probably working to quietly convince the US about India's positions'.[39]

Except for the diaspora in the US, which is an important vote bank for the BJP and was the object of massive mobilization efforts on the part of Modi (Rana 2023; Dubey 2024), mobilization around stronger India-US ties was not very prevalent, except at the beginning, around Obama's 2015 visit. At that time, Modi invited the US president to participate in his Mann Ki Baat radio address to the people, even replying to questions asked by ordinary Indians (narendramodi.in 2015). Interestingly, Modi did not further harness the overall favourable views of the US held by Indians, which remained constant over time. According to Pew Research surveys, in the years between 2002 and 2010, on average 65.7% of Indians held favourable views of the United States (Pew Research Center 2010), and also in 2023, the share of Indians seeing the US in favourable terms was 65% (Huang, Fagan, and Gubbala 2023). By contrast, according to an expert interviewed, in the BJP basis, there is 'a lot of anti-Western sentiment. But there is a large diaspora and he [Modi] can unilaterally make decisions'.[40] Despite all the rapprochement to the US, however, we also saw the Modi government antagonizing India's Western partners. In 2023, the Indian intelligence service reportedly assassinated a separatist Sikh activist in Canada, and it tried to assassinate another activist, who held US citizenship, on US soil (Bal 2023). Widely seen as both unprecedented and unexpected, this led to the breakdown of relations with Canada and major

---

[37] I16, Indian journalist, New Delhi, 7 March 2023.
[38] I01.
[39] Interview I03, Indian journalist, New Delhi, 22 February 2023.
[40] Interview I06, Indian scholar and observer, New Delhi, 28 February 2023.

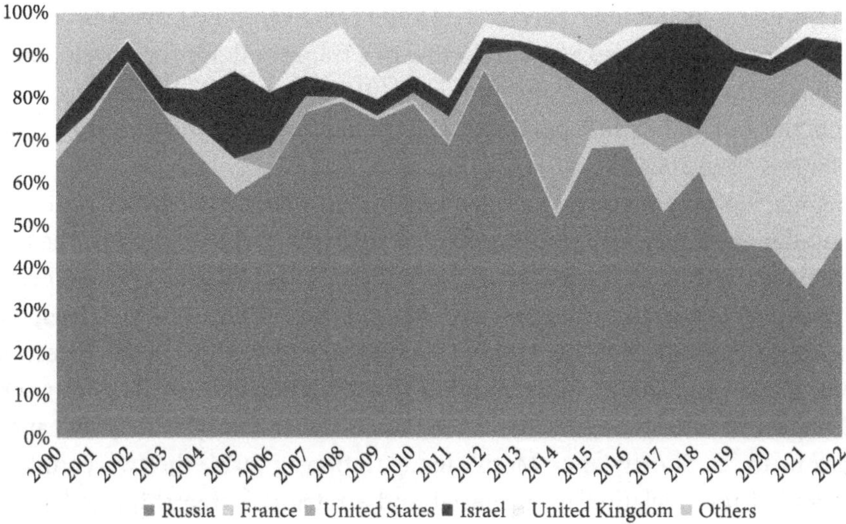

Figure 6.1 India's arms imports
Source: SIPRI Arms Transfers Database (2 April 2023)

diplomatic irritations with Washington, revealing to what extent the Indian government was willing to challenge the relationship with the US to pursue domestic goals.

However, in its turn to the West the Modi government has not focused on the US alone. As Figure 6.1 shows, France too has become a major security partner. As a fellow proponent of a 'multipolar world', aligning with France promises greater leeway and fewer strings attached: 'India's institutional hesitations are plausibly less intense in relation to France, a middle power that comes with much less political baggage than the United States' (C. R. Mohan and Baruah 2018, 2). The election of Emmanuel Macron as president in 2017 energized bilateral relations, especially so in arms procurement and maritime security. Enthusiastically adopting the 'Indo-Pacific' in his geopolitical vocabulary, keen on showcasing France's global role, and open to French arms manufacturers' interests, Macron successfully sought to deepen ties with the world's largest arms importer. For India, France's liberal policies on arms exports including in high-tech products as well as its geopolitical vocabulary around strategic autonomy and a multipolar world promised an alternative to the US-China binary abhorred in New Delhi. Beyond security, the two countries cooperate in energy and they established trilaterals with Australia and the United Arab Emirates (Malhotra 2023). Macron and Modi displayed their personal affinity at multiple visits and return visits, including as chief guests to India's Republic Day in 2024 and France's Bastille Day a year earlier. The latter occasion also saw the signing of a framework for the development of bilateral relations under the grandiose title 'Horizon 2047', referring to the centenary of India's independence as well as the establishment of bilateral relations (Rao 2024).

Albeit less focused on arms procurement, Indo-Japanese relations followed a similar trajectory with traditionally friendly relations energized by the personal involvement of the two countries' leaders. Like Macron, Japanese Prime Minister Abe was an early proponent of the Indo-Pacific, on which he spoke to India's parliament in his famous 'Confluence of the Two Seas' speech in 2007 (S. V. Singh 2022). Moreover, like France, Japan is a middle power with strengths in industry and science seen as complementary to its own capacities in India. Shortly after Modi's inauguration in 2014, the two countries upgraded their relation to a 'special and strategic partnership', and Japan became the first country with which India established a yearly 2+2 dialogue of ministers of defence and foreign affairs (Miller 2022). Under Modi, Japan began exporting its Shinkansen bullet train to India and, in 2016, the two countries signed a civil nuclear pact. Moreover, Japan is one of the few donor countries with a visible presence in India, including in India's fragile northeastern region (Borah 2022). Calling him a 'dear friend' with a 'personal bond', Modi declared a day of national mourning upon Abe's assassination in 2022 (Miller 2022).

In parallel to the improvement of relations with Western countries, under Modi, India's relations with Russia remained close. Although Russia remained an important provider of weapons, the share of arms imports from Russia declined over time. As illustrated in Figure 6.1, while in the early 2000s, almost 90% of the weapons imported by India came from Russia, and in 2011 that share was still similar, in 2016, India imported around 65% of its weapons from Russia, while in 2022 that share amounted to less than 50%. India under Modi's government very visibly diversified its weapons purchases, with the US, Israel, and France becoming important additional arms exporters to India.

The Indian prime minister's response to Russia's full-scale invasion of Ukraine in February 2022 exemplified his efforts at cultivating multiple international partnerships in parallel. Numerous European heads of government visited New Delhi in 2022 to bring India into the Western camp, but to no avail. India for long refrained from condemning Russia and refused to participate in the imposition of sanctions promoted by Western countries (Zakharov 2024; Warren and Ganguly 2022). Modi's government made use of this peculiar situation in which the West was courting India: as an interviewee at a government-friendly think tank put it in March 2023, 'India is now in a sweet spot'.[41] Indeed, the Indian economy benefitted tremendously from cheap oil imports from Russia, which contributed to a growth rate of 7.6% in 2023 (World Bank 2024). In September 2022, Modi addressed Putin by stating, 'I know that today's era is not of war and we have talked to you many times over the phone on the subject that democracy and diplomacy and dialogue are all these things that touch the world [sic]' (Pratap 2022)—a formulation that was sure not to offend the Russian president (see Chapter 4).

And indeed, in relations with Russia, the personal component of Modi's affinity for Putin played an important role, reinforcing a long-established partnership. At the same time, according to an interviewee, India's approach to Russia under Modi's populist government first and foremost exemplifies the government's new pragmatism: 'What is different [under Modi is that] these people are not afraid to seem opportunistic': India bought Russian oil because it was cheap, and there was 'no moralizing about this. Previously, that used to be cloaked under moralistic stuff'.[42] Also, 'buying [cheap] oil from Russia [was] framed [to the domestic public in India] as "We are taking care of the people's interests"'.[43] This policy found broad support among the Indian public: according to a survey by Pew Research, in spring 2023, 71% of Indians interviewed thought that their country should maintain access to Russia's oil and gas reserves (Fagan, Poushter, and Gubbala 2023).

A further remarkable development in India's foreign policy was a broad diversification of international partnerships that Prime Minister Modi pursued in virtually all world regions: 'Broadening the bandwidth of India's international diplomacy, via an ever-widening multi-directional diplomatic strategy, illustrates this aim as New Delhi seeks new trade and energy partners across Asia, Africa, and South America' (Ogden 2018, 9). Within single regions, this frequently meant cooperating with different, even opposed partners at the same time. This was most evident in India's approach to the Middle East. There, New Delhi's relations with the UAE, but also with Saudi Arabia as well as with Iran, improved considerably. As Blarel (2022, 100) puts it, 'Modi's multiple and repeated visits to the Gulf countries have been an effort to build on and consolidate existing economic ties', but they also increasingly had a security dimension: 'These interactions and agreements have included high-level strategic security dialogues (UAE), inter-state defence cooperation agreements (Qatar, Oman, UAE, Saudi Arabia), intelligence and counter-terrorism cooperation (Saudi Arabia, UAE, Bahrain, Qatar) and convergence

---

[41] Interview I12, retired Indian diplomat at think tank, New Delhi, 2 March 2023.
[42] Interview I01.
[43] Interview I03.

in enhancing maritime security in the Indian Ocean region' (Blarel 2022, 100). The sizeable Indian diaspora in countries such as Saudi Arabia (around 2 million Indians in 2019) and the UAE (around 2.3 million) (Blarel 2019, 28) increased the salience of these countries for Modi. This improvement of relations with Muslim-majority countries that traditionally had had close relations with Pakistan again reveals how Hindu-nationalist ideology, with its Islamophobic reverberations, was used strategically for mobilization mostly against Pakistan in the context of the bilateral India-Pakistan conflict, but rarely with reference to other countries.

At the same time, Modi also personally promoted closer cooperation with Israel, another change of course, as India had traditionally supported the Palestinian cause. In 2018, Modi broke protocol by welcoming his right-wing populist counterpart from Israel, Benjamin Netanyahu, at the airport (Ministry of Foreign Affairs 2018). This visit was preceded by an equally much-publicized visit by Modi to Israel—the first by an Indian prime minister to that country. Images of Netanyahu and Modi wading barefoot in the sea at a beach in northern Israel provided a visualization of the 'bromance' between the two leaders (AFP 2017). In fact, this was the culmination of a longer process of deepening diplomatic ties between India and Israel (Blarel 2015). While the two countries had established diplomatic relations only in 1992, already the government led by Manmohan Singh had started establishing defence ties with Israel. Modi made that cooperation public and gave it greater impetus (Blarel 2019). Thus, a strategic partnership was established with Israel, weapons are being co-produced, and India became the largest importer of weapons from Israel (SIPRI 2024; Scharf 2024). Publicization of this notwithstanding, Modi did not mobilize much around the relations with Israel given the overall still very sceptical attitudes of the Indian public vis-à-vis that country. This became all the more evident after 7 October 2023 and Israel's war against Hamas in Gaza, which was much criticized among the Indian public (Jangid 2023) and forced Modi to slightly tone down his support for Netanyahu. For example, after abstaining on an UNGA resolution calling for a ceasefire but failing to condemn Hamas shortly after 7 October, India voted in favour of a very similar resolution two months later (Ali Abbas 2024). Moreover, External Affairs Minister Jaishankar repeatedly called for a two-state solution (e.g., The Indian Express 2024).

Finally, another component of India's intensified multi-alignment was a renewed interest in the wider 'Global South'. This manifested in a greater engagement in development cooperation (see Chapter 4), understood as South-South cooperation (Destradi and Gurol 2022) as well as in diplomatic initiatives. Modi reformulated India's decades-old 'Look East Policy' into 'Act East', thus emphasizing the importance of deepening ties with South-east Asia. In his second year in office, Modi revived the triennial India-Africa Forum Summit first held in 2008, inviting African leaders to New Delhi. India remained an active member of the BRICS, which in 2024 gained four new members, and it successfully sought full membership of the Shanghai Cooperation Organization in 2017. Moreover, in January 2023 India for the first time hosted a virtual summit titled 'Voice of the Global South', uniting government representatives from Africa, Latin America, Southeastern Europe, the Middle East, and Asia (a second summit took place in 2024). The Indian government also used its presidency of the G-20 to formalize an invitation for the African Union to join the grouping. Although a fairly consensual move, New Delhi referred to this as proof of its role as leading power in the Global South (India Today 2024a). However, the Global South remains a vague category with relatively little concrete policy content beyond expressions of solidarity. The India-Africa Forum Summit failed to meet for nine years after 2015, a lacuna that cannot solely be attributed to the pandemic, and India's engagement, overall, stood in continuity with its long tradition of claiming to represent the Global South.

To conclude, the transition from the non-populist Congress-led governments of Manmohan Singh to the BJP-led populist governments of Narendra Modi led to a partial reorientation of India's foreign policy. We consider this partial because the strengthening of new partnerships and especially the shift towards the US and the Quad did not involve a break with or a neglect of traditional partnerships such as that with Russia. Instead of a full-fledged reorientation, we observed a re-calibration of partnerships and an even stronger pursuit of a foreign policy of 'multialignment' than in the past (I. Hall 2016). Mobilization around this recalibration was not consistent or systematic. Whereas we saw instances of mobilization in relations with the US, as well as with regard to energy imports from Russia, other foreign policy issues such as the G-20 presidency or the conflict with Pakistan were used more systematically to mobilize support. At the same time, improved relations with several countries in the Middle East were more difficult to frame in terms of Hindu-nationalist thick ideology and mobilization around the rapprochement with Israel would have been counter-productive beyond the Hindu-nationalist core of Modi's supporters. In any case, India's recalibration of its international partnerships was clearly personally driven by Modi. Especially relationships with countries governed by fellow populist leaders such as Trump or Netanyahu were cherished, but at the same time populism 'as such' was not a sufficient driver for a radical reorientation—for example, there was not much room for a deepening of ties with fellow populists Erdoğan and

Duterte. Ultimately, India continued its course of pursuing an independent foreign policy, just with a new *verve*. As a retired diplomat summarized India's more pragmatic and diversified foreign relations, 'we have nobody we can call untouchable, this is our unique selling point'.[44]

The Philippines

The other case in which we saw a partial reorientation of international partnerships, mainly driven by strong personalization, was that of the Philippines. As we discussed in Chapter 3, the country had traditionally cultivated close relations with the United States. The Philippines had been a colony of the US from 1898, when Spain ceded it to the US, until 1946. After independence, relations remained close: the US maintained a number of military bases in the former colony (Supreme Court of the Philippines 2019), and in 1951 a mutual defence treaty was signed. Further, the two countries signed the Visiting Forces Agreement (VFA), which came into force in 1999 and revived military cooperation especially in view of growing Chinese expansionism in the South China Sea (De Castro 2010). Ultimately, being one of the so-called major non-NATO allies of the US, the Philippines relied on close relations with the US, and President Aquino's foreign policy followed this tradition (see Chapter 3). By contrast, relations with China were tense under his non-populist government, mainly due to maritime disputes in the South China Sea. As a senior military official put it, 'We were completely anti-China'.[45]

After coming to power, Duterte tried to change these fundamental tenets of the Philippines' foreign policy, and to give it a new imprint by developing the notion of an 'Independent Foreign Policy' (IFP). Duterte announced his IFP in September 2016, and he described the policy as one being founded on the observation of the 'time-honored principle of sovereignty, sovereign equality, non-interference and the commitment of peaceful settlements of dispute' (Philstar 2016). A month later, during a state visit to China, he declared his 'separation from the US, both in military and economics' and his realignment with China's 'ideological flow', further stating: 'There are 3 of us against the world—China, Philippines, Russia' (ABS-CNB 2016). Despite such bold statements, calling the IFP a new doctrine would be an overstatement. For instance, the government never developed a full-fledged document outlining the new parameters of the country's foreign policy. In particular, it was not detailed what 'independence' should mean exactly. According to most

---

[44] Interview I08, retired Indian diplomat, New Delhi, 1 March 2023.
[45] P06, senior military official, Manila, 4 October 2022.

experts interviewed in the Philippines, the IFP was not a genuine effort to devise a new international role for the country, but primarily a rationalization of Duterte's personal preference for a shift away from dependence on the US.

As discussed in Chapter 3, Duterte had long harboured a personal aversion towards the US, grounded, among other things, in a sense of injustice about the colonial past and the atrocities committed by the Americans at that time. One of our interviewees recalls Duterte's behaviour at a ceremony that saw the returning of the Balangiga Bells to their original location. Those church bells had been seized by the US as a war trophy in 1901 during the Philippine-American war. The bells had a highly symbolical value because their ringing had alerted American soldiers to an upcoming ambush by Filipino forces, which were killed as a consequence:

> We watched him put them back in the church they were taken from—by right of the rules of war: to the victor goes the spoils and trophies of war. What more that [*sic*] the ringing of those bells was the signal for the Filipinos to stage an ambush of American soldiers. But all the tolling of the bells achieved was to alert the Americans of the Filipino intention. [With] the tolling of the bells the initiative went to the Americans and the Filipinos were dead. Duterte stood in a small chapel and ran his hands slowly over the names of the dead etched in stone; his eyes tearing as if they had just been killed before his eyes and they were his kinsmen. At that moment Philippine foreign policy crossed a century wide divide to draw inspiration from the Balangiga massacre. Take it or leave it, that is how the policy was made. This was payback time. We [. . .] advised him not to take it so far; he took it farther. He remembered the wrongs done and unrequited; the good promised never delivered.[46]

Besides this sense of historical injustice, rumours abound that Duterte's aversion of the US was further driven by very personal issues: 'His visa was cancelled in 2003 [. . .]. They cancelled it because he was linked to the Davao Death Squad. He was forced to bring home Honeylet and Kitty (his second family) and this led to him divulging his secret'.[47] According to a Filipino senator, the US 'didn't know that they were doing this to the future president of the Philippines who has a vindictive character. When he became president, it was his golden opportunity to hit back at them'.[48] Also a former high-ranking

---

[46] Interview P01, former high-ranking government official, Manila, 26 September 2022.

[47] Interview P09, Filipino academic, Manila, 10 October 2022. See also P17, e-mail communication with former senior national security official under Aquino, 8 December 2022.

[48] Interview P07, Filipino Senator 2007 to 2019, Manila, 5 October 2022.

government official confirmed that calling into question the Philippines' traditional ties with the US was 'his way of getting back to those who oppressed him'.[49]

Ultimately, this detachment from the US manifested in a short-lived retraction of the Philippines from the Visiting Forces Agreement, which was personally ordered by Duterte, virtually without any consultation.[50] According to a journalist interviewed, 'both [Secretary of Defense] Lorenzana and [Secretary of Foreign Affairs] Locsin did not want to terminate the VFA. They stated this at the senate hearing. But they couldn't do anything about it. I think Lorenzana and Locsin were on the same team, pro-US. They seem to balance Duterte's Chinese pivot. I don't think Lorenzana was consulted on the termination of the VFA. He really seemed surprised when the news came out'.[51] A Filipino academic shared the assessment that the withdrawal from the VFA was entirely Duterte's personal project and met little support among the bureaucracies tasked with managing relations with the US: 'The DFA [Department of Foreign Affairs] and DND [Department of National Defence] were only expected to implement. Lorenzana tried to convince him, but days after [*sic*], Duterte ordered Locsin to submit the official letter of withdrawal. Locsin couldn't do anything about it anymore. They realized never to challenge him publicly'.[52] At the level of concrete interactions with the US, military exercises continued, but Duterte wanted them to be carried out on a lower scale and in a manner that did not look as directed against China:[53]

> The military activities with the US were continuous. The Balikatan exercises remained, also Kamandag and Sama-Sama but the nature changed. [. . .] What the US did was to simply move away from activities perceived as direct[ed] against China to humanitarian assistance and risk reduction. No combat scenarios and away from the WPS [West Philippine Sea] until the Marawi incident which made the AFP [Armed Forces of the Philippines] realize they need live fire exercises. So Duterte agreed to it and live fire exercises were back in place.[54]

Indeed, as Duterte backtracked from his hostile course towards Washington, and especially after he left office, military exercises resumed in full scale: 'they

---

[49] Interview P10 former high-ranking government official, Manila, 10 October 2022.

[50] Interview P10.

[51] Interview P08, Filipino military affairs journalist, Manila, 7 October 2022.

[52] Interview P09.

[53] Interview P08. According to a senior military official, 'Exercises, like the Balikatan, continued albeit on a limited level, only within the territorial waters. He [Duterte] does not want to provoke China. He approves of exercises that are not anti- China. For example, those related to anti-terrorism'. Interview P11 senior military official, Manila, 11 October 2022.

[54] Interview P09.

are all out on it. For the first time they are going to deploy the most advanced fighter jet. Now they don't have to pretend anymore.'[55] More generally, already under the Trump administration, relations with the US improved, again driven by Duterte's personal affinity with Trump.[56] An illustration of the latter was the curious episode of Duterte singing a song called 'You Are the Light' at an ASEAN gala dinner at the request of Trump (Jimeno 2017). Among the factors contributing to such personal affinity might have been the fact that, other than Obama, Trump refrained from criticizing Duterte's human rights record.

It was also under the Trump administration that Duterte backtracked from his previous efforts at improving the Philippines' relations with China (see Chapter 3).[57] The move towards China had been primarily driven by the hope to benefit from Chinese investments—a hope that was ultimately disappointed. Some of our interviewees also claimed that Chinese businesspeople might have financially supported Duterte's campaign and that he pursued a pro-China policy to pay them back,[58] but there is no reliable evidence for such allegations.

Coming back to the IFP, this was entirely driven personally by Duterte, without consultation with the National Security Council[59] or with other members of the government. Most interviewees agreed that the main driver of the IFP was Duterte's anti-Americanism,[60] and its introduction was a 'pretext to veer away from the traditional western-centric Philippine foreign policy'.[61] According to a former high-ranking government official, '[Secretary of Foreign Affairs] Cayetano came up with the name "IFP", otherwise it would be "I'm getting even for what you did to us". So, he created the name, "friends to all, enemies to none"'.[62]

Besides the distancing from the US and the rapprochement with China, the third component of Duterte's IFP was an '"improvement of relations with non-traditional partners", including Russia, Japan, and India' (Galang 2017). Indeed, relations with Russia developed remarkably under Duterte, very much driven, again, by Duterte's personal sympathy for fellow strongman Putin. Duterte called Putin 'my favorite hero' (Gonzales 2016) and his 'idol' (Romero 2016a), and he told reporters: 'He [Putin] has no illusions

---

[55] Interview P08.
[56] Interview P09.
[57] Interview P15, former senior navy official under Aquino and Duterte, Manila, 13 October 2022.
[58] Interviews P03, senior staff to opposition senator under Duterte, Manila, 29 September 2022; P07.
[59] Interviews P08; P14, senior government official, Manila, 12 October 2022.
[60] Interview P05.
[61] Interview P07.
[62] Interview P01, former high-ranking government official, Manila, 26 September 2022.

about himself. He knows that he was not trained for politics, nor to be a statesman. He acts just like a president. My characterization of Putin is what I would describe myself' (Romero 2016c). Duterte's adulation of Putin was reflected in this interview given after an APEC meeting in 2016 in Peru: 'You know, we have become fast friends, President Putin and (China) President Xi Jinping', Duterte said. 'His (Putin) smile was wide. According to news reports, he does not laugh. But he was smiling all along. He said "do not forget to visit Russia. I reserved something for you there". "True?" "Gun". He loves guns', Duterte said, adding that the Russian president is fond of hunting. 'It seemed like we've known each other for so long' (Romero 2016a).

On his first state visit to Russia in 2017 (another one followed in 2019), Duterte signed a number of agreements in fields ranging from tourism to agriculture, but also in matters of defence and intelligence sharing (Ranada 2017). Further, in 2017 Russia offered the Philippines training of the Presidential Security Group (PSG) (Department of Foreign Affairs 2018) and provided for the transfer of military equipment after the Philippines signed a contract with Rosoboronexport, a Russian state-owned company selling defence equipment (Mogato 2017). But the most remarkable instance of defence procurement from Russia, driven personally by Duterte, was the Philippines' acquisition of sixteen military heavy-lift helicopters. According to a former high-ranking government official with first-hand insights into the process, '[t]he helicopter deal was made by Duterte and Putin [. . .]. [Duterte] told him "I will buy helicopters from you", and he asks me every time for an update. That's why the contract was signed, the president really wanted for it to push through [. . .]. Every time PRRD [President Rodrigo Roa Duterte] visits a country, he asks what military equipment we can buy from them. [. . .] in Russia, Putin told him: "We have helicopters here. You want them?" Duterte said yes and the deal was passed on to us'.[63] Also according to other interviewees, Duterte was really keen to acquire those Russian helicopters, despite opposition from the military,[64] and he made other procurements conditional on that deal: 'Duterte wanted to get Black Hawks but not from the US. So it was agreed to get them from a company in Poland which was American-owned but Duterte's condition was to also get them from Russia. That's why a deal was made despite the opposition from the AFP to procure Russian helicopters'.[65] However, the Russian invasion of Ukraine of February 2022 brought the deal, for which the Philippines had already paid 2 billion pesos as an advance, to a sudden end. Fearing Western sanctions, the Philippines

---

[63] Interview P10.
[64] Interview P11.
[65] Interview P09. As another interviewee put it, 'I think he wanted to impress Putin and to kick the Americans in the ass'. Interview P33, former Filipino justice, Manila, 27 November 2024.

exited the deal before the end of Duterte's term in office (Gomes 2022). As an interviewee recalled, 'PRRD asked me to tell my American counterpart if they return to us the two billion pesos we initially paid the Russians (which will be forfeited) and then sell us a similar helicopter with the same price as those we were supposed to buy, we will cancel the deal. [Later], I was told they were accepting the deal. We shook on it. So, we cancelled the deal with the Russians'.[66]

As the Philippines had already started moving back towards cooperating with the US, Russia's attack against Ukraine propelled a further and very explicit distancing of Duterte from his idol Putin. On 2 March 2022, the Philippines voted in favour of UNGA resolution ES-11/1, which deplored Russia's invasion of Ukraine and demanded an immediate, complete, and unconditional withdrawal of all Russian forces from Ukrainian territory as well as a reversal of its decision to recognize the self-declared People's Republics of Donetsk and Luhansk (UNGA 2022). Moreover, even if Duterte on 17 March 2022 stated, 'that's not our fight. Let's not interfere' (Gita-Carlos 2022), in April the DFA declared that the Philippines was ready to welcome Ukrainian refugees (Noriega 2022), reiterating a commitment already articulated in early March by Justice Secretary Guevarra (The Philippine Star 2022). Even more remarkably, Duterte publicly spoke up against Putin, stating: 'I am just hurt seeing innocent people being killed. Many are saying that Putin and I are the same. We are killers. You know, I want all you Filipinos to know that I really kill. I told you that even before, but I am only killing criminals. I do not kill children, the elderly. Putin and I have different worlds' (Lalu 2022). Thus, relations with Russia followed a similar pattern to those with China: after an initial effort to reorient the Philippines' relations towards this new partner, driven by Duterte's personal interest in closer ties with Putin, Duterte ultimately reversed his foreign policy course and returned to the conventional partnership with the US. Also in this case, the president's policy was not accompanied by significant mobilization and did not enjoy particular public support.

Beyond these key partnerships, Duterte also tried to reach out to a number of other international partners. Japan was particularly relevant—according to one interviewee even more than China[67]—and Duterte cultivated a personal friendship with Shinzo Abe.[68] Further, Duterte travelled to South Korea and

---

[66] Interview P10.
[67] Interview P06, senior military official, Manila, 4 October 2022.
[68] Interview P01.

deepened relations with fellow ASEAN members with a view to 'broaden[ing] our vision of our neighbourhood'.[69] Beyond that, however, alternative partnerships remained shallow.[70] In February 2021, the Philippines joined China, Russia, Venezuela, and Bolivia in dissociating itself from a UN resolution on human rights violations in the Rohingya crisis in Myanmar. Also with Turkey, relations improved under Duterte, and again the Philippines 'bought choppers from Turkey because Duterte does not want us to keep buying from the US'.[71] Thus, the diversification of partnerships is reflected in arms procurement under Duterte. Here, after 2016, the countries of origin of weapons imports displayed much greater variation as compared to previous years, including imports not only from the US and South Korea but also Israel, Spain, Indonesia, Germany, and others (SIPRI, n.d.).

In sum, the case of the Philippines was one in which the transition to a populist government led to an initial effort towards a radical reorientation of the country's international partnership towards authoritarian regimes (China, Russia). Primarily driven personally by the populist leader, this attempted policy shift away from Washington did not meet public support, given the Philippine public's affinity with the US (see Chapter 3). Moreover, it encountered massive opposition from both the foreign policy bureaucracy and the military.[72] According to a former senior navy official, 'Duterte mentioned during a ceremony [. . .] that the AFP was pro-American and he was pro-China. We took it as he will let us be and we also let him be. [. . .] it was taken as we secure our national interests but we also allow the president to do his style of leadership [. . .].'[73] Another former senior navy official confirmed this approach: The navy was ordered to participate in the ASEAN-China naval exercise. They did as instructed, but altered the order as much as they could to send a message that the Navy as an institution did not agree with Duterte's pivot to China: 'This was our subliminal message to China: "You being friends with Duterte does not mean we will be too. We will follow the instructions but not 100%".'[74] Ultimately, given the low potential for mobilization and the rather substantial pushback from relevant domestic actors, as well as the limited success of economic cooperation with China, Duterte reverted back to the Philippines' traditional partnership with Washington. The result was more incoherence than radical change. While the IFP virtually died, in the

---

[69] Interview P10.
[70] Interview P10.
[71] Interview P08.
[72] Interview P05, Filipino scholar, Manila, 30 September 2022.
[73] Interview P15, former senior navy official under Aquino and Duterte, Manila, 13 October 2022.
[74] Interview P12 former senior navy official, Manila, 11 October 2022.

meantime the Philippines had built a number of new ties, thus leading to a partial reorientation of its foreign policy partnerships.

Conclusion

In all four country cases, we saw the transition to a populist government leading to a reorientation in the country's international partnerships. Such reorientation was most pronounced in Bolivia, with Morales overthrowing his country's traditional partnership with the US in the context of very strong personalization of decision making and mobilization around foreign policy issues. In the case of Turkey, the disruption of existing partnerships was less marked, mainly because Turkey remained a member of NATO and instances of collaboration with Western countries remained in place also during Erdoğan's populist phase. However, relations with the West were severely disrupted as Erdoğan became increasingly populist and authoritarian over time. This was paralleled by a clear reorientation towards alternative partners, mostly driven personally by Erdoğan and promoted among the Turkish population in the context of an increasingly politicized foreign policy. Yet, unlike the MAS in Latin America in the 2000s, Turkey's AKP post–Arab Spring had far fewer natural allies with shared thick ideologies in its immediate surrounding. The extent to which Morales was able to re-orient his country's foreign policy thus was at least partially a result of the availability of ideologically aligned partners.

The cases of India and the Philippines, by contrast, saw only a partial reorientation of international partnerships after the formation of populist governments. In India, Prime Minister Modi continued a pre-existing trend of rapprochement with the United States while also pursuing a multi-aligned policy of improved relations with all sorts of partners across world regions. In the Philippines, Duterte tried to re-direct the country away from the alliance with the US and towards closer cooperation with China, but ultimately failed to do so, reverting back to business as usual. The partial reorientation of international partnerships in the cases of the Philippines and India was mostly driven by personalized decision making, but it was not backed up by substantial mobilization. This gave Duterte the flexibility to revert back to closely cooperating with the US without losing credibility vis-à-vis his domestic audience.

Overall, what Duterte, Modi, Erdoğan, and Morales had in common was a clear striving for an 'independent' foreign policy, a foreign policy that gave them room to manoeuvre and allowed them to sometimes play out different partners against each other. This seems to be an important feature of populist foreign policy, much in line with the literature that emphasizes populists' preference for sovereignty: populists in power try to pursue an 'independent' foreign policy that claims to put the 'people' first and does not shy away from being openly transactional.

7

Populism and Foreign Policy in European Cases

While much effort has been invested in recent years towards moving the disciplines of International Relations and social sciences more generally away from a mainly Western canon, old patterns persist. Most theory building still happens on the basis of Western/Global North cases, and existing theories are often just 'applied' to Global South cases. In this book, we took a different approach as we based the development and first application of our theory of populism and foreign policy on four country cases from the Global South. Overall, they confirmed that different intensities of mobilization and personalization drive variations in foreign policy change under populist governments. However, our initial expectations were also disconfirmed in some fields, most notably in global public goods provision and in some instances of engagement in multilateral institutions.

In this chapter, we apply our theoretical framework to three additional cases from the Global North. We do so much in the spirit of abductive research, which calls for successive refinements to theory via the inclusion of a greater number of cases (Tavory and Timmermans 2014). We thus analyse the impact of the formation of populist governments in Hungary under Viktor Orbán of the party Fidesz (Hungarian Civil Alliance; from 2010 until the time of writing in March 2025); in the United Kingdom under Boris Johnson of the Conservative Party (2019–2022); and in Italy under the all-populist 'yellow-green' coalition of Lega and Five Star Movement (Movimento Cinque Stelle, M5S) (2018–2019). More specifically, we again identify whether and how populism led to foreign policy change as compared to previous non-populist governments. Table 7.1 provides an overview of the non-populist and populist government analysed.

Due to space constraints, in this chapter we do not go into similar detail as for our main case studies, and we proceed country-case-wise. However, we broadly maintain our focus on the foreign policy issues analysed so far. We start with the cases of Hungary and the UK, both of which have been

Populism and Foreign Policy. Sandra Destradi and Johannes Plagemann, Oxford University Press.
© Oxford University Press (2025). DOI: 10.1093/9780197695012.003.0007

Table 7.1 Selection of cases for additional analysis of non-populist and populist governments

Hungary	2004–2009	Ferenc Gyurcsány/Hungarian Socialist Party MSZP
	2009–2010	Gordon Bajnaj (independent)
	Since 2010	Viktor Orbán/Fidesz
UK	July 2016–July 2019	Theresa May/Conservative Party
	July 2019–September 2022	Boris Johnson/Conservative Party
Italy	December 2016–June 2018	Paolo Gentiloni/Partito Democratico (PD)
	June 2018–September 2019	Giuseppe Conte/coalition government among Lega and Five Star Movement

amply documented in the secondary literature. The case of Italy adds further complexity and nuance to our analysis because of the peculiar populist coalition government constellation. Here, the two party leaders, rather than the weak prime minister, Giuseppe Conte, dominated decision making and employed selective foreign policy issues for mobilizing public support. Given the additional complexity of this case, we complemented the secondary literature and available primary sources with novel primary data collected via expert interviews.

Hungary

One of the populist governments that has received most media attention in recent years, not the least because of its controversial foreign policy, is the right-wing authoritarian populist government of Viktor Orbán in Hungary.[1] Orbán came to power with a landslide victory in 2010, which gave his party Fidesz (Hungarian Civic Alliance) a two-thirds supermajority in Parliament. His success was mainly driven by voters' disaffection with the ruling Socialist government. Widely perceived as corrupt, it had failed to protect Hungary from the severe consequences of the global financial crisis (Visnovitz and Jenne 2021). Orbán was re-elected in 2014, 2018, and 2022, becoming the longest-serving prime minister of Hungary.

Orbán had led Fidesz already since the early 1990s, and had been prime minister of Hungary between 1998 and 2002. His ideology can be defined as

---

[1] On Orbán's classification as a populist, see, e.g., Jenne et al. (2021); Söderbaum et al. (2021); Spandler and Söderbaum (2023); or Csehi and Zgut (2021).

right-wing ethno-nationalism, and since 2010 it was increasingly combined with a populist thin-centred ideology. Over time, his understanding of the 'elite' evolved. Initially, the 'elite' was identified domestically with the corrupt previous political establishment and 'political hedonists', as a think tank close to Fidesz called them (Visnovitz and Jenne 2021, 692). Moreover, it comprised cosmopolitan and liberal actors in academia and the media. Over time, Orbán's focus shifted towards 'Brussels' or 'European bureaucrats' (Csehi 2019, 1016), frequently described as a far-detached group of technocrats aiming to undermine Hungarian sovereignty and to harm the Hungarian people (Dessewffy 2023). As Orbán put it while campaigning ahead of the European Parliament elections of 2024: 'We need to win in such a way that Brussels' bureaucrats will be so frightened that they open the city gates for us and flee from their offices' (Kovács 2024). Further, Orbán and his supporters portrayed liberal NGOs as a fifth column of 'foreigners' (Csehi 2019, 1016), as part of a detached and corrupt elite. Moreover, philanthropist George Soros was the object of the Orbán government's attacks, which became increasingly conspiratorial and antisemitic (Subotic 2022, 466). At times, Soros and the EU were conflated as the enemy elite, such as on posters ahead of the 2019 and 2024 European Parliament elections (Dessewffy 2023). By contrast, the 'true people' that Orbán claimed to represent were the hard-working people of Hungary, with Orbán portraying himself as the 'defender of the cultural nation, [and] the traditionalist rural and religious social strata' (Pappas 2014, 14). Such 'national historical' (Bozóki 2011, 650) understanding of the people was extended to also include Central Europeans more broadly, as well as other Europeans working in the agricultural sector or in manufacturing jobs (Lamour 2024, 1309). As Csehi (2019, 1017) puts it, Orbán constantly reinterpreted the 'people', 'as he transformed it from "we, Hungarians" through "we, (Central) Europeans" to "we the sovereign nations"'.

Under Orbán's long government, Hungary shifted towards what he himself proudly called 'illiberal democracy'. In fact, democratic backsliding over the past decades has been extensive. According to the Bertelsmann Transformation Index 2024, '[m]ost formal veto players, such as the president, the Constitutional Court and oversight institutions like the State Audit Office, the Competition Authority and the ombudsperson are politically aligned with Fidesz and—with few exceptions—do not function as checks and balances' (Bertelsmann Stiftung 2024, 4). In 2024, Hungary ranked 67th out of 180 countries in the Press Freedom Index of Reporters without Borders (2024). Academic freedom was severely curtailed, and Orbán's campaign against Soros ultimately forced the Central European University (CEU), funded by Soros, to move to Vienna (Walker 2019). Moreover, the Orbán government kept prolonging a state of emergency established during the Covid-19 pandemic, which allowed it to rule by decree, often bypassing parliament (Bertelsmann Stiftung 2024, 11).

Orbán, Disputes with the EU, and Multilateralism

In foreign policy, Orbán's government broadly follows our expectations concerning the impact of populism. As Visnovitz and Jenne (2021, 687) put it, 'It is hard to imagine a case better suited to study the effects of populism on foreign policy than contemporary Hungary. [. . .] Orbán [. . .] has governed the country with a veto-proof parliamentary supermajority. Not only has he made consistent use of populist rhetoric during that time, but he has faced few internal constraints on his foreign policy action'.

The probably most visible manifestation of a shift in Hungary's foreign policy under Orbán has been its hostile approach towards the European Union. Hungary had become a member of the EU in 2004, after a referendum held in 2003. The governments preceding Orbán's had followed a pro-European consensus. For example, in 2008, Prime Minister Gyurcsány (2008) stated:

> I shall start with the basics. It is seemingly an easy job involving useless repetition, but all of us must be reminded that an integrated, democratic Europe is our most admirable and far-reaching historical achievement. It is therefore worth confirming our full commitment to that achievement, and our deep belief in it and in our capability to protect and develop it. Democratic values, especially freedom, democracy and human rights, as well as non-discrimination, are the starting point and our ultimate goal as well.

While Fidesz had originally been a traditional pro-European national-conservative party, after 2010 Orbán profoundly changed its discourse to, indeed, circulate around criticizing the EU. Ultimately, he repeatedly challenged the European Union on a range of issues, ranging from migration to the rule of law and democratic backsliding in Hungary. All this was clearly driven by a mix of strong mobilization as well as personalized decision making.

Accusing the European Union of endangering Hungary via its migration policies was one of the themes for mobilization that Orbán most relied on. Among his most visible policies in this regard was the construction of a fence to stop migration flows outside Hungary's borders in 2015 (Korte 2022). Orbán also mixed the issue of migration with his conspiracy theories about

George Soros, claiming that '[i]n line with George Soros' proposal, an EU-level Asylum and Migration Agency will be established that will further weaken national competencies in the area of immigration. If immigration quotas come into force, Hungarians will no longer have a say in who they want to live with' (quoted in Visnovitz and Jenne 2021, 694). Moreover, Orbán decried the EU's emphasis on LGBTQ+ rights and more generally called into question key EU values of democracy and the rule of law (European Parliament 2024). Beyond his scathing rhetoric, Orbán very concretely undermined the EU's external policies, especially by threatening to block and by delaying military aid to Ukraine after the Russian invasion in 2022. All this was accompanied by a discourse in which 'EU elites and domestic opposition were framed as warmongers trying to drag the country into the war' (Kopper, Szalai, and Góra 2023, 110).[2]

Interestingly, although Orbán focused extensively on the EU in his mobilization efforts, he was not particularly successful in re-shaping Hungarians' attitudes towards it: according to the Eurobarometer survey from spring 2024, Hungarians' views of the EU were similar to (and at times even slightly more positive than) the EU average, with 53% of Hungarians declaring that they tended to trust the EU (as opposed to 49% of Europeans); and 42% of Hungarians saying that the EU conjures up a positive image for them (as opposed to 44% of Europeans) (European Union 2024). Nevertheless, the EU remained the central object around which Orbán mobilized public support.

Besides mobilization, also personalization was decisive in shaping Hungary's approach to the European Union under Orbán's populist leadership. The literature on populism in Hungary has amply documented the gradual increase in the personalization of power around Orbán, who 'conquered and transformed firstly his party (beginning in 1994), then the right-wing political community (starting in 2002) [. . .] and finally the Hungarian party system [. . .] and the political regime' (Metz and Oross 2020, 147). Visnovitz and Jenne (2021) show in great detail how this extended to the field of foreign policy, with Orbán fundamentally restructuring the foreign ministry, especially after his re-election in 2014 and the nomination of Péter Szijjártó, his personal spokesperson, to the position of foreign minister. Specifically,

---

[2] Whereas Brussels for a long time chose not to react to democratic backsliding in Hungary (and Poland), in May 2018 the European Commission advanced a proposal for a rule-of-law budget conditionality, which was then activated in 2022. Since 2021, funds for Poland and Hungary from the Recovery and Resilience Facility were withheld, as well as funds under the Common Provisions Regulation (since 2022); moreover, €6.3 billion cohesion funding to Hungary were frozen by the Council in December 2022 (for an overview, see Blauberger and Sedelmeier 2024). In an unprecedented move, the European Parliament in January 2024 also proposed suspending Hungary's voting rights in EU institutions according to Article 7 of the Treaty on European Union (European Parliament 2024).

the important portfolio of EU affairs was also moved to the Prime Minister's Office, and a huge turnover in personnel among Hungarian diplomats was prompted by Orbán. Alongside personalization, as Visnovitz and Jenne (2021, 694) show, there was a high degree of centralization of decision making that played a role in shaping Orbán's approach to multilateral institutions: within the MFA, '[t]he departments dealing with the UN and OSCE were first lumped together under "global affairs" (2010–2013), then "security policies" (2014), and still later "international cooperation" (2014–2017)', and they were later further downgraded and subordinated to 'a rebranded deputy state secretary for "Handling the Challenges of Migration"' (Visnovitz and Jenne 2021, 694).

Although challenging the EU time and again, Orbán did not lead Hungary out of the EU. As one of its poorer member states, Hungary benefitted substantially from the EU's various financial support schemes. According to Söderbaum et al. (2021), ultimately Orbán was not opposed to regionalism or to the EU as such. Instead, he primarily rejected the liberal components of the European integration project. In his populist discourse, Orbán thus mainly sought to delegitimize the EU on the basis of its inability to represent the true people (Spandler and Söderbaum 2023). In parallel, Orbán promoted the notion of an alternative Europe, true to its Christian values and moral roots and to the respective nation states. This kind of discourse was especially pursued in the context of the Visegrad Group (V4), an informal group comprising the Czech Republic, Hungary, Poland, and Slovakia and presented as 'the vanguard in the effort to (re-)establish popular sovereignty within Europe and the EU' (Spandler and Söderbaum 2023, 1032). The peculiar engagement for the EU displayed by Orbán was reflected in the adoption of the Trump-inspired motto for the Hungarian presidency of the Council of the European Union in 2024: 'Make Europe Great Again' (Hungarian Presidency Council of the European Union 2024).

We found similar patterns of critiquing multilateralism without fully disengaging from it in Hungary's approach to the United Nations (Visnovitz and Jenne 2021, 693). For one, Orbán used an anti-UN discourse for political mobilization. This went so far that ahead of the 2018 elections, there were government billboards stating, 'The UN wants us to accept migrants on a continuous basis. HUNGARY DECIDES, NOT THE UN'. Very similar to the case of Duterte's approach to the UN (see Chapter 5), the Hungarian government at times also strongly criticized the UN. For instance, Budapest called for the resignation of United Nations High Commissioner for Human Rights Zeid bin Ra'ad al-Hussein, who had criticized Orbán's racist statements on immigration at the UN Human Rights Council (Human Rights Watch 2018).

Orbán's Pan-Populist Overtures

Another highly visible change in foreign policy under the populist government of Orbán has been the country's friendly approach to fellow populist parties and governments in Europe and beyond, as well as to authoritarian regimes. In fact, by the 2020s Budapest had become the mecca for the populist right across the Western world. Orbán was a celebrated speaker at the US Republicans' Conservative Political Action Conference (CPAC) in Dallas in 2022 and in the same year he hosted an offshoot (CPAC Hungary) of it in Budapest, thus uniting members of the international right from Argentina to the US and Israel, and from Portugal to Poland. Donald Trump praised Orbán as 'fantastic' (Dessewffy 2024) and the two politicians have met frequently, among others at Mar-a-Lago in the run-up to the US presidential election in March 2024. Orbán attended the inauguration of President Javier Milei in Argentina 2023, where the two discussed a 'more effective fight against international leftist forces' (Donnelly 2023). In 2024 former Brazilian president and fellow right-wing populist Jair Bolsonaro hid two days at the US Embassy, ostensibly in fear of Brazilian law enforcement (Nicas et al. 2024). In Europe, Orbán cooperated with various populist and radical right parties. In 2021, Orbán's Fidesz left the European People's Party (EPP) group, the centre-right bloc in the European Parliament. It did so as it had become evident that Fidesz members were to be expulsed (Politico 2021), after Fidesz had already been suspended from the group in 2019 (Macek 2021). While Fidesz MEPs were *Non-Inscrits* for some years, in June 2024 Orbán announced the formation of a new group called Patriots for Europe (PE). Other members include the Rassemblement National from France, the Lega from Italy, the Austrian Freiheitliche Partei Österreichs (FPÖ), and Spain's VOX. Moreover, according to the *Financial Times*, Marine Le Pen's Rassemblement National received a loan from a Hungarian bank with close connection to Orbán, and the Hungarian government sponsored Polish anti-immigration adverts ahead of elections there in 2022 (B. Hall, Dunai, and Foy 2024).

Beyond this rapprochement to right-wing populist and radical right parties internationally, Orbán in 2011 announced his 'Global Opening' policy, which sought to 'diversify Hungary's EU-centric external relations, especially towards emerging economies' by way of increasing foreign loans, scholarships to Christians from developing countries, as well as high-profile visits mostly to Africa and Asia (Szent-Ivanyi and Kugiel 2020, 126). Moreover, Orbán moved Hungary closer to China and Russia—a policy that contrasted sharply with those of preceding non-populist Hungarian governments. This amounted to an obvious and consistent reorientation of

Hungary's international partnerships. For instance, in October 2023, Orbán was the only European head of government to participate in China's BRI forum (Mistreanu 2023). During a visit by Xi Jinping to Hungary, Orbán was full of praise for China:

> Then we were living in a unipolar world order, and now we live in a multipolar world order—and one of the structural pillars of this new world order is the People's Republic of China. It is the country that is now determining the course of world economic and political developments. (About Hungary 2024)

During the Covid-19 pandemic, Orbán got vaccinated with the Sinopharm BBIBP-CorV vaccine, in a much-publicized and highly performative show of trust towards China (Marton, Matura, and Somogyvári 2023). An increasing economic interest in Asia on the part of Orbán played an important role in the rapprochement, and it was also relevant in Orbán's justifications for it vis-à-vis a domestic audience. Moreover, the shift was related to his anti-EU mobilization efforts, including references to Chinese initiatives for peace in Ukraine, as in this quote by Orbán during Xi Jinping's visit in 2024:

> The President's visit is particularly needed at a time when war is raging in our neighbourhood, and when the world is debating whether to continue this war or instead make efforts leading towards peace. Our voice, the voice of Hungary, is a lone voice in Europe. Today Europe stands on the side of war, the only exception being Hungary, which is calling for an immediate ceasefire and peace negotiations, and supporting all international efforts aimed at peace—including the Chinese peace initiative presented by President Xi Jinping. (About Hungary 2024)

An even more remarkable shift in Hungary's approach under the Orbán government was the rapprochement with Russia. Hungary had had a difficult relationship with its eastern neighbour due to the Soviet past and vivid memories of the violent suppression of the 1956 revolution by Soviet troops. According to Kopper et al. (2023), the shift under Orbán was the outcome of his personal agenda and changing beliefs. While in 1989 Orbán had called for Soviet troops to leave Hungary and continued to be sceptical of Russia in the early 2000s, '[h]e changed his mind following a visit to the Kremlin in 2009. What caused the change is unclear' (Kopper, Szalai, and Góra 2023, 102). Among the possible explanations for such shift, the authors mention the personal preferences of Orbán such as 'mak[ing] friends with a likeminded leader' and 'beliefs about a decline of the West' (Kopper, Szalai, and Góra 2023, 102).

Hungary's pro-Russian turn had already manifested in the 2010s. After Russia's annexation of Crimea in 2014, Hungary sought a balance between supporting EU sanctions against Russia and the simultaneous adoption of a range of Russia-friendly policies such as inviting Putin to visit Budapest in 2015 (Baczynska 2014; Deutsche Welle 2015). Also, Hungary used its veto in NATO to prevent NATO-Ukraine military exercises from happening (Kopper, Szalai, and Góra 2023, 103). The decision was driven by the new friendliness towards Russia but also by difficult relations with Ukraine deriving from disagreements over the treatment of Hungarian minorities in that country. In any case, the new friendship with Russia became most evident after Russia's attack on Ukraine in February 2022. This coincided with electoral campaigning in Hungary ahead of the April 2022 elections, and it forced Orbán to find new ways to justify his pro-Russian stance vis-à-vis his domestic audience. Ultimately, and similar to Donald Trump in his campaign for re-election in 2024, Orbán chose to frame his policies as peace-promoting, claiming that only dialogue with Russia could save Europe from a larger war, and that providing military support for Ukraine was a war-mongering policy on the part of European countries. This kind of narrative continued in the following years and it was similarly used by Orbán for mobilization ahead of the European Parliament elections in 2024, when he claimed that a victory of the left would bring war to Hungary: 'We are the only pro-peace government. A vote for Fidesz-KDNP today saves lives' (Kovács 2024). Beyond rhetoric, Hungary repeatedly blocked military aid to Ukraine via the European Peace Fund, which reimburses EU countries for providing weapons to Ukraine (Rankin 2024). Further, Orbán opposed EU accession talks with Ukraine (Camut 2023), and he diluted EU sanctions against Russia. Finally, together with Turkey, Hungary hampered Finland's and Sweden's accession to NATO (P. Müller and Slominski 2024).

Hungary and Global Public Goods

Beyond framing appeasement for Russia in peace-promoting terms, Orbán also tried to act as a peace broker between Ukraine and Russia. For example, at the end of June 2024, he paid a surprise visit to Kyiv, followed a few days later by a visit to Russian President Putin in Moscow. Since Hungary had just taken over the rotating presidency of the Council of the European Union on 1 July 2024, this prompted Josep Borrell, the High Representative of the Union for Foreign Affairs and Security Policy, to clarify that the Hungarian prime minister was 'not representing the EU in any form' (Sauer 2024) on his trip. Immediately afterwards, Orbán also flew to China, and posted on X 'Peace mission 3.0 #Beijing' (@PM_ViktorOrban 2024). Although inconsequential at that time, these efforts were much in line with other instances of personalized 'populist peacemaking' (Landau and Lehrs 2022) such as those by Erdoğan discussed in Chapter 4, entailing both personalization and mobilization. Conversely, during the years of Orbán's governments, we saw a lower emphasis on the provision of other global public goods. For example, Hungarian average yearly troop contributions to the UN declined from around 120 in the pre-Orbán years to just 25 in 2019 and 36 in 2023 (United Nations Peacekeeping 2024). Hungary's foreign aid increased somewhat in the early 2010s, but additional resources for concessional loans for infrastructure projects (tied to procurement from Hungarian companies) as well as scholarships for Christian students from developing countries very much reflected the Orbán government's foreign policy priorities of both supporting the Hungarian economy and expanding Hungary's foreign relations beyond the EU (Szent-Ivanyi and Kugiel 2020, 126). A notable initiative under Orbán was the 'Hungary Helps Program'. Launched in 2017, it provides aid to Christian minority communities in conflict zones as well as emergency aid. Aligning with both Orbán's anti-migration and pro-Christian rhetoric, the programme is designed to help communities stay in their homelands rather than migrating to Europe. Despite its symbolic importance, financial resources devoted to the programme seem to be relatively modest. With only sporadic data available, the budget for it in 2017 is estimated to have been around €6.3 million, with an additional €5 million allocated in 2018 (Szent-Ivanyi and Kugiel 2020, 130).

When it comes to climate change mitigation, Hungary's position under Orbán's populist government also broadly confirmed our expectations. Over time, successive Orbán governments shifted from climate denialism towards the promotion of a 'new conservative green agenda' (Antal 2021, 209). When climate change was acknowledged as a problem, it was discursively tied to criticism of the EU and framed in terms of the costs of providing the global public good of mitigation. For example, Orbán stated that he would 'not allow[. . .] the Brussels bureaucrats to make the poor and poorer member states bear the costs of the fight against climate change' (About Hungary 2019). The Hungarian government's approach to climate change under Orbán was framed in genuinely right-wing populist terms, also bringing in religious elements (note the parallels in the use of right-wing religious thick ideology in this case and in India, see Chapter 4). Thus, in an article in Politico, Hungary's minister of justice Judit Varga in 2020 called for a 'Christian conservative green policy':

> To truly address the challenge, we need an alternative approach to Green liberalism—something Europe's Christian conservative parties are well-placed to put forward. Conservatism has always attached special importance to the support of rural communities and local initiatives [. . .]. Multilateral environmental treaties, such as the 2015 Paris Agreement, have only a limited effect on the biggest polluting countries, which typically fall short of meeting their commitments under such agreements. Instead, it should be primarily incumbent on the individual states to develop a system of environmental regulation that is based on their local environment and its needs [. . .]. It is, of course, in our shared interest to preserve the Earth for our grandchildren. But we must understand that this is a huge undertaking with a significant price tag. The cost of protecting our environment cannot be shifted to poorer countries or to the most vulnerable citizens, employees or pensioners. 'The costs of a climate-neutral economy', as Hungarian Prime Minister Viktor Orbán said recently, 'should primarily be borne by the climate wreckers: the large polluting countries and large companies'. The largest burden should not be placed on the shoulders of those least equipped to bear it. (Varga 2020)

As we see from this quote, the Orbán government entwined right-wing thick ideological elements with typical populist themes, leading to arguments sceptical of global public goods provision and of multilateralism, emphasizing sovereignty, and blaming others for the burdens that the people had to carry. Besides this rhetoric, the populist government of Hungary also took concrete measures that weakened climate change mitigation efforts. For example, the independent Ministry of the Environment was subsumed under the Ministry of Rural Development, and other institutions such as an 'independent ombudsman for future generations' were eliminated (Antal 2021). Also, Hungary was, after fellow right-wing populist-governed Poland, the country that most frequently voted against EU energy-related legislation, thus undermining common European policies on that matter (Ćetković and Buzogány 2019).

To conclude, Hungarian foreign policy shifted in numerous fundamental ways under the populist governments of Orbán. Those shifts took place in line with our expectations, with strong mobilization and personalization as well as centralization of decision making being key drivers. A more confrontational approach towards the European Union as well as the reorientation of Hungary's international partnerships towards China and Russia stand out as particularly visible. At the same time, Hungary became more sceptical of contributions to global governance and to multilateralism generally. However, similar to what we have seen in our four main case studies, such scepticism neither applied to all sorts of multilateral engagements nor did it lead Orbán to adopt the most radical of options, such as ending EU membership or exiting other relevant multilateral institutions. Instead, he emphasized engagements in line with his 'illiberal' preferences. Further, the populist leader was willing to contribute to the provision of global public goods where this could be presented as a personal achievement and could be used to further other goals, as in the case of the promotion of 'peace' as a way of cultivating ties with Russia against opposition from the EU.

The United Kingdom

In the United Kingdom, Boris Johnson of the Conservative Party became prime minister in July 2019, leading the government until September 2022. He succeeded fellow Tory politician Theresa May, who had served as prime minister for three years starting in July 2016. In this section, we assess foreign policy changes from the non-populist government led by Theresa May to the populist one of Boris Johnson. The categorization of May as non-populist may require some explanation given that, for instance, Team Populism classifies May's rhetoric as prime minister as 'somewhat populist' (Lewis, Clarke, and Barr 2019). However, such assessment is driven primarily by Team Populism's analysis of one speech with particularly strong populist overtures that May gave to Conservative Party members in October 2016.[3] By contrast, the other three speeches analysed were not classified as populist. Thus, as others have pointed out and despite 'incorporat[ing] aspects of the populist style into [her] political practice', we consider May not to be a populist (Margulies 2019). For one, a 'remainer' on Brexit with a long history as a loyal party member and former home minister under the more clearly non-populist prime minister David Cameron, May was not an outsider, nor did she pretend to be one. Although at times employing anti-elitist language and pursuing a harder Brexit than many had expected (Pickard 2019), she did not represent anti-elitism personally, nor did she incorporate it into her way of governing as was the case under Boris Johnson (see below). Moreover, she became prime minister following the Brexit referendum of 2016 and Cameron's resignation

---

[3] Its author, Chris Wilkins, later said he 'massively' regretted the speech's arguably most populist line ('But if you believe you're a citizen of the world, you're a citizen of nowhere') because of its divisiveness (Lewis, Clarke, and Barr 2019).

afterwards because she convinced her party and its majority in parliament, not the people. In fact, nicknamed 'the Maybot' in the national and international media (Atkins and Gaffney 2020, 305), the awkward May lacked the ability to directly connect with the people all the while she 'was in charge of a populist project' (Stefanowitsch 2019, 232). More important, rather than fuelling the polarization emanating from the close Brexit referendum, in the 2017 election and aided by her 'agnosticism on Brexit', she presented 'herself as the unity candidate' capable of healing 'the wounds inflicted by a bitter referendum campaign' (Atkins and Gaffney 2020, 298). As a result, rather than leading it, May became increasingly haunted by the populist right of her own party.

By contrast, Boris Johnson can unequivocally be defined as a populist leader (Beck 2023; Lacatus and Meibauer 2022; J. Ward and B. Ward 2023). In his discourse he habitually resorted to people-centrism, anti-elitism, and the notion of politics as an expression of the general will of the people. As Lacatus and Maibauer (2022, 448) show in their analysis of Johnson's tweets, the British prime minister claimed to speak for the people, understood as 'the "everyman", [. . .] a fictitious, homogeneous British folk'. Despite his elitist upbringing, Johnson performed 'authenticity' by displaying 'typically British' preferences and emphasizing his belonging to the 'people' (Lacatus and Meibauer 2022, 448). The authentic British people was defined in opposition to migrants, much in line with Johnson's right-wing thick ideology—think of Johnson vowing an 'end to migrants "treating Britain as their own"' (Swinford 2019). At the same time, the 'elite' was primarily identified with the EU, as the topic at the core of Johnson's government were negotiations with the EU over the implementation of Brexit. Johnson himself had played a key role in the 'leave' campaign ahead of the 2016 referendum, in which a slim majority of 51.9% of the UK population voted for their country's exit from the European Union (BBC News, n.d.).

Three years later, his 2019 election campaign came under the motto 'getting Brexit done'. Winning him the largest conservative majority in decades, Johnson's populism successfully targeted voters in left-behind English rural districts traditionally inclined towards the Labour Party. By adopting a hardline stance on Brexit and presenting himself as the leader who could deliver on the referendum's promise, he also successfully reclaimed voters from radical-right parties (Evans, de Geus, and Green 2023). By emphasizing British sovereignty from the EU as well as the failures of parliament, including Tory and Labour party members opposed to a 'hard Brexit', his nationalist populism substantially relied on foreign affairs in its efforts to mobilize public support (Courea 2020; Cooper and Cooper 2020). In fact, given the depth of the UK's political, economic, and societal integration within the EU, the controversies over how to implement Brexit were destined to systematically conflate domestic and foreign politics. When it comes to the claim to represent the 'general will' of the people, this aspect of populist thin-centred ideology was also very much present during Johnson's government: the very ambition of getting Brexit done was presented as a mission to finally realize the British people's wish to leave the European Union, as displayed in the 2016 referendum (Courea 2019). As a former tabloid journalist with a history of blaming the EU for all sorts of ills, Johnson habitually accused both parliament and judges of opposing his commonsense policies over Brexit and, in fact, of acting as enemies of the people (Alexandre-Collier 2022, 538). He expelled MPs from his own party who held differing views on Brexit and, shortly after his election in 2019, he sought the prorogation of parliament to prevent it from interfering in his negotiations with the EU (Alexandre-Collier 2022, 538). All these aspects of populism in the ideational sense were flanked with performative and stylistic elements that also sought to display Johnson's identification with the 'people', among other things a targeted use of humour and his notoriously imperfect apparel and hairstyle.

In terms of actual governance, Johnson personalized policymaking to a degree unseen before. Indeed, besides Brexit, the prime minister's agenda focused on a much wider reform of the British (elitist, pro-European) civil service deemed detached from the people. Whereas supporters applauded the decentralization of power away from metropolitan elites, critics described the endeavour as a 'concentration of power in the hands of a tightly-knit group of Leavers' (Bush 2020). Interestingly, the feat was driven less by Johnson himself than by his Cabinet Office Minister Michael Gove and, especially, the prime minister's controversial Chief Advisor Dominic Cummings. In his long blog posts, Cummings attacked what he called 'the blob'—the 'elitist' (and pro-European) bureaucratic establishment, unions, and civil society organizations, which he depicted as representing the mainstream but crowding out innovation, talent, and those unwilling to conform (Payne 2020). As was the case with Gove, Cummings's considerable authority rested on his personal proximity to Johnson as well as on his role as Brexit's lead strategist. Described as a 'career psychopath' by former prime minister Cameron, and as brilliant albeit polarizing by Brexit-loyalists (Boscia 2024), Cummings was notorious for his dislike of the bureaucratic establishment. As chief advisor to Johnson, he fought with 'all around him' insulting 'every established elite' and he was 'unworried at being pervasively loathed' (Dunleavy 2020). To his critics, Cummings was 'an embodiment of many malignant dark forces on the right, pushing for an unrestrained populist assault on any constitutional element force constraining No. 10's privatizing freedom of action' (Dunleavy 2020). As such, he was the ideological complement to Johnson's ideationally more superficial populism. Cummings resigned in November 2020 in response to mounting critique of his flagrant breaches of Covid-lockdown measures. Whereas his dismissal alleviated some of the tensions between the political leadership and Britain's traditionally influential civil service officers, it did not end the ongoing process of centralization and personalization under Johnson (B. Ward and J. Ward 2022).

Foreign policy was particularly affected by these trends. A former foreign minister himself and with a background as Brexit's star campaigner, foreign policy naturally dominated Johnson's three years as prime minister. More than that, he emphasized the centrality of his persona to take matters in his own hands and solve the country's problems by swiftly concluding negotiations with the EU to then focus again on the people's priorities, from health to regional infrastructure. For example, Johnson equated himself with the Incredible Hulk, implying that his superpowers were needed in negotiations with the EU (Beck 2023). Another theme closely connected to Johnson was the 'Global Britain' slogan first adopted by Theresa May post-2016 (with Johnson as foreign minister) and actively promoted by Johnson as prime minister. Here, the aim was to redefine the UK's role in a post-Brexit environment, emphasizing a more assertive global presence from Asia to Africa and the Middle East, building upon Britain's history. In fact, '[the British] empire stood in Johnson's rhetoric as a mark of virility; evidence of what Britain could still achieve if it recovered its national mojo' (Saunders 2020, 1163). Moreover, Johnson publicly cultivated his celebration of Winston Churchill, a defender of British colonialism, among other things by authoring a biography of him in 2014. As prime minister, Johnson frequently drew parallels with the UK's leader throughout World War II.

In institutional terms, some major shifts towards greater centralization took place under Johnson. In particular, the Department for International Development (DfID) was merged into the Foreign and Commonwealth Office (FCO) in 2020. The merger—de facto a subordination of development affairs to foreign policy—reflected the conservative media's and the Tory's right-wing critiques of British development aid and foregrounded a reduction in aid overall (see below). While significantly enlarging the FCO's budget (and, thus, authority), it also contributed to a centralization of foreign policy. Another key institution within the foreign policy making process is the National Security Council (NSC), a cabinet committee also including heads of British intelligence, and the Chief of Defence Staff. Established in 2010, its purpose was to integrate British foreign and security policies and to counter allegations of foreign and security decision making in unaccountable small groups of political loyalists to the prime minister (Elliott and Goodman 2020). According to former members of the council, the NSC's prominence had started to decline under Theresa May already, who also merged the roles of the National Security Advisor with that of the Cabinet Secretary, the UK's most senior civil servant. Yet, it clearly deteriorated soon after Johnson took office (Elliott and Goodman 2020). While the NSC was supposed to meet once a week after cabinet, under Johnson its structures reverted to 'ad-hoc arrangements and improvisation', as put in a highly critical parliamentary report from 2021 (Sky News 2021). In fact, with the beginning of the Covid-19 pandemic, the NSC failed to meet at all over months. Moreover, changes to the working procedures of the NSC devised under Johnson's national security advisor Stephen Lovegrove would reduce the prime minister's attendance by around two-thirds, thus further diminishing the body's authority, the parliamentary report stated in an alarmist tone (Merrick 2021). The approach to the NSC not only illustrates the Johnson government's inclination towards personalizing decision making but also its disdain for bureaucratic processes and its animosity towards parliamentary oversight. The latter was also evident in Johnson's 2020 decision to appoint then Chief Negotiator for Exiting the European Union, David Frost, a former diplomat and CEO of the Scotch Whisky Association, as national security advisor. This choice of a political appointee rather than a senior bureaucrat from the security sphere broke with past precedent (Elliott and Goodman 2020) and led to much public and parliamentary criticism, among others, by Johnson's predecessor Theresa May (BBC 2021). Illustrating the intensity of political infighting and turmoil characterizing the Johnson government, Frost ultimately never took up the position.

A More Aggressive Foreign Policy?

Pushing for a hardline negotiation position with the EU to reclaim British 'sovereignty' had propelled the former mayor of London Boris Johnson to become prime minister. It is thus unsurprising that the British tone towards Brussels was more confrontational following the transition from the non-populist government of May to the populist one of Johnson. There are multiple accounts of hostile encounters between British and EU representatives from negotiation insiders on both sides (e.g., Stone and Woodcock 2019). Moreover, unlike May, Johnson entered the negotiation process with maximalist demands destined to infuriate his counterparts from Brussels.

His government's negotiation position was complicated, on the one hand, by an unexpected European unity and, on the other, by unrealistic promises made to the British public both during the referendum campaign and throughout May's three-year stint as prime minister. As a result, negotiations on the British side did not revolve around the more pragmatic question of what was best for the British economy or other key sectors, but around the question of how to achieve maximum market access while ensuring complete British freedom from EU regulation. The *Financial Times* quotes one member of the negotiating team as saying: 'The process just wasn't driven by thinking about what the UK really wanted from a deal, but to justify the claims to sovereignty. It was quite astonishing' (Brunsden et al. 2021). This very point was driven home relentlessly by Johnson and his chief negotiator, David Frost, both in internal British meetings and vis-à-vis EU negotiators. Moreover, Johnson was adamant in reaching a deal by the end of 2020 (Brunsden et al. 2021), thus fulfilling his core campaign promise, even at the cost of further worsening his country's negotiating position. In sum, ideology, mobilization, and personalization drove the British towards a bitter negotiation process with erstwhile partners, eventually resulting in a deal that according to multiple accounts was unnecessarily harmful to the British economy—and much less in the European interest than what optimists had hoped for. For example, the *Financial Times* quotes a senior executive from London's financial industry as saying: 'The Conservative party is controlled by ideologues who were allowed to define what Brexit meant. It came to mean a purist view of sovereignty at the expense of the economy'. With reference to the importance of fishing to British negotiators, another bank executive added: 'We rank lower than fish and we know it' (Brunsden et al. 2021). In sum then, in comparison with May, the populist Johnson government was significantly less accommodative to EU demands. Its tone was harsher, and it continuously resorted to Brexit as a key theme to mobilize domestic support both against foreign (EU) adversaries and their domestic allies in parliament, the media, business, and academia.

With European partners out of the picture, the UK was keen to demonstrate its attractiveness for alternative partners from the US to Canada, Japan, or Australia (see below), a circumstance that contributed to numerous diplomatic outreach initiatives under the 'Global Britain' banner. In terms of adversarial relationships, the Johnson government continued the May government's relatively hawkish positions on Russia and China. Johnson in 2020 authorized the 'largest sustained increase in the core defence budget for 30 years' (Kirk-Wade 2024, 5). In line with his predecessor May, the UK under Johnson was among NATO's most consistent supporters of Ukraine following the Russian invasion in early 2022. A year earlier the Johnson government saw the largest deployment of Royal Navy warships since the 1982 Falklands War, including the aircraft carrier HMS *Queen Mary*, to the Indo-Pacific (Chuter 2021). Visiting dozens of countries en route, the naval mission was meant to carry the banner of 'Global Britain' and underline its support for the freedom of the seas, displeasing Chinese authorities (Gardner 2021).

Johnson and Global Public Goods

The Johnson government offers a mixed picture on global public goods. By merging the DFID and the FCO, it diminished the political importance of development aid. Moreover, the government assigned significantly fewer financial resources to aid, the 'Global Britain' pledges notwithstanding. Reducing the ODA budget from 0.7% to 0.5% of the UK's gross national income (GNI) in 2021 was justified by Johnson as a necessary measure following the Covid pandemic's economic impact. The cut led to a £4 billion shortfall compared to previous levels, causing closures and reductions in numerous development programmes, particularly in health, education, and humanitarian assistance. It was criticized by former prime minister Theresa May and other prominent figures, who argued that it would have devastating effects on the world's poorest people and undermine the UK's global influence (Webber 2021). Critics also pointed out that the UK was the only G-7 country to reduce its aid budget during the pandemic, damaging its reputation as a leader in international development (Wintour 2021). At the same time, the reduction in aid corresponded with the preferences of Johnson's support base, which was sceptical of foreign aid.

We found a different picture in the domain of climate change mitigation. Although expressing doubts about climate science in a 2015 column for the *Daily Telegraph*, once prime minister, Johnson pushed for more, not less, British engagement. In stark contrast to some other right-wing populists such as President Trump in the US, Johnson launched a 10-Point Plan for a Green Industrial Revolution in 2020 (Johnson 2021), he energetically hosted the COP26 summit in Glasgow in 2021, and his government pledged a 68% reduction by 2030 and net-zero carbon emissions by 2050. Also, Johnson in 2021 promised £11.6 billion (over five years) to support climate action in developing countries, thus demonstrating his commitment to international climate finance. According to detailed reporting by the Carbon Brief, the prime minister's office was doubtful about climate science, and it did express its doubts behind closed doors in the initial months in power. Yet, in an illustration of the importance of personal leadership, according to this reporting Johnson changed his mind following a scientific briefing as prime minister in 2019 (Carbon Brief Staff 2022). In fact, speaking to journalists ahead of the Glasgow summit he admitted having had doubts about climate change and that a briefing by the government's scientific advisors had changed his mind (Walker 2021). Thus, unlike what our theory suggests, personalization under Johnson—possibly helped by the opportunity for mobilization as the host to the COP in Scotland—led to the reinforcement of climate change mitigation efforts, rather than their diminishment.

When it comes to peacekeeping missions, the UK under Johnson did not alter its commitment. Troop contributions did not change fundamentally from the Cameron to May and Johnson cabinets (United Nations Peacekeeping 2024), and the UK remained one of the UN's top contributors to the peacekeeping budget (United Nations Peacekeeping, n.d.). Keen to dilute the impression of an isolationist turn following Brexit and to rebuild global status, the Johnson government was an outspoken supporter of the United Nations and its peacekeeping (Foreign & Commonwealth Office 2020). The Integrated Review of Security, Defence, Development, and Foreign Policy devised under Johnson ('Global Britain in a Competitive Age') not only underlined the importance of British military force but also emphasized the importance of international cooperation and the UK's role in addressing global security challenges, including nuclear non-proliferation and conflict resolution (Boulton 2021). However, absorbed by Brexit, Covid, the Russian attack on Ukraine, plus preparations for a modestly successful COP in Glasgow, Johnson did not figure personally in any major mediation effort, nor did peacekeeping and mediation play a prominent role in mobilization efforts.

The EU and Beyond: Johnson and Multilateralism

Johnson's demonization of the European Union's regulatory regime and the rejection of the common market, despite ample evidence of significant economic costs attached to it, constitute a primary example of populists' disdain for multilateral institutions. Flooding public debates over the course of at least five years—from the lead-up to the referendum in June 2016 to the eventual Brexit deal in December 2020—mobilization around the issue was intense. In fact, the Brexit campaign and its success allowed for Johnson to emerge as its leader and generated a new support base for him in a transformed Conservative party. He clearly was its most visible spokesperson. Thus, Brexit defined Johnson's political career as much as he defined Brexit. In fact, what Brexit actually entailed was initially rather unclear. Simply asking, 'Should the

United Kingdom remain a member of the European Union or leave the European Union?' and offering two options ('Remain' or 'Leave') as response, the referendum did not specify what kind of arrangements the UK should maintain with its European neighbours. May pursued a Brexit deal with the EU that would retain much of the considerable benefits that market and regulatory integration had in store for the UK. None of this was satisfying Brexit hardliners, with Boris Johnson as the most prominent figure among them. Thus, Johnson, once prime minister, found himself struggling with internal dissent as much as with Brussels. Indeed, the seemingly endless saga of negotiations and debates was paralleled by an ongoing radicalization of the pro-Brexit camp and ensured a continuously high degree of mobilization around the issue up until an eventual deal was reached (Martill 2022). Hence, maximum degrees of personalization and mobilization contributed to a negotiated outcome that yielded much less benefits for the UK than what most observers and, arguably, voters had expected in 2016. In this sense, Brexit and the populist leadership by Boris Johnson are among the most vivid illustrations of the outcomes of populist foreign policy.

However, Brexit notwithstanding, the Johnson government was not opposed to multilateralism per se. In fact, Johnson's foreign policy thinking throughout his career was focused on the defence of the West and its normative stature and legacy in global politics, epitomized in Johnson's celebration of Churchill, his support for free trade globally (rather than within Europe), his admiration for the US, and his habitual references to past British glories. Alongside this came an instinctive disregard for the achievements and grievances of the post-colonial world, a circumstance that greatly complicated the 'Global Britain' agenda (see below). Another corollary was the conviction that western alliances—Brexit apart—increased the UK's strength. Johnson frequently spoke out in favour of NATO, and the UK was among the alliance's most active supporters for Ukraine. Moreover, in 2020 Johnson suggested a new alliance of ten leading democracies—the G-7 plus Australia, India, and South Korea—as an effective forum to counter Chinese economic statecraft (the initiative died only weeks later once Trump suggested to also add Russia to the club [Fishman and Mohandas 2020]). Under his 'Global Britain' banner, Johnson further underscored London's emphatic support for the United Nations, global cooperation, as well as—ironically—for free trade. Whereas the trade agenda was pursued mostly bilaterally, the UK also sought membership of the Comprehensive and Progressive Agreement for Transpacific Partnership (CPTPP) comprising numerous East and Southeast Asian as well as some Latin American nations (it became a full member in 2023) (Department for Business and Trade 2023). In any case, Johnson's defence of the 'liberal international order'—in the Indo-Pacific, via the UK's support for embattled Ukraine, or elsewhere—stood in contrast to his disregard for international law around issues such as migration. His government's plans to deport asylum seekers to autocratic Rwanda conflicted with Britain's international legal obligations. Both on this issue and over Brexit, Johnson openly stated he was prepared to break international law to reinstate British sovereignty (Parker et al. 2020; Mason and Elgot 2022). Thus, mobilization and his personal commitment to the Brexit agenda drove his government towards a visible disregard for the so-called international rules-based order.[4] This attitude was mirrored in his scepticism of institutional checks and balances domestically. Ultimately, it was the lack of respect for professional ethics, the courts, and parliament in his scandal-soaked government which led to his premature downfall as party leader and prime minister in 2022.

'Global Britain' and the Search for New Partners

Among the Johnson government's foreign policy priorities was its desire to prove that Brexit was not isolating Britain, that the UK had allies overseas, and that it was capable of deepening ties with them in a post-Brexit context. Despite having served as foreign minister tasked with outlining 'Global Britain', Johnson's discourse on the UK's post-Brexit foreign policy was vague and reliant on a few but often repeated slogans: The British people voted to 'leave the EU and embrace the world' (Oppermann, Beasley, and Kaarbo 2020, 138) and independence from the EU's common market gave London the opportunity to enter new trade deals with overseas partners. However, unlike our cases from the Global South in the previous chapters, the Johnson government turned less towards new partners. Instead, it sought revigorated ties with traditional ones. Johnson, as well as his predecessor May, habitually underlined the importance of the UK's 'special relationship' with the US, sometimes with reference to the new freedom in cooperating with Washington (Stewart, Makortoff, and Wintour 2019; Forgey 2021). Moreover, the UK sought to deepen relations with other Anglo-Saxon countries from Canada to Australia and New Zealand. Johnson and his cabinet members sought free trade deals with, among others, Japan (concluded in 2020), Australia (signed in 2021), India (formal negotiations began in 2022), the Gulf Cooperation Council (under negotiation since 2022), and (unsuccessfully) the US. Joining free trade agreements with non-European countries was a priority not

---

[4] Past his tenure as prime minister, he vocally criticized the return of British administered Chagos Islands to Mauritius, as called for repeatedly by the UN's International Court of Justice (Daly 2023).

the least since it was meant to support a key argument for Brexit, that is, the new freedom to enter into trading agreements that would 'unleash' the British economy. Thus, such agreements received considerable media interest and high-level political attention. Both in terms of trade and beyond it, there was much talk about 'Global Britain' and a revived Commonwealth (in Johnson's own words: 'Like the Queen, we should all cherish the Commonwealth' [Johnson 2022]), although eventually little came out of this (Gallardo 2022). Even though he employed a more careful rhetoric while in office, Johnson's reputation in the Global South suffered from his 'track record of misrepresenting and offending foreign peoples, leaders, and entire countries' (Połońska-Kimunguyi and Kimunguyi 2017, 325).[5]

Declaring an 'Indo-Pacific Tilt' in its Integrated Review of Security, Defence, Development, and Foreign Policy, the Johnson government emphasized the UK's involvement in the Indo-Pacific, including in security terms. Most visibly, the UK partook in the establishment of AUKUS, a security cooperation scheme with Australia and the US with the immediate ambition to provide Australia with nuclear powered submarines. AUKUS received enormous media attention and may figure prominently among Johnson's foreign policy legacies. Yet, it also greatly harmed relations with France as Paris until the very publication of AUKUS was convinced it had struck its own submarine deal with Australia, only to be later told that Canberra had already decided against it (Remeikis 2021).

The UK's emphasis on the Indo-Pacific as well as its proximity to Washington naturally reduced its chances to significantly improve relations with China. Hampered by a deep disappointment over Hong Kong, the 'golden age' of UK-China relations of David Cameron's times was a thing of the past as Boris Johnson moved into Downing Street (Leoni 2022). Yet, observers and former aides describe his approach to China as essentially unchanged from his time as mayor of London (2008–2016): While enjoying the benefits of alignment with the US, the self-described 'Sinophile' also pragmatically sought to maintain business relations with significant Chinese investment flowing into London and the UK (Courea 2022). The result of contradicting forces—Johnson's personal history and economic pragmatism vs. his pro-democracy stance in foreign affairs and alliance commitments—was a paradoxical policy of diplomatically boycotting Beijing's Winter Olympics (over human rights) in 2022 while at the same time (unsuccessfully) seeking

---

[5] Johnson described Labour Party politics as 'Papua New Guinea–style orgies of cannibalism and chief-killing' and Africans as 'flag-waving picaninnies' and 'tribal warriors [breaking] out in watermelon smiles'. In an article on Africa from 2002 for *The Spectator* he stated: 'The problem is not that we were once in charge, but that we are not in charge any more' (Połońska-Kimunguyi and Kimunguyi 2017, 325).

trade talks with China. Overall, we therefore see that the shift to Johnson's populist government led to a reorientation of international partnerships, albeit without a strong preference for populist and authoritarian regimes, as we had hypothesized. Rather, Johnson attempted to diversify the UK's foreign relations while firmly sticking to and further expanding cooperation with non-European Western partners.

Italy

On 1 June 2018, an all-populist coalition government was formed in Italy. Elections of March 2018 had led to a hung parliament, leaving none of the traditional political groupings with a majority. After as many as eighty-nine days, an unlikely coalition government was formed, comprising two rather different populist parties, the Five Star Movement (Movimento 5 Stelle; M5S) and the Lega. The government was led by Giuseppe Conte, an independent law professor, who was close to the M5S but had not held any political positions up to that point and thus played the role of a rather weak technocratic prime minister (President of the Council of Ministers, according to the official denomination). This government is sometimes called the 'yellow-green' (from the colours of the parties' logos) or the 'Conte I' government (referring to the fact that, later, Conte again served as prime minister in a different constellation). To assess foreign policy change, we compare the Conte I government to the preceding non-populist government led by Paolo Gentiloni of the Partito Democratico, which had been in power from December 2016 to May 2018.

The Lega and the M5S have very different histories and thick-ideological orientations. The Lega originated from the regionalist Lega Nord, a party founded in northern Italy in 1991[6] and rebranded as a national party with the name 'Lega' by Matteo Salvini in 2017. As its undisputed leader, Salvini transformed the regionalist force 'into a nationalist, radical right profile, strengthening its nativist focus on security and hostility to immigration' (Baldini and Giglioli 2021, 113). By contrast, the 5 Star Movement, founded in 2009, had emerged as a populist party under the leadership of popular comedian Beppe Grillo via an online platform called Rousseau, which sought to promote direct democracy and principles such as participation and equality among members. Over time, the party combined a top-down approach with its traditional horizontal structures, for example when in 2017 it carried

---

[6] A federation of smaller regionalist parties had been created already in 1989.

out a survey on foreign policy among its members (Diodato 2023). Scholars agree that the M5S 'appears to lack a host ideology' (Baldini and Giglioli 2021, 513) or that its thick ideology is 'difficult to classify' (Verbeek and Zaslove 2017, 410). Especially at its origins, the Movement had an anti-globalist and a Eurosceptic approach, but it mostly focused on issues such as environmentalism or opposing multinationals and the banking system (Tarchi 2015). On foreign policy, the M5S espoused pacifist ideals and was interested in humanitarian issues (Coticchia and Vignoli 2020), but it did not have a clearly defined stance on most other topics.

The yellow-green government was thus a genuinely populist government, with no clearly predominating thick ideology. This makes it a particularly interesting case study for the analysis of how populism plays out in foreign policy. A number of caveats are necessary. The main peculiarity of the yellow-green government was its being an uneasy coalition between two parties with diverging thick ideologies (Conti, Pedrazzani, and Russo 2020, 344) held together by a weak prime minister. For the two mechanisms we are interested in, mobilization and personalization, this means that we will not so much focus on Giuseppe Conte,[7] but on the two de facto leaders, Luigi Di Maio, the head of the M5S, and Matteo Salvini, the head of the Lega. Both were deputy prime ministers under Conte. Moreover, Di Maio was nominated minister of economic development, labour and social policies, while Salvini became minister of the interior. Both roles involved 'a concentration of responsibilities, very rare in the history of republican Italy' meant to 'compensate for the a-political nature of the premiership' (Marangoni and Verzichelli 2019, 270). In the post-electoral coalition agreement set up by the M5S and the Lega, foreign policy issues did not figure prominently and details on implementation were lacking (Giannetti, Pinto, and Plescia 2020, 191). This led to foreign policy receiving a clear imprint by the leaders of the two parties in distinct issue areas that were particularly relevant to each of them. The centrality of Di Maio and Salvini became evident from the very beginning of the coalition, as only they signed the coalition agreement, without involving their respective parliamentary groups (Musella 2020, 418). The prime minister was largely marginalized from important decisions, and he did not even manage to serve as a mediator between his two deputies when they had disagreements (Conti, Pedrazzani, and Russo

---

[7] According to one of our interviewees directly involved in the yellow-green government, Conte during the yellow-green government did not personalize and centralize decision making: 'Conte had an approach very much focused on listening. He let everybody speak as much as they wanted, the civil society groups. There were meetings that started at one and ended at one in the night. He gave [everybody] the feeling that he wanted to participate [in discussions]'. Interview IT10, former high-ranking officer, Italian Ministry of Foreign Affairs and International Cooperation, online, 12 October 2022.

2020, 342). It is thus not surprising that Di Maio and Salvini were the actors driving the most significant foreign policy changes during the Conte I government.

The Ministry of Foreign Affairs and International Cooperation (MAECI), colloquially called Farnesina from the name of the building that houses it, was led by Enzo Moavero Milanesi, a technocrat coming from within the ministry, and ultimately a weak figure. As a high-ranking former government official at his ministry put it, 'Moavero was a minister who was not loved [in the ministry], he was afraid of making any decision.'[8] The minister of defence was Elisabetta Trenta of the M5S. Both Di Maio and Salvini expanded their ministries' respective responsibilities to issues related to foreign policy, thus weakening the foreign ministry, much in line with our expectation concerning the centralization and personalization of power. In particular, Salvini made migration policy a key element driving Italy's foreign policy during his time in government. Di Maio and his ministry, in turn, were the driving force in negotiations over Italy joining China's Belt and Road Initiative (De Maio 2020, 12), which was probably the most visible instance of foreign policy change under the yellow-green government. All this led to a clear increase in the politicization of foreign policy, with the two coalition partners competing by setting different priorities in the foreign policy realm. Indeed, Prime Minister Conte 'was at the mercy of those two [Salvini and Di Maio]'.[9] At the same time, at least to some extent, the foreign ministry's bureaucracy resisted efforts at weakening it (Lequesne 2021).[10]

The second peculiarity of the yellow-green government concerns the strong role that the president of the republic, Sergio Mattarella, exercised in the phase of government formation, in line with the Italian constitution. In fact, Mattarella directly interfered with government formation as he refused to nominate the Eurosceptic economics professor Paolo Savona as minister of finance and economy, fearing negative responses from markets and investors (Agi 2018b). Moreover, via the technocrat Conte and a number of other nonpartisan ministers such as Minister of Economy and Finance Giovanni Tria, there was an understanding of the government as having a 'third leg' related to 'a "Rome–Brussels" axis between the president of the Republic Sergio Mattarella and the EU Commission' (Baldini and Giglioli 2021, 514).

Finally, the third peculiarity of the Italian case is its very short duration in power: the yellow-green coalition government only survived for

---

⁸ Interview IT10.
⁹ Interview IT03, Italian journalist, online, 20 September 2022.
¹⁰ Interview IT10; Interview IT01, Italian scholar, Florence, 12 September 2022.

fifteen months, from June 2018 to September 2019,[11] thereby making this case different from the populist governments analysed in the previous chapters, which all had much longer durations in power.

International Disputes under the Yellow-Green Coalition Government

Focusing on Italy's bilateral relationships, and particularly on its approach to international disputes, the one with France stands out. Relations with France had been relatively tense already under the non-populist Gentiloni government. Among the main issues of contention were competing claims for influence in Libya, a former Italian colony. There, during the period analysed, Italy supported the internationally recognized Government of National Accord of Fayez al-Sarraj. French President Macron in 2017 invited both al-Sarraj and his rival Khalifa Haftar, the leader of the Libyan Armed Forces, to Paris—a move that 'angered Italian officials' (Balmer 2017), who had not been consulted on this matter. A further source of tensions with France was an already negotiated merger between Italian state-owned ship maker Fincantieri and French STX Shipyard, which Macron stopped, much to the disappointment of Italy's non-populist Gentiloni government (Darnis 2019). Finally, towards the end of the Gentiloni government, another episode led to new tensions: in March 2018, French police officials raided a migration management centre on Italian territory, at the railway station of Bardonecchia in Piedmont, without fulfilling the requirement of having an Italian officer present. In response to this, the Italian foreign ministry summoned the French ambassador, a highly unusual step in inner-European diplomacy (Rai News 2018a).

While the Gentiloni government had ultimately managed all these tensions diplomatically, avoiding an escalation, things changed under the populist yellow-green government. The growing tensions with France were mainly provoked by the M5S, and personally by Di Maio. Interestingly, it proceeded in parallel with a worsening of the M5S's position in opinion polls vis-à-vis the Lega. While the M5S had won nearly double the share of votes as compared to the Lega in the 2018 elections (32.7% M5S; 17.4% Lega) (Agi 2018a), its share of support in opinion polls declined after the formation of the Conte I government in June. By the end of February 2019, support for the two parties

---

[11] It fell when Salvini decided to leave the coalition hoping to exploit the electoral successes of the Lega and the weakening of the M5S at the 2019 European election, which had amounted to a 'reversal of the coalition's informal balance of power' (Capati and Improta 2021, 6).

was nearly inverted (21.2% M5S; 35.9% Lega) (Pagnoncelli 2019). Faced with such poor results in opinion polls, Di Maio stoked tensions with France for domestic mobilization. Despite the two countries' many commonalities, according to several interviewees there is a deep suspicion among Italians vis-à-vis France, partially driven by a latent sense of inferiority as well as by more concrete issues like several takeovers of Italian fashion companies by French businesses (Darnis 2019).[12] Against this backdrop, after French President Macron called Italy 'cynical and irresponsible' on the issue of migration in June 2018, Italy summoned the French ambassador (Repubblica 2018a) for the second time in one year. Moreover, Di Maio on his Facebook page stated that Macron risked becoming Italy's 'enemy number one' (Montefiori 2018). The relationship further deteriorated when Di Maio in January 2019 addressed the 'yellow vests' movement in France. Di Maio urged the bottom-up movement staging massive protests against Macron 'not [to] give up' and promised the M5S's support (Istituto Cattaneo 2019). Further, in an interview in January 2019 Di Maio accused France of pursuing 'colonial' economic policies in Africa, which 'impede the development of dozens of states', thus leading to migration (Schianchi 2019). The M5S even called for the EU to impose sanctions on France over such 'colonial' policies (Repubblica 2019), inducing France to summon the Italian ambassador in Paris. The next step in the escalation, with France recalling its ambassador from Rome, was a much-publicized trip by Di Maio to France to meet Christophe Chalençon, a leader of the 'yellow vests' movement who had advocated for a military coup against Macron (Darnis 2019). According to our interviewees, this trip was a personal decision by Di Maio, not supported by the bureaucracy: 'It was an impulsive decision by him to stand by [such] a group. It was a mistake, it would have been better to express a political opinion, but not to go to the streets. Later there was [...] an adjustment [...]. Di Maio then said himself that he realized that such an instinctive expression [of support] had not been a good move.'[13] Or, as a retired Italian diplomat put it, this was 'embarrassing [...]. It was an effort by Di Maio to present himself as some sort of Italian Che Guevara. [...] A populist government tried to cultivate its image, and this is dangerous because abroad this is perceived as a change [in foreign policy].'[14] In sum, the deterioration of Italy's bilateral relations with France was very much driven by the Five Star Movement and specifically by personalized politics on the part of Di Maio and by the need of the M5S to mobilize support against the backdrop of increasingly unfavourable opinion poll results.

[12] Interviews IT01; IT02, Italian academic, online, 19 September 2022; IT03.
[13] Interview IT10.
[14] Interview IT05, retired Italian diplomat, telephone interview, 22 September 2022.

Italy's Populist Coalition and Global Public Goods

Italy's readiness to contribute to global public goods did not change markedly under the populist yellow-green government as compared to the previous non-populist Gentiloni government. The issue of climate change mitigation was only mentioned *in passim* in the government 'contract' (Movimento 5 Stelle and Lega 2018)—despite environmental issues traditionally being a topic of concern to the M5S. The low salience of the topic became evident already during the 2018 election campaign, from which it was virtually absent (La Repubblica 2018). During the Conte I government, the minister for environment, Sergio Costa (M5S), was quite active, for example at the COP24 in Katowice (Bianchi 2019), but this did not reflect the more general position of the government. For instance, when three opposition parties presented motions in the Senate to declare a climate emergency for Italy, the government opposed them (De Francesco 2019). However, the governing populist parties did not openly negate climate change or oppose mitigation policies per se (Bianchi 2019). Overall, the government's approach to climate change was considered insufficient by the Italian Alliance for Sustainable Development (ASviS), which however acknowledged that this was in line with the approach of previous governments: 'Italy continues to lag behind, because of the inertia shown by the last three governments and a lack of interest among the general public' (Alleanza Italiana per lo Sviluppo Sostenibile/Italian Alliance for Sustainable Development 2019). In other words, since there was not much to mobilize around, or a personal interest of the two main leaders of the yellow-green coalition in climate change mitigation, Italian policies ultimately displayed a high degree of continuity.

The same applies for the field of peace contributions, where the government did not call into question existing peacekeeping commitments (Coticchia and Vignoli 2020; Ceccorulli, Coticchia, and Gianfreda 2023, 438). Also, the number of Italian troops in UN peacekeeping missions did not change significantly. This was in line with the broader tenets of defence policy under the Conte I government, which continued that of previous governments, mainly due to the 'lower political salience of defence policy compared to foreign policy' (Cladi and Locatelli 2021, 468). Correspondingly, defence issues were 'mostly excluded from public debate' (Ceccorulli, Coticchia, and Gianfreda 2023, 433).

Development cooperation, the other public good we looked into in our previous cases, was consistently framed by Salvini as a tool to curb migration by helping migrants at home (*'aiutiamoli a casa loro'*) (Agi 2018c), but these instances of mobilization did not lead to substantial policy changes.

According to a former high-ranking officer at the Ministry of Foreign Affairs, 'there was no hostility by Salvini [towards the field of development cooperation], there was at most an ideologization in talking about the need to help them at home, thus conveying the message that it's rational to help so-called third countries'.[15] At the same time, the Conte I government showed little interest in development cooperation. For example, the director position of the Italian Agency for Development Cooperation (AICS), an operational body created in the context of a broader reform of Italy's development cooperation in 2014 (Coticchia and Vignoli 2021),[16] remained vacant for over a year (Narada 2019). In terms of geographic priorities, Italy's development aid had for some years focused especially on Africa, which in 2019 received 54% of Italy's total bilateral aid expenditures. Yet, the rhetorically much-emphasized link to migration was not obvious in all cases: Pakistan, which after Tunisia was the second main country of origin of immigrants to Italy in 2019 (Ministero dell'Interno 2019), was only the third recipient country of Italian bilateral aid in the already neglected region labelled as 'Asia and Oceania', and it saw a decline of bilateral aid from 2018 to 2019 (MAECI 2019; 2020). Overall, thus, beyond anti-immigration rhetoric, the populist government did not leave a major imprint on Italy's development policy.

Whither the EU?

When it comes to Italy's engagement in multilateral institutions, the European Union obviously was the coalition government's first frame of reference—and scepticism towards the EU was one of the few issues on which there was a 'common ground' between M5S and Lega (Capati and Improta 2021, 13). Correspondingly, the goal of reforming European Union policies on matters of migration and on austerity measures was one of the very few foreign policy topics mentioned in the 'Contract of the government of change' between M5S and Lega (Capati and Improta 2021, 16; Cladi and Locatelli 2021, 465).

Migration to Italy from African countries was one of the main topics in Italian politics throughout the 2010s. The migration policies of the non-populist Gentiloni government had sought a solution in negotiations with the EU while at the same time pursuing unilateral approaches. Interior Minister Minniti had been actively involved in efforts to limit migration—thus setting a precedent for the Interior Ministry's leadership on the matter that Salvini later

---

[15] Interview IT10.

[16] It was in the context of that reform and in order to increase the visibility of development cooperation that the foreign ministry was renamed to MAECI.

followed.[17] Among other things, Minniti cooperated bilaterally with the Serraj government of Libya and hosted several rounds of talks with representatives of Libyan factions in Rome (Felsen 2018, 372). The Gentiloni government 'reformed the migrant detention centres, accelerated the expulsion of irregular immigrants, and most remarkably, on [*sic*] February 2017, signed the memorandum of understanding with the Libyan Government of National Accord (GNA). It gave Italian assistance to the Libyan Navy and Coast Guard to rescue migrants in the Libyan waters and take them to detention camps in Libya' (Attinà 2018, 5). In the EU, Minniti sought to gain support for his migration policy via regular contact with his French and German counterparts. As a result, French, Italian, Spanish, German, and several African states' leaders met at a summit in Paris in 2017 (Aliboni 2018, 140), agreeing to support Italy in the migration 'emergency' (Istituto Cattaneo 2019). Overall, under the non-populist Gentiloni government, Italian migration policies challenged the EU, but not in a fundamental way. For example, Italy at the last minute agreed to a prolongation of the EU military mission European Union Naval Force Mediterranean (EUNAVFOR MED) Operation Sophia in exchange for the promise to relocate refugees across Europe as well as the provision of additional financial support (Deutsche Welle 2017b).

Things changed with the populist yellow-green government, whose agenda both in domestic and foreign policy very much centred on the 'migrant crisis' (Strazzari and Grandi 2019). As under the previous government, the interior minister played a crucial role in shaping migration policies, which in many ways displayed continuity with those of the Gentiloni government (Zotti and Fassi 2020, 100). However, under Salvini, the approach to migration was more clearly personalized and more visibly used for domestic political mobilization, and this contributed to increased tensions between Italy and the EU. Salvini's approach was framed in line with his party's right-wing thick ideology as one based on 'security and intransigence' (Strazzari and Grandi 2019, 337). Most notably, Salvini illegally closed Italian ports to NGO ships carrying migrants, as in the case of a rescue vessel of the Spanish NGO Open Arms, which Salvini banned from entering Italian territorial waters in August 2019 (an issue over which he later faced trial) (Gozzi 2024). Salvini thus adopted a blackmailing bargaining style vis-à-vis the EU, including over Italy's participation in the EUNAVFOR MED mission, threatening that Italy would not participate in it if migrants were to be taken mostly to Italian ports: 'We remain firmly unavailable to landing procedures that include the

---

[17] Interview IT07, Italian academic, Florence, 26 September 2022.

landing only in Italian ports' (Del Re 2018). Salvini used the issue to mobilize against the EU by attacking EU High Representative for Foreign Policy Mogherini, a former Italian foreign minister under the Renzi government, whom he accused of 'forgetting that she is Italian' (Cartaldo 2019). How this clash was used for mobilization could further be seen one day later on Salvini's Twitter channel, where he posted a video presenting the Sophia Mission as the failed mission of Renzi, Mogherini, the European Commission, and the PD (Salvini 2019). Thus, Salvini politicized the issue of migration by trying to mobilize domestic support against 'Europeanist' Italian parties identified with the EU Commission as an external foe. According to Baldini and Giglioli (2021, 519), 'In terms of spectacularization [. . .] the "closed ports" policy was a domestic public relations triumph. Particularly successful was the attack on international NGOs assisting migrants in the central Mediterranean (although they were responsible for less than 10% of arrivals in the country). Salvini's mediatization of the issue, especially on Twitter (where he is by far the most active of Italian political leaders), was extremely effective'. In fact, according to a May 2019 survey, 67% of Italians were in favour of keeping ports closed for ships carrying migrants (De Sio and Angelucci 2019). Ultimately, Salvini's hard-line policies led to the termination of Operation Sophia, something that an intervention by the defence and foreign affairs ministers, who had been totally marginalized in the process, and by President Mattarella, could not prevent (Ceccorulli, Coticchia, and Gianfreda 2023, 442).

The topic of 'austerity' and the state of Italy's public finances had been another major issue of contention between Italy and the EU for many years before the yellow-green government took over. The Gentiloni government diverged from the German line by arguing that the time of austerity was over, but Italy's approach under this non-populist government had overall been rather constructive. For instance, the Gentiloni government responded to a EU Commission letter asking for 'a detailed package of specific commitments' to correct the deficit for 2017, by agreeing to 'limited spending cuts, with a reduction in tax breaks, and new revenues, thanks to the fight against tax evasion and a tweak to excise taxes' (Istituto Cattaneo 2019). After the populist Conte I government took over, Italy's approach to the EU became more confrontational, and this was driven mainly by the two populist leaders, Salvini and Di Maio. In October 2018, the European Commission rejected the Conte I government's budget plan for 2019 because it seriously 'fell short of the Commission's country-specific recommendations and SGP [Stability and Growth Pact] rules', and it undertook first steps towards an Excessive Deficit Procedure (EDP) when a nearly identical budget plan was sent again (Capati and Improta 2021, 16–17). Ultimately, a last-minute agreement was reached and the Conte I government gave in to the Commission's demands. Nevertheless, the resistance on the part of the Italian government was remarkable, and it was driven by Di Maio and Salvini trying to capitalize on the issue with Italian voters. In October 2018, with reference to the letter sent by the European Commission on the Italian budget, Salvini commented: 'Brussels can send 12 little letters, from now until Christmas, but the budget does not change, we stick to it. What is happening is an attack on the Italian economy' (Rai News 2018b). Later, when the Commission responded to the Italian government's response, Salvini dismissed its critique by saying: 'The letter from Brussels has arrived. Well, I was also waiting for the letter from Santa Claus' (Il fatto quotidiano 2018). Di Maio was less harsh but equally intransigent: 'If this government is in the right, it will have nothing to fear. And since we are in the right because we are on the side of the citizens, we should do nothing more than explain and keep our reasons' (Il Mattino 2018). Ultimately, the two populist leaders used the spat with the European Commission to mobilize support ahead of the 2019 European elections, while the more moderate camp in government composed of Prime Minister Conte and Economy Minister Tria sought to find a compromise. Mobilization was particularly promising as the issue was highly salient to Italian voters. According to a May 2019 survey, 70.7% of Italians were in favour of more flexibility on economic policies on the part of the EU and 75.6% wanted greater EU support for the countries most heavily affected by economic crises (De Sio and Angelucci 2019).

Interestingly, the yellow-green government's confrontational line towards the EU did not extend to other multilateral organizations in a wholesale manner and should thus not be mistaken for a general rejection of multilateralism (Monteleone 2021). Yet, where the government saw the opportunity to mobilize against multilateral institutions, it did so. This became evident again around the issue of migration in 2018–2019, as the Conte I government refused to ratify the Global Compact for Safe, Orderly and Regular Migration (GC), a non-binding inter-governmentally negotiated agreement, prepared under the auspices of the United Nations, aiming to regulate international migration. As Ceccorulli et al. (2023, 441) put it, '[t]he negotiation of the GC shows that the populist parties in government decided to politicize salient issues in the interests of short-term electoral success, regardless of the risk of remaining isolated at an international level'. On other issues that could not be easily politicized or were of lesser importance to the two party leaders, there was no foreign policy change. For example, PM Conte emphasized his government's continued commitment to NATO, and there were no instances of wholesale criticism of the United Nations or of disengagement from the organization.[18] The yellow-green government did however slightly cut its financial contributions to the UN budget (Monteleone 2021; Repubblica 2018b). A real clash only took place, again, around the issue of migration, as the yellow-green government 'entered a feud with the UN High Commissioner for Human Rights', who had criticized increasing anti-immigrant violence and racism in Italy (Monteleone 2021, 555).

Italy's Populist Coalition and New Partners

When it comes to the question of whether Italy's all-populist government promoted a reorientation of the country's partnerships towards populist and authoritarian regimes, some important developments took place. First of all, the yellow-green government did not call into question Italy's traditional transatlantic alliance with the United States, which at that time was governed by Trump, whom Salvini admired (Evolvi 2023). At the same time, the government was 'keen to dialogue with Russia' (Marrone 2018, 3). On the one hand, the coalition proposed to review sanctions against Russia, while on the other hand it paid attention to reassure the G-7 that Italy would not act unilaterally (Marrone 2018, 3). The notion of a rapprochement with Russia was mainly driven by the Lega and by Salvini's personal sympathy for Putin. Ultimately, however, 'despite the display of friendship, on sanctions, Italy never defected from the European position' (Monteleone 2021, 554). Also at the UNGA, Italy continued to align with EU states, as revealed by the co-sponsoring of resolutions (Monteleone 2021).

The most dramatic shift in Italy's international partnerships took place as the populist Conte I government in March 2019 signed a Memorandum of Understanding (MoU) with China, becoming the first (and only) G-7 country to officially join the Belt and Road Initiative (BRI). While the decision to sign the MoU had already been prepared under the previous non-populist government,[19] the push for the rapprochement with China was clearly and personally driven by Di Maio, with the institutional support of his ministry of economic development. It broadly reflected the preferences of the M5S, with its belief in an approach to foreign policy that should not be driven by partisan ideologies as well as its latent anti-Americanism. Moreover, it entailed the hope for substantial Chinese investments.[20] The leading architect

---

[18] Interview IT08, retired Italian ambassador, telephone interview, 3 October 2022.

[19] As a former high-ranking government official in the Ministry of Foreign Affairs and International Cooperation put it, 'the issue of China was not something new, it was a continuation [of previous policies]' (Interview IT10).

[20] Interview IT02.

of the deal with China was Michele Geraci, an academic who taught at foreign universities based in China and who was nominated by the Lega undersecretary of state with responsibility for trade (De Maio 2020, 12).[21] The Lega itself was split on the China issue, with Salvini not being interested in it, but the traditional power base of the Lega, the manufacturing sector in northern Italy, favouring stronger relations with Beijing.[22] Thus Di Maio 'took control of the China dossier' (Pugliese, Ghiretti, and Insisa 2022, 1039), completely marginalizing the foreign ministry in the process.[23] As an interviewee put it: 'Then comes Di Maio, who signs everything without understanding that in port technology there are sensitive dossiers. [...] Then the American embassy in Rome sets everyone in motion to put things in order again. Ambassador Heisenberg expresses his perplexity. And then Conte intervenes'.[24]

In sum, the transition from the non-populist Gentiloni government to the all-populist M5S-Lega coalition government led to a number of changes in Italian foreign policy, mostly in line with our expectations about populists' foreign policy. Where mobilization and personalization were strong, such as around the issue of migration but also in bilateral relations with France and in Italy's approach to the European Union over 'austerity', foreign policy change was more marked. In fact, in those cases, the populist government pursued a more confrontational policy vis-à-vis its European partners and France in particular. The shift towards new partners, most notably towards China, was mainly driven by personalization but less by mobilization. While certainly a highly visible foreign policy shift, joining the BRI was not paralleled by a disruption of existing partnerships and alliances. Thus, it did not amount to a complete re-orientation of the country's international partnerships. Rather, Italy's yellow-green government followed a pattern similar to those observed in some of the other cases discussed in Chapter 6, trying to diversify its international partnerships. Finally, in policy areas that were not particularly salient to the public, and in which none of the leaders had a personal interest, foreign policy did not change much: this was the case with regard to Italy's readiness to contribute to the provision of the global public goods of climate change mitigation and peace, as well as development. Thus, the case of Italy, despite being an unstable populist coalition with an unclear thick ideology and despite of having only a very short duration in power,

---

[21] According to a journalist interviewed, Geraci was not a prominent figure in the Lega, there 'nobody knows him. [...] It has never been entirely clear how he came into government'. Interview I03.

[22] Interview IT04, Italian academic, online, 21 September 2022.

[23] According to a retired diplomat interviewed, however, also within the Farnesina there is a pro-China faction. Interview IT05.

[24] Interview IT02.

overall displays similar patterns as the other case studies. Given the peculiar structure of the government with the two party leaders playing the most prominent roles in decision making, we observed a parallel personalization around specific issues related to the respective party's thick ideology. Moreover, the two leaders at times competed in their mobilization efforts around foreign policy issues, which exacerbated the drive for change, as seen in Italy's approach to France, driven by Di Maio, or in the migration issue, driven by Salvini.

Conclusion

In this chapter, we applied our theoretical framework to the analysis of three European cases that displayed variation along a number of relevant theoretical dimensions: the thick ideologies of populist governments (right-wing populists in Hungary and the UK, and an all-populist government with a mixed thick ideology in Italy), the countries' embeddedness in international institutions (with Hungary and Italy facing the peculiar constraints of EU membership and the UK negotiating its exit from the EU), the constraints on the governing populist party (one-party government in Hungary and the UK, coalition government in Italy), and the governments' duration in power (from the fourteen years in power of Orbán to the fifteen months in office of the Conte I government).

Regardless of the specific context, populism drives foreign policy change via mobilization and personalization, as outlined in our theoretical model. The intertwining of domestic and international politics peculiar to populism greatly contributes to explaining foreign policy change. In the case of Hungary, we saw that mobilization against the EU was not necessarily successful across the Hungarian population, but it was still used by Orbán to project the enemy image of an elite detached from the 'people', thus underpinning the importance of the thin ideology of populism. The UK under Johnson further exposed the value foreign policy may have as a mobilizing device for ambitious populist leaders. Moreover, Brexit and the central role played in the campaign around it by Boris Johnson illustrate how mobilization and personalization reinforce each other, eventually resulting in the reversal of decades of British foreign policy and a fulsome distancing from the UK's European partners. Moreover, Johnson was prepared to break international law to realize Brexit-hardliners' demands, again pointing at the interrelation of domestic and foreign politics that is characteristic of populists in power. Personalization also matters enormously in creating the space for populist leaders to change foreign policy. The UK under Johnson significantly reduced its widely acclaimed foreign aid but invested in climate change mitigation, at least partially due to the prime minister changing his mind. Orbán cultivated ties with Russia as well as a host of right-wing populists across the Western world and Latin America. Italy severed ties with France as Di Maio personally chose to abandon diplomatic convention, and Rome broke ranks with its Western allies in signing up to China. The Italian case especially revealed how the personalization on the part of two party leaders and members of cabinet, Di Maio and Salvini, led to a spiralling of foreign policy changes driven by the leaders' desire to perform well in front of their domestic audience and to cater to their constituents.

8

Conclusion

Claiming to be different from the 'establishment', populists introduce reforms that alter state institutions, often ending up weakening democracy and increasing societal polarization. This all happens in the name of a 'thin' ideology, which focuses on pitting the true people against an evil elite. How such an ideology, which is primarily focused on some basic features of domestic society, would impact the way a populist-governed country interacts with the world—that was the main question of this book.

The impact of populist thin-centred ideology on foreign policy is not immediate, simply because such ideology is limited to domestic issues. Yet, a number of expectations about populist governments' foreign policy flow from the basic tenets of it. Overall, we expect populist governments to be less willing than non-populist ones to compromise in bilateral disputes, more 'egoistic' in their approach to global public goods provision, more sovereigntist in their interactions with multilateral organizations, and more independent in their approach to international partners—but we expect this to manifest to varying degrees depending on procedural factors. Where populist leaders personally take interest in an issue and marginalize foreign policy bureaucracies and advisors, that is, where they strongly personalize foreign policy making, the impact of populism will be stronger, making foreign policy change more likely. Similarly, if populist governments use a foreign policy issue to mobilize domestic support, that is, if they deeply intertwine foreign affairs with the fight against their domestic opponents in their indefinite political campaigning, this will also increase the likelihood of foreign policy change under populist governments. A combination of both strong personalization and strong mobilization will thus lead to the most intense foreign policy change.

And in fact, we saw that some populists in power fundamentally change their country's foreign policy. They escalated bilateral tensions, complicated rapprochements with their adversaries, and personally insulted leaders of foreign countries and international institutions. In several cases, populist governments shifted alliances away from traditional partners, forging ties with

Populism and Foreign Policy. Sandra Destradi and Johannes Plagemann, Oxford University Press.
© Oxford University Press (2025). DOI: 10.1093/9780197695012.003.0008

new and more autocratic ones, thus fundamentally reshaping their countries' foreign policy orientation. Bolivia's president Morales traded his country's development and security cooperation with the US against alignments with Venezuela, other leftist regional governments, as well as Russia, China, and Iran. Erdoğan, after eliminating the Kemalist establishment's control of Turkish foreign and security affairs, antagonized his Western NATO allies. He oversaw a naval stand-off with Greece and sent Turkish soldiers to Syria and Syrian militias to Libya, all the while reaching out to Russia and damaging relations with the EU beyond repair. Boris Johnson as member of the British parliament, as foreign minister, and most visibly as prime minister was a key force driving his country towards a 'hard Brexit', a significantly more substantive break away from the EU than the outcome of the 2016 referendum required, and one that neither of his Tory predecessors Theresa May and David Cameron had been prepared for. Viktor Orbán turned Hungary into a meeting ground for the populist right across the Western world, thus derailing relations with its non-populist partners in Europe and North America. In Italy's short yellow-green coalition government, Salvini as a central actor expressed his admiration for Vladimir Putin while his coalition partner Di Maio broke a diplomatic taboo by publicly supporting the populist 'yellow vests' movement in France.

Yet, other populist governments examined in this book did not alter their countries' foreign policy fundamentals, or only selectively pushed for change. Under the banner of his barely thought-through 'Independent Foreign Policy', Duterte in the Philippines threatened to dismantle the long-standing alliance with the US, turning instead to China, Japan, and Russia, whose president, Putin, he personally admired. However, faced with resistance internally and unfulfilled promises from China, the Philippines' foreign policy returned to its usual pattern of close security relations with the US and vocal complaints over Chinese encroachments in the South China Sea before the Duterte presidency's end. The other less-than-radical case in this book is India under Modi. Rather than building on his predecessor's dialogue with Pakistan, the populist prime minister, ahead of the 2019 elections, authorized air strikes on Pakistani soil while seeking to isolate the neighbouring country internationally. Yet, this and other policy changes notwithstanding, Modi maintained the core principles of India's traditional foreign policy orientation, pursuing them with greater vigour. He continued the previous government's policy of deepening security ties with the US while remaining close to Russia and reaching out to a diverse array of new and old partners in security and beyond, from Israel to Saudi Arabia, and from Iran to Japan and France.

Explaining Radical Change

Our theory of populism and foreign policy accounts for the variations above. In fact, one of the primary purposes of this book was the theorization of both foreign policy change *and* its absence once populists come to power. Through our abductive research process, we identified two mechanisms—personalization and mobilization—that, if prevalent at the same time, tend to produce significant foreign policy change. In all our cases examined in detail we found traces of the two mechanisms. Denouncing US interference in Bolivia's internal affairs—framed as 'anti-imperialism'—was a key plank of Morales's domestic discourse throughout his fourteen years in power. Similarly, the more populist Erdoğan became and the longer he remained in office—first as prime minister and, from 2014 onwards, as president, and later as executive president—the more his public discourse turned anti-Western, increasingly using his country's foreign relations in mobilizing public support. In India, tension with Pakistan escalated just before national elections in 2019, securing Modi's party a resounding majority in parliament. His mobilization around Indian air strikes on Pakistan was substantial. Meanwhile, Duterte's threats of subverting long-standing foreign policy tenets were most extreme, and his language was most improper when responding to foreign critiques of the brutal 'war on drugs', his hallmark domestic policy around which much of his public mobilization circulated. Johnson's Brexit negotiations with the EU dominated campaigning in 2019 and were driven by populist hardliners' public promises rather than cool-headed calculations of British interests. Orbán habitually campaigned with resisting the EU's migration regime and combatting other forms of foreign influence, from US philanthropy to 'LGBT ideology'. Italy's two populist parties both pre- and post-election mobilized support by opposing EU policies. In all these cases, the transition to a populist government led to a closer intertwining of domestic and foreign issues, which had tangible foreign policy consequences.

At the same time, our interviews as well as media reporting and academic sources confirmed the pronounced personalization in the foreign policy making processes in several of the cases and fields analysed. Morales's persona and charisma as one of the world's few Indigenous leaders provided him with an unusual degree of global attention, which his foreign policy team sought to leverage to a maximum degree. The Philippines' pivot towards China under Duterte was driven by his very personal dislike of the US. Turkish observers describe foreign policy under Erdoğan after the introduction of the executive presidency as hinging almost entirely on the president's whims, thus rendering it more transactional but also less reliable than before.

Although foreign policy in India under Modi seems less erratic than in Turkey or the Philippines, our sources also indicate the extent to which domestic actors outside the Prime Minister's Office have been marginalized in foreign policy making. This may explain provocations such as the killing of a Sikh activist in Canada in 2023 and an assassination attempt in the US at the hand of Indian intelligence personnel—possible alarming signals of an enclosed foreign policy circle prioritizing domestic concerns over foreign policy foresight. Orbán, over his many years in power, significantly centralized and personalized foreign policy making. In the UK, Boris Johnson's premiership ended early, not the least because of his antipathy to parliament, the bureaucratic elite, and the courts. And Salvini and Di Maio successfully monopolized authority over issues relevant to their respective political agendas.

The more personalized and politicized a bilateral relation or foreign policy issue was, the more radical the changes we observed. Across our four policy fields and cases from the Global South, Bolivia's turn away from the US, the worsening of relations with Greece under Erdoğan and his wider recalibration of Turkey's relations with the West, and Modi's unwillingness to engage Pakistan stand out as examples of change combining both high degrees of personalization and mobilization. Likewise, Johnson's pursuit of 'getting Brexit done', Orbán's continuous haggling with EU institutions and members states' governments, and Salvini's actions on migration combine strong mobilization with strong personalization.

Less-than-Radical Foreign Policy Change across Issues

However, many foreign policy issues hardly arouse any public interest and thus do not lend themselves to mobilization efforts. At the same time, even the most hard-working populist leaders have limited time, thus forcing them to prioritize among foreign policy themes and bilateral relations. Our theory captures these variations in mobilization and personalization across dossiers. As a result, changes were less radical or did not occur at all.

In fact, in our sample of issue areas and bilateral relations we also found numerous cases of continuity or stasis. The Philippines' commitment to the promotion of peace did not change much. Bolivia's involvement in climate change mitigation was somewhat trickier to categorize, given its interrelations with elements of the MAS's thick ideology—the discourse around *Pachamama* in particular—and its initial activist international position. Yet, following the departure of Pablo Solón as ambassador to the UN in 2011,

Bolivia returned to positions similar to those of pre-Morales years, and all the while resource extractivism and deforestation intensified. The Modi government did not alter India's commitment to UN peacekeeping and development aid, nor did it transform its relations with the United Nations. Likewise, New Delhi did not touch SAARC, the only regional organization involving all South Asian states, thus cementing stasis. Turkey's commitment to the UN remained steady, nor did we see much of a change in terms of Ankara's involvement in climate change mitigation. In all the above cases we found indications of only weak personalization and mobilization.

Particularly interesting are the in-between cases, in which only either mobilization or personalization is strong, while the other mechanism is weak. In those cases, foreign policy change is less pronounced. With no mobilization around it, Duterte delegated climate change issues to his finance secretary. As a result, the Philippines' climate policies became more centralized, less transparent, and also less ambitious than those of Duterte's non-populist predecessor Aquino. As described vividly by our interviewees, Duterte's 'Independent Foreign Policy' was driven almost exclusively by his personal dislike of the US. However, it lacked the potential to mobilize support among the US-friendly Filipino public and thus was unsustainable. By contrast, given the high salience of the Indo-Chinese disputes, Modi could have used bilateral tensions to mobilize support. Yet, he chose not to do so to avoid public pressures for military action against a clearly superior rival. Ultimately, India's response to Chinese incursions, devised in the Prime Minister's Office, did not prevent Beijing from eating away portions of Indian territory and sought to avoid escalation.

The converse cases of strong mobilization with weak personalization were much harder to find, but not entirely absent. Bolivia's approach to its age-old conflict over access to the sea under Morales at times featured strong mobilization by the ruling MAS. However, it also turned into a sophisticated campaign involving former Bolivian presidents and other senior opposition figures as well as an elaborate judicial case made before the International Court of Justice. Bolivia's approach to peacebuilding also fell under this category. The Bolivian armed forces throughout the first few years of Morales's presidency ensured continuity in providing the highest number of peacekeepers (to Haiti and the Congo) in the history of the country. As shown in Chapter 4, the MAS's ideology and its proponents within the Foreign Ministry opposed UN peacekeeping as an extension of great power interventionism, but Morales did not enforce his party's stance against the military; as a consequence, the number of Bolivian peacekeepers only decreased in the second half of his presidency.

In sum, these cases confirm that the transition to a populist government leads to moderate foreign policy change where one of the two mechanisms of populist foreign policy making plays out forcefully, but the other one does not. At the same time, our findings show a certain prevalence of personalization over mobilization as a driver of populists' foreign policy change. The two mechanisms are analytically separate—and this is confirmed by our empirical finding that in many instances they do not go hand in hand. However, a combination of weak personalization and strong mobilization could only be found in the case of Bolivia, concerning the territorial conflict with Chile and the readiness to contribute to the global public good of peace. The occurrence of a combination of weak personalization and strong mobilization in Bolivia might be related to limited interest in peacekeeping on the part of Morales as well as to the peculiarities of the dispute with Chile, which did not lend itself to high-stakes leader-level involvement given the rather low likelihood of eventual success. It could also be traced back to the origins of Morales's populist government in a broader social movement, even though we found that personalization was strong in other fields. In any case, our analysis reveals that although not a necessary condition for foreign policy change, personalization in many cases is its main driver.

Populists' Perplexing Involvement in Global Governance and Multilateralism

However, we also came across cases and issue areas in which the four populists from the Global South did not conform to our theoretical model. The exploration of such cases and a comparison with the findings from our three European cases reveal more about how domestic and international contexts shape the foreign policy of populist governments.

In Chapter 4 we saw that, contrary to our theoretical expectations, in none of our cases populists substantially reduced their country's involvement in global public goods provision compared to their predecessor governments across the three fields we examined in detail. However, most surprising from the standpoint of our theory is that two of our four populist leaders were substantially *more* personally engaged in at least one issue area of global governance than their non-populist predecessors, and that they even leveraged it for mobilization purposes, advocating *for*—not against—the provision of global public goods. Modi in India endorsed climate change mitigation and habitually referred to this issue in his public appearances, even though it was not a priority for Indian voters. He shifted India's traditionally intransigent international negotiation position towards one that, according to foreign observers and domestic experts, was both more constructive and more ambitious than under Manmohan Singh—while also maintaining key planks of the previous government's agendas. Moreover, domestically and internationally he adopted new policy initiatives to facilitate the transition towards clean energy. To be sure, India under Modi continued to rely on domestic coal as the country's primary source of energy. Yet, unlike populist climate change obstructionists from Trump to Bolsonaro or Orbán, Modi never left a doubt about his conviction that climate change was real, and that India would need to change to address this global challenge.

Turkey under Erdoğan, the other country aspiring for a greater role in world politics, increasingly invested in the provision of global public goods, both politically and financially. Particularly noticeable was Ankara's growing involvement in development and humanitarian aid. Not only did the ODA budget rise sharply during Erdoğan's populist period as Turkey officially adopted the notion of being a 'humanitarian power'. Visiting dozens of African countries, Erdoğan also personally appeared in numerous Turkish aid activities, thus substantially increasing their visibility to the domestic public. Besides aid, Erdoğan also played a prominent role with his personal mediation efforts, both during his non-populist and his populist phase. He frequently told his domestic audiences about his involvement in the resolution of foreign conflicts, which, so he claimed, would elevate Turkey's status in international politics.

Therefore, the four cases explored in detail suggest that the broader fear of a fundamental populist opposition to the resolution of global problems is misplaced. None of the four populist leaders from the Global South, all of which were in power for a considerable time, contested the necessity of global governance per se, or the importance of the three global public goods in question. Not one of them vilified development aid, climate change mitigation, or peacekeeping to mobilize public support while also personalizing decision making around them.

By contrast, two of the three European populist governments analysed in Chapter 7 align more closely with our theoretical expectations. Viktor Orbán was a quintessential climate obstructionist, casting doubt about Brussels' preoccupation with climate change mitigation and the allegedly paternalistic policies emanating from it. Orbán also reduced the number of Hungarian soldiers in UN peacekeeping (though his government emphasized its utility in combating migration). Despite overseeing the establishment of Hungary's aid agency in 2017, its resources were directed at addressing the 'root causes' of migration (primarily in Africa) as well as assisting persecuted Christians abroad, both issues that aligned with Orbán's thin and thick ideologies and which he frequently used for mobilization. In the UK, Boris Johnson cut the aid budget at the same time as he diminished the DFID's political clout by merging it with the foreign ministry. Yet, here like in the case of emerging powers, the picture is blurred. Johnson, albeit a climate sceptic in the past, actively worked towards an agreement as host of the COP26 in Glasgow. Moreover, his 'Global Britain' agenda foresaw sustained British involvement in the resolution of armed conflicts and peacekeeping. Italy's short-lived yellow-green populist coalition displayed primarily continuity in all three areas, none of which was used for mobilization purposes. Thus, of the three Western cases only Hungary under Orbán resembled the vocal Trump-style rejection of contributing to global public goods per se. Still, overall, the European cases conformed more neatly with our expectations.

The analysis of populists' involvement in global and regional multilateral arrangements yielded similar results. In line with our expectations, the populist Erdoğan reversed Turkey's relations with the EU by deepening rifts with member states and vocally denouncing the EU as racist, anti-Islam, and hypocritical. Erdoğan clearly took personal control of Turkey's relations with the EU, leveraging his critique of Brussels for domestic mobilization. However, in our analysis of Global South cases we also identified three instances in which populist leaders exhibited significantly more support for multilateral institutions than their non-populist predecessors. Bolivia, the weakest country in our sample, created new regional institutions in Latin America and reinvigorated existing ones. Moreover, Morales's government was more proactive and the president more visible on the UN level than his predecessors, with Bolivia's initiatives closely connected with key domestic issues, ranging from coca cultivation to the pursuit of Bolivian access to the sea. Indian Prime Minister Modi arranged India's G-20 presidency in late 2023 ahead of national elections, literally bringing the summit to the people with billboards and events across the entire country. Notably, we found no equivalent to the Trumpist rejection of the UN or the hardcore Brexiteers' demonization of the EU as threats to sovereignty and the will of the people. Thus, our cases from the Global South do not support an understanding of populism as a threat to multilateral institutions per se.

By comparing our findings from the Global South with those from Europe, we may develop some explanations as to why we find relatively low levels of opposition to the provision of global public goods as well as multilateral arrangements on the part of the former. At the broadest level, irrespective of whether they are populist-led or not, countries in the Global South have a shared history in international affairs, which may drive them towards approaches to global governance and multilateralism that differ from those of Western governments. With hardly any exceptions, colonial and post-colonial societies have long remained at the margins of international politics. Four of the five permanent members of the UNSC pertain to the Global North. The US maintains its veto power within the International Monetary Fund. Heads of the World Bank and the International Monetary Fund following an unwritten rule have always been American and European, respectively. Post–World War II, even large countries like India at times were highly dependent on Western handouts in form of food and other aid. In the 1980s and 1990s economic reforms along the 'Washington Consensus' enforced by the IMF and World Bank as well as individual Western donor countries prescribed market liberalization, privatization of public entities, and deregulation. All of this fuelled resentment, a deeply ingrained desire for autonomy, and strong resistance against foreign intrusions as well as a more pronounced attention towards the politics in the Western world than vice versa. These dynamics have had rather concrete consequences for the two foreign policy areas—public goods and multilateralism—discussed above.

First, constraints on Global South countries' agency in the post–World War II world meant that expectations for their contribution to the provision of global public goods have remained limited. Traditionally, this has been the domain of rich industrialized countries, and more recently, China. This is most obvious when it comes to development aid, but it also extends to other fields. Thus, portraying the contribution to climate change mitigation, development, or peacekeeping as an undue infringement on national autonomy per se makes little sense for those countries that traditionally stood to gain more from increased contributions from the West. Of course, important differences within the Global South remain, as reflected in the different approaches by Turkey and India, on the one hand, and Bolivia and the Philippines, on the other. Whereas the economically stronger India and Turkey do face certain expectations at least regionally to contribute to the provision of public goods, this is much less the case for Bolivia as well as the Philippines. For instance, neither of the two latter countries runs its own development agency. Moreover, the changing international context has had deep impacts on India and Turkey as aspiring great or global middle powers. With an increasingly global reach, both countries more than ever seek ways to undergird their status demands (Destradi 2023). Turkey has done so, among others, by way of vastly increasing its ODA budget, while India has taken a more proactive role in international climate negotiations and climate change mitigation policies. To be sure, other factors more related to the populist character of each government have played into each of the three issue areas, and we detailed the politics around them in Chapter 4. Yet, in counterfactual terms, a hypothetical non-populist government in Ankara or New Delhi would presumably also have felt the need to more visibly contribute to global public goods to bolster the country's global standing. As discussed in Chapter 4, India changed its target year for net zero emissions following a more ambitious target set by China, thus revealing the status-competition element inherent in these policies. Indeed, on a fundamental level, vocally rejecting the responsibility to contribute to public goods would contradict each aspiring country's status claims in a world characterized by intensifying transnational problems.

However, on a more concrete level, the specificities of the global public goods we examined also play a role. Most obviously, if Global South countries rejected global efforts at climate change mitigation as unnecessary, futile, or unjustified, this would legitimize rich countries abandoning past pledges for recompensation and investments in transitioning towards a cleaner economy. The climate agenda neatly fits into some populists' anti-imperialist, anti-colonial discourse, (correctly) blaming the industrialization of the Global North for climate change while highlighting its negative consequences to the Global South. This alone has made the issue politically appealing to populist leaders from Morales to Modi. In any case, as global warming has intensified over the past two decades and its consequences have become more visible across the globe, calls for climate action have become more pressing, thus also complicating our comparison with past pre-populist governments, some of which were in power in the 1990s and early 2000s, when the issue was less salient. Also, large developing and middle-income countries—like India or Turkey—today make up for much larger shares of global emissions (although the change is less pronounced on a per capita basis), at the same time that the economic benefits attached to transitioning to clean energy have become more obvious and easier to harvest. In other words, comparing the climate agenda of any government in the early 2020s with that of its historical predecessor of the 2000s is fraught with difficulties, given the vastly different context with both stronger economic (e.g., prospects for clean energy) and political incentives (e.g., frequency of extreme weather).

Having said that, our findings also show that none of the four populists in the Global South was a climate change denialist at the same time that climate denialism has become a key feature of the populist right in the US as well as in European countries (with the UK under Johnson as an exception). This is all the more noteworthy given that some of the populists we studied were prone to conspiracy theorizing and promoted pseudo-science in other fields. Thus, climate denialism, the rejection of the scientific evidence of climate change, very much appears to be a peculiarity of the West, rather than a phenomenon characteristic of populism per se – with Brazilian president Bolsonaro and Argentinian president Milei as notable exceptions. Our comparison allows us to speculate about the reasons for this. For instance, whereas all populists invoke and cater to a certain longing for the past, the historical reference points differ greatly. To Western populists, the golden age usually is an idealized version of the post–World War II industrialization and boom years, epitomized by America's 'Greatest Generation', the *Trente Glorieuses* in France, or Germany's *Wirtschaftswunder*. In the public memory this was a time of intact social mores, growing economic prosperity, cultural and ethnic homogeneity, Western preponderance in international politics—and the absence of environmental concerns. In stark contrast, populists in the Global South expectedly draw on different historical reference points. The populist-right in India celebrates Hinduism's mythology, the Vedic era, and an idealized history of pre-Mughal India as key reference points. Erdoğan's AKP dwells on the Ottoman Empire's glory. Morales in his discourse idealized indigenous traditions and their harmony with nature as formulated in notions like *Pachamama* and *vivir bien*. What unites these diverse historical and cultural points of reference is the absence of carbon intensive industrialization, resource extractivism, and excessive consumerism. This allows populists in the Global South to embrace environmentalist and climate change–related themes and to promote related policies while emphasizing their peoples' moral superiority and building upon existing tropes to discursively justify global engagement.

A note on aid as a public good is also warranted here. Contrary to our expectations, populist governments in Turkey and India did not abandon or substantially scale back their incipient roles as donor countries. The Modi government prided itself for delivering Covid-19 vaccines, for its humanitarian assistance under the motto 'the world is one family', and for successfully rescuing not only Indian but also other nationals from various conflict zones. However, as outlined in Chapter 4, the bulk of India's aid goes to strategically relevant and politically aligned countries, and those where China threatens to undermine Indian regional supremacy. Turkey under Erdoğan substantially increased its aid to states in Africa and the Middle East. Erdoğan in his frequent references to Turkey's aid efforts describes them as 'humanitarian' in nature. Yet, much of it has been spent on refugees within Turkey and some of it in places where Turkey has growing business interests, from selling drones to infrastructure. Moreover, with a worsening economic situation in Turkey and growing opposition to Erdoğan, criticism of his humanitarian focus mounted, leading to a decline in Turkey's official ODA by the time this book was written. In any case, albeit a noteworthy phenomenon, in Turkey (as well as India), the overall spending on aid even in peak years was comparable to that of mid-sized donors such as the Netherlands or Canada and thus significantly below the world's largest donors like the US pre 2025, Germany, the EU, Japan, or the UK (OECD 2024).

Another consequence of the historical marginalization of post-colonial states in the international order of the twentieth century is the desire for a voice in existing international institutions, rather than their rejection. This is most visible when it comes to the UN. Whereas the populist right in the US regards the UN as a threat to Washington's freedom of action, for societies and governments in the Global South the UN remains one of the few global institutions that gives them a voice in international politics. And whereas populists in the West often focus on the UN's bureaucratic overreach, unchecked spending, or defence of pariah states in its subgroupings, governments and societies in the Global South tend to underline the UN Charter's formal commitment to national sovereignty and non-interference. Senior UN representatives from the Global South often occupy prominent political positions in domestic politics, either before or after their posts in New York. Gaining and maintaining membership in many cases were key elements in the nation-building of countries in Asia, Africa, and the Middle East. Moreover, financial contributions of Global South countries tend to be negligible, thus providing little reason for mobilization against the UN. As the literature on weak or small states tells us, countries that do not and will not belong to the exclusive club of great powers tend to appreciate inclusive multilateralism—and this logic, according to our findings, also applies to weak states run by populist governments. Thus, rather than calling for its abandonment, both large and small powers in the Global South call for reforming the UN so that it more accurately reflects today's international politics rather than the political context of the immediate postwar period. Of the three European populist cases we looked at in Chapter 7, Orbán in Hungary used opposition to the UN for mobilization—but his government underlined the importance of UN peacekeeping to combat migration. In Italy, the yellow-green populist coalition publicly feuded with the UN High Commissioner for Human Rights over migration—a key domestic policy issue—but otherwise did not show much policy change. Much in contrast, Johnson went out of his way to emphasize the UK's support for the UN to affirm the global relevance of London in a post-Brexit environment. Thus, even among the European cases—none of them a great power—the relationship with the UN is more complex and ambiguous, rather than simply antagonistic.

This leads us to another factor explaining the relative absence of opposition to multilateralism on the part of populists in the Global South.

In terms of market and policy integration, the EU is unmatched in its depth. None of the regional institutions in Latin America, Africa, the Middle East, or Asia comes even close to the level of authority ceded to Brussels. Thus, a Brexit-style campaign (or its equivalent under Trump—the 'renegotiation' of NAFTA) against, say, SAARC in South Asia or ASEAN in Southeast Asia makes no sense to populists, not the least since domestic publics rarely take note of the regional organizations their governments are involved in anyways. To the contrary, some of these regional institutions do grant populist leaders the personal visibility they aspire to, given that (unlike the EU) these institutions usually are leader-level driven and strictly inter-governmental. The various regional bodies supported by Morales in Latin America illustrate this well. Relatedly, Erdoğan's worsening of relations with the EU may have been partially driven by fears of losing sovereignty and control. Yet, his discourse did not reflect this. Rather than adopting a Brexit-style depiction of Brussels as a threat to national self-determination, he mobilized public support by portraying the EU as part of a hostile West intent on subjugating Islam and Turkey in particular. Hence, as outlined in our previous writings, populists' opposition to regional multilateralism hinges on the level of authority ceded to regional organizations in the first place (Destradi and Plagemann 2019). From this perspective, Trump, Brexit, and Orbán are the outliers rather than the populist norm.

Returning to our theoretical model, with the above considerations around diverging meanings of public goods and multilateralism across the world, we observe that populists in power may well be more invested than their non-populist domestic opponents in various aspects of global governance, if such investments allow them to mobilize support and shine personally. Moreover, the above tells us that theorizing primarily based on cases from the Global South not only helps in detecting Western peculiarities but also reveals commonalities among populists of all stripes and origins with regard to the foreign policies they pursue. Thus, whereas regional specificities clearly matter, our model still demonstrates the similar mechanisms at play in populist governments all over the world.

Is There a 'Populist Foreign Policy'?

What do the preceding chapters reveal about the very nature of populists' foreign policies? Given the 'thin' nature of populist ideology, does it make sense at all to talk about a 'populist foreign policy'? And if so, what does the continuing appeal of populists across the world then beckon for international politics?

First, as we mentioned above, populism is too thin as an ideology to make concrete prescriptions to leaders about what foreign policy to pursue. At the same time, our analysis has shown that the anti-elitism and the people-centrism that constitute a populist thin-centred ideology profoundly reshape the procedural aspects of foreign policy making. Populists in power personalize decision making and use foreign policy for domestic mobilization. They do so to varying degrees across issue areas and policy fields, but they are more prone than non-populists to concentrating power in their own hands and to intertwining domestic and foreign issues, thus politicizing foreign policy. Therefore, once populists take over power, foreign policy change is driven by the mechanisms of personalization and mobilization. The impact of populism on foreign policy outcomes is thus an indirect one, but still consequential.

Second, populists tend to adopt 'thick' ideologies which, if spelled out consistently, have the potential to challenge key bilateral relations as well as the wider strategic outlook of their respective countries. At the same time, such thick ideologies increase the predictability of populists' foreign policy by providing blueprints for action on specific issues. Erdoğan's Muslim nationalism increasingly translated into the adoption of an anti-Western discourse that greatly complicated Turkey's traditional role in NATO and ran counter to previous policies on EU accession and traditional close relations with individual Western countries. The breakdown of relations with the US under Morales was clearly driven by a combination of thin and thick ideology. Modi's Hindu-nationalist thick ideology predictably impacted India's approach to Pakistan. As our theory suggested, the more unequivocally foreign policy was personalized and the more the populists' thick ideology lent itself to mobilization, the more radical foreign policy change was. Thus, while thick ideologies indicate a direction for populists' foreign policy, it is the thin-centred ideology of populism, with the procedural changes it provokes, that drives foreign policy change, and its varying intensities.

While populist foreign policy is shaped by both thick and thin ideology, our analysis also reveals that ideology and pragmatism often go hand in hand, and that populists indeed often are extremely pragmatic and transactional. For one, although most populist governments covered in this book were ready to antagonize traditional partners in the name of a reorientation of their countries' foreign policies, they were not revisionists seeking to militarily overthrow borders or to fundamentally alter existing regional orders, an agenda that would threaten their domestic support and accrue incalculable risks. Arguably, Turkey's military intervention in Syria from 2016 onwards was an exception to this (see Chapter 3). However, while carefully avoiding a direct confrontation with Russian (and US) forces, Ankara's primary aim was the prevention of a Kurdish state regarded as a core threat to the integrity of Turkey, a goal that was much in line with past Turkish policies. And albeit in conflict with Russian interest over Syria and Azerbaijan, Erdoğan succeeded in deepening, rather than breaking, ties with Putin (see Chapter 6). More generally, it is important to note the pragmatism involved in the loosening of traditional bonds. Being open to all sorts of partners is a pragmatic choice in a multipolar world, with the US-led West widely seen as in decline (especially so in the Global South), and given the weakening of international institutions driven by intensifying great power rivalries (Plagemann 2021; Goh 2008; Laksmana 2020). Thus, our in-depth analysis confirms what we argued elsewhere: that populists tend to deepen pre-existing trends in international politics rather than necessarily introduce new ones (Destradi and Plagemann 2019). The intensification of South-South relations, the celebration of multipolarity, and the readiness to challenge Western prerogatives are chief among these trends. Indeed, populists are particularly prone to displaying scepticism—if not outright hostility—to the West, a sentiment widely shared across the Global South. This is partly because such stances are effective in mobilizing public support, and alternatives to the West from China to Russia—are now a much-appreciated reality. More surprisingly perhaps, the affinity to new partners extends to populists in the Global North, as epitomized by their Russophile tendencies, both on the right and the left (with Johnson's UK being a stark exception). Pragmatism, moreover, has other manifestations, as we have seen in the preceding chapters. Erdoğan backtracked on some of his most radical demands vis-à-vis the West in times of economic crisis. The Modi government refrained from using Chinese intrusion into its northern borders for domestic mobilization while deepening ties with Muslim-majority Bangladesh under Sheik Hasina. Duterte's 'Independent Foreign Policy' was de facto scrapped as the hoped-for gains from Beijing were not forthcoming. The Morales government maintained relations with its Western partners other than the US while also being open to partnerships with ideologically less aligned governments in Latin America and elsewhere. Thus, the extent to which populists are willing to balance ideology and pragmatism hinges on their respective context and the vulnerabilities emanating from it. With these in mind, populists pick and choose among the potential foreign policy prescriptions they draw from their thin and their respective thicker ideologies.

Understanding a populist government's foreign policy thus requires knowledge of the populist leader's personal beliefs and characteristics, the respective thick ideology as well as of the specific political context and vulnerabilities vis-à-vis foreign countries. In highly asymmetric relationships, populist governments will not differ much from non-populist ones. Thus, we should expect populism, including its negative consequences, to play out most forcefully in powerful states, where governments have greater leeway for substantial foreign policy change. This explains why Donald Trump throughout his first administration was able to impart a substantially different course to the United States' foreign policy and promised to do so even more radically in his second. On the one hand, actual constraints for the US in terms of international dependencies in security, energy, or technology are much more limited than in any of the other cases discussed in this book; on the other hand, Trump and his MAGA acolytes revel in the illusion of almost unlimited US power, a mindset that might clash with reality at some point. By contrast, as we mentioned above, actual vulnerabilities explain the ultimate continuity in the Philippines' foreign policy, as Duterte was unable to emancipate his country from dependency on the US. Still, Bolivia shows that there are exceptions, if there is a charismatic leader monopolizing decision making, if thick ideology is strong and coherent enough to mobilize support—and if the context conditions (a boom in commodity exports and the availability of alternative partners) are favourable. In that case, the populist government of a small state radically subverted the country's foreign policy tradition. Moreover, the case of Bolivia shows that mobilizing around specific bilateral relations is most effective if these are, in fact, consequential. This, in turn, is more likely in weak states with asymmetric relations to individual major powers than in strong ones. Anti-US sentiments in Bolivia were rife, not the least because Washington's reach into the country's domestic politics—over its coca policy and beyond—was pronounced in the pre-Morales era.

Another insight from the preceding chapters defining what is characteristic of populists' foreign policies concerns their transnational connections. In fact, we found that the turn towards new or alternative partners was a (if not the most) common thread across cases from both the Global South and Europe. Thus, whereas 'programme changes' across the various domains of foreign affairs we looked at in Chapters 3–5 were less systematic, the more fundamental dimension of 'international orientation change' was prevalent across cases. However, this did not translate into the formation of something like a transnational populist coalition. The populist right both in and outside government over the past decade has become more of a transnational force including populist parties and leaders from South and North America, Europe, and Israel. Yet, while we observed hints of populist overtures between single leaders such as Trump and Modi, Duterte, and Erdoğan, none of these proved to be particularly consequential. Not all populists (and not even all populist strongmen who share similar leadership styles) automatically like each other. Moreover, whereas Trump, Orbán, Bolsonaro, or Argentina's Javier Milei may rely on shared ideological tropes from climate denialism to identity politics, the populist right in the Global South—Erdoğan and Modi but also Duterte—have much less in common ideologically. In fact, *Hindutva's* anti-Muslim streaks might have all but prevented a rapprochement between populist-led India and Turkey. The populist left in power so far has built bonds especially in Latin America, where political and personal alignments of its leaders ran deep. Overall, as a thin ideology alone, populism does not appear to be strong enough to foster bonds across the world's deeper ideological and cultural divides. For instance, presenting the Hindu-nationalist Modi or the Muslim-nationalist Erdoğan as ideological allies may not be appealing to members of the MAGA support base in the US simply because of the huge cultural differences.

Contradicting interests clearly are another reason for the lack of a populist international so far. Populists' opposition to migration exemplifies this well. For Orbán, Trump, and many other Western populists, opposing migration is the single most important element to mobilize around, as it captures core elements of both their thick and thin ideologies. Some populists in the Global South also vocally oppose migration into their countries. Modi's refusal to allow persecuted Muslim Rohingya into India is but one example. Yet, Indian nationals abroad, Turkish citizens in Germany, and Filipino workers in North America constitute important support bases for Modi, Erdoğan, and Duterte respectively. In fact, a key element for Indian foreign policy under Modi has been to facilitate Indian migration into Western countries and Duterte too sought to alleviate the plight of Filipino workers abroad, thus running counter to Western populists' core agenda. In other words, whereas the populist right in the western hemisphere clearly consolidated its transnational connections, our findings do not support fears of a 'Third Position' uniting populists across the world.

Finally, populists are not isolationists. Or at least, not necessarily so. If anything, Modi, Morales, and Erdoğan have been decidedly more active internationally than their non-populist predecessors, giving their countries an entirely new clout in world politics. The Philippines under Duterte deviates somewhat from this pattern, possibly because of the president's more superficial interest in foreign affairs, more driven by his personality than by strategic calculation. Overall, thus, it would be fatally wrong to generalize based on cases such as the Trump's first adminstration or Brexit. Populists see considerable merit in their involvement in foreign policy making, and at times in increasing their countries' international say. In specific foreign policy areas, populist governments seek to achieve substantial change, albeit not always successfully. Thus, their foreign policy approach is more accurately described as sovereigntist. The populist instinct in foreign policy is to zealously guard their country's autonomy and preserve their governments' room to manoeuvre. Here, populists from the Global South in particular build on a history of their respective countries' struggle for autonomy, thus reducing the scope for radical change. Correspondingly, international organizations are rejected where they are seen as intrusive and as limiting the country's sovereignty. However, populists' inherent scepticism of intermediate institutions that might hinder their personal control of events does not translate into a wholesale rejection of multilateralism.

Thus, the good news is that populists do not necessarily stand in the way of deepening international cooperation via inter-governmental agreements and institutions. They are not necessarily more 'egoistic' or more unilateralist than their non-populist counterparts. Those with great power aspirations in particular may even emerge as forceful providers of selective global public goods for as long as a certain recognition of it is attached to their efforts.

However, our findings also carry a note of caution. Populists tend to prefer minilateral fora or multilateral organizations that do not go beyond inter-governmentalism—but in many ways, strictly inter-governmental agreements are only second-best solutions to global governance problems. New mottos or a summit's headlines may be more important to populists in power than the actual implementation of policies, which arouses less public interest. Moreover, the profound personalization of foreign policy by populists may render their countries less reliable partners on the international stage. At the same time, the longer populists are in power—and their autocratic impulses may lengthen their tenure considerably—the more they fundamentally transform their respective foreign policy apparatuses, and the world views cultivated by them, thus mainstreaming even the more obscure elements of their thick ideologies. This, in turn, may make their imprint on international politics all the more lasting.

Future Research

The preceding chapters answered our main question of how and why the formation of populist governments leads to changes in foreign policy. Yet, our findings also raise a number of new questions that will need to be addressed in future research.

First, among them is the temporal dimension of populist rule. The study of some populist governments, especially of the two decades under Erdoğan in Turkey, has revealed that populism evolves over time. This has important domestic implications, as populism gradually 'disfigures' democracy by undermining and eroding democratic institutions (Urbinati 2019b), but it equally seems to have an impact on foreign policy. In Turkey, we saw that, as Erdoğan became increasingly populist and authoritarian, his foreign policy also became more confrontational, marked by a conspiratorial rhetoric and by a growing unwillingness to compromise. In the case of India, after ten years of BJP-led governments under the leadership of populist Prime Minister Modi, these developments were similarly linear on the domestic front, but less unequivocal when it comes to foreign policy. Such differences across cases calls for a more detailed investigation of the connections between the increasingly authoritarian traits of populist governments and their impact on foreign policy (Wajner, Destradi, and Zürn 2024). Furthermore, the temporal dimension also matters from a longer-term perspective: populists in many cases eventually lose elections to other, possibly non-populist political parties or leaders. Yet, the centralization of power and personalization of foreign policy decision making under populist governments can be expected to endure long after populists leave office. Future research will need to address the question of whether there is indeed a long-term populist legacy and how this works.

A second important area for future research concerns the personalization of decision making by populist leaders. We found that personalization was a hallmark of populist rule, including on matters of foreign policy, albeit with some variation across cases and issue areas. Future research should harness the potential of interdisciplinary dialogue with political psychology and studies in Foreign Policy Analysis that focus on the specific characteristics of individual decision makers. While some important research has already been made on the operational codes and the leadership traits of populist leaders, it will be important to delve deeper into how decisions are made. One way of addressing this question could be by tracing the cognitive processes of leaders, trying to reconstruct the way they made decisions (Mintz and Tal-Shir 2019). Specifically, it would be interesting to assess if populist leaders share similarities in how they arrive at their decisions, that is, if there is anything like a distinctively populist way of decision making in foreign policy. Moreover, more research is needed around the question of which topics populist leaders will tend to prioritize: as we have seen that leaders are selective in their personalization, we need a better understanding of the drivers of such selective engagement.

Third, future research will need to explore in greater detail how non-populist actors in the international sphere respond to populist governments and to the challenges that populism poses to the international order. Some research has started addressing issues like the responses of the foreign policy establishment in the US to the Trump administration (Biegon and Hamdaoui 2024). Besides this, it is worth exploring how non-populist foreign governments as well as international organizations deal with populists in power. In fact, the prevalence of populist governments already has led to public as well as less visible and even pre-emptive responses. For instance, recent research has shown that international institutions can mitigate populists' 'sovereigntism' by adopting redistributionist policies (Giurlando and Monteleone 2024). However, we might also expect international organizations to take measures aimed at avoiding deeper integration in order not to alienate populist actors and to prevent a populist backlash by anticipating it (Wajner, Destradi, and Zürn 2024). We thus need a better knowledge of how international institutions as well as non-populist governments deal with populists' quest for inter-governmental forms of international cooperation as well as with their tendency to diversify their countries' international partnerships.

References

About Hungary. 2019. 'PM Orbán: Hungary Committed to Achieving Climate Neutrality by 2050'. 13 December 2019. https://abouthungary.hu//news-in-brief/pm-orban-hungary-committed-to-achieving-climate-neutrality-by-2050.

ABS-CNB. 2016. 'Duterte: It's Russia, China, PH "against the World"'. ABS-CBN News. 20 October 2016. https://news.abs-cbn.com/news/10/20/16/duterte-its-russia-china-ph-against-the-world.

Acharya, Amitav. 1997. 'Ideas, Identity, and Institution-building: From the "ASEAN Way" to the "Asia-Pacific Way"?' *Pacific Review* 10 (3): 319–46.

Adar, Sinem, and Günter Seufert. 2021. 'Turkey's Presidential System after Two and a Half Years'. SWP Research Paper. Berlin: SWP. https://www.swp-berlin.org/publikation/turkeys-presidential-system-after-two-and-a-half-years.

ADB Institute. 2015. 'ASEAN Governing Mechanisms'. In *The 3rd ASEAN Reader*, edited by Kee Beng Ooi, Sanchita Basu Das, Terence Chong, Malcolm Cook, Cassey Lee, and Michael Yeo Chai Ming, 184–88. Singapore: ISEAS Publishing.

Adler-Nissen, Rebecca, and Ayşe Zarakol. 2021. 'Struggles for Recognition: The Liberal International Order and the Merger of Its Discontents'. *International Organization* 75 (2): 611–34. https://doi.org/10.1017/S0020818320000454.

AFP. 2017. 'Beach Stroll by Modi, Netanyahu Makes Internet Waves'. 6 July 2017. http://www.timesofisrael.com/beach-stroll-by-modi-netanyahu-causes-internet-waves/.

Agarwal, Anil, and Sunita Narain. 2019. 'Global Warming in an Unequal World: A Case of Environmental Colonialism'. In *India in a Warming World*, edited by Navroz K. Dubash, 81–91. Delhi: Oxford University Press. https://doi.org/10.1093/oso/9780199498734.003.0005.

Agence France-Presse. 2014. 'Syrian Rebels Surround Filipino UN Peacekeepers in Golan Heights'. *The Guardian*, 29 August 2014. World news. https://www.theguardian.com/world/2014/aug/29/syria-rebels-filipino-un-peacekeepers-golan-heights.

Agence France-Presse. 2016a. 'Philippines Police Chief Echoes President's Call to Kill Drug Traffickers'. *The Guardian*, 26 August 2016. World news. https://www.theguardian.com/world/2016/aug/26/philippines-police-chief-echoes-presidents-call-to-kill-drug-traffickers.

Agence France-Presse. 2016b. 'UN Chief Slams Duterte's Remarks on Media Killings'. *Rappler*, 9 June 2016. https://www.rappler.com/nation/135933-un-chief-slams-duterte-philippine-killings/.

Agencia de Noticias Fides Bolivia. 2016. 'Tras nueve años de mantener Cascos Azules en Haití, Evo asegura que sirven para el "reparto imperial"'. https://www.noticiasfides.com/nacional/politica/tras-nueve-anos-de-mantener-cascos-azules-en-haiti-evo-asegura-que-sirven-para-el-reparto-imperial—370118-370014.

Agencia EFE. 2017. 'Evo Morales amenaza con expulsar al representante de EEUU por "Conspiración"'. https://www.youtube.com/watch?v=yLo1ZmjtRVA.

Aggarwal, Arshi. 2021. 'PM Modi at Davos: Despite Doomsday Predictions, India Defeated Covid and Helped 150 Other Countries'. *India Today*, 28 January 2021. https://www.indiatoday.in/india/story/pm-modi-at-davos-despite-doomsday-predictions-india-defeated-covid-and-helped-150-other-countries-1763662-2021-01-28.

Agi. 2018a. 'Come si sono evoluti i consensi dei partiti nel 2018'. Agi. https://www.agi.it/blog-italia/youtrend/sondaggi_partiti_supermedia-4776395/post/2018-12-28/.

Agi. 2018b. 'Perché Mattarella ha detto no a Paolo Savona'. 28 May 2018. https://www.agi.it/politica/news/2018-05-28/discorso_mattarella_governo-3957981/.

Agi. 2018c. 'Un miliardo per "aiutarli a casa loro". Il piano di Salvini per l'Africa'. Agi. 1 January 2018. https://www.agi.it/politica/salvini_piano_africa-4237200/news/2018-08-04/.

Aguirre, Jessica Camille, and Elizabeth Sonia Cooper. 2010. 'Evo Morales, Climate Change, and the Paradoxes of a Social-Movement Presidency'. *Latin American Perspectives* 37 (4): 238–44. https://doi.org/10.1177/0094582X10376362.

Aiolfi, Théo. 2023. 'Performing the Populist Repertoire on the Global Stage: A Critical Approach to IR and Populist Communication'. In *Political Communication and Performative Leadership: Populism in International Politics*, edited by Corina Lacatus, Gustav Meibauer, and Georg Löfflmann, 203–24. Cham: Springer International Publishing. https://doi.org/10.1007/978-3-031-41640-8_11.

Akkerman, Agnes, Cas Mudde, and Andrej Zaslove. 2014. 'How Populist Are the People? Measuring Populist Attitudes in Voters'. *Comparative Political Studies* 47 (9): 1324–53. https://doi.org/10.1177/0010414013512600.

Akkoyunlu, Karabekir. 2021. 'The Five Phases of Turkey's Foreign Policy under the AKP'. *Social Research: An International Quarterly* 88 (2): 243–70.

AKP. 2015. *1 kasım 2015 genel seçimleri beyannamesi [1 November 2015 General Election Manifesto]*. Ankara: Ak Parti. https://cdnuploads.aa.com.tr/uploads/TempUserFiles/ak_parti_beyanname.pdf.

AKP. 2018. *Cumhurbaşkanlığı seçimleri ve genel seçimler seçim beyannamesi [The Presidential and General Elections Manifesto]*. Ankara: AK Parti. https://cdnuploads.aa.com.tr/uploads/userFiles/c09e217d-a61f-47f8-a355-ddf8004cfef9/Beyanname23May%C4%B1s18-icSayfalar.pdf.

Al Jazeera. 2017. 'Erdoğan: Türkiye'nin Afrika'da sömürgeci geçmişi olmadı: Al Jazeera Turk - Ortadoğu, Kafkasya, Balkanlar, Türkiye ve çevresindeki bölgeden son dakika haberleri ve analizler'. 1 January 2017. https://www.aljazeera.com.tr/haber/erdogan-turkiyenin-afrikada-somurgeci-gecmisi-olmadi

Al Jazeera. 2018. 'UN General Assembly 2018: All the Latest Updates'. 29 September 2018. https://www.aljazeera.com/news/2018/9/29/un-general-assembly-2018-all-the-latest-updates.

Alemdar, Zeynep. 2021. 'The State and Future of Turkey and Germany Relations: The Political Backdrop | EDAM'. *Foreign Policy & Security*, March. https://edam.org.tr/en/foreign-policy-and-security/the-state-and-future-of-turkey-and-germany-relations-the-political-backdrop.

Alexandre-Collier, Agnès. 2022. 'David Cameron, Boris Johnson and the "Populist Hypothesis" in the British Conservative Party'. *Comparative European Politics* 20 (5): 527–43. https://doi.org/10.1057/s41295-022-00294-5.

Algo, John Leo. 2021. 'Exclusion of Civil Society: Activists Criticise the Philippine COP26 Delegation'. Friedrich Ebert Stiftung. 12 November 2021. https://www.fes.de/en/shaping-a-just-world/article-in-shaping-a-just-world/exclusion-of-civil-society-activists-criticise-the-philippine-cop26-delegation.

Ali Abbas, Bashir. 2024. 'Analysis of India's Voting Patterns on Israel-Palestine Issues at the United Nations'. *Hindustan Times*, 21 March 2024. https://www.hindustantimes.com/analysis/analysis-of-indias-voting-patterns-on-israel-palestine-issues-at-the-united-nations-101710950988836.html.

Aliboni, Roberto. 2018. 'Il cimento libico'. In *L'Italia al bivio: rapporto sulla politica estera italiana*, edited by Ettore Greco, 129–43. Rome: Edizioni Nuova Cultura.

Alleanza Italiana per lo Sviluppo Sostenibile/Italian Alliance for Sustainable Development. 2019. 'Italy and the Sustainable Development Goals. ASviS Report 2019'. https://asvis.it/public/asvis2/files/Rapporto_ASviS/Report_ASviS_2019_ENG.pdf.

Alpan, Başak. 2016. 'From AKP's "Conservative Democracy" to "Advanced Democracy": Shifts and Challenges in the Debate on "Europe"'. *South European Society & Politics* 21 (1): 15–28. https://doi.org/10.1080/13608746.2016.1155283.

Altunışık, Meliha Benli. 2022. 'Change in Turkey's Foreign Policy'. In *The Routledge Handbook of Diplomacy and Statecraft*, edited by B. J. C. McKercher, 2nd ed., 171–81. London: Routledge. https://doi.org/10.4324/9781003016625-17.

Alvarez, Nahiomy. n.d. 'Can a Developing Country Shape Climate Change Aid Negotiations? Bolivia's Stance in Paris | Williams and COP21'. Accessed 27 June 2024. https://sites.williams.edu/cop21/blog-posts/can-a-developed-country-shape-climate-change-aid-negotiations-bolivias-stance-in-paris/.

americaeconomia.com. 2015. 'Bolivia relanzó el G77 con la tarea de eliminar la pobreza hasta 2030'. http://www.sela.org/es/prensa/servicio-informativo/20150112/si/19808/bolivia-relanzo-el-g77-con-la-tarea-de-eliminar-la-pobreza-hasta-2030.

Amnesty International Philippines. 2024. 'International Justice and the ICC'. Amnesty Philippines. https://www.amnesty.org.ph/campaigns/intl-justice-icc/.

Andersen, Walter, and Shridhar D. Damle. 2019. *Messengers of Hindu Nationalism: How the RSS Reshaped India*. London: Hurst.

Anria, Santiago. 2013. 'Social Movements, Party Organization, and Populism: Insights from the Bolivian MAS'. *Latin American Politics and Society* 55 (3):19–46.

Anria, Santiago. 2019. *When Movements Become Parties: The Bolivian MAS in Comparative Perspective*. Cambridge: Cambridge University Press.

Antal, Attila. 2021. 'Authoritarian Populism, Environmentalism and Exceptional Governance in Hungary'. *Czech Journal of Political Science/Politologický Časopis* 28 (3): 209–28. https://doi.org/10.5817/PC2021-3-209.

AP. 2019. 'Bolivian President Visits Russia to Discuss Expanding Ties'. *Associated Press*, 11 June 2019. https://apnews.com/general-news-792c7ab267254a26a598d0f374fe0630.

Aras, Damla. 2011. 'Turkey's Ambassadors vs. Erdoğan'. *Middle East Forum* 18 (1): 47–57.

Arbell, Dan. 2018. 'Pragmatism Pays Off for Erdogan—How Long Can He Keep It Up?' IISS. 2018. https://www.iiss.org/online-analysis/online-analysis/2018/11/pragmatism-pays-off-erdogan/.

Arkan, Zeynep, and Müge Kınacıoğlu. 2016. 'Enabling "ambitious activism": Davutoğlu's vision of a new foreign policy identity for Turkey'. *Turkish Studies* 17 (3): 381–405, DOI: 10.1080/14683849.2016.1185943

Arhirova, Hanna. 2024. 'Indian Prime Minister Modi Offers to Help "as a Friend" to Bring Peace to Ukraine'. New Delhi: Associated Press. https://apnews.com/article/india-ukraine-modi-zelenskyy-visit-b633d7c646b801117106f5500a138493.

Arugay, Aries A. 2022. 'When Populists Perform Foreign Policy: Duterte's China Pivot and the South China Sea Dispute'. In *Populism, Nationalism and South China Sea Dispute: Chinese and Southeast Asian Perspectives*, edited by Nian Peng and Chow-Bing Ngeow, 25–46. Springer.

Arzheimer, Kai. 2023. 'To Russia with Love? German Populist Actors' Positions vis-à-vis the Kremlin'. In *The Impacts of the Russian Invasion of Ukraine on Right-Wing Populism in Europe*, edited by Gilles Ivaldi and Emilia Zankina,157–67. Brussels: European Center for Populism Studies (ECPS).

ASEAN Ministerial Meeting on Transnational Crime (AMMTC). 2017. 'ASEAN Plan of Action in Combating Transnational Crime (2016–2025)'. https://asean.org/wp-content/uploads/2021/01/ASEAN-Plan-of-Action-in-Combating-TC_Adopted-by-11th-AMMTC-on-20Sept17.pdf.

ASEAN Secretariat, ed. 2017. *ASEAN Document Series on Transnational Crime: Terrorism and Violent Extremism, Drugs, Cybercrime, and Trafficking in Persons*. Jakarta: ASEAN Secretariat.

Aslanidis, Paris. 2016. 'Is Populism an Ideology? A Refutation and a New Perspective'. *Political Studies* 64 (January): 88–104.

Aslanidis, Paris. 2017. 'Populism and Social Movements'. In *The Oxford Handbook of Populism*, edited by Cristóbal Rovira Kaltwasser, Paul Taggart, Paulina Ochoa Espejo, and Pierre Ostiguy. Oxford University Press. https://doi.org/10.1093/oxfordhb/9780198803560.013.23.

Asmussen, Jan. 2004. 'Cyprus after the Failure of the Annan-Plan: ECMI Brief #11'. Flensburg. https://www.files.ethz.ch/isn/34229/brief_11.pdf.

Atkins, Judi, and John Gaffney. 2020. 'Narrative, Persona and Performance: The Case of Theresa May 2016–2017'. *British Journal of Politics and International Relations* 22 (2): 293–308. https://doi.org/10.1177/1369148120910985.

Attinà, Fulvio. 2018. 'EU Management of Migration Crisis: Policy Responses from Italy'. Policy Brief 2018.1. Izmir: Yasar University.

Avila, Ava Patricia C., and Justin Goldman. 2015. 'Philippine-US Relations: The Relevance of an Evolving Alliance'. *Bandung: Journal of the Global South* 2 (1): 1–18. https://doi.org/10.1186/s40728-015-0021-y.

Aytaç, S. Erdem, and Ezgi Elçi. 2019. 'Populism in Turkey'. In *Populism around the World: A Comparative Perspective*, edited by Daniel Stockemer, 89–108. Cham: Springer.

Azcui, Mabel. 2008. 'Morales expulsará al embajador de EE UU por "divider" Bolivia'. *El País*, 11 September 2008. https://elpais.com/diario/2008/09/11/internacional/1221084007_850215.html.

Azcui, Mabel. 2013. 'Morales expulsa de Bolivia a la agencia oficial de cooperación de EEUU'. *El País*, 1 May 2013. https://elpais.com/internacional/2013/05/01/actualidad/1367416943_964674.html.

Baczynska, Gabriela. 2014. 'Russia's Relations with Hungary Warm as Ties with West Chill'. *Reuters*, 19 November 2014. https://www.reuters.com/article/world/russias-relations-with-hungary-warm-as-ties-with-west-chill-idUSKCN0J3261/.

Badie, Dina. 2010. 'Groupthink, Iraq, and the War on Terror: Explaining US Policy Shift toward Iraq'. *Foreign Policy Analysis* 6 (4): 277–96.

Bajpai, Kanti. 2017. 'Narendra Modi's Pakistan and China Policy: Assertive Bilateral Diplomacy, Active Coalition Diplomacy'. *International Affairs* 93 (1): 69–91. https://doi.org/10.1093/ia/iiw003.

Bajpai, Kanti. 2018. 'Modi's China Policy and the Road to Confrontation'. *Pacific Affairs* 91 (2): 245–60.

Baker, Peter, and Choe Sang-Hun. 2017. 'Trump Threatens "Fire and Fury" against North Korea If It Endangers U.S'. *New York Times*, 8 August 2017. https://www.nytimes.com/2017/08/08/world/asia/north-korea-un-sanctions-nuclear-missile-united-nations.html.

Bal, Hartosh Singh. 2023. 'The Mystery of India's Assassination Plots'. *Foreign Affairs*, 8 December 2023. https://www.foreignaffairs.com/india/mystery-indias-assassination-plots.

Baldini, Gianfranco, and Matteo F. N. Giglioli. 2021. 'Bread or Circuses? Repoliticization in the Italian Populist Government Experience'. *Government and Opposition* 56 (3): 505–24. https://doi.org/10.1017/gov.2020.5.

Baldini, Gianfranco, Filippo Tronconi, and Davide Angelucci. 2022. 'Yet Another Populist Party? Understanding the Rise of Brothers of Italy'. *South European Society & Politics* 27 (3): 385–405. https://doi.org/10.1080/13608746.2022.2159625.

Balkan, Neşecan, and Sungur Savran, eds. 2002. *The Politics of Permanent Crisis: Class, Ideology and State in Turkey*. New York: Nova.

Balmer, Crispian. 2017. 'Italy Upset over French Diplomatic Intervention in Libya'. *Reuters*. https://www.reuters.com/article/us-italy-france-libya-idUSKBN1A926W.

Balta, Evren. 2018. 'The AKP's Foreign Policy as Populist Governance'. Middle East Report. https://merip.org/2018/12/the-akps-foreign-policy-as-populist-governance/.

Barbier, Chrystelle. 2015. 'Bolivia Resists Global Pressure to Do Away with Coca Crop'. *The Guardian*, 24 April 2015. https://www.theguardian.com/world/2015/apr/24/bolivia-coca-growing-cocaine.

Bashirov, Galib, and Ihsan Yilmaz. 2020. 'The Rise of Transactionalism in International Relations: Evidence from Turkey's Relations with the European Union'. *Australian Journal of International Affairs* 74 (2): 165–84. https://doi.org/10.1080/10357718.2019.1693495.

Basile, Linda, and Oscar Mazzoleni. 2020. 'Sovereignist Wine in Populist Bottles? An Introduction'. *European Politics and Society* 21 (2): 151–62.

Basrur, Rajesh. 2017. 'Modi's Foreign Policy Fundamentals: A Trajectory Unchanged'. *International Affairs* 93 (1): 7–26. https://doi.org/10.1093/ia/iiw006.

Bauer, Michael W. 2024. 'Public Administration under Populist Rule: Standing Up against Democratic Backsliding'. *International Journal of Public Administration* 47 (15): 1019–31.

Bauer, Michael W., and Stefan Becker. 2020. 'Democratic Backsliding, Populism, and Public Administration'. *Perspectives on Public Management and Governance* 3 (1): 19–31. https://doi.org/10.1093/ppmgov/gvz026.

Baum, Matthew A., and Philip B. K. Potter. 2008. 'The Relationships between Mass Media, Public Opinion, and Foreign Policy: Toward a Theoretical Synthesis'. *Annual Review of Political Science* 11 (1): 39–65. https://doi.org/10.1146/annurev.polisci.11.060406.214132.

Bayer, Lili. 2017. 'Hungarian Law Targets Soros, Foreign-Backed NGOs'. *Politico*, 7 March 2017. https://www.politico.eu/article/hungary-vs-civil-society/.

Baykal, Fide. 2022. 'Turkish Press Climate Crisis Coverage (2018–2019): Elements of Disconnect in Discourses and the Representation of Solutions'. *New Perspectives on Turkey* 67: 32–56.

BBC. 2016. 'Bolivia Opens "Anti-Imperialist" School to Counter US'. *BBC News*, 18 August 2016. https://www.bbc.com/news/world-latin-america-37114191.

BBC. 2019. '"Howdy, Modi!": Trump Hails Indian PM at "Historic" Texas Rally'. *BBC*, 22 September 2019. https://www.bbc.com/news/world-us-canada-49788492.

BBC. 2020. 'Donald Trump: Huge Crowds Welcome US President to India'. *BBC News*, 24 February 2020. https://www.bbc.com/news/world-asia-india-51611949.

BBC. 2021. 'No 10 Replaces Frost as National Security Adviser Days before He Starts'. *BBC*, 29 January 2021. https://www.bbc.com/news/uk-politics-55854541.

BBC. 2023. 'How Modi and Biden Turbocharged India-US Ties'. *BBC*, 23 June 2023. https://www.bbc.com/news/world-asia-india-65982053.

BBC Mundo. 2018. 'La bandera 'más grande del mundo' que desplegó Bolivia para reclamar a Chile una salida al mar'. *BBC*, 10 March 2018. https://www.bbc.com/mundo/noticias-america-latina-43359404.

BBC News. 2015. 'India PM Narendra Modi's "1m-Rupee Name Suit" Criticised'. *BBC News*, 29 January 2015. India. https://www.bbc.com/news/world-asia-india-31034110.

BBC News. 2016. 'Philippines' Rodrigo Duterte Threatens to Leave UN'. *BBC News*, 21 August 2016. Asia. https://www.bbc.com/news/world-asia-37147630.

BBC News. n.d. 'EU Referendum Results—BBC News'. Accessed 12 August 2024. https://www.bbc.co.uk/news/politics/eu_referendum/results.

Bechev, Dimitar. 2022. *Turkey under Erdogan: How a Country Turned from Democracy and the West*. New Haven, CT: Yale University Press.

Bechev, Dimitar. 2024. 'Closer Ties to the West Don't Mean Turkey Will Give Up on Russia'. Carnegie Politika, 7 February 2024. https://carnegieendowment.org/russia-eurasia/politika/2024/02/closer-ties-to-the-west-dont-mean-turkey-will-give-up-on-russia?lang=en.

Beck, Daniel. 2023. 'Humorous Parodies of Popular Culture as Strategy in Boris Johnson's Populist Communication'. *British Journal of Politics and International Relations* 26 (3). https://doi.org/10.1177/13691481231174165.

Belder, Ferit, and Samiratou Dipama 2018. 'A Comparative Analysis of China and Turkey's Development Aid Activities in Sub-Saharan Africa'. In *Middle Powers in Global Governance: The Rise of Turkey*, edited by Emel Parlar Dal, 231-254, Basingstoke: Palgrave Macmillan.

Belder, Ferit, Sandra Destradi, Julia Gurol, Carlos Heras Rodríguez, Melih Kölük, Jameson Martins, Shaked Rogel, and Swarati Sabhapandit. 2023. 'Patterns of Populist Mobilization: Comparing Narratives on COVID-19 in the Global South'. *International Affairs* 99 (1): 337–55.

Benasaglio Berlucchi, Antonio, and Marisa Kellam. 2023. 'Who's to Blame for Democratic Backsliding: Populists, Presidents or Dominant Executives?' *Democratization* 30 (5): 815–35.

Bercovitch, Jacob, J. Theodore Anagnoson, and Donnette L. Wille. 1991. 'Some Conceptual Issues and Empirical Trends in the Study of Successful Mediation in International Relations'. *Journal of Peace Research* 28 (1): 7–17. https://doi.org/10.1177/0022343391028001003.

Berg, Ryan C., and Henry Ziemer. 2023. 'Paper Tiger or Pacing Threat? China's Security and Defense Engagement in Latin America and the Caribbean'. Center for Strategic and International Studies. https://www.csis.org/analysis/paper-tiger-or-pacing-threat.

Berg, Ryan C., and Henry Ziemer. 2024. 'Exporting Autocracy. China's Role in Democratic Backsliding in Latin America'. Center for Strategic and International Studies. https://csis-website-prod.s3.amazonaws.com/s3fs-public/2024-02/240215_Berg_Exporting_Autocracy.pdf.

Bermeo, Nancy. 2016. 'On Democratic Backsliding'. *Journal of Democracy* 27 (1): 5–19.

Berridge, G. R. 2011. *The Counter-Revolution in Diplomacy and Other Essays*. London: Palgrave Macmillan UK. https://doi.org/10.1057/9780230309029.

Bertelsmann Stiftung. 2006. 'Bolivia Country Report 2006'. https://bti-project.org/fileadmin/api/content/en/downloads/reports/country_report_2006_BOL.pdf.

Bertelsmann Stiftung. 2010. 'Bolivia Country Report 2010'. https://bti-project.org/fileadmin/api/content/en/downloads/reports/country_report_2010_BOL.pdf.

Bertelsmann Stiftung. 2024. 'Hungary Country Report 2024'. Gütersloh: Bertelsmann Stiftung. https://bti-project.org/en/reports/country-report?isocode=HUN&cHash=23ec19955473853989c4feaeadb3b2bb.

Bhagavan, Manu. 2010. 'A New Hope: India, the United Nations and the Making of the Universal Declaration of Human Rights'. *Modern Asian Studies* 44 (2): 311–47.

Bharatiya Janata Party. 2024. 'Salient Points of Speech of Hon'ble Prime Minister of Shri Narendra Modi Ji While Addressing Public Rallies in Bardhaman-Durgapur, Krishnanagar & Bolpur (West Bengal)'. https://www.bjp.org/.

Bhatt, Yagyavalk, Aljawhara Al Quayid, and Nourah Al Hosain. 2018. 'India's Balancing Act to Address Climate Change Under the Paris Agreement'. KAPSARC, 12 December 2018. https://new.kapsarc.org/our-offerings/publications/india-s-balancing-act-to-address-climate-change-under-the-paris-agreement/.

Bhattarai, Kamal Dev. 2022. 'Does SAARC Still Have Some Life Left in It?' *Annapurna Express*, 4 June 2022. https://annapurna-express.prixa.net/news/does-saarc-still-have-some-life-left-in-it-6308/.

Bianchi, Margherita. 2019. 'Clima: La finestra è stretta e l'ambizione è poca'. https://www.affarinternazionali.it/archivio-affarinternazionali/2019/03/clima-finestra-stretta-ambizione-poca/.

Bianet. 2003. 'Denktaş: Türk subaylarına söz verdim'. 1 January 2003. https://m.bianet.org/bianet/print/25354-denktas-turk-subaylarina-soz-verdim.

Biegon, Rubrick. 2019. 'A Populist Grand Strategy? Trump and the Framing of American Decline'. *International Relations* 33 (4): 517–39.

Biegon, Rubrick, and Soraya Hamdaoui. 2024. 'Anti-Populism and the Trump Trauma in US Foreign Policy'. *International Affairs* 100 (5): 1857–75. https://doi.org/10.1093/ia/iiae174.

Binder, Amy J., Daniel B. Davis, and Nick Bloom. 2016. 'Career Funneling: How Elite Students Learn to Define and Desire "Prestigious" Jobs'. *Sociology of Education* 89 (1): 20–39. https://doi.org/10.1177/0038040715610883.

Binder, Martin, and Monika Heupel. 2020. 'Rising Powers, UN Security Council Reform, and the Failure of Rhetorical Coercion'. *Global Policy* 11 (S3): 93–103. https://doi.org/10.1111/1758-5899.12857.

Bir, Burak. 2021. 'Turkey expects up to 21% drop in emissions until 2030'. Anadolu Agency, 23 May 2021. https://www.aa.com.tr/en/energy/regulation-renewable/turkey-expects-up-to-21-drop-in-emissions-until-2030/32513.

Birns, Larry, and Alex Sanchez. 2011. 'From Obscurity to Center Stage: The Architectonics of Bolivia's Foreign Policy'. In *Latin American Foreign Policies*, edited by Gian Luca Gardini and Peter Lambert, 103–18. New York: Palgrave Macmillan. https://doi.org/10.1057/9780230118270_7.

Blarel, Nicolas. 2015. *The Evolution of India's Israel Policy: Continuity, Change, and Compromise since 1922*. New Delhi: Oxford University Press.

Blarel, Nicolas. 2019. 'Looking West? Evaluating Change and Continuity in Modi's Middle East Policy'. *International Studies Perspectives* 20 (1): 25–29. https://doi.org/10.1093/isp/eky008.

Blarel, Nicolas. 2022. 'Modi Looks West? Assessing Change and Continuity in India's Middle East Policy since 2014'. *International Politics* 59 (1): 90–111. https://doi.org/10.1057/s41311-021-00314-3.

Blauberger, Michael, and Ulrich Sedelmeier. 2024. 'Sanctioning Democratic Backsliding in the European Union: Transnational Salience, Negative Intergovernmental Spillover, and Policy Change'. *Journal of European Public Policy* 32 (2): 365–391. https://doi.org/10.1080/13501763.2024.2318483.

Blavoukos, Spyros, and Dimitris Bourantonis. 2014. 'Identifying Parameters of Foreign Policy Change: An Eclectic Approach'. *Cooperation and Conflict* 49 (4): 483–500. https://doi.org/10.1177/0010836713517568.

Bojanic, Alan H. 2001. 'Bolivia's Participation in the UN Framework on Climate Change'. London: Overseas Development Institute. https://media.odi.org/documents/4727.pdf.

Bollettino, Vincenzo, Tilly Alcayna-Stevens, Manasi Sharma, Philip Dy, Phuong Pham, and Patrick Vinck. 2020. 'Public perception of climate change and disaster preparedness: Evidence from the Philippines'. *Climate Risk Management* 30: 1–14. https://doi.org/10.1016/j.crm.2020.100250.

Bonansinga, Donatella. 2022. '"A Threat to Us": The Interplay of Insecurity and Enmity Narratives in Left-Wing Populism'. *British Journal of Politics and International Relations* 24 (3): 511–25. https://doi.org/10.1177/13691481221078187.

Bonikowski, Bart. 2016. 'Three Lessons of Contemporary Populism in Europe and the United States'. *Brown Journal of World Affairs* 23 (1): 9–24.

Borah, Rupakjyoti. 2022. 'Japan's Infrastructure Investment in Northeast India'. *The Diplomat*, 8 February 2022. https://thediplomat.com/2022/02/japans-infrastructure-investment-in-northeast-india/.

Bornschier, Simon. 2017. 'Populist Mobilization across Time and Space: An Introduction'. *Swiss Political Science Review* 23 (4): 301–12. https://doi.org/10.1111/spsr.12282.

Börzel, Tanja A., and Michael Zürn. 2021. 'Contestations of the Liberal International Order: From Liberal Multilateralism to Postnational Liberalism'. *International Organization* 75 (2): 282–305. https://doi.org/10.1017/S0020818320000570.

Boscia, Stefan. 2024. 'Dominic Cummings Steps Up Plan to Replace Tories with New Party'. *Politico*, 9 May 2024. https://www.politico.eu/article/dominic-cummings-steps-up-plan-to-replace-tories-with-new-party/.

Bose, Sumantra. 2005. *Kashmir: Roots of Conflict, Paths to Peace*. Cambridge, MA: Harvard University Press.

Boucher, Jean-Christophe, and Cameron G. Thies. 2019. '"I Am a Tariff Man": The Power of Populist Foreign Policy Rhetoric under President Trump'. *Journal of Politics* 81 (2): 712–22.

Boulton, Frank. 2021. 'Response to the UK Government's Integrated Review of Security, Defence, Development and Foreign Policy'. *Medicine, Conflict and Survival* 37 (2): 102–11. https://doi.org/10.1080/13623699.2021.1914807.

Bozóki, András. 2011. 'Occupy the State: The Orbán Regime in Hungary'. *Debatte: Journal of Contemporary Central and Eastern Europe* 19 (3): 649–63. https://doi.org/10.1080/0965156X.2012.703415.

Brautigam, Deborah. 2020. 'A Critical Look at Chinese "Debt-Trap Diplomacy": The Rise of a Meme'. *Area Development and Policy* 5 (1): 1–14. https://doi.org/10.1080/23792949.2019.1689828.

Briceño-Ruiz, José, and Andrea Ribeiro Hoffmann. 2015. 'Post-Hegemonic Regionalism, UNASUR, and the Reconfiguration of Regional Cooperation in South America'. *Canadian Journal of Latin American and Caribbean Studies/Revue canadienne des études latino-américaines et caraïbes* 40 (1): 48–62. https://doi.org/10.1080/08263663.2015.1031475.

Brummer, Klaus. 2024. 'A Leader-Centered Theory of Foreign Policy Change'. Bristol: Bristol University Press.

Brummer, Klaus, and Kai Oppermann. 2024. *Foreign Policy Analysis*. New York: Oxford University Press.

Brunsden, Jim, Peter Foster, Sam Fleming, and George Parker. 2021. 'Inside the Brexit Deal: The Agreement and the Aftermath'. *Financial Times*, 22 January 2021. FT Magazine. https://www.ft.com/content/cc6b0d9a-d8cc-4ddb-8c57-726df018c10e.

Bruslé, Laetitia. 2015. 'La integración continental sudamericana, inscripción espacial y dispositivo discursivo. Apuntes desde Bolivia, el "país de contactos"'. *Journal of Latin American Geography* 14 (2): 101–28.

Bunde, Tobias, Benedikt Franke, Quirin Maderspacher, Adrian Oroz, Lukas Schwemer, Lisa Marie Ullrich, Lukas Werner, and Kai Witteck. 2017. 'Munich Security Report 2017: Post-Truth, Post-West, Post-Order?' Munich: Münchner Sicherheitskonferenz. https://doi.org/10.47342/TJBL3691.

Bundesministerium für Ernährung und Landwirtschaft. 2024. 'Außenhandel mit der Türkei'. BMEL-Statistik. https://www.bmel-statistik.de/aussenhandel/deutscher-aussenhandel/aussenhandel-mit-der-tuerkei.

Bush, Stephen. 2020. 'The Contradiction at the Heart of Dominic Cummings' Vision of Civil Service Reform'. *New Statesman* (blog), 29 June 2020. https://www.newstatesman.com/politics/uk-politics/2020/06/contradiction-heart-dominic-cummings-vision-civil-service-reform.

Cadier, David. 2021. 'Populist Politics of Representation and Foreign Policy: Evidence from Poland'. *Comparative European Politics* 19 (6): 703–21. https://doi.org/10.1057/s41295-021-00257-2.

Cadier, David. 2024. 'Foreign Policy as the Continuation of Domestic Politics by Other Means: Pathways and Patterns of Populist Politicization'. *Foreign Policy Analysis* 20 (1): orad035.

Cadier, David, Angelos Chryssogelos, and Sandra Destradi, eds. 2025. *Routledge Handbook of Populism and Foreign Policy*. Abingdon and New York: Routledge.

Cadier, David, and Kacper Szulecki. 2020. 'Populism, Historical Discourse and Foreign Policy: The Case of Poland's Law and Justice Government'. *International Politics* 57 (6): 990–1011.

CAF. 2010. 'Study for Gas Pipeline to Connect Bolivia, Paraguay and Uruguay'. https://www.caf.com/en/currently/news/2010/03/study-for-gas-pipeline-to-connect-bolivia-paraguay-and-uruguay/.

Camut, Nicolas. 2023. 'Hungary's Orbán Rejects Talks on Ukraine's EU Bid'. *Politico*, 4 December 2023. https://www.politico.eu/article/hungary-pm-viktor-orban-rejects-talks-on-ukraine-eu-membership-bid/.

Canes-Wrone, Brandice. 2021. *Who Leads Whom?: Presidents, Policy, and the Public*. Chicago: University of Chicago Press.

Canovan, Margaret. 1999. 'Trust the People! Populism and the Two Faces of Democracy'. *Political Studies* 47 (1): 2–16.

Capati, Andrea, and Marco Improta. 2021. 'Dr. Jekyll and Mr. Hyde? The Approaches of the Conte Governments to the European Union'. *Italian Political Science* 16 (1): 1–22.

Caramani, Daniele. 2017. 'Will vs. Reason: The Populist and Technocratic Forms of Political Representation and Their Critique to Party Government'. *American Political Science Review* 111 (1): 54–67. https://doi.org/10.1017/s0003055416000538.

Caramel, Laurence. 2017. 'Marine Le Pen, son programme Afrique: « L'aide, seul rempart contre l'immigration massive »'. *Le Monde Afrique*, 11 April 2017. https://www.lemonde.fr/afrique/article/2017/04/11/marine-le-pen-son-programme-en-afrique-l-aide-seul-rempart-contre-l-immigration-massive_5109633_3212.html.

Carbon Brief Staff. 2022. 'Revealed: The 11 Slides That Finally Convinced Boris Johnson about Global Warming'. Carbon Brief, 1 February 2022. https://www.carbonbrief.org/revealed-the-11-slides-that-finally-convinced-boris-johnson-about-global-warming/.

Cardoso, Fernando Henrique, and Enzo Faletto. 1979. *Dependency and Development in Latin America*. Berkeley: University of California Press. https://doi.org/10.1525/9780520342118.

Carlsnaes, Walter. 2002. 'Foreign Policy'. In *Handbook of International Relations*, edited by Walter Carlsnaes, Thomas Risse, and Beth Simmons, 331–50. London: SAGE Publications. https://doi.org/10.4135/9781848608290.n17.

Carrión, Julio F. 2022. *A Dynamic Theory of Populism in Power*. New York: Oxford University Press.

Cartaldo, Claudia. 2019. 'Sophia, Salvini attacca La Mogherini: "Dimentica di essere Italiana"'. *Il Giornale*, 23 January 2019. https://www.ilgiornale.it/news/cronache/sophia-salvini-attacca-mogherini-dimentica-essere-italiana-1633300.html.

Cason, Jeffrey W., and Timothy J. Power. 2009. 'Presidentialization, Pluralization, and the Rollback of Itamaraty: Explaining Change in Brazilian Foreign Policy Making in the Cardoso-Lula Era'. *International Political Science Review* 30 (2): 117–40.

Castro, Renato Cruz de. 2020. 'The Death of EDCA and Philippine-U.S. Security Relations'. 1 January 2020. https://www.iseas.edu.sg/wp-content/uploads/2020/03/ISEAS_Perspective_2020_42.pdf.

Ceccorulli, Michela, Fabrizio Coticchia, and Stella Gianfreda. 2023. 'The Government of Change? Migration and Defence Policy under Giuseppe Conte's First Cabinet'. *Contemporary Italian Politics* 15 (4): 432–49.

Cem, İsmail. 1999. 'Statement by Foreign Minister İsmail Cem on the European Union November 30, 1999. Republic of Türkiye Ministry of Foreign Affairs'. https://www.mfa.gov.tr/_p_statement-by-foreign-minister-ismail-cem-on-the-european-union_br_november-30_-1999__p_.en.mfa.

Centellas, Miguel. 2013. 'Bolivia's New Multicultural Constitution: The 2009 Constitution in Historical and Comparative Perspective'. In *Latin America's Multicultural Movements: The Struggle between Communitarianism, Autonomy, and Human Rights*, edited by Todd A. Eisenstadt, Michael S. Danielson, and Moisés Jaime Bailón Corres, 88–110. New York: Oxford University Press.

Ćetković, Stefan, and Aron Buzogány. 2019. 'The Political Economy of EU Climate and Energy Policies in Central and Eastern Europe Revisited: Shifting Coalitions and Prospects for Clean Energy Transitions'. *Politics and Governance* 7 (1): 124–38.

Cevallos, Melo. 2013. 'Documento descriptivo, analítico y comparativo de las políticas públicas sobre cambio climático en Colombia, Ecuador, Perú y Bolivia y su relación con el conocimiento tradicional'. Agencia Española de Cooperación Internacional para el Desarrollo (AECID), 1 November 2013. https://www.aecid.es/Centro-Documentacion/Documentos/Publicaciones%20coeditadas%20por%20AECID/2013_03_consultoria_politicas_publicas__cc_y_conoc_tradicional_docx.pdf.

Cha, Jeremiah. 2020. 'Asia-Pacific Nations Regard the U.S. More Favorably than China, but Trump Gets Negative Marks'. *Pew Research Center* (blog), 25 February 2020. https://www.pewresearch.org/short-reads/2020/02/25/people-in-asia-pacific-regard-the-u-s-more-favorably-than-china-but-trump-gets-negative-marks/.

Chakravartty, Paula, and Srirupa Roy. 2015. 'Mr. Modi Goes to Delhi: Mediated Populism and the 2014 Indian Elections'. *Television & New Media* 16 (4): 311–22. https://doi.org/10.1177/1527476415573957.

Chaturvedi, Sachin. 2012. 'India's Development Partnership: Key Policy Shifts and Institutional Evolution'. *Cambridge Review of International Affairs* 25 (4): 557–77.

Chaturvedi, Sachin. 2016. *The Logic of Sharing: Indian Approach to South-South Cooperation*. New Delhi: Cambridge University Press.

Chaudhuri, Rudra, and Shreyas Shende. 2020. 'Dealing with the Taliban: India's Strategy in Afghanistan after U.S. Withdrawal'. Washington, DC: Carnegie Endowment for International Peace. https://carnegieendowment.org/research/2020/06/dealing-with-the-taliban-indias-strategy-in-afghanistan-after-us-withdrawal?lang=en¢er=europe.

Christou, Jean. 2001. 'Clerides: Denktash Must Not Be Allowed to Bypass UN Process'. *Cyprus Mail*, 1 January 2001. https://www.khas.edu.tr/tr/arastirma/khasta-arastirma/khas-arastirmalari/turk-dis-politikasi-kamuoyu-algilari-arastirmasi-2021.

Chryssogelos, Angelos. 2017. 'Populism in Foreign Policy'. In *Oxford Research Encyclopedia of Politics*, http://politics.oxfordre.com/view/10.1093/acrefore/9780190228637.001.0001/acrefore-9780190228637-e-467.

Chryssogelos, Angelos. 2020. 'State Transformation and Populism: From the Internationalized to the Neo-Sovereign State?' *Politics* 40 (1): 22–37.

Chryssogelos, Angelos. 2021. 'The Dog That Barked but Did Not Bite: Greek Foreign Policy under the Populist Coalition of SYRIZA-Independent Greeks, 2015–2019'. *Comparative European Politics* 19 (2): 722–38.

Chryssogelos, Angelos, Erin K. Jenne, Christopher David LaRoche, Bertjan Verbeek, Andrej Zaslove, Sandra Destradi, David Cadier, Fabrizio Coticchia, Federico Donelli, and Christian Lequesne. 2023. 'New Directions in the Study of Populism in International Relations'. *International Studies Review* 25 (4): viad035. https://doi.org/10.1093/isr/viad035.

Chu, Sinan, Heike Holbig, Amrita Narlikar, and Johannes Plagemann. 2024. 'In the Eyes of the Beholders: The Legitimacy of Global Governance Institutions under Multipolarity'. *International Studies Quarterly* 68 (2): sqae034. https://doi.org/10.1093/isq/sqae034.

Chuter, Andrew. 2021. 'British Name Enormous Carrier Strike Group Heading for the Indo-Pacific'. *Defense News*, 26 April 2021. https://www.defensenews.com/global/europe/2021/04/26/british-name-enormous-carrier-strike-group-heading-for-the-indo-pacific/.

Cinco, Maricar. 2016. 'Duterte: I'm a Socialist, Not a Communist; Last Card'. Inquirer.net, 18 April 2016. https://newsinfo.inquirer.net/779984/duterte-im-a-socialist-not-a-communist-last-card.

Cizre, Ümit. 2003. 'Demythologyzing the National Security Concept: The Case of Turkey'. *Middle East Journal* 57 (2): 213–29.

Çınar, Menderes. 2019. 'Turkey's "Western" or "Muslim" Identity and the AKP's Civilizational Discourse'. In *Islamism, Populism, and Turkish Foreign Policy*, edited by Burak Bilgehan Özpek and Bill Park, 8–29. Abingdon and New York: Routledge.

Cladi, Lorenzo, and Andrea Locatelli. 2021. 'Explaining Italian Foreign Policy Adjustment after Brexit: A Neoclassical Realist Account'. *Journal of European Integration* 43 (4): 459–73.

Clary, Christopher. 2022. *The Difficult Politics of Peace: Rivalry in Modern South Asia*. Oxford: Oxford University Press. https://ebookcentral.proquest.com/lib/kxp/detail.action?docID=6970185.

Climate Action Tracker. 2023. 'India'. 4 December 2023. https://climateactiontracker.org/countries/india/.

CND Blog. 2013. 'Opening Session: Plenary Address by Evo Morales President of Bolivia'. CND Blog. 11 March 2013. https://cndblog.org/2013/03/opening-session-plenary-address-by-evo-morales-president-of-bolivia/.

CNN. 2018. 'Cayetano: Leave DFA, Career Officials out of Call for My Resignation'. *CNN Philippines*, 3 May 2018. https://www.cnnphilippines.com/news/2018/05/03/alan-cayetano-DFA-career-officials-resignation.html.

Coelho Farias de Souza, André Luiz, Clayton M. Cunha Filho, and Vinicius Santos. 2020. 'Changes in the Foreign Policy of Bolivia and Ecuador: Domestic and International Conditions'. *Brazilian Political Science Review* 14 (3). https://doi.org/10.1590/1981-3821202000030004.

Colgan, Jeff D., and Robert O. Keohane. 2017. 'The Liberal Order Is Rigged: Fix It Now or Watch It Wither'. *Foreign Affairs* 96 (3): 36–44.

Coman, Ramona, and Cécile Leconte. 2019. 'Contesting EU Authority in the Name of European Identity: The New Clothes of the Sovereignty Discourse in Central Europe'. *Journal of European Integration* 41 (7): 855–70. https://doi.org/10.1080/07036337.2019.1665660.

Comissão Parlamentar de Inquérito da Pandemia. 2021. 'Minuta contendo resumo dos trabalhos da CPI da pandemia até 17 de outubro de 2021'. https://static.poder360.com.br/2021/10/Relatorio_CPI-da-Covid-19.out_.2021.pdf.

Conti, Nicolò, Andrea Pedrazzani, and Federico Russo. 2020. 'Policy Polarisation in Italy: The Short and Conflictual Life of the "Government of Change" (2018–2019)'. *South European Society and Politics* 25 (3–4): 317–50. https://doi.org/10.1080/13608746.2020.1840110.

Cooper, Andrew F. 2010. 'The G20 as an Improvised Crisis Committee and/or a Contested "Steering Committee" for the World'. *International Affairs* 86 (3): 741–57. https://doi.org/10.1111/j.1468-2346.2010.00909.x.

Cooper, Luke, and Christabel Cooper. 2020. '"Get Brexit Done": The New Political Divides of England and Wales at the 2019 Election'. *Political Quarterly* 91 (4): 751–61. https://doi.org/10.1111/1467-923X.12918.

Cop, Burak, and Özge Zihnioğlu. 2017. 'Turkish Foreign Policy under AKP Rule: Making Sense of the Turbulence'. *Political Studies Review* 15 (1): 28–38.

Copelovitch, Mark, and Jon C. W. Pevehouse. 2019. 'International Organizations in a New Era of Populist Nationalism'. *The Review of International Organizations* 14:169–86.

Corz, Carlos. 2015. 'Correa, Maduro y Morales asumen compromiso de incluir en la Cumbre de París conclusiones de Tiquipaya'. *La razón*, 12 October 2015. https://www.la-razon.

com/sociedad/2015/10/12/correa-maduro-y-morales-asumen-compromiso-de-incluir-en-la-cumbre-de-paris-conclusiones-de-tiquipaya/.

Corz, Carlos. 2016. 'Reunión de Países sin litoral concluye con llamado a uniformar condiciones de tránsito al mar'. *La razón*, 14 October 2016. https://www.la-razon.com/nacional/2016/10/14/reunion-de-paises-sin-litoral-concluye-con-llamado-a-uniformar-condiciones-de-transito-al-mar/.

Coticchia, Fabrizio, and Valerio Vignoli. 2020. 'Populist Parties and Foreign Policy: The Case of Italy's Five Star Movement'. *British Journal of Politics and International Relations* 22 (3): 523–41. https://doi.org/10.1177/1369148120922808.

Coticchia, Fabrizio, and Valerio Vignoli. 2021. 'Italian Foreign Policy: Still the Days Seem the Same?' In *Foreign Policy Change in Europe since 1991*, edited by Jeroen K.Joly and Tim Haesebrouck, 179–204. Cham: Springer International Publishing. https://doi.org/10.1007/978-3-030-68218-7_8.

Courea, Eleni. 2019. 'Boris Johnson Welcomes "Powerful New Mandate"'. *Politico*, 13 December 2019. https://www.politico.eu/article/boris-johnson-hails-powerful-new-mandate/.

Courea, Eleni. 2020. 'Boris Johnson Heralds "Recaptured Sovereignty" after Brexit'. *Politico*, 31 January 2020. https://www.politico.eu/article/boris-johnson-heralds-recaptured-sovereignty-after-brexit/.

Courea, Eleni. 2022. 'Boris Johnson's China Problem'. *Politico*, 5 April 2022. https://www.politico.eu/article/boris-johnson-china-ukraine-putin-war-invasion/.

Crabtree, John. 2013. 'From the MNR to the MAS: Populism, Parties, the State, and Social Movements in Bolivia since 1952'. In *Latin American Populism in the Twenty-First Century*, edited by Carlos de la Torre and Cynthia J. Arnson, 269–95. Washington, D.C. and Baltimore, MD: Woodrow Wilson Center Press / Johns Hopkins University Press

Csehi, Robert. 2019. 'Neither Episodic, nor Destined to Failure? The Endurance of Hungarian Populism after 2010'. *Democratization* 26 (6): 1011–27. https://doi.org/10.1080/13510347.2019.1590814.

Csehi, Robert, and Edit Zgut. 2020. '"We Won't Let Brussels Dictate Us": Eurosceptic Populism in Hungary and Poland'. *European Politics and Society* 22 (1): 53–68. https://doi.org/10.1080/23745118.2020.1717064.

Culp, Julian. 2018. 'International Responsibilities'. In *Routledge Handbook of Development Ethics*, edited by Jay Drydyk and Lori Keleher, 333–45. London: Routledge. https://doi.org/10.4324/9781315626796-37.

Cumbre de Jefas y Jefes de Estado y de Gobierno del Grupo de los 77. 2014. 'Por un nuevo orden mundial para vivir bien "Declaración de Santa Cruz"'. Santa Cruz: Estado Plurinacional de Bolivia. https://cedla.org/wp-content/uploads/2014/06/Declaraci%C3%B3n-de-Santa-Cruz.pdf.

Cumhurbaşkanlığı, T. C. 2021. İklim Liderler Zirvesi'nde Yaptıkları Konuşma. Presidency of the Republic of Türkiye,22 May, 2021. https://www.tccb.gov.tr/konusmalar/353/127662/iklim-liderler-zirvesi-nde-yaptiklari-konusma.

Curato, Nicole. 2016. 'Politics of Anxiety, Politics of Hope: Penal Populism and Duterte's Rise to Power'. *Journal of Current Southeast Asian Affairs* 35 (3): 91–109.

Dalaman, Cem. 2023. 'The Image of Germany in Türkiye: An Analysis of the Perspective of the Turkish Media over the Last 20 Years'. Istanbul: Istanbul Policy Center. Policy Commons. https://policycommons.net/artifacts/11206822/the-image-of-germany-in-turkiye-an-analysis-of-the/.

Daly, Patrick. 2023. 'Foreign Office Rejects Boris Johnson's Chagos Islands Handover Fears'. *The Independent*, 22 September 2023. https://www.independent.co.uk/news/uk/boris-johnson-britain-chagos-islands-mauritius-international-court-of-justice-b2416963.html.

Danforth, Nick, and Aaron Stein. 2024. 'Coming to Terms with the Loss of Turkey'. War on the Rocks, 7 June 2024. https://warontherocks.com/2024/06/coming-to-terms-with-the-loss-of-turkey/.

Darnis, Jean-Pierre. 2019. 'The Political Rollercoaster of Italian-French Relations'. IAI Commentaries. https://www.iai.it/sites/default/files/iaicom1914.pdf.

Dasgupta, Sravasti. 2024. '"Jai Jagannath" Instead of Jai Shree Ram, No Mention of UP, Maharashtra in Modi's Victory Speech'. *The Wire*, 2024. https://thewire.in/politics/jai-jagannath-instead-of-jai-shree-ram-no-mention-of-up-maharashtra-in-modis-victory-speech.

David, Randy. 2016. 'Dutertismo'. *Philippine Daily Inquirer*, 1 May 2016. https://opinion.inquirer.net/94530/dutertismo#ixzz5MnDSO63X.

Davutoğlu, A. 2013. 'Turkey's humanitarian diplomacy: objectives, challenges and prospects'. *Nationalities Papers* 41 (6): 865–870. doi:10.1080/00905992.2013.857299

De Castro, Renato Cruz. 2010. 'Weakness and Gambits in Philippine Foreign Policy in the Twenty-First Century'. *Pacific Affairs* 83 (4): 697–717.

De Castro, Renato Cruz. 2016. 'The Duterte Administration's Foreign Policy: Unravelling the Aquino Administration's Balancing Agenda on an Emergent China'. *Journal of Current Southeast Asian Affairs* 35 (3): 139–59. https://doi.org/10.1177/186810341603500307.

De Castro, Renato Cruz. 2020. 'The Limits of Intergovernmentalism: The Philippines' Changing Strategy in the South China Sea Dispute and Its Impact on the Association of Southeast Asian Nations (ASEAN)'. *Journal of Current Southeast Asian Affairs* 39 (3): 335–58. https://doi.org/10.1177/1868103420935562.

De Castro, Renato Cruz. 2022. 'From Appeasement to Soft Balancing: The Duterte Administration's Shifting Policy on the South China Sea Imbroglio'. *Asian Affairs: An American Review* 49 (1): 35–61.

De Cleen, Benjamin, Benjamin Moffitt, Panos Panayotu, and Yannis Stavrakakis. 2020. 'The Potentials and Difficulties of Transnational Populism: The Case of the Democracy in Europe Movement 2025 (DiEM25)'. *Political Studies* 68 (1): 146–66. https://doi.org/10.1177/0032321719847576.

De Francesco, Stefania. 2019. 'Cambiamento climatico, il Senato boccia l'emergenza—Istituzioni e UE—ANSA.it'. 5 June 2019. https://www.ansa.it/canale_ambiente/notizie/istituzioni/2019/06/05/cambiamento-climatico-il-senato-boccia-lemergenza-_3e638c77-fee8-4db9-bff5-0b95449a3379.html.

De la Torre, Carlos. 2017. 'A Populist International? ALBA's Democratic and Autocratic Promotion'. *SAIS Review of International Affairs* 37 (1): 83–93.

De Maio, Giovanna. 2020. 'Playing with Fire: Italy, China, and Europe'. Washington, DC: Brookings.

De Sá Guimarães, Feliciano, and Irma Dutra de Oliveira e Silva. 2021. 'Far-Right Populism and Foreign Policy Identity: Jair Bolsonaro's Ultra-Conservatism and the New Politics of Alignment'. *International Affairs* 97 (2): 345–63. https://doi.org/10.1093/ia/iiaa220.

De Sio, Lorenzo, and Davide Angelucci. 2019. 'Italiani ancora europeisti, ma ormai critici e sfiduciati: il super-sondaggio CISE con 19 domande sull'Europa'. *CISE* (blog), 9 May 2019. https://cise.luiss.it/cise/2019/05/09/italiani-ancora-europeisti-ma-ormai-critici-e-sfiduciati-il-super-sondaggio-cise-con-19-domande-sulleuropa/.

Del Re, Giovanni Maria. 2018. 'La sfida degli arrivi. Politiche migratorie, il fallimento dell'Europa'. *Avvenire*, 6 December 2018. https://www.avvenire.it/attualita/pagine/politiche-migratorie-il-fallimento-delleuropa.

Dellmuth, Lisa, Jan Aart Scholte, Jonas Tallberg, and Soetkin Verhaegen. 2022. *Citizens, Elites, and the Legitimacy of Global Governance*. New York: Oxford University Press. https://library.oapen.org/handle/20.500.12657/59282.

Department for Business and Trade. 2023. 'The UK and the Comprehensive and Progressive Agreement for Trans-Pacific Partnership (CPTPP)'. Gov.uk, 17 July 2023. https://www.gov.uk/government/collections/the-uk-and-the-comprehensive-and-progressive-agreement-for-trans-pacific-partnershipcptpp.

Department of Foreign Affairs. 2016a. 'Letting Go as Interdependent Brothers'. 1 January 2016. https://shanghaipcg.dfa.gov.ph/index.php/newsroom/consulate-news/210-statement-of-secretary-perfecto-r-yasay-jr.

Department of Foreign Affairs. 2016b. 'Yasay: America Has Failed Us'. 1 January 2016. https://dfa.gov.ph/dfa-news/news-from-our-foreign-service-postsupdate/10586-statement-of-secretary-perfecto-r-yasay-jr.

Department of Foreign Affairs. 2018. 'Key PH-Russia Security Agreement Enters into Force'. 1 January 2018. https://dfa.gov.ph/dfa-news/news-from-our-foreign-service-postsupdate/15277-key-ph-russia-security-agreement-enters-into-force.

Department of Trade and Industry. 2017. 'PRRD Calls on ASEAN Trade Officials to Substantially Conclude RCEP'. Department of Trade and Industry Philippines. 7 September 2017. https://www.dti.gov.ph/archives/news-archives/prrd-calls-on-asean-trade-officials-conclude-rcep/.

Dessewffy, Tibor. 2023. 'Populist Gegenpressing: Why the EU Shouldn't Expect Orban to Back Off'. ECFR. 5 December 2023. https://ecfr.eu/article/populist-gegenpressing-why-the-eu-shouldnt-expect-orban-to-back-off/.

Dessewffy, Tibor. 2024. 'Why MAGA Republicans Are Obsessed with Viktor Orbán'. *Time*, 28 June 2024. https://time.com/6993483/budapest-playbook-orban-trump/.

Destradi, Sandra. 2012a. 'India and Sri Lanka's Civil War: The Failure of Regional Conflict Management in South Asia'. *Asian Survey* 52 (3): 595–616. https://doi.org/10.1525/as.2012.52.3.595.

Destradi, Sandra. 2012b. 'India as a Democracy Promoter? New Delhi's Involvement in Nepal's Return to Democracy'. *Democratization* 19 (2): 286–311. https://doi.org/10.1080/13510347.2011.584452.

Destradi, Sandra. 2012c. *Indian Foreign and Security Policy in South Asia*. Abingdon and New York: Routledge. https://doi.org/10.4324/9780203152744.

Destradi, Sandra. 2014. 'India: A Reluctant Partner for Afghanistan'. *Washington Quarterly* 37 (2): 103–17.

Destradi, Sandra. 2019. 'The Finances of the Association of Southeast Asian Nations (ASEAN)'. In *The Finances of Regional Organisations in the Global South*, edited by Ulf Engel and Frank Mattheis, 206–20. London and New York: Routledge.

Destradi, Sandra. 2023. 'Populism and Status Seeking in World Politics'. *International Studies Review* 25 (4). https://doi.org/10.1093/isr/viad035.

Destradi, Sandra. 2025a. 'The Ideational Approach to Populism and Foreign Policy'. In *Routledge Handbook of Populism and Foreign Policy*, edited by David Cadier, Angelos Chryssogelos, and Sandra Destradi, 17–33. Abingdon and New York: Routledge.

Destradi, Sandra. 2025b. 'The South Asian Association for Regional Cooperation (SAARC)'. In *The Globalization Projects of Regional Organizations*, edited by Ulf Engel, Jens Herpolsheimer, and Frank Mattheis, 467–82. Göttingen: Vandenhoeck & Ruprecht.

Destradi, Sandra, David Cadier, and Johannes Plagemann. 2021. 'Populism and Foreign Policy: A Research Agenda (Introduction)'. *Comparative European Politics* 19 (6): 663–82. https://doi.org/10.1057/s41295-021-00255-4.

Destradi, Sandra, and Julia Gurol. 2022. 'South-South Cooperation: Between Cooperation at Eye Level and Accusations of Neo-Colonialism'. In *Handbook on Global Governance and Regionalism*, edited by Jürgen Rüland and Astrid Carrapatoso, 160–70. Cheltenham and Northampton, MA: Edward Elgar Publishing.

Destradi, Sandra, and Johannes Plagemann. 2019. 'Populism and International Relations: (Un)Predictability, Personalisation, and the Reinforcement of Existing Trends in World Politics'. *Review of International Studies* 45 (5): 711–30.

Destradi, Sandra, and Johannes Plagemann. 2024. 'Do Populists Escalate International Disputes?' *International Affairs* 100 (5): 1919–40. https://doi.org/10.1093/ia/iiae172.

Destradi, Sandra, Johannes Plagemann, Ege Husemoglu, Vihang Jumle, Alyssa Santiago, and Ronald Schleehauf. 2023. 'Populists' Foreign Policy Rhetoric: More Confrontational, Less Consensual?' In *Political Communication and Performative Leadership*, edited by Corina Lacatus, Gustav Meibauer, and Georg Löfflmann, 279–98. Cham: Springer International Publishing. https://doi.org/10.1007/978-3-031-41640-8_15.

Destradi, Sandra, Johannes Plagemann, and Hakkı Taş. 2022. 'Populism and the Politicisation of Foreign Policy'. *British Journal of Politics and International Relations* 24 (3): 475–92. https://doi.org/10.1177/13691481221075944.

Destradi, Sandra, and Johannes Vüllers. 2024. 'Populism and the Liberal International Order: An Analysis of UN Voting Patterns'. *Review of International Organizations* (October). https://doi.org/10.1007/s11558-024-09569-w.

Deutsche Welle. 2015. 'Hungarian PM Gives Putin a Warm Welcome'. Dw.com, 17 February 2015. https://www.dw.com/en/hungarian-prime-minister-gives-putin-warm-welcome-in-budapest/a-18264810.

Deutsche Welle. 2017a. 'Germany Blocks Arms Sales to Turkey'. dw.com, 22 March 2017. https://www.dw.com/en/germany-blocks-arms-sales-to-turkey-report/a-38059815.

Deutsche Welle. 2017b. 'Marine-Mission "Sophia" bis 2018 verlängert'. dw.com, 25 July 2017. https://www.dw.com/de/marine-mission-sophia-bis-2018-verl%C3%A4ngert/a-39828579.

Deutschlandfunk. 2018. 'Erdogan bei Moschee-Eröffnung in Köln—"Ein erfolgreicher Besuch"'. 29 September 2018. https://www.deutschlandfunk.de/erdogan-bei-moschee-eroeffnung-in-koeln-ein-erfolgreicher-100.html.

Dingwerth, Klaus, and Philipp Pattberg. 2006. 'Global Governance as a Perspective on World Politics'. *Global Governance: A Review of Multilateralism and International Organizations* 12 (2): 185–204.

Diodato, Emidio. 2023. 'The UE Turn of a Populist Movement: At the Roots of the Five-Star Movement's Foreign-Policy Agenda'. *Contemporary Italian Politics* 15 (1): 60–74. https://doi.org/10.1080/23248823.2022.2059900.

Diodato, Emidio, and Federico Niglia. 2019. *Berlusconi 'The Diplomat': Populism and Foreign Policy in Italy*. Cham: Palgrave Macmillan.

Directorate of Climate Change. 2024. 'About Us—İklim değişikliği başkanlığı'. 2024. https://iklim.gov.tr/en/about-us-i-75.

Dizdaroğlu, Cihan. 2023. *Turkish-Greek Relations: Foreign Policy in a Securitisation Framework*. Edinburgh: Edinburgh University Press.

Donelli, Federico. 2024. 'Red Sea Politics: Why Turkey Is Helping Somalia Defend Its Waters'. The Conversation, 28 February 2024. http://theconversation.com/red-sea-politics-why-turkey-is-helping-somalia-defend-its-waters-224377.

Donnelly, Dylan. 2023. 'Javier Milei Flanked by Volodymyr Zelenskyy and Far-Right Viktor Orban and Jair Bolsonaro as Argentina's President Sworn In'. *Sky News*, 11 December 2023. https://news.sky.com/story/javier-milei-flanked-by-volodymyr-zelenskyy-and-far-right-viktor-orban-and-jair-bolsonaro-as-argentinas-president-sworn-in-13028062.

Donthi, Praveen. 2017. 'Ajit Doval in Theory and Practice'. *The Caravan*. https://caravanmagazine.in/reportage/ajit-doval-theory-practice.

Doyle, Michael W. 1983. 'Kant, Liberal Legacies, and Foreign Affairs'. *Philosophy & Public Affairs* 12 (3): 205–35.

Drezner, Daniel W. 2000. 'Ideas, Bureaucratic Politics, and the Crafting of Foreign Policy'. *American Journal of Political Science* 44 (4): 733–49. https://doi.org/10.2307/2669278.

Drezner, Daniel W. 2019. 'Present at the Destruction: The Trump Administration and the Foreign Policy Bureaucracy'. *Journal of Politics* 81 (2): 723–30. https://doi.org/10.1086/702230.

Dubash, Navroz K. 2019. 'An Introduction to India's Evolving Climate Change Debate: From Diplomatic Insulation to Policy Integration'. In *India in a Warming World*, edited by Navroz K. Dubash, 1–28. Delhi: Oxford University Press. https://doi.org/10.1093/oso/9780199498734.003.0001.

Dubey, Ajay. 2024. 'The Influence of Indian Diaspora: 2024 Election Dynamics'. Heinrich Böll Stiftung. 2024. https://in.boell.org/en/2024/04/29/influence-indian-diaspora-2024-election-dynamics.

Dunleavy, Patrick. 2020. 'A Modern "Rasputin", or the UK's "Vice-Premier"? Whichever View You Take, Cummings's Role Is Unprecedented'. *British Politics and Policy at LSE* (blog), 27 May 2020. https://blogs.lse.ac.uk/politicsandpolicy/dominic-cummings-row/.

Duterte, Rodrigo. 2017. 'Remarks of President Rodrigo Roa Duterte at the Opening Ceremony of the 30th ASEAN Summit, PICC, Manila, Philippines, 29 April 2017'. 1 January 2017. https://asean.org/remarks-of-president-rodrigo-roa-duterte-at-the-opening-ceremony-of-the-30th-asean-summit-picc-manila-philippines-29-april-2017/.

Duterte, Rodrigo. 2020. 'Philippine Statement'. Presented at the 75th Session of the United Nations General Assembly, 22 September. https://estatements.unmeetings.org/estatements/10.0010/20200922/cVOfMr0rKnhR/onTeYkHGFL0t_en.pdf.

Duterte, Rodrigo. 2021. 'President Duterte's Speech at 2021 UN General Assembly'. Rappler, 1 January 2021. https://www.rappler.com/nation/full-text-duterte-speech-united-nations-general-assembly-2021/.

Dymek, Jakub. 2016. 'Poland's Rightward Turn'. *Dissent* 63 (2): 121–27.

The Economic Times. 2019. 'Pakistan Expels Indian Envoy Ajay Bisaria'. *The Economic Times*, 7 August 2019. https://economictimes.indiatimes.com/news/politics-and-nation/pakistan-expels-indian-envoy-ajay-bisaria/articleshow/70577351.cms?from=mdr.

The Economist. 2021. 'How Many People Have Been Killed in Rodrigo Duterte's War on Drugs?' *The Economist*, 22 November 2021. https://www.economist.com/graphic-detail/2021/11/22/how-many-people-have-been-killed-in-rodrigo-dutertes-war-on-drugs.

The Economist. 2023. 'India Is Getting an Eye-Wateringly Big Transport Upgrade'. *The Economist*, 13 March 2023. https://www.economist.com/asia/2023/03/13/india-is-getting-an-eye-wateringly-big-transport-upgrade.

Edwards, George C., Kenneth R. Mayer, and Stephen J. Wayne. 2022. *Presidential Leadership: Politics and Policy Making*. Lanham, MD: Rowman & Littlefield.

Efe, Mehmet. 2000. 'Atina'yla kardeş olduk'. 1 January 2000. https://www.yenisafak.com/arsiv/2000/ocak/21/dunya.html.

Eksi, Betul, and Elizabeth A. Wood. 2019. 'Right-Wing Populism as Gendered Performance: Janus-Faced Masculinity in the Leadership of Vladimir Putin and Recep T. Erdogan'. *Theory and Society* 48 (5): 733–51.

El Espectador. 2009. 'Presidente de Bolivia dice que Rusia volvió a Latinoamérica'. elespectador.com, 24 February 2009. https://www.elespectador.com/mundo/america/presidente-de-bolivia-dice-que-rusia-volvio-a-latinoamerica-article-121143/.

Elliott, Edward, and Sam Goodman. 2020. '"Global Britain"? Assessing Boris Johnson's Major Changes to National Security and Foreign Policy'. *British Politics and Policy at LSE* (blog), 14 July 2020. https://blogs.lse.ac.uk/politicsandpolicy/johnson-natsec-and-fp/.

Ellis, Evan R. 2016. 'Chinese Engagement with Bolivia—Resources, Business Opportunities, and Strategic Location'. *Air and Space Power Journal*, no. 2: 3–19.

Ellis-Petersen, Hannah. 2020. 'Indians Call for Boycott of Chinese Goods after Fatal Border Clashes'. *The Guardian*, 18 June 2020. https://www.theguardian.com/world/2020/jun/18/indians-call-for-boycott-of-chinese-goods-after-fatal-border-clashes.

Erdoğan, Recep Tayyip. 2019a. 'AK Parti 1. Olağan Büyük Kongresi, 12.10.2003'. *Kurumsal İletişim Başkanlığı* Yeni Türkiye Vizyonu—Beraber Yürüdük Biz Bu Yollarda-1.

Erdoğan, Recep Tayyip. 2019b. 'AK Parti 3. Olağan Büyük Kongresi, 03.10.2009'. *Kurumsal İletişim Başkanlığı* Yeni Türkiye Vizyonu—Beraber Yürüdük Biz Bu Yollarda-6.

Erdoğan, Recep Tayyip. 2019c. 'AK Parti 4. Büyükelçilerle İftar Buluşması, 12.08.2010'. *Kurumsal İletişim Başkanlığı* Yeni Türkiye Vizyonu—Beraber Yürüdük Biz Bu Yollarda-7.

Erdoğan, Recep Tayyip. 2019d. 'AK Parti 13. İstişare ve Değerlendirme Toplantısı, 29.11.2008'. *Kurumsal İletişim Başkanlığı*, no. Yeni Türkiye Vizyonu—Beraber Yürüdük Biz Bu Yollarda-5.

Erdoğan, Recep Tayyip. 2019e. 'AK Parti TBMM Grup Toplantısı, 13.01.2004'. *Kurumsal İletişim Başkanlığı*, no. Yeni Türkiye Vizyonu—Beraber Yürüdük Biz Bu Yollarda-1.

Erdoğan, Recep Tayyip. 2019f. *Yeni Türkiye vizyonu—Beraber yürüdük biz bu yollarda-2*. Ankara: Kurumsal İletişim Başkanlığı.

Erdoğan, Recep Tayyip. 2021. "Bölgesinin ve dünyanın siyasette sözü dinlenen, ekonomisi güçlü, sosyal ve kültürel etki alanı geniş Türkiye'sine hiç olmadığımız kadar yakınız". Türkiye Cumhuriyeti Cumhurbaşkanlığı. 23 November 2021. https://www.tccb.gov.tr/haberler/410/133579/-bolgesinin-ve-dunyanin-siyasette-sozu-dinlenen-ekonomisi-guclu-sosyal-ve-kulturel-etki-alani-genis-turkiye-sine-hic-olmadigimiz-kadar-yakiniz-.

Erdoğan, Recep Tayyip. 2022. 'Enerji ve İklim Konulu Büyük Ekonomiler Forumu'nda Yaptıkları Konuşma', TC Cumhurbaşkanlığı, 17 June. https://www.tccb.gov.tr/konusmalar/353/138440/enerji-ve-iklim-konulu-buyuk-ekonomiler-forumu-nda-yaptiklari-konusma

Erdoğan, Recep Tayyip. 2023. 'Türkiye yüzyılı için doğru adımlar—Seçim beyannamesi 2023'. Ankara: AK Parti. https://www.akparti.org.tr/media/dwyd05pu/tu-rkiye-yu-zy%C4%B1l%C4%B1-ic-in-dog-ru-ad%C4%B1mlar-2023-sec-im.pdf.

Ernst, Nicole, Frank Esser, Sina Blassnig, and Sven Engesser. 2019. 'Favorable Opportunity Structures for Populist Communication: Comparing Different Types of Politicians and Issues in Social Media, Television and the Press'. *International Journal of Press/Politics* 24 (2): 165–88. https://doi.org/10.1177/1940161218819430.

Escudero, María Cristina, and Leslie Wehner. 2022. 'Populismo y política exterior'. *Política. Revista de ciencia política* 60 (2): 7–8. https://doi.org/10.5354/0719-5338.2022.69322.

Esmaquel II, Paterno R. 2016a. 'Philippine President-Elect Duterte Curses UN'. *Rappler* (blog), 3 June 2016. https://www.rappler.com/philippines/135179-philippines-president-duterte-curses-united-nations/.

Esmaquel II, Paterno. 2016b. 'Cambodia: Yasay Dropped Bid for ASEAN to Cite Hague Ruling'. *Rappler* (blog), 27 July 2016. https://www.rappler.com/philippines/141131-cambodia-philippines-yasay-asean-hague-ruling/.

Esmaquel II, Paterno. 2017. 'ASEAN 2017: A Wasted Opportunity for the West Philippine Sea'. *Rappler* (blog), 20 November 2017. https://www.rappler.com/newsbreak/in-depth/188948-asean-summit-2017-philippines-assessment-south-china-sea/.

European Council. 2016. 'EU-Turkey Statement, 18 March 2016'. https://www.consilium.europa.eu/en/press/press-releases/2016/03/18/eu-turkey-statement/.

European Parliament. 2024. 'The Hungarian Government Threatens EU Values, Institutions, and Funds, MEPs Say'. 18 January 2024. https://www.europarl.europa.eu/news/en/press-room/20240112IPR16780/the-hungarian-government-threatens-eu-values-institutions-and-funds-meps-say.

European Union. 2024. 'Standard Eurobarometer 101—Spring 2024'. https://europa.eu/eurobarometer/surveys/detail/3216.

Evans, Geoffrey, Roosmarijn de Geus, and Jane Green. 2023. 'Boris Johnson to the Rescue? How the Conservatives Won the Radical-Right Vote in the 2019 General Election'. *Political Studies* 71 (4): 984–1005. https://doi.org/10.1177/00323217211051191.

Evolvi, Giulia. 2023. '"Europe Is Christian, or It Is Not Europe": Post-Truth Politics and Religion in Matteo Salvini's Tweets'. In *Europe in the Age of Post-Truth Politics: Populism, Disinformation and the Public Sphere*, edited by Maximilian Conrad, Guðmundur Hálfdanarson, Asimina Michailidou, Charlotte Galpin, and Niko Pyrhönen, 129–48. Cham: Springer International Publishing. https://doi.org/10.1007/978-3-031-13694-8_7.

Express News Service. 2008. 'Modi Poses as Warlord, Targets "Delhi Sultanate"—Indian Express'. 21 January 2008. http://archive.indianexpress.com/news/modi-poses-as-warlord-targets--delhi-sultanate-/263689/.

Fabricant, Nicole, and Bret Gustafson. 2020. 'The Political Economy of Gas, Soy and Lithium in Morales's Bolivia'. *Bolivian Studies Journal* 25 (May): 45–59. https://doi.org/10.5195/bsj.2019.220.

Fagan, Moira, Jacob Poushter, and Sneha Gubbala. 2023. 'Large Shares See Russia and Putin in Negative Light, While Views of Zelenskyy More Mixed'. *Pew Research Center* (blog), 10 July 2023. https://www.pewresearch.org/global/2023/07/10/attitudes-toward-russian-oil-and-gas/.

Falkner, Gerda, and Georg Plattner. 2020. 'EU Policies and Populist Radical Right Parties' Programmatic Claims: Foreign Policy, Anti-discrimination and the Single Market'. *JCMS: Journal of Common Market Studies* 58 (3): 723–39. https://doi.org/10.1111/jcms.12963.

Farias, Deborah Barros Leal, Guilherme Casarões, and Daniel F. Wajner. 2024. 'Populist International (Dis)Order? Lessons from World-Order Visions in Latin American Populism'. *International Affairs* 100 (5): 2003–24. https://doi.org/10.1093/ia/iiae179.

Farnham, Barbara. 2004. 'Impact of the Political Context on Foreign Policy Decision-Making'. *Political Psychology* 25 (3): 441–63. https://doi.org/10.1111/j.1467-9221.2004.00379.x.

Farthing, Linda, and Thomas Grisaffi. 2024. 'From Alternative Development to Decolonisation: Transforming Drug Crop Policies in Bolivia'. *Journal of Development Studies* 60 (7): 985–1001. https://doi.org/10.1080/00220388.2024.2328035.

Fasola, Nicolò, and Sonia Lucarelli. 2024. 'The "Pragmatic" Foreign Policy of the Meloni Government: Between "Euro-Nationalism", Atlanticism and Mediterranean Activism'. *Contemporary Italian Politics* 16 (2): 198–213. https://doi.org/10.1080/23248823.2024.2335847.

Fearon, James D. 1994. 'Domestic Political Audiences and the Escalation of International Disputes'. *American Political Science Review* 88 (3): 577–92. https://doi.org/10.2307/2944796.

Felsen, David. 2018. 'Italian Foreign Policy under the Gentiloni Government: Do the "Three Circles" Hold in 2017?' *Contemporary Italian Politics* 10 (4): 363–76. https://doi.org/10.1080/23248823.2018.1544352.

Fishman, Edward, and Siddharth Mohandas. 2020. 'A Council of Democracies Can Save Multilateralism'. *Foreign Affairs*, 3 August 2020. https://www.foreignaffairs.com/articles/asia/2020-08-03/council-democracies-can-save-multilateralism.

Food and Agriculture Organization of the United Nations. 2024. 'Quinoa'. http://www.fao.org/quinoa/en/.

Foreign & Commonwealth Office. 2020. 'Supporting UN Peacekeeping'. gov.uk, 4 May 2020. https://www.gov.uk/government/speeches/supporting-un-peacekeeping.

Forgey, Quint. 2021. 'Biden, Johnson Talk "Global Vision" for U.S.-U.K. Relationship'. *Politico*, 10 June 2021. https://www.politico.com/news/2021/06/10/biden-johnson-us-uk-relationship-493162.

FORUM. 2019. 'Duterte Calls on ASEAN Leaders to Redouble Efforts in Combating Common Challenges'. *Indo-Pacific Defense Forum* (blog), 18 July 2019. https://ipdefenseforum.com/2019/07/duterte-calls-on-asean-leaders-to-redouble-efforts-in-combating-common-challenges/.

Fouquet, Stephan, and Klaus Brummer. 2023. 'Profiling the Personality of Populist Foreign Policy Makers: A Leadership Trait Analysis'. *Journal of International Relations and Development* 26 (1): 1–29. https://doi.org/10.1057/s41268-022-00270-2.

Foyle, Douglas. 2017. 'Public Opinion and Foreign Policy'. In *Oxford Research Encyclopedia of Politics*, by Douglas Foyle. Oxford University Press. https://doi.org/10.1093/acrefore/9780190228637.013.472.

France24. 2019. 'Macron Calls out Bolsonaro's "Extraordinarily Rude" Insults against Wife Brigitte'. France 24, 26 August 2019. https://www.france24.com/en/20190826-macron-calls-out-bolsonaros-extraordinarily-rude-insults-against-wife-brigitte.

Frangie-Mawad, Tony. 2024. 'Chavismo's Latest Target'. *Foreign Policy* (blog), 24 July 2024. https://foreignpolicy.com/2022/09/25/ngos-venezuela-law-humanitarian-crisis-chavismo-caracas/.

Frankfurter Allgemeine Zeitung. 2016. 'Satire-Streit: Böhmermann steht unter Polizeischutz'. faz.net, 12 April 2016. https://www.faz.net/aktuell/politik/inland/satire-streit-boehmermann-steht-unter-polizeischutz-14174326.html.

Fraser, Suzan, and Derek Gatopoulos. 2020. 'German FM Warns of "Abyss", Calls for Greek-Turkish Talks'. *AP News*, 25 August 2020. https://apnews.com/general-news-d660f1d6963b9c1ed30f930b1009b737.

Friedrichs, Gordon M. 2022. 'Populist Minds Think Alike? National Identity Conceptions and Foreign Policy Preferences of Populist Leaders'. *Foreign Policy Analysis* 18 (2): orac004.

Fuchs, Andreas, and Krishna Chaitanya Vadlamannati. 2013. 'The Needy Donor: An Empirical Analysis of India's Aid Motives'. *World Development* 44:110–28.

G20 India. 2023. 'G20 New Delhi Leaders' Declaration'. https://www.g20.in/content/dam/gtwenty/gtwenty_new/document/G20-New-Delhi-Leaders-Declaration.pdf.

g20.in. 2023. 'India's G20 Presidency: A Synopsis'. 2023. https://www.g20.in/content/dam/gtwenty/Indias_G20_Presidency-A_Synopsis.pdf.

Galang, Mico. 2017. 'US, China, and Duterte's "Independent Foreign Policy"'. 6 April 2017. https://thediplomat.com/2017/04/us-china-and-dutertes-independent-foreign-policy/.

Gallardo, Cristina. 2022. 'The Incredible Shrinking Global Britain'. *Politico*, 19 May 2022. https://www.politico.eu/article/the-incredible-shrinking-global-britain/.

Gamarra, Eduardo A. 2007. 'Bolivia on the Brink'. New York: Council on Foreign Relations.

Ganguly, Sumit. 2002. *Conflict Unending: India-Pakistan Tensions Since 1947*. New York: Columbia University Press.

Ganguly, Sumit. 2016. *Deadly Impasse: Indo-Pakistani Relations at the Dawn of a New Century*. Cambridge: Cambridge University Press. https://doi.org/10.1017/CBO9781139019477.

Ganguly, Sumit, and Manjeet S. Pardesi. 2009. 'Explaining Sixty Years of India's Foreign Policy'. *India Review* 8 (1): 4–19. https://doi.org/10.1080/14736480802665162.

Ganguly, Sumit, Manjeet S. Pardesi, and William R. Thompson. 2023. *The Sino-Indian Rivalry: Implications for Global Order*. Cambridge: Cambridge University Press. https://doi.org/10.1017/9781009193542.

Garcés, Pablo. 2020. 'Between Hierarchy and Individuality: The Andean Community of Nations' Historical Rationalities'. *Comentario internacional: Revista del Centro Andino de Estudios Internacionales*, no. 20, 57–79. https://doi.org/10.32719/26312549.2020.20.1.4.

Gardner, Frank. 2021. 'China Warns UK as Carrier Strike Group Approaches'. *BBC*, 30 July 2021. https://www.bbc.com/news/world-asia-58015367.

Gayle, Damien. 2016. 'Barack Obama Cancels Meeting after Philippines President Calls Him "Son of a Whore"'. *The Guardian*, 5 September 2016. https://www.theguardian.com/world/2016/sep/05/philippines-president-rodrigo-duterte-barack-obama-son-whore.

Gazprom International. 2024. 'Gazprom International in Bolivia'. Gazprom. https://www.gazprom-international.com/operations/bolivia/.

Gerbaudo, Paolo. 2023. 'From Occupy Wall Street to the Gilets Jaunes: On the Populist Turn in the Protest Movements of the 2010s'. *Capital & Class* 47 (1): 107–24. https://doi.org/10.1177/03098168221137207.

Gerhards, Jürgen, and Dieter Rucht. 1992. 'Mesomobilization: Organizing and Framing in Two Protest Campaigns in West Germany'. *American Journal of Sociology* 98 (3): 555–96. https://doi.org/10.1086/230049.

Germani, Gino. 1978. *Authoritarianism, Fascism, and National Populism*. New Brunswick, NJ: Transaction Books.

Ghose, Sagarika. 2018. 'Gandhi Bashing Is a Tired Old Formula That's Not Paying Off'. *Times Of India*, 15 December 2018. https://timesofindia.indiatimes.com/blogs/bloody-mary/gandhi-bashing-is-a-tired-old-formula-thats-not-paying-off/?source=app&frmapp=yes.

Giannetti, Daniela, Luca Pinto, and Carolina Plescia. 2020. 'The First Conte Government: "Government of Change" or Business as Usual?' *Contemporary Italian Politics* 12 (2): 182–99. https://doi.org/10.1080/23248823.2020.1745512.

Gita-Carlos, Ruth Abbey. 2022. 'Duterte Maintains "Neutral" Stance on Russia-Ukraine Conflict'. Philippine News Agency. https://www.pna.gov.ph/articles/1170053.

Giurlando, Philip. 2021. 'Populist Foreign Policy: The Case of Italy'. *Canadian Foreign Policy Journal* 27 (2): 251–67. https://doi.org/10.1080/11926422.2020.1819357.

Giurlando, Philip, and Carla Monteleone. 2024. 'Institutional Change, Sovereigntist Contestation and the Limits of Populism: Evidence from Southern Europe'. *International Affairs* 100 (5): 2047–67. https://doi.org/10.1093/ia/iiae058.

Giurlando, Philip, and Daniel F. Wajner. 2023. *Populist Foreign Policy: Regional Perspectives of Populism in the International Scene*. Cham: Springer Nature.

Gladstone, Rick, and William Newman. 2013. 'New Rumor of Snowden Flight Raises Tensions'. *New York Times*, 2 July 2013. https://www.nytimes.com/2013/07/03/world/europe/snowden.html.

Glinski, Stefanie. 2024. '"New Turks" Are All In for Erdogan'. *Foreign Policy* (blog), 28 June 2024. https://foreignpolicy.com/2023/05/10/turkey-election-erdogan-kilicdaroglu-immigration/.

Gök, Oğuz and Emel P. Dal 2016. 'Understanding Turkey's Emerging "Civilian" Foreign Policy Role in the 2000s through Development Cooperation in the Africa Region'. *Perceptions* XXI (3-4), 67–100.

Goh, Evelyn. 2008. 'Great Powers and Hierarchical Order in Southeast Asia: Analyzing Regional Security Strategies'. *International Security* 32 (3): 113–57. https://doi.org/10.1162/isec.2008.32.3.113.

Goldstein, Joshua S. 1992. 'A Conflict-Cooperation Scale for WEIS Events Data'. *Journal of Conflict Resolution* 36 (2): 369–85.

Gomes, Jim. 2022. 'Philippines to Buy US Aircraft after Scrapping Russia Deal'. *AP News*, 20 October 2022. https://apnews.com/article/russia-ukraine-europe-moscow-philippines-manila-c7bd86a34a7586d114d516c359007960.

Gonzales, Yuji Vincent. 2016. 'Clinton? Trump? Duterte Says Putin "My Favorite Hero"'. *Philippine Daily Inquirer*, 23 October 2016. https://globalnation.inquirer.net/147585/duterte-trump-airing-valid-issues-putin-my-favorite-hero.

Görener, Aylin Ş., and Meltem Ş. Ucal. 2011. 'The Personality and Leadership Style of Recep Tayyip Erdoğan: Implications for Turkish Foreign Policy'. *Turkish Studies* 12 (3): 357–81.

Gozzi, Laura. 2024. 'Matteo Salvini: Italian Deputy PM Takes Stand in Migrant Kidnap Trial'. *BBC*, 12 January 2024. https://www.bbc.com/news/world-europe-67958284.

Grigoriadis, Ioannis N. 2022. 'Between Escalation and Détente: Greek-Turkish Relations in the Aftermath of the Eastern Mediterranean Crisis'. *Turkish Studies* 23 (5): 802–20. https://doi.org/10.1080/14683849.2022.2087509.

Grisaffi, Thomas. 2019. *Coca Yes, Cocaine No: How Bolivia's Coca Growers Reshaped Democracy*. Durham, NC: Duke University Press.

Gross, Stephen G. 2023. 'Understanding Europe's Populist Right: The State of the Field'. *Contemporary European History* 32 (3): 489–97. https://doi.org/10.1017/S0960777322000261.

Grzymala-Busse, Anna. 2019. 'How Populists Rule: The Consequences for Democratic Governance'. *Polity* 51 (4): 707–17. https://doi.org/10.1086/705570.

The Guardian. 2010a. 'Bolivia Creates a New Opportunity for Climate Talks That Failed at Copenhagen'. *The Guardian*, 19 March 2010. https://www.theguardian.com/environment/cif-green/2010/mar/19/bolivia-conference-on-climate-change.

The Guardian. 2010b. 'Why Bolivia Stood Alone in Opposing the Cancún Climate Agreement'. *The Guardian*, 21 December 2010. https://www.theguardian.com/environment/cif-green/2010/dec/21/bolivia-oppose-cancun-climate-agreement.

Guimarães, Feliciano de Sá, and Martin Egon Maitino. 2019. 'Socializing Brazil into Regional Leadership: The 2006 Bolivian Gas Crisis and the Role of Small Powers in Promoting Master Roles Transitions'. *Foreign Policy Analysis* 15 (1): 1–20. https://doi.org/10.1093/fpa/orx010.

Guinness World Records. 2017. 'Largest Yoga Lesson: 54,522 Participants Break Record in India'. Guinness World Records. 10 July 2017. https://www.guinnessworldrecords.com/news/commercial/2017/7/largest-yoga-lesson-54-522-participants-break-record in india-480870.

Gül, Abdullah. 2004. 'Turkey's Role in a Changing Middle East Environment'. *Mediterranean Quarterly* 15 (1): 1–7.

Gul, Nabiha. 2008. 'Pakistan-India Composite Dialogue'. *Pakistan Horizon* 61 (3): 11–17.

Gülen, Berkay. 2019. 'Why Doesn't Israel Have a Minister of Foreign Affairs?' *UW Stroum Center for Jewish Studies* (blog), 9 March 2019. https://jewishstudies.washington.edu/israel-hebrew/israel-minister-of-foreign-affairs-diplomacy-modern-era/.

Günay, Cengiz. 2016. 'Foreign Policy as a Source of Legitimation for "Competitive Authoritarian Regimes": The Case of Turkey's AKP'. *Georgetown Journal of International Affairs* 17 (2): 39–46.

Gupta, Surupa, Rani D. Mullen, Rajesh Basrur, Ian Hall, Nicolas Blarel, Manjeet S. Pardesi, and Sumit Ganguly. 2019. 'Indian Foreign Policy under Modi: A New Brand or Just Repackaging?' *International Studies Perspectives* 20 (1): 1–45. https://doi.org/10.1093/isp/eky008.

Guzman, Chad de. 2023. 'What to Know about the ICC Probe Into the Philippines' Drug War'. *Time*, 27 November 2023. https://time.com/6339873/rodrigo-duterte-drug-war-international-criminal-court-investigation/.

Gyurcsány, Ferenc. 2008. 'Speech Made to the Assembly: Tuesday, 22 January 2008'. https://assembly.coe.int/nw/xml/Speeches/Speech-XML2HTML-EN.asp?SpeechID=84.

Haber7. 2016. 'Erdoğan ABD'ye sert çıkıştı: Tarafını seç'. *Haber7*, 10 February 2016. https://www.haber7.com/guncel/haber/1789234-erdogan-abdye-sert-cikisti-tarafini-sec.

Habermas, Jürgen. 1998. 'Die postnationale Konstellation und die Zukunft der Demokratie'. https://library.fes.de/pdf-files/akademie/online/50332.pdf.

Hacaoglu, Selcan. 2022. 'Turkey Plans Return of a Million Syrians as Refugee Critics Grow'. *Bloomberg.com*, 3 May 2022. https://www.bloomberg.com/news/articles/2022-05-03/turkey-plans-return-of-a-million-syrians-as-refugee-critics-grow.

Haesebrouck, Tim, and Jeroen Joly. 2021. 'Foreign Policy Change: From Policy Adjustments to Fundamental Reorientations'. *Political Studies Review* 19 (3): 482–91.

Hafezi, Parisa. 2010. 'Turkey, Brazil Seal Deal on Iran Nuclear Fuel Swap'. *Reuters*, 16 May 2010. https://www.reuters.com/article/world/turkey-brazil-seal-deal-on-iran-nuclear-fuel-swap-idUSTRE64F29P/.

Haggard, Stephan, and Robert Kaufman. 2021. 'The Anatomy of Democratic Backsliding'. *Journal of Democracy* 32 (4): 27–41.

Haidar, Suhasini. 2021. 'In Policy Shift Narendra Modi Brings Up Balochistan Again'. *The Hindu*, 4 December 2021. https://www.thehindu.com/news/national/In-policy-shift-Narendra-Modi-brings-up-Balochistan-again/article14572650.ece.

Haidar, Suhasini, and Kallol Bhattacherjee. 2021. 'Analysis | Backchannel Diplomacy Played Its Part in India, Pakistan Decision to Cease Fire along LoC'. *The Hindu*, 25 February 2021. https://www.thehindu.com/news/national/analysis-indications-that-india-and-pakistan-have-been-in-back-channel-talks/article33935351.ece.

Hall, Ben, Marton Dunai, and Henry Foy. 2024. 'Viktor Orbán: What Is the Endgame for Europe's Chief Disrupter?' *Financial Times*, 1 February 2024. https://www.ft.com/content/e158834e-1860-4dee-9d2f-3458ec71f287.

Hall, Ian. 2016. 'Multialignment and Indian Foreign Policy under Narendra Modi'. *The Round Table* 105 (3): 271–86.

Hall, Ian. 2017. 'Narendra Modi and India's Normative Power'. *International Affairs* 93 (1): 113131. https://doi.org/10.1093/ia/iiw004.

Hall, Ian. 2019. *Modi and the Reinvention of Indian Foreign Policy*. Bristol: Bristol University Press. https://doi.org/10.46692/9781529204612.

Hall, Ian. 2021. 'Narendra Modi: Elected Authoritarian (Born 1950)'. In *Dictators and Autocrats: Securing Power across Global Politics*, edited by Klaus Larres, 191–203. London: Routledge.

Hall, Ian 2023. 'India pushes China to the margins of the G20'. The Interpreter. 11 September 2023. https://www.lowyinstitute.org/the-interpreter/india-pushes-china-margins-g20 pushes China to the margins of the G20 | Lowy Institute.

Harshe, Rajen. 1990. 'India's Non-Alignment: An Attempt at Conceptual Reconstruction'. *Economic and Political Weekly* 25 (7/8): 399–405.

Haugom, Lars. 2019. 'Turkish Foreign Policy under Erdogan: A Change in International Orientation?' *Comparative Strategy* 38 (3): 206–23. https://doi.org/10.1080/01495933.2019.1606662.

Jeannine Hausmann, and Erik Lundsgaarde. 2015. Turkey's Role in Development Cooperation. United Nations University Centre for Policy Research, November 2015. https://digitallibrary.un.org/record/4076698?v=pdf

Hawkins, Kirk A. 2009. 'Is Chávez Populist?' *Comparative Political Studies* 42 (8): 1040–67.

Hawkins, Kirk A., Ryan E. Carlin, Levente Littvay, and Cristóbal Rovira Kaltwasser. 2018. *The Ideational Approach to Populism: Concept, Theory, and Analysis*. London and New York: Routledge.

Hawkins, Kirk A., and Cristóbal Rovira Kaltwasser. 2017. 'The Ideational Approach to Populism'. *Latin American Research Review* 52 (4): 513–28. https://doi.org/10.25222/larr.85.

He, Kai. 2015. 'Power and Risk in Foreign Policy: Understanding China's Crisis Behavior'. *Political Science Quarterly* 130 (4): 701–33. https://doi.org/10.1002/polq.12396.

Heibach, Jens, and Hakkı Taş. 2024a. 'Beyond the Soft–Hard Power Binary: Resource Control in Turkey's Foreign Policy Towards Sub-Saharan Africa'. *Journal of Balkan and Near Eastern Studies* 26 (3): 311–26.

Heibach, Jens, and Hakkı Taş. 2024b. 'Infrastructural Power in Foreign Policy: Conceptualising States' Efforts to Mobilise Non-State Actors'. *International Relations*. https://doi.org/10.1177/00471178241265615.

Hellwig, Timothy. 2014. 'The Structure of Issue Voting in Postindustrial Democracies'. *Sociological Quarterly* 55 (4): 596–624. https://doi.org/10.1111/tsq.12072.

Henke, Marina, and Richard Maher. 2021. 'The Populist Challenge to European Defense'. *Journal of European Public Policy* 28 (3): 389–406. https://doi.org/10.1080/13501763.2021.1881587.

Hermann, Charles F. 1990. 'Changing Course: When Governments Choose to Redirect Foreign Policy'. *International Studies Quarterly* 34 (1): 3–21. https://doi.org/10.2307/2600403.

Hernández Bermúdez, Orietta E. 2020. 'La política exterior del Estado Plurinacional de Bolivia en el marco del proceso de cambio (2009–2019)'. *Universidad de La Habana* 290: 250–67.

Heydarian, Richard. 2017. *The Rise of Duterte: A Populist Revolt against Elite Democracy.* Singapore: Palgrave Pivot.

Heydarian, Richard. 2018. 'The Implications of Duterte's Proposed Constitutional Changes'. 1 January 2018. https://www.cfr.org/blog/implications-dutertes-proposed-constitutional-changes.

Heydarian, Richard. 2021. 'After Duterte: Is the Philippines Pivoting Back to the U.S.?' 1 January 2021. https://www.chinausfocus.com/foreign-policy/after-duterte-is-the-philippines-pivoting-back-to-the-us.

Hincks, Joseph. 2016. 'A Brief History of U.S.-Philippine Relations'. *Time*, 26 October 2016. https://time.com/4543996/history-of-us-philippine-relations/.

Hincks, Joseph. 2020. 'What to Know about Greece and Turkey's Mediterranean Standoff'. TIME. 28 August 2020. https://time.com/5884397/turkey-greece-tensions/.

Hindustan Times. 2019. '"They Want to Be Pak's Heroes": Modi's Jibe at Balakot Air Strike "Doubters"'. 28 March 2019. https://www.youtube.com/watch?v=FxvT_jXk0Ng.

Hintz, Lisel. 2019. 'Rethinking Turkey's "Rapprochements": Trouble with Germany and Beyond'. *Survival* 61 (3): 165–86. https://doi.org/10.1080/00396338.2019.1614787.

Hofstadter, Richard. 1965. *The Paranoid Style in American Politics and Other Essays.* New York: Alfred A. Knopf.

Holliday, Shabnam J. 2019. 'Populism, the International and Methodological Nationalism: Global Order and the Iran–Israel Nexus'. *Political Studies* 68 (1): 3–19.

Holsti, Kalevi Jaako. 2015. *Why Nations Realign: Foreign Policy Restructuring in the Postwar World.* London: Routledge.

Hooghe, Liesbet, Gary Mark, Tobias Lenz, Jeanine Bezuijen, Besir Ceka, and Svet Derderyan. 2017. *Measuring International Authority: A Postfunctionalist Theory of Governance*, Vol. III. Oxford: Oxford University Press. https://doi.org/10.1093/oso/9780198724490.003.0007.

Huang, Christine, Moira Fagan, and Sneha Gubbala. 2023. 'Views of India Lean Positive across 23 Countries'. 29 August 2023. https://www.pewresearch.org/global/2023/08/29/indians-views-of-other-countries/.

Huber, Daniela, and Barbara Pisciotta. 2023. 'From Democracy to Hybrid Regime. Democratic Backsliding and Populism in Hungary and Tunisia'. *Contemporary Politics* 29 (3): 357–78. https://doi.org/10.1080/13569775.2022.2162210.

Huber, Robert A., Esther Greussing, and Jakob-Moritz Eberl. 2022. 'From Populism to Climate Scepticism: The Role of Institutional Trust and Attitudes towards Science'. *Environmental Politics* 31 (7): 1115–38. https://doi.org/10.1080/09644016.2021.1978200.

Huju, Kira. 2022. 'Saffronizing Diplomacy: The Indian Foreign Service under Hindu Nationalist Rule'. *International Affairs* 98 (2): 423–41. https://doi.org/10.1093/ia/iiab220.

Human Rights Watch. 2017. '"License to Kill": Philippine Police Killings in Duterte's "War on Drugs"'. 1 January 2017. https://www.hrw.org/report/2017/03/02/license-kill/philippine-police-killings-dutertes-war-drugs.

Human Rights Watch. 2018. 'Hungary's Government Turns on the UN | Human Rights Watch'. 15 March 2018. https://www.hrw.org/news/2018/03/15/hungarys-government-turns-un.

Hungarian Presidency Council of the European Union. 2024. 'Make Europe Great Again: The Official Priorities, Social Media Pages and Visuals of the Hungarian Presidency Unveiled'. 19 June 2024. https://hungarian-presidency.consilium.europa.eu/en/news/make-europe-great-again-the-official-priorities-social-media-pages-and-visuals-of-the-hungarian-presidency-unveiled/.

Hürriyet. 2001. 'Her söze evet denmeyecek'. 8 March 2001. https://bigpara.hurriyet.com.tr/haberler/ekonomi-haberleri/her-soze-evet-denmeyecek_ID360830/.

Hyde, Susan D. 2020. 'Democracy's Backsliding in the International Environment'. *Science* 369 (6508): 1192–96.

Ikenberry, G. John. 2018. 'The End of Liberal International Order?' *International Affairs* 94 (1): 7–23.

Il fatto quotidiano. 2018. 'Ue, Salvini: "Arrivata lettera Bruxelles? Aspettiamo anche quella di Babbo Natale. Ci confronteremo ma vado avanti"'. *Il fatto quotidiano*, 21 November 2018. https://www.ilfattoquotidiano.it/2018/11/21/ue-salvini-arrivata-lettera-bruxelles-aspettiamo-anche-quella-di-babbo-natale-ci-confronteremo-ma-vado-avanti/4781226/.

Il Mattino. 2018. 'Manovra, Di Maio: «Noi nel giusto, non abbiamo paura della Commissione Ue»'. *Il Mattino*, 22 October 2018. https://www.ilmattino.it/video/primopiano/manovra_di_maio_giusto_non_abbiamo_paura_commissione_europea-4056520.html?refresh_ce.

India Exim Bank. 2024. 'Lines of Credit Statistics—India Exim Bank'. 2024. https://www.eximbankindia.in/lines-of-credit-GOILOC.aspx.

India Today. 2024a. 'Countries Trusted India in Global South, China Skipped Meetings: S Jaishankar'. *India Today*, 8 March 2024. https://www.indiatoday.in/india/story/eam-jaishankar-says-global-south-believes-in-india-china-does-not-participate-in-voicing-their-concerns-2512299-2024-03-08.

India Today. 2024b. 'Will India Play Mediator's Role to End Russia-Ukraine War? Jaishankar Responds'. *India Today*, 21 February 2024. https://www.indiatoday.in/india/story/s-jaishankar-on-india-mediating-to-end-russia-ukraine-war-we-are-open-if-approached-2504955-2024-02-21.

India Today Web Desk. 2019. 'India Withdraws Most Favoured Nation Status to Pakistan: What It Means'. *India Today*. https://www.indiatoday.in/india/story/india-withdraws-most-favoured-nation-status-to-pakistan-what-it-means-1456746-2019-02-15.

The Indian Express. 2023. 'PM Narendra Modi Independence Day Speech Full Text'. *The Indian Express* (blog), 15 August 2023. https://indianexpress.com/article/india/prime-minister-narendra-modi-independence-day-speech-2023-full-text-8893141/.

The Indian Express. 2024. 'Jaishankar Reiterates Two-State Solution for Israel-Palestine Issue'. *The Indian Express* (blog), 23 March 2024. https://indianexpress.com/article/india/jaishankar-two-state-solution-israel-palestine-issue-9230649/.

Integrated Values Surveys, and Our World in Data. 2022. 'Trust: Confidence in the United Nations. Integrated Values Surveys'. Integrated Values Surveys (IVS). https://ourworldindata.org/grapher/confidence-in-un-wvs.

International Court of Justice. 2018. 'Obligation to Negotiate Access to the Pacific Ocean'. 1 January 2018. https://www.icj-cij.org/public/files/case-related/153/153-20181001-JUD-01-00-EN.pdf.

Ionescu, Ghita, and Ernest Gellner, eds. 1969. *Populism: Its Meaning and National Characteristics*. London: Weidenfeld & Nicolson.

ISEAS-Yusof Ishak Institute. 2019. 'The State of Southeast Asia: 2019 Survey Report'. https://www.iseas.edu.sg/centres/asean-studies-centre/state-of-southeast-asia-survey/test-state-of-southeast-asia-survey-01/.

Istituto Cattaneo. 2019. 'Gli avvenimenti del 2017'. https://www.cattaneo.org/gli-avvenimenti-del-2017/.

Jack, Victor. 2024. 'How Turkey Became Putin's "Pit Stop" for Selling Camouflaged Fuel to the EU'. *Politico*, 15 May 2024. https://www.politico.eu/article/how-turkey-become-vladimir-putin-pit-stop-sell-camouflage-fuel-eu/.

Jacobs, Lawrence R., and Benjamin I. Page. 2005. 'Who Influences U.S. Foreign Policy?' *American Political Science Review* 99 (1): 107–23.

Jacobs, Lawrence R., and Robert Y. Shapiro. 1999. 'Lyndon Johnson, Vietnam, and Public Opinion: Rethinking Realist Theory of Leadership'. *Presidential Studies Quarterly* 29 (3): 592–616. https://doi.org/10.1111/j.0268-2141.2003.00051.x.

Jaffrelot, Christophe. 2010. 'Hindu Nationalism and Power'. In *The Oxford Companion to Politics in India*, edited by Niraja Gopal Jayal and Pratab Bhanu Mehta, 205–18. New Delhi: Oxford University Press.

Jaffrelot, Christophe. 2021. *Modi's India: Hindu Nationalism and the Rise of Ethnic Democracy*. Princeton, NJ: Princeton University Press. https://press.princeton.edu/books/hardcover/9780691206806/modis-india.

Jaffrelot, Christophe, and Louise Tillin. 2017. 'Populism in India'. In *The Oxford Handbook of Populism*, edited by Cristóbal Rovira Kaltwasser, Paul Taggart, Paulina Ochoa Espejo, and Pierre Ostiguy, 179–94. Oxford University Press. https://doi.org/10.1093/oxfordhb/9780198803560.013.7.

Jaffrelot, Christophe, and Gilles Verniers. 2020. 'The BJP's 2019 Election Campaign: Not Business as Usual'. *Contemporary South Asia* 28 (2): 155–77.

Jahn, Beate. 2018. 'Liberal Internationalism: Historical Trajectory and Current Prospects'. *International Affairs* 94 (1): 43–61.

Jangid, Khinvraj. 2023. 'India's Uneasy Standoff on Gaza War: Hosting Hamas vs. Standing with Israel'. *Haaretz*, 8 November 2023. https://www.haaretz.com/opinion/2023-11-08/ty-article-opinion/.premium/indias-uneasy-standoff-on-gaza-war-hosting-hamas-vs-standing-with-israel/0000018b-aa9f-db59-a9ab-bedf5d650000.

Janis, Irving L. 1982. *Groupthink: Psychological Studies of Policy Decisions and Fiascoes*. Boston: Houghton Mifflin.

Jansen, Robert S. 2011. 'Populist Mobilization: A New Theoretical Approach to Populism'. *Sociological Theory* 29 (2): 75–96.

Jenne, Erin K. 2021. 'Populism, Nationalism and Revisionist Foreign Policy'. *International Affairs* 97 (2): 323–43.

Jenne, Erin K., Kirk A. Hawkins, and Bruno Castanho Silva. 2021. 'Mapping Populism and Nationalism in Leader Rhetoric across North America and Europe'. *Studies in Comparative International Development* 56 (2): 170–96.

Jenne, Nicole. 2019. 'Peacekeeping, Latin America and the UN Charter's Chapter VIII: Past Initiatives and Future Prospects'. *International Peacekeeping* 26 (3): 327–53. https://doi.org/10.1080/13533312.2019.1588729.

Jesse, Neal. 2016. *Small States in the International System: At Peace and at War*. Lanham, MD: Lexington Books.

Jha, Prashant. 2008. 'Nepal at the Crossroads'. *Seminar: The Monthly Symposium, Web Edition* 584 (April 2008).

Jha, Prashant. 2017. *How the BJP Wins: Inside India's Greatest Election Machine*. New Delhi: Juggernaut Books.

Jha, Prashant. 2023. 'What the G20 Summit Success Means for India and the World'. *Hindustan Times*, 11 September 2023. https://www.hindustantimes.com/india-news/what-the-g20-summit-success-means-for-india-and-the-world-101694371976835.html.

Jha, Vyoma. 2022. 'India and Climate Change: Old Traditions, New Strategies'. *India Quarterly* 78 (2): 280–96. https://doi.org/10.1177/09749284221089553.

Jimeno, Karen. 2017. 'Duterte Sings for Trump: "You Are the Light"—Video'. *The Guardian*, 13 November 2017, sec. World news. https://www.theguardian.com/world/video/2017/nov/13/duterte-sings-for-trump-you-are-the-light-video.

Johnson, Boris. 2021. 'PM Boris Johnson's Address to the UN Security Council on Climate and Security: 23 February 2021'. gov.uk, 23 February 2021. https://www.gov.uk/government/speeches/pm-boris-johnsons-address-to-the-un-security-council-on-climate-and-security-23-february-2021.

Johnson, Boris. 2022. 'PM Boris Johnson: The Commonwealth Gives Britain a Boost'. gov.uk, 19 June 2022. https://www.gov.uk/government/speeches/pm-boris-johnson-the-commonwealth-gives-britain-a-boost.

Johnson, David T. 2008. 'Remarks on Release of the Annual Report on the Major Illicit Drug Producing Countries for Fiscal Year 2008'. Washington, DC: U.S. Department of State. https://2001-2009.state.gov/p/inl/rls/rm/109783.ht.

Joshi, Shashank. 2015. 'India and the Middle East'. *Asian Affairs* 46 (2): 251–69.

Jumle, Vihang, Johannes Plagemann, Sandra Destradi, Elena Dressler, Alyssa Santiago, and Ronald Schleehauf. 2025. 'Populism and the Centralisation of Foreign Policy Decision-Making: Paths and Patterns'. In *The Routledge Handbook of Populism and Foreign Policy*, edited by David Cadier, Angelos Chryssogelos, and Sandra Destradi, 233–250. Abingdon and New York: Routledge.

Kaarbo, Juliet, and Cameron G. Thies. 2024a. 'Repositioning Foreign Policy Analysis in International Relations'. In *The Oxford Handbook of Foreign Policy Analysis*, edited by Juliet Kaarbo and Cameron G. Thies, 1–21. Oxford and New York: Oxford University Press.

Kaarbo, Juliet, and Cameron G. Thies, eds. 2024b. *The Oxford Handbook of Foreign Policy Analysis*. Oxford and New York: Oxford University Press.

Kabiling, Genalyn. 2021. 'Nation in serious trouble because of climate change — Duterte'. Manila Bulletin, 2 May 2021. https://mb.com.ph/2021/02/25/nation-in-serious-trouble-because-of-climate-change-duterte/?utm_source=rss&utm_medium=rss&utm_campaign=nation-in-serious-trouble-because-of-climate-change-duterte.

Kallis, Aristotle. 2018. 'Populism, Sovereigntism, and the Unlikely Re-Emergence of the Territorial Nation-State'. *Fudan Journal of the Humanities and Social Sciences* 11 (3): 285–302. https://doi.org/10.1007/s40647-018-0233-z.

Karnitschnig, Matthew, and Jacopo Barigazzi. 2016. 'EU and Turkey Reach Refugee Deal'. *Politico*, 18 March 2016. https://www.politico.eu/article/eu-and-turkey-finalize-refugee-deal/.

Kars Kaynar, Ayşegül. 2017. 'Political Activism of the National Security Council in Turkey after the Reforms'. *Armed Forces & Society* 43 (3): 523–44.

Katigbak, Jovito Jose. 2017. 'RCEP and the Future of Asian Free Trade Agreements: A Philippine Perspective'. *Center for International Relations and Strategic Studies* 4 (2). https://fsi.gov.ph/rcep-and-the-future-of-asian-free-trade-agreements-a-philippine-perspective/.

Katsambekis, Giorgos. 2022. 'Constructing "the People" of Populism: A Critique of the Ideational Approach from a Discursive Perspective'. *Journal of Political Ideologies* 27 (1): 53–74. https://doi.org/10.1080/13569317.2020.1844372.

Kaul, Inge, Isabelle Grunberg, and Marc Stern, eds. 2004. *Global Public Goods: International Cooperation in the 21st Century*. Oxford: Oxford University Press. http://www.loc.gov/catdir/enhancements/fy0604/99010940-d.html.

Kaup, Brent Z. 2010. 'A Neoliberal Nationalization?: The Constraints on Natural-Gas-Led Development in Bolivia'. *Latin American Perspectives* 37 (3): 123–38. https://doi.org/10.1177/0094582X10366534.

Kaura, Vinay, and Meena Rani. 2020. 'India's Neighbourhood Policy during 2014–2019: Political Context and Policy Outcomes'. *Indian Journal of Public Administration* 66 (1): 10–27.

Keenleyside, T. A. 1980. 'Prelude to Power: The Meaning of Non-Alignment before Indian Independence'. *Pacific Affairs* 53 (3): 461–83. https://doi.org/10.2307/2757304.

Kemahlıoğlu, Özge, and Yeğen, Oya. 2021. 'Surviving the Covid-19 Pandemic under Right-wing Populist Rule: Turkey in the First Phase'. *South European Society and Politics* 27 (4): 577–606.

Kenny, Paul. 2020. 'Why Is There No Political Polarization in the Philippines?' 1 January 2020. https://carnegieendowment.org/2020/08/18/why-is-there-no-political-polarization-in-philippines-pub-82439.

Khan, Owais Hasan. 2021. *Strengthening Regional Trade Integration in South Asia*. Singapore: Springer.

Khilnani, Sunil. 2010. 'Politics and National Identity'. In *The Oxford Companion to Politics in India*, edited by Niraja Gopal Jayal and Pratap Bhanu Mehta, 192–204. Oxford: Oxford University Press.

Khilnani, Sunil, Rajiv Kumar, Pratap Bhanu Mehta, Prakash Menon, Nandan Nilekani, Srinath Raghavan, Shyam Saran, and Siddharth Varadarajan. 2012. 'Nonalignment 2.0: A Foreign and Strategic Policy for India in the Twenty First Century'. New Delhi: Centre for Policy Research. https://cprindia.org/wp-content/uploads/2021/12/NonAlignment-2.pdf.

Kim, Abraham. 2014. 'The Plight of Bolivian Coca Leaves: Bolivia's Quest for Decriminalization in the Face of Inconsistent International Legislation'. *Washington University Global Studies Law Review* 13 (3): 559–83.

Kınıklıoğlu, Suat. 2002. 'The Democratic Left Party: Kapikulu Politics Par Excellence'. *Turkish Studies* 3 (1): 4–24. https://doi.org/10.1080/714005696.

Kirk-Wade, Esme. 2024. 'UK Defence Spending'. London: House of Commons Library. https://researchbriefings.files.parliament.uk/documents/CBP-8175/CBP-8175.pdf.

Kohl, Benjamin. 2010. 'Bolivia under Morales: A Work in Progress'. *Latin American Perspectives* 37 (3): 107–22. https://doi.org/10.1177/0094582X10366533.

Kopper, Akos, András Szalai, and Magdalena Góra. 2023. 'Populist Foreign Policy in Central and Eastern Europe: Poland, Hungary and the Shock of the Ukraine Crisis'. In *Populist Foreign Policy: Regional Perspectives of Populism in the International Scene*, edited by Philip Giurlando and Daniel F. Wajner, 89–116. Cham: Springer.

Korte, Kristina. 2022. '"Who Is the Animal in the Zoo?" Fencing In and Fencing Out at the Hungarian-Serbian Border. A Qualitative Case Study'. *Journal of Borderlands Studies* 37 (3): 453–74. https://doi.org/10.1080/08865655.2020.1787188.

Kösebalaban, Hasan. 2011. *Turkish Foreign Policy: Islam, Nationalism, and Globalization*. New York: Springer.

Kovács, Zoltán. 2024. 'PM Orbán: Hungary Must Stay Out of the War'. 1 June 2024. https://abouthungary.hu//blog/pm-orban-hungary-must-stay-out-of-the-war.

Krastev, Ivan, and Stephen Holmes. 2019. *The Light That Failed: A Reckoning*. London: Penguin Books.

Krebs, Ronald R. 2021. 'Pluralism, Populism, and the Impossibility of Grand Strategy'. In *The Oxford Handbook of Grand Strategy*, edited by Thierry Balzacq and Ronald R. Krebs, 673–98. New York: Oxford University Press.

Krebs, Ronald R. 2025. 'Trump vs. the Military: Why Populists Turn Against Their Armed Forces–and Degrade National Power'. *Foreign Affairs*, 10 January 2025. https://www.foreignaffairs.com/united-states/trump-vs-military.

Krejsa, Harry. 2016. 'Rodrigo Duterte's Turn in the South China Sea'. *The Diplomat*, 15 July 2016. https://thediplomat.com/2016/07/rodrigo-dutertes-turn-in-the-south-china-sea/.

Kreuzer, Peter. 2020. 'A Patron-Strongman Who Delivers: Explaining Enduring Public Support for President Duterte in the Philippines'. PRIF Report 1/2020, Peace Research Institute Frankfurt. https://www.jstor.org/stable/resrep26192.5.

Krommes-Ravnsmed, Jeppe. 2019. 'The Frustrated Nationalization of Hydrocarbons and the Plunder of Bolivia'. *Latin American Perspectives* 46 (2): 65–83. https://doi.org/10.1177/0094582X18820294.

Kumar, Ajay, and Tejas Bharadwaj. 2024. 'One Year of the INDUS-X: Defense Innovation Between India and the U.S'. Carnegie Endowment for International Peace. 18 June 2024. https://carnegieendowment.org/research/2024/06/one-year-of-the-indus-x-defense-innovation-between-india-and-the-us.

Kutlu, Erdi, Çağdaş Cengiz, Murat Necip Arman, and Emir Ozeren. 2021. 'Understanding the Role of Leadership Styles of Erdogan and Merkel in Sustainability of Turkey-European Union Relations: A Leadership Trait Analysis'. *Sustainability* 13 (16): 9258. https://doi.org/10.3390/su13169258.

La Opinión/Agencias. 2008. 'Gobierno suspende indefinidamente las actividades de la DEA en Bolivia'. *La Opinión*, 1 November 2008. https://www.opinion.com.bo/articulo/el-pais/gobierno-suspende-indefinidamente-actividades-dea-bolivia/20081101210658296026.html.

La Repubblica. 2018. 'Elezioni, i leader politici non parlano di ambiente: Greenpeace lancia campagna di finti manifesti'. *La Repubblica*, 1 January 2018. https://www.repubblica.it/speciali/politica/elezioni2018/2018/02/23/foto/elezioni_greenpeace_ambiente_campagna_leader_politici-189583392/1/.

Lacatus, Corina. 2021. 'Populism and President Trump's Approach to Foreign Policy: An Analysis of Tweets and Rally Speeches'. *Politics* 41 (1): 31–47.

Lacatus, Corina, and Gustav Meibauer. 2022. '"Saying It Like It Is": Right-Wing Populism, International Politics, and the Performance of Authenticity'. *British Journal of Politics and International Relations* 24 (3): 437–57. https://doi.org/10.1177/13691481221089137.

Lacatus, Corina, Gustav Meibauer, and Georg Löfflmann. 2023. *Political Communication and Performative Leadership: Populism in International Politics*. Cham: Springer Nature.

Laclau, Ernesto. 1977. *Politics and Ideology in Marxist Theory*. London: NLB.

Laclau, Ernesto. 2005. *On Populist Reason*. London: Verso.

Lake, David A., Lisa L. Martin, and Thomas Risse. 2021. 'Challenges to the Liberal Order: Reflections on International Organization'. *International Organization* 75 (2): 225–57. https://doi.org/10.1017/S0020818320000636.

Laksmana, Evan A. 2020. '4. Pragmatic Equidistance: How Indonesia Manages Its Great Power Relations'. In *China, the United States, and the Future of Southeast Asia*, edited by David B. H. Denoon, 113–35. New York: New York University Press. https://doi.org/10.18574/nyu/9781479866304.003.0004.

Lalu, Gabriel Pabico. 2022. 'Duterte on Sharing "Killer" Tag with Putin: "But I Only Kill Criminals"'. *Philippine Daily Inquirer*, 24 May 2022. https://newsinfo.inquirer.net/1601687/duterte-on-being-labeled-killer-together-with-putin-yup-but-i-only-kill-criminals.

Lalwani, Sameer P., and Vikram J. Singh. 2024. 'What's the Deal with INDUS-X?' United States Institute of Peace. 16 February 2024. https://www.usip.org/publications/2024/02/whats-deal-indus-x.

Lambah, Satinder Kumar. 2023. *In Pursuit of Peace: India-Pakistan Relations under Six Prime Ministers*. Gurugram: Viking.

Lamour, Christian. 2024. 'Orbán Placed in Europe: Ukraine, Russia and the Radical-Right Populist Heartland'. *Geopolitics* 29 (4): 1297–1323.

Landau, Dana M., and Lior Lehrs. 2022. 'Populist Peacemaking: Trump's Peace Initiatives in the Middle East and the Balkans'. *International Affairs* 98 (6): 2001–19. https://doi.org/10.1093/ia/iiac228.

Lanzona, Leonardo A. 2016. 'The Sustainability of Recent Philippine Economic Growth'. In *Southeast Asian Affairs 2016*, edited by Daljit Singh and Malcolm Cook, 281–92. Singapore: ISEAS Publishing. https://doi.org/10.1355/9789814695671-020.

Lasco, Gideon. 2020. 'Medical Populism and the COVID-19 Pandemic'. *Global Public Health* 15 (10): 1417–29.

Lassila, Jussi. 2018. 'Putin as a Non-Populist Autocrat'. *Russian Politics* 3 (2): 175–95.

Lavasa, Ashok. 2019. 'Reaching Agreement in Paris: A Negotiator's Perspective'. In *India in a Warming World*, edited by Navroz K. Dubash, 169–86. Delhi: Oxford University Press. https://doi.org/10.1093/oso/9780199498734.003.0010.

Leeds, Brett Ashley. 1999. 'Domestic Political Institutions, Credible Commitments, and International Cooperation'. *American Journal of Political Science* 43 (4): 979–1002.

Leeds, Brett Ashley, and Michaela Mattes. 2022. *Domestic Interests, Democracy, and Foreign Policy Change*. Cambridge: Cambridge University Press. https://doi.org/10.1017/9781009037938.

Lega. 2018. 'Elezioni 2018 programma di governo: Salvini premier, la rivoluzione del buon senso'. https://www.leganord.org/component/phocadownload/category/5-elezioni?download=1514:programma-lega-salvini-premier-2018.

Lemke, Christiane. 2020. 'Right-Wing Populism and International Issues: A Case Study of the AfD'. *German Politics and Society* 38 (2): 90–108.

Leon, Daniel S. 2022. 'Do International Rents Bolster Democratic Backsliding under Populist Governments? Evidence from Latin America'. *International Area Studies Review* 25 (4): 280–302. https://doi.org/10.1177/22338659221120976.

Leoni, Zeno. 2022. 'The End of the "Golden Era"? The Conundrum of Britain's China Policy Amidst Sino-American Relations'. *Journal of Current Chinese Affairs* 51 (2): 313–26. https://doi.org/10.1177/18681026221090315.

Lequesne, Christian. 2021. 'Populist Governments and Career Diplomats in the EU: The Challenge of Political Capture'. *Comparative European Politics* 19 (6): 779–95. https://doi.org/10.1057/s41295-021-00261-6.

Lewis, Paul, Seánn Clarke, and Caelainn Barr. 2019. 'Theresa May's Rhetoric Can Be as Populist as Trump's'. *The Guardian*, 6 March 2019. https://www.theguardian.com/world/2019/mar/06/theresa-may-british-prime-minister-populism-rhetoric-is-as-rife-as-in-donald-trump-speeches.

Liang, Christina Schori, ed. 2007a. *Europe for the Europeans: The Foreign and Security Policy of the Populist Radical Right*. Aldershot: Ashgate.

Liang, Christina Schori. 2007b. 'Europe for the Europeans: The Foreign and Security Policy of the Populist Radical Right'. In *Europe for the Europeans: The Foreign and Security Policy of the Populist Radical Right*, edited by Christina Schori Liang, 1–32. Aldershot: Ashgate.

Limaye, Yogita. 2020. 'Amnesty International to Halt India Operations'. *BBC News, Mumbai*, 29 September 2020. https://www.bbc.com/news/world-asia-india-54277329.

Lockwood, Matthew. 2018. 'Right-Wing Populism and the Climate Change Agenda: Exploring the Linkages'. *Environmental Politics* 27 (4): 712–32. https://doi.org/10.1080/09644016.2018.1458411.

Löfflmann, Georg. 2022a. '"Enemies of the People": Donald Trump and the Security Imaginary of America First'. *British Journal of Politics and International Relations* 24 (3): 543–60. https://doi.org/10.1177/13691481211048499.

Löfflmann, Georg. 2022b. 'Introduction to Special Issue: The Study of Populism in International Relations'. *British Journal of Politics and International Relations* 24 (3): 403–15. https://doi.org/10.1177/13691481221103116.

Lührmann, Anna, Düpont Nils, Masaaki Higashijima, Yaman Berkre Kavasoglu, Kyle M. Marquardt, Michael Bernhard, Holger Döring, et al. 2020. 'V-Party Dataset v1: Varieties of Democracy'. V-Dem Institute. https://doi.org/10.23696/VPARTYDSV1.

Macaraig, Mynardo. 2016. 'Duterte Wants to Shift Power from "Imperial Manila"'. *ABS-CBN News*. https://news.abs-cbn.com/focus/06/28/16/duterte-wants-to-shift-power-from-imperial-manila.

Macek, Lukáš. 2021. 'History of a Breakdown: Fidesz's Departure from the EPP Group at the European Parliament'. Institut Jacques Delors. 5 May 2021. https://institutdelors.eu/en/publications/chronique-dune-rupture-le-depart-du-fidesz-du-groupe-ppe-au-parlement-europeen/.

Madan, Tanvi. 2022. 'The Quad as a Security Actor'. *Asia Policy* 17 (4): 49–56. https://doi.org/10.1353/asp.2022.0065.

Madhi, Gentiola. 2021. *'Our Brother Erdogan'—From Official to Personal Relations of Political Leaders of Albania and Kosovo with the Turkish President*. Prague: Prague Security Studies Institute. https://www.pssi.cz/download/docs/8474_our-brother-erdogan-from-official-to-personal-relations-of-political-leaders-of-albania-and-kosovo-with-the-turkish-president.pdf.

MAECI. 2019. 'Relazione annuale sull'attuazione della politica di cooperazione allo sviluppo, anno 2018'. https://www.esteri.it/mae/resource/doc/2020/06/relazione_2018.pdf.

MAECI. 2020. 'Relazione annuale sull'attuazione della politica di cooperazione allo sviluppo, anno 2019'. https://www.esteri.it/wp-content/uploads/2021/11/Relazioneart12-4pereserciziofinanziario2019.pdf.

Magcamit, Michael I, and Aries A. Arugay. 2024. 'Explaining Populist Securitization and Rodrigo Duterte's Anti-Establishment Philippine Foreign Policy'. *International Affairs* 100 (5): 1877–97. https://doi.org/10.1093/ia/iiad248.

Malhotra, Shairee. 2023. '25 Years of India-France Strategic Partnership: Resilient in the Darkest Storms'. Observer Research Foundation. https://www.orfonline.org/expert-speak/25-years-of-india-france-strategic-partnership.

Malig, Jun. 2016. 'Duterte to UN Rights Chief: Shut Up, We Pay Your Salary'. *Rappler*, 22 December 2016. https://www.rappler.com/nation/156339-duterte-united-nations-salary-shut-up/.

Mance, Henry. 2016. 'Britain Has Had Enough of Experts, Says Gove'. *Financial Times*, 3 June 2016. https://www.ft.com/content/3be49734-29cb-11e6-83e4-abc22d5d108c.

Marangoni, Francesco, and Luca Verzichelli. 2019. 'Goat-Stag, Chimera or Chameleon? The Formation and First Semester of the Conte Government'. *Contemporary Italian Politics* 11 (3): 263–79. https://doi.org/10.1080/23248823.2019.1645998.

March, Luke. 2023. 'Putin: Populist, Anti-Populist, or Pseudo-Populist?' *Journal of Political Ideologies*: 1–23. https://doi.org/10.1080/13569317.2023.2250744.

Mardin, Şerif. 1973. 'Center-Periphery Relations: A Key to Turkish Politics?' *Daedalus* 102 (1): 169–90.

Margulies, Ben. 2019. 'The Accidental Populists: Why May and Corbyn Ended Up Being Isolated and Unpopular'. *British Politics and Policy at LSE* (blog), 11 July 2019. https://blogs.lse.ac.uk/politicsandpolicy/the-accidental-populists-why-may-and-corbyn-ended-up-being-isolated-and-unpopular/.

Marquardt, Jens, M. Cecilia Oliveira, and Markus Lederer. 2022. 'Same, Same but Different? How Democratically Elected Right-Wing Populists Shape Climate Change Policymaking'. *Environmental Politics* 31 (5): 777–800.

Marrone, Alessandro. 2018. 'The Conte Government: Radical Change or Pragmatic Continuity in Italian Foreign and Defence Policy?' Rome: IAI Commentaries. https://www.iai.it/sites/default/files/iaicom1833.pdf.

Martill, Benjamin. 2022. 'Prisoners of Their Own Device: Brexit as a Failed Negotiating Strategy'. *British Journal of Politics and International Relations* 24 (4): 582–97. https://doi.org/10.1177/13691481211044645.

Martin, Lenore G. 2019. 'Analysing a Tumultuous Relationship: Turkey and the US in the Middle East'. *Asian Journal of Middle Eastern and Islamic Studies* 13 (2): 262–77. https://doi.org/10.1080/25765949.2019.1605571.

Marton, Péter, Tamás Matura, and Csendike Somogyvári. 2023. '"Dracunculus against the Dragon": Hungarian Prime Minister Viktor Orbán's Public Vaccination as Simultaneous Enactment of Public Health and Foreign Policy'. *Journal of Contemporary Central and Eastern Europe* 31 (2): 409–28. https://doi.org/10.1080/25739638.2023.2221923.

Mason, Rowena, and Jessica Elgot. 2022. 'The Week Boris Johnson Went to War with the Law'. *The Guardian*, 17 June 2022. https://www.theguardian.com/politics/2022/jun/17/the-week-boris-johnson-went-to-war-with-the-law.

Mathur, Ajay. 2019. 'India and Paris: A Pragmatic Way Forward'. In *India in a Warming World*, edited by Navroz K. Dubash, 222–29. Delhi: Oxford University Press. https://doi.org/10.1093/oso/9780199498734.003.0013.

Mattes, Michaela, and Mariana Rodríguez. 2014. 'Autocracies and International Cooperation'. *International Studies Quarterly* 58 (3): 527–38.

Mattoo, Shashank. 2024. 'India to Push SAARC Countries to Restart Funding of South Asian University'. *Mint*, 2 April 2024. https://www.livemint.com/news/world/india-to-push-saarc-countries-to-restart-funding-of-south-asian-university-11712059166587.html.

Maynard, Jonathan Leader, and Mark L. Haas. 2021. 'Introduction: Ideology and the Study of World Politics'. In *Routledge Handbook of Ideology and International Relations*, edited by Jonathan Leader Maynard and Mark L. Haas, 1–21. London and New York: Routledge.

Mazumdar, Tulip. 2021. 'India's Covid Crisis Hits Covax Vaccine-Sharing Scheme'. 17 May 2021. https://www.bbc.com/news/world-57135368.

McCargo, Duncan. 2016. 'Duterte's Mediated Populism'. *Contemporary Southeast Asia: A Journal of International and Strategic Affairs* 38 (2): 185–90.

McKay, Ben M., and Gonzalo Colque. 2021. 'Populism and Its Authoritarian Tendencies: The Politics of Division in Bolivia'. *Latin American Perspectives*, November, 1–17. https://doi.org/10.1177/0094582X211052980.

McKibben, Charlene. 2023. 'Populism on the Periphery of Democracy: Moralism and Recognition Theory'. *Critical Review of International Social and Political Philosophy* 26 (6): 897–917. https://doi.org/10.1080/13698230.2020.1799159.

McMaster, H. R. 2024. *At War with Ourselves: My Tour of Duty in the Trump White House*. New York: Harper.

McNeish, John-Andrew. 2013. 'Extraction, Protest and Indigeneity in Bolivia: The TIPNIS Effect'. *Latin American and Caribbean Ethnic Studies* 8 (2): 221–42. https://doi.org/10.1080/17442222.2013.808495.

Meier, Oliver, and Maren Vieluf. 2021. 'Upsetting the Nuclear Order: How the Rise of Nationalist Populism Increases Nuclear Dangers'. *Nonproliferation Review* 28 (1–3): 13–35.

Meislová, Monika Brusenbauch, and Angelos Chryssogelos. 2024. 'The Ambiguous Impact of Populist Trade Discourses on the International Economic Order'. *International Affairs* 100 (5): 1941–57. https://doi.org/10.1093/ia/iiad296.

MENA Research Center. 2021. 'Erdogan's U-turn in climate policy'. MENA Research Center, 14 October 2021. https://www.mena-researchcenter.org/erdogans-u-turn-in-climate-policy/

Mendez, Christina. 2019. 'Duterte Presses ASEAN on Sea Code of Conduct'. *Philippine Star*, 24 June 2019. https://www.philstar.com/headlines/2019/06/24/1929103/duterte-presses-asean-sea-code-conduct.

MercoPress. 2009. 'Iran Loans Bolivia 280 Million USD to Develop Industry and Energy Sector'. *MercoPress*, 31 July 2009. https://en.mercopress.com/2009/07/30/iran-loans-bolivia-280-million-usd-to-develop-industry-and-energy-sector.

MercoPress. 2011. 'South American Countries Divided over Allied Bombings of Libya'. *MercoPress*, 23 March 2011. https://en.mercopress.com/2011/03/23/south-american-countries-divided-over-allied-bombings-of-libya.

Merez, Arianne, and Kristine Sabillo. 2020. 'Philippines Sends Notice of VFA Termination to US'. *ABS CBN News*, 11 February 2020. https://news.abs-cbn.com/news/02/11/20/philippines-sends-notice-of-vfa-termination-to-us.

Merrick, Rob. 2021. 'Boris Johnson Accused of Neglecting National Security as He Prepares to Skip Meetings'. *The Independent*, 18 September 2021. https://www.independent.co.uk/news/uk/politics/boris-johnson-national-security-covid-afghanistan-b1922642.html.

Metz, Rudolf, and Daniel Oross. 2020. 'Strong Personalities' Impact on Hungarian Party Politics: Viktor Orbán and Gábor Vona'. In *Party Leaders in Eastern Europe: Personality, Behavior and Consequences*, edited by Sergiu Gherghina, 145–70. Cham: Springer International Publishing. https://doi.org/10.1007/978-3-030-32025-6_7.

Michael, Arndt. 2013. *India's Foreign Policy and Regional Multilateralism*. Basingstoke and New York: Palgrave Macmillan.

Miller, Manjari Chatterjee. 2022. 'India's Special Relationship with Abe Shinzo'. *Council on Foreign Relations* (blog), 14 July 2022. https://www.cfr.org/blog/indias-special-relationship-abe-shinzo.

Ministerio de Relaciones Exteriores del Estado Plurinacional de Bolivia. 2018. 'Presidente Morales exhorta a garantizar la soberanía de los pueblos de América Latina y el Caribe'. 14 December 2018. https://www.cancilleria.gob.bo/webmre/node/2979.

Ministero Dell'interno. 2019. 'Cruscotto statistico al 31 dicembre 2019'. 1 January 2019. http://www.libertaciviliimmigrazione.dlci.interno.gov.it/sites/default/files/allegati/cruscotto_statistico_giornaliero_31-12-2019.pdf.

Ministry of External Affairs. 2024a. 'Annual Reports'. Ministry of External Affairs. https://mea.gov.in/Annual_Reports.htm?57/Annual_Reports.

Ministry of External Affairs. 2024b. 'India-Bangladesh Bilateral Relations'. https://www.mea.gov.in/Portal/ForeignRelation/Bilateral-Brief-Bangladesh-February-2024.pdf.

Ministry of Foreign Affairs. 2018. 'PM Netanyahu's State Visit to India'. https://www.gov.il/en/pages/pm-netanyahus-official-visit-to-india-14-january-2018.

Mintz, Alex, and Eldad Tal-Shir. 2019. 'Introduction: How Do Leaders Make Decisions? An Applied Decision Analysis Account'. In *Contributions to Conflict Management, Peace Economics and Development*, edited by Alex Mintz and Dmitry (Dima) Adamsky, 28 (A): 1–12. https://doi.org/10.1108/S1572-832320190000028003.

Mistreanu, Simina. 2023. 'Here Are the Key Leaders Joining the Belt and Road Forum and Their Wish Lists to Beijing'. *AP News*, 17 October 2023. https://apnews.com/article/belt-road-forum-china-putin-xi-orban-beijing-b248ad6f710bfcf9aea62e916239a37d.

Modi, Narendra. 2011. *Convenient Action: Gujarat's Response to Challenges of Climate Change*. New Delhi: Macmillan Publishers India.

Modi, Narendra. 2014. 'English Rendering of the Text of Prime Minister's "Mann Ki Baat" on All India Radio on 14th December 2014'. https://www.pmindia.gov.in/en/news_updates/english-rendering-of-the-text-of-prime-ministers-mann-ki-baat-on-all-india-radio-on-14th-december-2014/.

Modi, Narendra. 2017a. 'English Rendering of the Text of PM's "Mann Ki Baat" Programme on All India Radio on 29.10.2017'. https://pib.gov.in/pib.gov.in/Pressreleaseshare.aspx?PRID=1507411.

Modi, Narendra. 2017b. 'PM's "Mann Ki Baat" Programme on All India Radio'. 30 July 2017. https://www.pmindia.gov.in/en/news_updates/pms-mann-ki-baat-programme-on-all-india-radio-4/.

Modi, Narendra. 2018. 'PM's Mann Ki Baat Programme on All India Radio'. 30 December 2018. https://www.pmindia.gov.in/en/news_updates/pms-mann-ki-baat-programme-on-all-india-radio-19/.

Moffitt, Benjamin. 2015. 'How to Perform Crisis: A Model for Understanding the Key Role of Crisis in Contemporary Populism'. *Government and Opposition* 50 (2): 189–217. https://doi.org/10.1017/gov.2014.13.

Moffitt, Benjamin. 2016. *The Global Rise of Populism: Performance, Political Style, and Representation.* Stanford, CA: Stanford University Press.

Moffitt, Benjamin. 2020. 'Populism'. Medford, MA: Polity Press.

Moffitt, Benjamin, and Simon Tormey. 2014. 'Rethinking Populism: Politics, Mediatisation and Political Style'. *Political Studies* 62 (2): 381–97.

Mogato, Manuel. 2017. 'Philippines, Russia Sign Two Military Deals'. 25 October 2017. https://www.reuters.com/article/philippines-russia-defence-idINKBN1CU1JH.

Mohan, Aniruddh. 2017. 'From Rio to Paris: India in Global Climate Politics'. *Rising Powers Quarterly* 2 (3): 39–61.

Mohan, Aniruddh, and Timon Wehnert. 2019. 'Is India Pulling Its Weight? India's Nationally Determined Contribution and Future Energy Plans in Global Climate Policy'. *Climate Policy* 19 (3): 275–82. https://doi.org/10.1080/14693062.2018.1503154.

Mohan, C. Raja, and Darshana M. Baruah. 2018. 'Deepening the India-France Maritime Partnership'. Carnegie India. https://carnegie-production-assets.s3.amazonaws.com/static/files/Mohan_Baruah_Deepening_The_India_France_Maritime_Partnership.pdf.

Monsonis, Guillem. 2010. 'India's Strategic Autonomy and Rapprochement with the US'. *Strategic Analysis* 34 (4): 611–24. https://doi.org/10.1080/09700161003802802.

Montefiori, Stefano. 2018. 'Macron alza il tiro su Roma. Il premier spagnolo: «Italia egoista»'. *Corriere della Sera*, 23 June 2018. https://www.corriere.it/politica/18_giugno_24/macron-alza-tiro-roma-maio-nemico-numero-d3944580-7720-11e8-b055-7e55445aba73.shtml.

Monteleone, Carla. 2021. 'Foreign Policy and De-Europeanization under the M5S–League Government: Exploring the Italian Behavior in the UN General Assembly'. *Journal of European Integration* 43 (5): 551–67.

Montgomery, Martin. 2017. 'Post-Truth Politics? Authenticity, Populism and the Electoral Discourses of Donald Trump'. *Journal of Language and Politics* 16 (4): 619–39.

Morales, Evo. 2008a. 'Palabras del presidente de la republica, Evo Morales Ayma, en el congreso cocalero en la Cuidad de Cochabamba'. Ministerio de Communicación, Estado Plurinacional de Bolivia.

Morales, Evo. 2008b. 'Salvemos al planeta del capitalismo'. La Paz. http://latinoamericana.org/2010/info/docs/MoralesSalvemosAlPlaneta.pdf.

Morales, Evo. 2009. 'Palabras del presidente de la republica, Evo Morales Ayma, en su informe ante el congreso nacional en los tres años de gestion'. Parlamento Nacional, La Paz.

Morales, Evo. 2016. 'Entrevista al presidente del Estado Plurinacional de Bolivia, Evo Morales Ayma, en el programa diálogo en panamericana de Radio Panamericana'. Ministerio de Communicación, Estado Plurinacional de Bolivia.

Morgül, Kerem. 2023. 'Sending "Our Brothers" Back "Home": Continuity and Change in President Erdoğan's Discourse on Syrian Refugees'. *New Perspectives on Turkey* 69 (November): 30–51. https://doi.org/10.1017/npt.2023.23.

Morin, Jean-Frédéric, and Jonathan Paquin. 2018. *Foreign Policy Analysis: A Toolbox*. Cham: Springer. https://doi.org/10.1007/978-3-319-61003-0.

Moss, Trefor. 2016. 'Behind Duterte's Break with the U.S., a Lifetime of Resentment'. *Wall Street Journal*, 21 October 2016. https://www.wsj.com/articles/behind-philippine-leaders-break-with-the-u-s-a-lifetime-of-resentment-1477061118.

Movimento 5 Stelle, and Lega. 2018. 'Contratto per il governo del cambiamento'. https://www.ansa.it/documents/1526568727881_Governo.pdf.

Mudde, Cas. 2004. 'The Populist Zeitgeist'. *Government and Opposition* 39 (4): 541–63.

Mudde, Cas, and Cristóbal Rovira Kaltwasser. 2012. *Populism in Europe and the Americas: Threat or Corrective for Democracy?* Cambridge: Cambridge University Press.

Mudde, Cas, and Cristóbal Rovira Kaltwasser. 2013. 'Exclusionary vs. Inclusionary Populism: Comparing Contemporary Europe and Latin America'. *Government and Opposition* 48 (2): 147–74.

Mudde, Cas, and Cristóbal Rovira Kaltwasser. 2017. *Populism: A Very Short Introduction*. New York: Oxford University Press.

Muhr, Thomas. 2011. 'Conceptualising the ALBA-TCP: Third Generation Regionalism and Political Economy'. *International Journal of Cuban Studies* 3 (2/3), 98–115.

Muhr, Thomas. 2012. 'Bolivarian Globalization? The New Left's Struggle in Latin America and the Caribbean to Negotiate a Revolutionary Approach to Humanitarian Militarism and International Intervention'. *Globalizations* 9 (1): 145–59. https://doi.org/10.1080/14747731.2012.627725.

Mukherjee, Bhaswati. 2017. 'India and the UN: Reform and Role in a Globalised World'. *Indian Foreign Affairs Journal* 12 (2): 119–32.

Mukherjee, Rohan. 2015. 'India's International Development Program'. In *The Oxford Handbook of Indian Foreign Policy*, edited by David M. Malone, C. Raja Mohan, and Srinath Raghavan, 173–87. New York: Oxford University Press. https://doi.org/10.1093/oxfordhb/9780198743538.013.13.

Mukherji, Rahul. 2020. 'Covid vs. Democracy: India's Illiberal Remedy'. *Journal of Democracy* 31 (4): 91–105.

Müller, Jan-Werner. 2016. *What Is Populism?* Philadelphia: University of Pennsylvania Press.

Müller, Patrick, and Peter Slominski. 2024. 'Hungary, the EU and Russia's War against Ukraine: The Changing Dynamics of EU Foreign Policymaking'. In *The War against Ukraine and the EU: Facing New Realities*, edited by Claudia Wiesner and Michèle Knodt, 111–31. Cham: Springer Nature Switzerland. https://doi.org/10.1007/978-3-031-35040-5_6.

Murthy, C. S. R. 2010. 'Assessing India at the United Nations in the Changing Context'. *International Studies* 47 (2–4): 205–23.

Musella, Fortunato. 2020. 'The Personalization of Italian Political Parties in Three Acts'. *Contemporary Italian Politics* 12 (4): 411–24. https://doi.org/10.1080/23248823.2020.1838870.

Narada, Eliseo. 2019. 'Il governo non ha ancora nominato il capo dell'Agenzia italiana cooperazione sviluppo'. linkiesta.it, 19 March 2019. https://www.linkiesta.it/2019/03/cooperazione-nomine-conte/.

Narang, Vipin, and Paul Staniland. 2018. 'Democratic Accountability and Foreign Security Policy: Theory and Evidence from India'. *Security Studies* 27 (3): 410–47.

narendramodi.in. 2015. 'Mann Ki Baat, January 2015'. https://www.narendramodi.in/mann-ki-baat.

Narlikar, Amrita. 2017. 'India's Role in Global Governance: A Modification?' *International Affairs* 93 (1): 93–111. https://doi.org/10.1093/ia/iiw005.

NATO. 2023. 'Press Statement Following the Meeting between Türkiye, Sweden, and the NATO Secretary General'. NATO, 10 July 2023. https://www.nato.int/cps/en/natohq/news_217147.htm.

Neumann, Iver B. 2007. '"A Speech That the Entire Ministry May Stand For", or: Why Diplomats Never Produce Anything New'. *International Political Sociology* 1 (2): 183–200. https://doi.org/10.1111/j.1749-5687.2007.00012.x.

News Wires. 2017. 'Germany's Merkel Looks to End Turkey's EU Membership Talks'. France 24. 3 September 2017. https://www.france24.com/en/20170903-germany-merkel-turkey-erdogan-diplomatic-eu-membership-talks.

Nicas, Jack, Christoph Koettl, Leonardo Coelho, and Paulo Motoryn. 2024. 'Video: Bolsonaro, Facing Investigations, Hid at Hungarian Embassy'. *New York Times*, 25 March 2024. https://www.nytimes.com/2024/03/25/world/americas/jair-bolsonaro-hungary-video.html.

Nolte, Detlef. 2021. 'From the Summits to the Plains: The Crisis of Latin American Regionalism'. *Latin American Policy* 12 (1): 181–92. https://doi.org/10.1111/lamp.12215.

Noriega, Richa. 2022. 'Philippines Ready to Welcome Ukrainian Refugees, Vows $100,000 Aid'. *GMA News*, 7 April 2022. https://www.gmanetwork.com/news/topstories/nation/827768/philippines-ready-to-welcome-ukrainian-refugees-pledges-100-000-in-humanitarian-aid/story/.

Nye, Joseph S. 2002. 'The American National Interest and Global Public Goods'. *International Affairs* 78 (2): 233–44.

O'Brien, Derek. 2024. 'Spread and Spread of the Sangh: The BJP-RSS Network Has Only Expanded under the Current Government'. *Indian Express*, 26 April 2024. https://indianexpress.com/article/opinion/columns/derek-obrien-writes-spread-and-spread-of-the-sangh-the-bjp-rss-network-has-only-expanded-under-the-current-government-9291581/.

Observatório do Clima. 2023. 'Nunca mais outra vez: 4 anos de desmonte ambiental sob Jair Bolsonaro'. https://www.oc.eco.br/wp-content/uploads/2023/03/AF_reduzido_20220323_individuais_nunca-mais-outra-vez-1.pdf.

Observer Research Foundation. 2023. 'Raisina 2023—The Quad Squad: Power and Purpose of the Polygon'. https://www.orfonline.org/videos/raisina-2023-the-quad-squad-power-and-purpose-of-the-polygon.

OECD. 2024. 'Official Development Assistance (ODA) in 2023, by Members of the Development Assistance Committee (Preliminary Data)'. https://data-explorer.oecd.org/vis?lc=en&tm=flows%20by%20donor&pg=0&snb=18&vw=tb&df[ds]=dsDisseminateFinalDMZ&df[id]=DSD_DAC1%40DF_DAC1&[ag]=OECD.DCD.FSD&df[vs]=1.2&dq=DAC1140%2B1160..Q.&lom=LASTNPERIODS&lo=10&to[TIME_PERIOD]=false&ly[cl]=TIME_PERIOD&ly[rs]=FLOW_TYPE&ly[rw]=MEASURE.

Official Gazette. 2013. 'Aquino Dinner Hosted for Sec. of State John Kerry'. 1 January 2013. https://www.officialgazette.gov.ph/2013/12/17/message-of-president-aquino-atthe-dinner-hosted-for-u-s-secretary-of-state-john-kerry-december-17-2013/.

Official Gazette. 2016. 'President Duterte Not Serious in Leaving UN, Says DFA Chief'. 1 January 2016. https://mirror.officialgazette.gov.ph/2016/08/23/president-duterte-not-serious-in-leaving-un-says-dfa-chief/.

Ogden, Chris. 2018. 'Tone Shift: India's Dominant Foreign Policy Aims under Modi'. *Indian Politics & Policy* 1 (1). https://doi.org/10.18278/inpp.1.1.2.

Oğuzlu, H. Tarik, and Uğur Güngör. 2006. 'Peace Operations and the Transformation of Turkey's Security Policy'. *Contemporary Security Policy* 27 (3): 472–88. https://doi.org/10.1080/13523260601060388.

OHCHR. 2016. 'UN Experts Urge the Philippines to Stop Unlawful Killings of People Suspected of Drug-Related Offences'. https://www.ohchr.org/en/press-releases/2016/08/un-experts-urge-philippines-stop-unlawful-killings-people-suspected-drug.

Oner, Imdat. 2020. 'Turkey and Venezuela: An Alliance of Convenience'. The Wilson Center, 1 January 2020. https://www.wilsoncenter.org/sites/default/files/media/uploads/documents/lap_200317_ven%20turkey_v2%20(1).pdf.

Öniş, Ziya. 2003. 'Domestic Politics versus Global Dynamics: Towards a Political Economy of the 2000 and 2001 Financial Crises in Turkey'. *Turkish Studies* 4 (2): 1–30. https://doi.org/10.1080/14683849.2003.9687227.

Öniş, Ziya. 2010. 'Contesting for Turkey's Political "Centre": Domestic Politics, Identity Conflicts and the Controversy over EU Membership'. *Journal of Contemporary European Studies* 18 (3): 361–76. https://doi.org/10.1080/14782804.2010.507919.

Öniş, Ziya, and Maimaiti Yalikun. 2021. 'Emerging Partnership in a Post-Western World? The Political Economy of China-Turkey Relations'. *Southeast European and Black Sea Studies* 21 (4): 507–29. https://doi.org/10.1080/14683857.2021.1981624.

Oppermann, Kai, Ryan Beasley, and Juliet Kaarbo. 2020. 'British Foreign Policy after Brexit: Losing Europe and Finding a Role'. *International Relations* 34 (2): 133–56. https://doi.org/10.1177/0047117819864421.

Oppermann, Kai, and Henrike Viehrig, eds. 2011. *Issue Salience in International Politics.* Milton Park: Routledge. https://doi.org/10.4324/9780203816950.

ORF. 2023. 'Kickl und Weidel: Schulterschluss von FPÖ und AfD'. news.ORF.at, 19 September 2023. https://orf.at/stories/3331697/.

Örmeci, Ozan. 2011. 'A Turkish Social Democrat: İsmail Cem'. *Turkish Studies* 12 (1): 101–14. https://doi.org/10.1080/14683849.2011.563504.

Ostermann, Falk, and Bernhard Stahl. 2022. 'Theorizing Populist Radical-Right Foreign Policy: Ideology and Party Positioning in France and Germany'. *Foreign Policy Analysis* 18 (3): orac006. https://doi.org/10.1093/fpa/orac006.

Ostiguy, Pierre. 2017. 'Populism: A Socio-Cultural Approach'. In *The Oxford Handbook of Populism,* edited by Cristóbal Rovira Kaltwasser, Paul A. Taggart, Paulina Ochoa Espejo, and Pierre Ostiguy, 73–97. Oxford: Oxford University Press.

Ostrom, Elinor. 1990. *Governing the Commons: The Evolution of Institutions for Collective Action.* Cambridge: Cambridge University Press.

Özdamar, Özgür, and Erdem Ceydilek. 2020. 'European Populist Radical Right Leaders' Foreign Policy Beliefs: An Operational Code Analysis'. *European Journal of International Relations* 26 (1): 137–62. https://doi.org/10.1177/1354066119850254.

Özdamar, Özgür, and Lerna K. Yanik. 2024. 'Populist Hyperpersonalization and Politicization of Foreign Policy Institutions'. *International Affairs* 100 (5): 1835–56. https://doi.org/10.1093/ia/iiae181.

Özerdem, Alpaslan, and Ahmet Erdi Öztürk, eds. 2023. *A Companion to Modern Turkey's Centennial: Political, Sociological, Economic and Institutional Transformations since 1923.* Edinburgh: Edinburgh University Press.

Ozkan, Mehmet, and Serhat Orakci. 2015. 'Turkey as a "political" actor in Africa – an assessment of Turkish involvement in Somalia'. *Journal of Eastern African Studies* 9 (2): 343–352. DOI: 10.1080/17531055.2015.1042629

Özkırımlı, Umut, ed. 2014. *The Making of a Protest Movement in Turkey: #occupygezi.* Hampshire: Palgrave Macmillan.

Özpek, Burak Bilgehan, and Nebahat Tanriverdi Yaşar. 2018. 'Populism and Foreign Policy in Turkey under the AKP Rule'. *Turkish Studies* 19 (2): 198–216.

Öztürk, Ahmet Erdi. 2020. 'Turkey's Hagia Sophia Decision: The Collapse of Multiculturalism and Secularism or Something More?' Contending Modernities. 3 August 2020. https://contendingmodernities.nd.edu/global-currents/hagia-sophia-multiculturalism/.

Pacciardi, Agnese, Kilian Spandler, and Fredrik Söderbaum. 2024. 'Beyond Exit: How Populist Governments Disengage from International Institutions'. *International Affairs* 100 (5): 2025–45. https://doi.org/10.1093/ia/iiae185.

Padmanabhan, Keshav. 2024. 'MEA Budget Sees 35% Cut in Contributions to International Bodies. UN, Nalanda University Top List'. *ThePrint*, 1 February 2024. https://theprint.in/diplomacy/mea-budget-sees-35-cut-in-contributions-to-international-bodies-un-nalanda-university-top-list/1949434/.

Pagnoncelli, Nando. 2019. 'I 5 Stelle crollano al 21,2%, la Lega sfiora il 36% e il Pd ritrova i consensi delle Ultime Politiche'. *Corriere della Sera*, 2 March 2019. https://www.corriere.it/politica/19_marzo_02/m5s-crolla-212percento-lega-sfiora-36percento-pd-ritrova-consensi-un-anno-fa-514fecb6-3c5d-11e9-8da9-1361971309b1.shtml.

Paliwal, Avinash. 2017. *My Enemy's Enemy: India in Afghanistan from the Soviet Invasion to the US Withdrawal.* London: Hurst.

Panda, Ankit. 2013. 'Indian PM Signs Border Defense Agreement with China'. *The Diplomat*, 24 October 2013. https://thediplomat.com/2013/10/indian-pm-signs-border-defense-agreement-with-china/.

Panizza, Francisco, and Romina Miorelli. 2009. 'Populism and Democracy in Latin America'. *Ethics & International Affairs* 23 (1): 39–46.

Pant, Harsh V. 2007. 'The US–India Nuclear Deal: The Beginning of a Beautiful Relationship?' *Cambridge Review of International Affairs* 20 (3): 455–72.

Pant, Harsh V., and Vivek Lall. 2024. 'Introduction: Modi Heralds a New Era in India-US Partnership'. In *Aligned but Autonomous: India-US Relations in the Modi Era*, edited by Harsh V. Pant and Vivek Lall, 6–13. New Delhi: ORF and Global Policy Journal. https://www.orfonline.org/research/aligned-but-autonomous-india-us-relations-in-the-modi-era.

Pappas, Takis S. 2014. 'Populist Democracies: Post-Authoritarian Greece and Post-Communist Hungary'. *Government and Opposition* 49 (1): 1–23.

Pappas, Takis S. 2019. *Populism and Liberal Democracy: A Comparative and Theoretical Analysis.* Oxford: Oxford University Press.

Parameswaran, Prashanth. 2017. 'The Truth about Duterte's ASEAN South China Sea Blow'. 1 January 2017. https://thediplomat.com/2017/05/the-truth-about-dutertes-asean-south-china-sea-blow/.

Parker, George, Sebastian Payne, Peter Foster, and Jim Pickard. 2020. 'UK Government Admits It Will Break International Law over Brexit Treaty'. *FT.com*, 8 September 2020. https://www.proquest.com/docview/2476113776/citation/FD78CD5AA4764317PQ/3.

Parlar Dal, Emel, and Ali Murat Kurşun. 2018. 'Turkey's Global Governance Strategies at the UN Compared to the BRICS (2008–2014): Clarifying the Motivation–Contribution Nexus'. *Third World Quarterly* 39 (9): 1770–90. https://doi.org/10.1080/01436597.2018.1438182.

Pathak, Swapna, and Christie Parris. 2021. 'India's Diplomatic Discourse and Development Dilemma in the International Climate Change Regime'. *India Review* 20 (1): 1–28. https://doi.org/10.1080/14736489.2021.1875699.

Payne, Sebastian. 2020. 'Cummings and Gove Join Forces in Battle against the Whitehall "Blob": PM's Chief Adviser and Cabinet Office Minister Target What They See as Ineffectual, pro-EU Officials'. *Financial Times*, 30 June 2020. https://www.proquest.com/docview/2428902592/citation/64D82990810B4042PQ/1.

Permanent Mission of the Republic of the Philippines to the United Nations. 2019. 'Philippine Defense Secretary Lorenza Announces Philippine Pledge at the 2019 UN Peacekeeping Ministerial Meeting in New York City | Philippines'. 3 April 2019. https://www.un.int/philippines/activities/philippine-defense-secretary-lorenza-announces-philippine-pledge-2019-un-peacekeeping.

Pew Research Center. 2010. 'Indians See Threat From Pakistan, Extremist Groups'. *Pew Research Center* (blog), 20 October 2010. https://www.pewresearch.org/global/2010/10/20/chapter-2-india-and-the-world/.

The Philippine Star. 2022. 'Philippines to Welcome Ukrainian Refugees — DOJ'. *The Philippine Star*, 3 March 2022. https://www.philstar.com/headlines/2022/03/03/2164637/philippines-welcome-ukrainian-refugees-doj.

Philstar. 2016. 'Government to Pursue Independent Foreign Policy, Says Duterte'. 10 September 2016. https://www.philstar.com/headlines/2016/09/10/1622357/government-pursue-independent-foreign-policy-says-duterte.

Piazza, James A. 2024. 'Populism and Support for Political Violence in the United States: Assessing the Role of Grievances, Distrust of Political Institutions, Social Change Threat, and Political Illiberalism'. *Political Research Quarterly* 77 (1): 152–66. https://doi.org/10.1177/10659129231198248.

Pickard, Jim. 2019. 'Theresa May's Five Big Mistakes: How They Stacked Up'. *Financial Times*, 19 May 2019. https://www.ft.com/content/2ea1b40c-7d7f-11e9-81d2-f785092ab560.

Pillai, Aditya Valiathan, and Navroz K. Dubash. 2021. 'The Limits of Opportunism: The Uneven Emergence of Climate Institutions in India'. *Environmental Politics* 30 (sup1): 93–117. https://doi.org/10.1080/09644016.2021.1933800.

Plagemann, Johannes. 2021. 'Small States and Competing Connectivity Strategies: What Explains Bangladesh's Success in Relations with Asia's Major Powers?' *Pacific Review*, January, 1–29. https://doi.org/10.1080/09512748.2021.1908410.

Plagemann, Johannes, and Sandra Destradi. 2019. 'Populism and Foreign Policy: The Case of India'. *Foreign Policy Analysis* 15 (2): 283–301. https://doi.org/10.1093/fpa/ory010.

Plagemann, Johannes, Carlo Heras Rodríguez, and Sandra Destradi. 2022. 'Populist Foreign Policy and Mobilization in Bolivia'. *Política/Revista de ciencia política* 60 (2): 9–32.

Plagemann, Johannes, and Miriam Prys-Hansen. 2020. '"Responsibility", Change, and Rising Powers' Role Conceptions: Comparing Indian Foreign Policy Roles in Global Climate Change Negotiations and Maritime Security'. *International Relations of the Asia-Pacific* 20 (2): 275–305. https://doi.org/10.1093/irap/lcy028.

Plurinational State of Bolivia. 2009. 'Bolivia (Plurinational State of)'. 2009. https://www.constituteproject.org/constitution/Bolivia_2009.

Plurinational State of Bolivia. n.d. 'Intended Nationally Determined Contribution from the Plurinational State of Bolivia'.

PM India. 2023. 'PM's Address in the 100th Episode of "Mann Ki Baat"'. 30 April 2023. https://www.pmindia.gov.in/en/news_updates/pms-address-in-the-100th-episode-of-mann-ki-baat/.

@PM_ViktorOrban. 2024. 'Peace Mission 3.0 #Beijing Https://T.Co/DZZFv4qAEH'. Tweet. *Twitter*. https://twitter.com/PM_ViktorOrban/status/1810085572758634995.

Podemos. 2022. 'Podemos ante el conflicto de Ucrania y el reconocimiento unilateral de Rusia de las autoproclamadas repúblicas del Donbás'. *Podemos*, 23 February 2022. https://podemos.info/podemos-ante-el-conflicto-de-ucrania-y-el-reconocimiento-unilateral-de-rusia-de-las-autoproclamadas-republicas-del-donbas/.

Politico. 2021. 'Orbán's Fidesz Quits EPP Group in European Parliament'. *Politico*, 3 March 2021. https://www.politico.eu/article/epp-suspension-rules-fidesz-european-parliament-viktor-orban-hungary/.

Połońska-Kimunguyi, Eva, and Patrick Kimunguyi. 2017. '"Gunboats of Soft Power": Boris on Africa and Post-Brexit "Global Britain"'. *Cambridge Review of International Affairs* 30 (4): 325–49. https://doi.org/10.1080/09557571.2018.1432565.

Poupeau, Franck. 2013. 'La Bolivie entre Pachamama et modèle extractiviste'. *Écologie & politique* 46 (1): 109–19.

Pratap, Rishabh, Larry Register, and Heather Chen. 2022. 'India's Modi Tells Putin: Now Is Not the Time for War'. *CNN*, 17 September 2022. https://www.cnn.com/2022/09/17/world/modi-putin-russia-ukraine-war-rebuke-intl-hnk/index.html.

Presidency of the Republic of Turkey. 2016. 'The Date of July 15, 2016 Is a Turning Point for Turkey'. https://www.tccb.gov.tr/en/news/542/58866/turk-milleti-15-temmuzda-sadece-bayragina-degil-hedeflerine-de-sahip-cikti.

Presidency of the Republic of Türkiye. 2016. 'European Union Should Question Its Manner and Integrity'. 24 June 2016. https://www.tccb.gov.tr/en/news/542/45519/european-union-should-question-its-manner-and-integrity.

Presidency of the Republic of Turkey. 2017. 'President Erdoğan Attends Dinner Hosted in His Honor by President Pavlopoulos of Greece'. 12 July 2017. https://www.tccb.gov.tr/en/news/542/87641/president-erdogan-attends-dinner-hosted-in-his-honor-by-president-pavlopoulos-of-greece.

Presidency of the Republic of Türkiye. 2017a. 'President Erdoğan Addresses Ambassadors at the Presidential Complex'. 9 January 2017. https://www.tccb.gov.tr/en/news/542/70698/mill-guvenligimizi-ilgilendiren-konularda-masada-ve-sahada-olmaya-devam-edecegiz.

Presidency of the Republic of Türkiye. 2017b. 'Some European Countries Are Disturbed by Our Fight against Terrorist Organizations'. 15 April 2017. https://www.tccb.gov.tr/en/news/542/74772/avrupa-ulkelerinin-bir-bolumu-teror-orgutleriyle-mucadelemizden-rahatsiz.

Presidency of the Republic of Türkiye. 2017c. 'Today's Sick Man is the European Union'. 5 April 2017. https://www.tccb.gov.tr/en/news/542/74629/bugunun-hasta-adami-artik-avrupa-birligidir.

Presidency of the Republic of Türkiye. 2017d. 'Turkey Proved Its Determination for Democracy and the Rule of Law on July 15'. 27 April 2017. https://www.tccb.gov.tr/en/news/542/74986/turkiye-demokrasi-ve-hukuk-devleti-konusundaki-kararliligini-15-temmuzda-ibra-etmistir.

Presidency of the Republic of Türkiye. 2020a. 'Presidency of the Republic of Turkey: "NATO Is Going through a Period of Critical Importance during Which It Should Display Alliance Solidarity with Turkey in a Clear Manner"'. 9 March 2020. https://www.tccb.gov.tr/en/news/542/116977/-nato-is-going-through-a-period-of-critical-importance-during-which-it-should-display-alliance-solidarity-with-turkey-in-a-clear-manner-.

Presidency of the Republic of Türkiye. 2020b. 'The Current Global System, Which Protects the Mighty Rather than Those Who Are Right, Cannot Continue as It Is'. 9 November 2020. https://www.tccb.gov.tr/en/news/542/122723/-the-current-global-system-which-protects-the-mighty-rather-than-those-who-are-right-cannot-continue-as-it-is-.

Presidency of the Republic of Türkiye. 2021. 'NATO Should Undertake More Effective Initiatives in the Face of Global Challenges'. 14 June 2021. https://www.tccb.gov.tr/en/news/542/128320/-nato-should-undertake-more-effective-initiatives-in-the-face-of-global-challenges-.

Presidency of the Republic of Turkey. 2022a. 'Türkiye Displays a Firm Stance Both at Home and Abroad'. 26 September 2022. https://www.tccb.gov.tr/en/news/542/139851/-turkiye-displays-a-firm-stance-both-at-home-and-abroad-.

Presidency of the Republic of Turkey. 2022b. 'We Work Tirelessly for the Establishment of Peace, Prosperity and Justice'. 16 November 2022. https://www.tccb.gov.tr/en/news/542/141733/-we-work-tirelessly-for-the-establishment-of-peace-prosperity-and-justice-.

Presidency of the Republic of Turkey. 2023. 'While Enhancing Our Relations with the U.S. on the Political Level, We Also Need to Diversify Our Cooperation in the Economic Field'. 21 September 2023. https://www.tccb.gov.tr/en/news/542/149555/-while-enhancing-our-relations-with-the-u-s-on-the-political-level-we-also-need-to-diversify-our-cooperation-in-the-economic-field-.

Presidency of the Republic of Türkiye. 2023a. 'President Erdoğan's Message on United Nations Day'. 24 October 2023. https://www.tccb.gov.tr/en/speeches-statements/558/149856/president-erdogan-s-message-on-united-nations-day.

Presidency of the Republic of Türkiye. 2023b. 'The Current Order, Which Confines the Humanity's Fate to the Mercy of Five Countries, Is Not Sustainable'. 4 April 2023. https://www.tccb.gov.tr/en/news/542/145578/-eu-membership-remains-a-strategic-goal-for-us-.

Presidency of the Republic of Türkiye. 2023c. 'Those Who Do Not Speak Out Against Israel's Crimes Against Humanity Are Just as Much an Accomplice in These Crimes as the Perpetrators'. 15 November 2023. https://www.tccb.gov.tr/en/news/542/150195/-those-who-do-not-speak-out-against-israel-s-crimes-against-humanity-are-just-as-much-an-accomplice-in-these-crimes-as-the-perpetrators-.

Presidency of the Republic of Türkiye. 2024. 'Türkiye Cannot Be Confined to a Single Bloc'. 16 July 2024. https://www.tccb.gov.tr/en/news/542/153041/-turkiye-cannot-be-confined-to-a-single-bloc-.

President Biden [@POTUS]. 2023. 'The Friendship between the United States and India Is among the Most Consequential in the World. And It's Stronger, Closer, and More Dynamic than Ever'. Tweet. *Twitter*. https://x.com/POTUS/status/1673028455506616321.

Pugliese, Giulio, Francesca Ghiretti, and Aurelio Insisa. 2022. 'Italy's Embrace of the Belt and Road Initiative: Populist Foreign Policy and Political Marketing'. *International Affairs* 98 (3): 1033–51. https://doi.org/10.1093/ia/iiac039.

Putnam, Robert D. 1988. 'Diplomacy and Domestic Politics: The Logic of Two-Level Games'. *International Organization* 42 (3): 428–60.

Queiroz-Stein, Guilherme de, Alfredo Alejandro Gugliano, Carlos Alberto Seifert Jr., and Aidee Maria Moser Torquato Luiz. 2023. 'Climate Change, Denialism, and Participatory Institutions in Brazil: Effects of the Bolsonaro Government's Environmental Strategy (2019–2022)'. *Brazilian Political Science Review* 17 (3): e0006.

Quitral Rojas, Máximo. 2014. 'La política exterior de Evo Morales', January. http://www.scielo.org.bo/pdf/rlde/n21/n21_a07.pdf.

Rachman, Gideon. 2017. *Easternization: Asia's Rise and America's Decline from Obama to Trump and Beyond*. New York: Other Press.

Rai News. 2018a. 'A Bardonecchia irruzione della polizia francese in centro migranti, è polemica'. *Rai News*, 31 March 2018. https://www.rainews.it/dl/rainews/articoli/A-Bardonecchia-irruzione-della-Polizia-francese-in-centro-migranti-polemica-politica-72c19c1f-aa32-44b0-a446-a14aacfae3a1.html.

Rai News. 2018b. 'Manovra. Salvini: Bruxelles può mandare 12 letterine, ma non cambia'. *Rai News*, 24 October 2018. https://www.rainews.it/archivio-rainews/articoli/salvini-bruxelles-puo-mandare-12-letterine-ma-la-manovra-non-cambia-122a4f3d-2246-456d-bba2-043779b01ca1.html?refresh_ce.

Raja Mohan, C. 2008. 'India's Great Power Burdens'. *India Seminar* 581. https://www.india-seminar.com/2008/581/581_c_raja_mohan.htm.

Ramos, Charmaine. 2020. 'Change without Transformation: Social Policy Reforms in the Philippines under Duterte'. *Development and Change* 51 (2): 485–505.

Ramos, Daniel. 2023. 'Bolivia Taps China, Russia's Rosatom in Bid to Unlock Huge Lithium Riches'. *Reuters*, 29 June 2023. https://www.reuters.com/world/americas/bolivia-seals-14-bln-lithium-deals-with-russias-rosatom-chinas-guoan-2023-06-29/.

Rana, Chetan. 2023. 'Populism beyond Borders: Modi's Discursive Strategy with the Indian Diaspora in the United States of America'. In *Political Communication and Performative Leadership: Populism in International Politics*, edited by Corina Lacatus, Gustav Meibauer, and Georg Löfflmann, 243–57. Cham: Springer International Publishing. https://doi.org/10.1007/978-3-031-41640-8_13.

Ranada, Pia. 2017. 'PH, Russia Sign Defense Agreement, 9 Other Deals'. *Rappler* (blog), 25 May 2017. https://www.rappler.com/nation/170877-philippines-russia-defense-agreement-deals/.

Ranada, Pia. 2019. 'Malacañang Suspends Talks on Loans, Grants from Countries Backing U.N. Probe into Drug War'. *Rappler* (blog), 21 September 2019. https://www.rappler.com/philippines/240669-philippines-suspends-talks-loans-grants-countries-support-un-resolution-drug-war/.

Ranada, Pia. 2021. 'In First, Finance Chief to Head PH Delegation to UN Climate Summit in Glasgow'. *Earth Journalism Network*, 26 October 2021. https://earthjournalism.net/stories/in-first-finance-chief-to-head-ph-delegation-to-un-climate-summit-in-glasgow.

Rankin, Jennifer. 2024. '"Make Europe Great Again": Hungary Sets Scene for Its EU Presidency'. *The Guardian*, 30 June 2024. https://www.theguardian.com/world/article/2024/jun/30/make-europe-great-again-hungary-sets-scene-eu-presidency.

Ranta, Eija M. 2014. 'In the Name of Vivir Bien: Indigeneity, State Formation, and Politics in Evo Morales' Bolivia'. Helsinki: University of Helsinki. https://helda.helsinki.fi/server/api/core/bitstreams/e9f9a808-44f9-4649-b28e-53e6c445f9eb/content.

Rao, Swasti. 2024. 'Beyond Macron-Modi Bromance—What's Next for India-France Partnership?' *ThePrint*, 26 January 2024. https://theprint.in/opinion/beyond-macron-modi-bromance-whats-next-for-india-france-partnership/1939623/.

Rappler. 2016. 'Obama to Duterte: Fight Crime, Terror "the Right Way"'. *Rappler*, 8 September 2016. https://www.rappler.com/nation/145619-obama-duterte-crime-war-right-way/.

Rathbun, Brian C. 2004. *Partisan Interventions: European Party Politics and Peace Enforcement in the Balkans*. Ithaca, NY: Cornell University Press.

Redo, Daniel, Andrew C. Millington, and Derrick Hindery. 2011. 'Deforestation Dynamics and Policy Changes in Bolivia's Post-Neoliberal Era'. *Land Use Policy* 28 (1): 227–41. https://doi.org/10.1016/j.landusepol.2010.06.004.

Remeikis, Amy. 2021. '"We Felt Fooled": France Still Furious after Australia Scraps $90bn Submarine Deal'. *The Guardian*, 20 September 2021. https://www.theguardian.com/world/2021/sep/20/we-felt-fooled-france-still-furious-after-australia-scraps-90bn-submarine-deal.

Reporters without Borders. 2024. 'Hungary'. 24 July 2024. https://rsf.org/en/country/hungary.

Repubblica. 2018a. 'Aquarius, niente scuse da Macron: "Non posso dare ragione a chi provoca". Conte orientato a disertare l'incontro col leader francese'. *La Repubblica*, 13 June 2018. https://www.repubblica.it/cronaca/2018/06/13/news/la_farnesina_convoca_l_ambasciatore_francese-198875992/.

Repubblica. 2018b. 'Manovra, l'Italia taglia i fondi all'Onu per 32 milioni all'anno'. *La Repubblica*, 24 December 2018. https://www.repubblica.it/politica/2018/12/24/news/manovra_taglio_fondi_onu-215011836/.

Repubblica. 2019. 'Di Maio e Di Battista: "La Francia sfrutta l'Africa, va sanzionata". Parigi convoca l'ambasciatrice italiana'. *La Repubblica*, 21 January 2019. https://www.repubblica.it/politica/2019/01/21/news/di_maio_e_di_battista_all_attacco_della_francia_sfrutta_l_africa_va_sanzionata_-217090366/.

Republic of Türkiye Ministry of Foreign Affairs. 1999a. 'The PKK Strategy in Europe to Place Turkey on Trial Foreign Policy Research Institute'. 1 March 1999. https://www.mfa.gov.tr/_p_the-pkk-strategy-in-europe-to-place-turkey-on-trial-foreign-policy-research-institute—michael-radu—_february-26_-1999__br_march-1_-1999__p____p____p_.en.mfa.

Republic of Türkiye Ministry of Foreign Affairs. 1999b. 'Turkey Reacts to Security Council Resolutions on Cyprus July 1, 1999'. 1 July 1999. https://www.mfa.gov.tr/turkey-reacts-to-security-council-resolutions-on-cyprus_br_july-1_-1999.en.mfa.

Republic of Türkiye Ministry of Foreign Affairs. 2022. 'Türkiye-Russia-Ukraine Trilateral Foreign Ministers Meeting, 10 March 2022'. 10 March 2022. https://www.mfa.gov.tr/turkiye-rusya-ukrayna-uclu-disisleri-bakanlari-toplantisi--10-mart-2022.en.mfa.

Reuters. 2009. 'Turkish Leader Calls Xinjiang Killings "Genocide"'. *Reuters*, 11 July 2009, sec. World. https://www.reuters.com/article/world/turkish-leader-calls-xinjiang-killings-genocide-idUSTRE56957D/.

Reuters. 2016. 'Bolivia Agrees $300 Million Nuclear Complex with Russia's Rosatom'. *Reuters*, 6 March 2016. https://www.reuters.com/article/business/environment/bolivia-agrees-300-million-nuclear-complex-with-russias-rosatom-idUSKCN0W80R2/.

Reuters. 2017. 'Philippines' Duterte Signs Paris Pact on Climate Change'. *Reuters*, 1 March 2017. https://www.reuters.com/article/world/philippines-duterte-signs-paris-pact-on-climate-change-idUSKBN168310/.

Reuters. 2024. 'Netanyahu Rejects International Pressure for Palestinian State'. *Reuters*, 16 February 2024. https://www.reuters.com/world/middle-east/netanyahu-rejects-international-pressure-palestinian-state-2024-02-16/.

Riedel, Bruce. 2009. 'The Mumbai Massacre and Its Implications for America and South Asia'. *Journal of International Affairs* 63 (1): 111–26.

Roberts, Hannah. 2024. 'As Meloni Embraces Africa, Europe Holds Its Breath'. *Politico*, 29 January 2024. https://www.politico.eu/article/meloni-italy-africa-energy-migration-far-right/.

Robinson, Neil, and Sarah Milne. 2017. 'Populism and Political Development in Hybrid Regimes: Russia and the Development of Official Populism'. *International Political Science Review* 38 (4): 412–25. https://doi.org/10.1177/0192512117697705.

Rochlin, James. 2007. 'Latin America's Left Turn and the New Strategic Landscape: The Case of Bolivia'. *Third World Quarterly* 28 (7): 1327–42. https://doi.org/10.1080/01436590701591838.

Rodrigues, Jeanette, and Bibhudatta Pradhan. 2017. 'Modi Takes a Swipe at Harvard Economists after India GDP Surprise'. *Bloomberg.com*, 2 March 2017. https://www.bloomberg.com/politics/articles/2017-03-02/harvard-economists-face-modi-s-censure-after-india-gdp-surprise.

Romero, Alexis. 2016a. 'Duterte on Putin: We Became "Fast Friends"'. *Philippine Star*, 21 November 2016. https://www.philstar.com/headlines/2016/11/21/1644167/duterte-putin-we-became-fast-friends.

Romero, Alexis. 2016b. 'Duterte Threatens to Scrap VFA after US-Led MCC Defers Aid Grant'. *Philippine Star*, 17 December 2016. https://www.philstar.com/headlines/2016/12/17/1654344/duterte-threatens-scrap-vfa-after-us-led-mcc-defers-aid-grant.

Romero, Alexis. 2016c. 'Rody on Idol Putin: We Have Similarities'. *Philippine Star*, 7 November 2016. https://www.philstar.com/headlines/2016/11/07/1640240/rody-idol-putin-we-have-similarities.

Romero, Simon. 2007. 'Venezuela Rivals U.S. in Aid to Bolivia'. *New York Times*, 23 February 2007. https://www.nytimes.com/2007/02/23/world/americas/23bolivia.html?searchResultPosition=6.

Rooduijn, Matthijs. 2014. 'The Mesmerising Message: The Diffusion of Populism in Public Debates in Western European Media'. *Political Studies* 62 (4): 726–44. https://doi.org/10.1111/1467-9248.12074.

Rooduijn, Matthijs, Sarah L. de Lange, and Wouter van der Brug. 2014. 'A Populist Zeitgeist? Programmatic Contagion by Populist Parties in Western Europe'. *Party Politics* 20 (4): 563–75. https://doi.org/10.1177/1354068811436065.

Room, Robin. 2012. 'Reform by Subtraction: The Path of Denunciation of International Drug Treaties and Reaccession with Reservations'. *International Journal of Drug Policy* 23 (January): 401–6.

Rosenstone, Steven J., and John Mark Hansen. 1993. *Mobilization, Participation, and Democracy in America*. New York: Macmillan.

Rowe, Paul S. 2012. *Religion and Global Politics*. Oxford: Oxford University Press.

Roy, Srirupa. 2024. *The Political Outsider: Indian Democracy and the Lineages of Populism*. South Asia in Motion. Stanford, CA: Stanford University Press.

Roy-Chaudhury, Rahul, and Kate Sullivan de Estrada. 2018. 'India, the Indo-Pacific and the Quad'. *Survival* 60 (3): 181–94.

Ruser, Nathan, and Baani Grewal. 2022. 'Zooming into the Tawang Border Skirmishes'. ASPI: International Cyber Policy Centre. https://pageflow.aspi.org.au/zooming-into-the-tawang-border-skirmishes.

Russett, Bruce. 1994. *Grasping the Democratic Peace: Principles for a Post–Cold War World*. Princeton, NJ: Princeton University Press.

SAARC. 2020. 'SAARC Summits'. 12 July 2020. https://saarc-sec.org/index.php/about-saarc/saarc-structure/saarc-summits.

Sagarzazu, Iñaki, and Cameron G. Thies. 2019. 'The Foreign Policy Rhetoric of Populism: Chávez, Oil, and Anti-Imperialism'. *Political Research Quarterly* 72 (1): 205–14.

Sajjanhar, Ashok. 2017. 'The Doklam Crisis Ends: A Diplomatic Victory for India'. Orfonline.org, 30 August 2017. https://www.orfonline.org/expert-speak/the-doklam-crisis-ends-a-diplomatic-victory-for-india.

Sakallioğlu, Ümit Cizre. 1997. 'The Anatomy of the Turkish Military's Political Autonomy'. *Comparative Politics* 29 (2): 151–66. https://doi.org/10.2307/422077.

Salvini, Matteo. 2019. 'Sapete qual è la percentuale di immigrati portati in Italia dalla missione internazionale #Sophia sottoscritta da Renzi nel 2015? 100%. Questo è il grande contributo fornito all'interesse nazionale dal PD. Qualcuno ritiene di far venire meno la missione? Ce ne faremo una ragione. https://t.co/px3FeLjwC9'. Tweet. *Twitter*. https://twitter.com/matteosalvinimi/status/1088332973596786688.

San Diego Union-Tribune. 2016. 'Morales dice que la OEA debe desaparecer si no respeta la soberania'. *San Diego Union-Tribune* (blog), 21 September 2016. https://www.sandiegouniontribune.com/2016/09/21/morales-dice-que-la-oea-debe-desaparecer-si-no-respeta-la-soberana/.

Sanger, David E. 2024. 'Trump Had an "America First" Foreign Policy. But It Was a Breakdown in American Policymaking'. *New York Times*, 31 October 2024. https://www.nytimes.com/2024/10/31/us/politics/trump-foreign-policy.html.

Santoro, Lauren Ratliff, Elias Assaf, Robert M. Bond, Skyler J. Cranmer, Eloise E. Kaizar, and David J. Sivakoff. 2021. 'Exploring the Direct and Indirect Effects of Elite Influence on Public Opinion'. *PLoS ONE* 16 (11): e0257335. https://doi.org/10.1371/journal.pone.0257335.

Saran, Samir, and Aled Jones. 2017. *India's Climate Change Identity: Between Reality and Perception*. Cham: Palgrave Macmillan.

Satana, Nil. 2013. 'Turkey'. In *Providing Peacekeepers: The Politics, Challenges, and Future of United Nations Peacekeeping Contributions*, edited by Alex J. Bellamy and Paul D. Williams, 355–75. Oxford: Oxford University Press.

Sauer, Pjotr. 2024. 'Viktor Orbán Visits Vladimir Putin to Condemnation from Fellow EU Leaders'. *The Guardian*, 5 July 2024. https://www.theguardian.com/world/article/2024/jul/05/viktor-orban-visits-vladimir-putin-to-condemnation-from-fellow-eu-leaders.

Saunders, Robert. 2020. 'Brexit and Empire: "Global Britain" and the Myth of Imperial Nostalgia'. *Journal of Imperial and Commonwealth History* 48 (6): 1140–74. https://doi.org/10.1080/03086534.2020.1848403.

Scazzieri, Luigi. 2024. 'The EU and Turkey after the Elections: The Start of a New Chapter?' Centre for European Reform. https://www.cer.eu/publications/archive/policy-brief/2023/eu-and-turkey-after-elections-start-new-chapter.

SCF. 2019. 'Erdoğan Calls Some EU Politicians "Enemies of Islam"'. *Stockholm Center for Freedom* (blog), 25 March 2019. https://stockholmcf.org/erdogan-calls-some-eu-politicians-enemies-of-islam/.

SCF. 2023. 'Anti-LGBT Rhetoric Becomes Pillar of Erdogan's Election Campaign'. *Stockholm Center for Freedom* (blog), 5 May 2023. https://stockholmcf.org/anti-lgbt-rhetoric-becomes-pillar-of-erdogans-election-campaign/.

Schafer, Mark, and Crichlow, Scott. 2010. *Groupthink VS. High-Quality Decision Making in International Relations.* New York: Columbia University Press.

Scharf, Avi. 2024. 'Top Israeli Arms Maker Unwittingly Reveals Its Largest Foreign Customer: India'. *Haaretz*, 9 May 2024. https://www.haaretz.com/israel-news/security-aviation/2024-05-09/ty-article/.premium/israeli-defense-giant-iai-unwittingly-reveals-its-largest-foreign-customer/0000018f-583d-d348-a7bf-febdda230000.

Schianchi, Francesca. 2019. 'Di Maio accusa la Francia di colonialismo, ambasciatore d'Italia convocato a Parigi'. *La Stampa*, 21 January 2019. https://www.lastampa.it/esteri/2019/01/21/news/di-maio-accusa-la-francia-di-colonialismo-ambasciatore-d-italia-convocato-a-parigi-1.33671714/.

Schilling-Vacaflor, Almut. 2011. 'Bolivia's New Constitution: Towards Participatory Democracy and Political Pluralism?' *Revista Europea de Estudios Latinoamericanos y del Caribe/European Review of Latin American and Caribbean Studies*, no. 90, 3–22.

Schmidt, Friedrich. 2019. 'Russischer Staatssender bietet Evo Morales Job an'. *Frankfurter Allgemeine Zeitung*, 12 November 2019. https://www.faz.net/aktuell/politik/ausland/was-verbindet-wladimir-putin-mit-evo-morales-16481753.html.

Schnabel, Chris. 2016. 'Beyond the Numbers: How Aquino Fueled the Economy'. *Rappler* (blog), 17 June 2016. https://www.rappler.com/business/economy/136536-president-aquino-economy-legacy/.

Schreier, Margrit. 2012. *Qualitative Content Analysis in Practice.* London: SAGE Publications.

Seelke, Clare Ribando. 2014. 'Bolivia: In Brief'. 17 April 2014, Congressional Research Service Report 7-5700. https://sgp.fas.org/crs/row/R43473.pdf.

Sehl, Annika, Felix M. Simon, and Ralph Schroeder. 2022. 'The Populist Campaigns against European Public Service Media: Hot Air or Existential Threat?' *International Communication Gazette* 84 (1): 3–23. https://doi.org/10.1177/1748048520939868.

Sengupta, Sandeep. 2020. 'Deciphering India's Foreign Policy on Climate Change: Role of Interests, Institutions, and Ideas'. In *India Rising: A Multi Layered Analysis of Ideas, Interests and Institutions*, edited by Johannes Plagemann, Sandra Destradi, and Amrita Narlikar, 167–94. New Delhi: Oxford University Press.

Sengupta, Shayak, and Abhinav Jindal. 2024. 'Are Global Climate Partnerships Fit for Purpose?' *Foreign Policy* (blog), 24 July 2024. https://foreignpolicy.com/2023/12/01/india-climate-finance-cop-energy-renewables/.

Serna Duque, Santiago. 2018. 'Evo Morales: "Luis Almagro no respeta la carta de la OEA"'. Bogotá: Agencia Anadolu. https://www.aa.com.tr/es/pol%C3%ADtica/evo-morales-luis-almagro-no-respeta-la-carta-de-la-oea/1114293.

Shaheen, Kareem. 2016. 'Turkey Sends Tanks into Syria in Operation Aimed at Isis and Kurds'. *The Guardian*, 24 August 2016. https://www.theguardian.com/world/2016/aug/24/turkey-launches-major-operation-against-isis-in-key-border-town.

Sharma, Chanchal Kumar, Sandra Destradi, and Johannes Plagemann. 2020. 'Partisan Federalism and Subnational Governments' International Engagements: Insights from India'. *Publius: The Journal of Federalism* 50 (4): 566–92. https://doi.org/10.1093/publius/pjaa017.

Sharma, Jyoti, and S. K. Varshney. 2021. 'India's Vaccine Diplomacy Aids Global Access to COVID-19 Jabs'. *Nature India*, 17 February 2021. https://doi.org/10.1038/nindia.2021.31.

Sharma, Mukul. 2023. 'Hindu Nationalism and Right-Wing Ecology: RSS, Modi and Motherland Post-2014'. *Studies in Indian Politics* 11 (1): 102–17. https://doi.org/10.1177/23210230231166197.

Sharman, John. 2020. 'Turkish and Greek Warships Collide in Eastern Mediterranean'. *The Independent*, 14 August 2020. https://www.independent.co.uk/news/world/europe/turkey-greece-war-mediterranean-erdogan-ships-collide-a9670416.html.

Sidhu, W. P. S. 2015. 'Looking Ahead: The Next 365 Days'. *Modi's Foreign Policy* 365. https://www.brookings.edu/wp-content/uploads/2015/06/modi365_wps.pdf.

Sidhu, W. P. S., and Shruti Godbole. 2015. 'Neighbourhood First: Bilateralism Trumps Regionalism'. *Brookings India*. https://www.brookings.edu/wp-content/uploads/2015/05/modi365_wps_godbole3.pdf.

Singh, Gurjit. 2024. 'NAM at a Crossroads: Analysing India's Diplomatic Choices and Priorities'. *Firstpost*, 4 February 2024. https://www.firstpost.com/opinion/nam-at-a-crossroads-analysing-indias-diplomatic-choices-and-priorities-13687512.html.

Singh, Jaswant. 1998. 'Against Nuclear Apartheid'. *Foreign Affairs* 77 (5): 41–52.

Singh, Suchet Vir. 2022. '"Confluence of Two Seas": Shinzo Abe's 2007 Speech That Shaped 21st-Century India-Japan Ties'. *ThePrint*, 8 July 2022. https://theprint.in/world/confluence-of-two-seas-shinzo-abes-2007-speech-that-shaped-21st-century-india-japan-ties/1031314.

SIPRI. 2024. 'Arms Transfer Database'. https://armstransfers.sipri.org/ArmsTransfer/CSVResult.

SIPRI. n.d. 'SIPRI Military Expenditure Database'. https://milex.sipri.org/sipri.

Skonieczny, Amy. 2018. 'Trading with the Enemy: Narrative, Identity and US Trade Politics'. *Review of International Political Economy* 25 (4): 441–62.

Skonieczny, Amy, and Ancita Sherel. 2024. 'The Trump Effect: The Perpetuation of Populism in US–China Trade'. *International Affairs* 100 (5): 1959–81. https://doi.org/10.1093/ia/iiae183.

Sky News. 2021. 'Boris Johnson Accused of Having a "Casual" Approach to Britain's National Security by Senior MPs'. *Sky News*, 19 September 2021. https://news.sky.com/story/boris-johnson-accused-of-having-a-casual-approach-to-britains-national-security-by-senior-mps-12411803.

Smith, David. 2019. 'Trump Hails "Good Man" Boris Johnson and Says of UK: "They Like Me over There"'. *The Guardian*, 23 July 2019. https://www.theguardian.com/us-news/2019/jul/23/trump-boris-johnson-britain-trump-uk-prime-minister.

Smith, Will. 2022. 'Climates of Control: Violent Adaptation and Climate Change in the Philippines'. *Political Geography* 99. https://www.sciencedirect.com/science/article/pii/S0962629822001548.

Söderbaum, Fredrik, Kilian Spandler, and Agnese Pacciardi. 2021. *Contestations of the Liberal International Order*. Cambridge: Cambridge University Press. https://doi.org/10.1017/9781009030915.

South China Morning Post. 2016. 'Philippine Presidential Front-Runner Rodrigo Duterte Open to Talks with Beijing to Resolve South China Sea Dispute'. *South China Morning Post*, 3 May 2016. https://www.scmp.com/news/asia/southeast-asia/article/1940708/philippine-presidential-front-runner-rodrigo-duterte-open.

Spandler, Kilian, and Fredrik Söderbaum. 2023. 'Populist (de)Legitimation of International Organizations'. *International Affairs* 99 (3): 1023–41.

Spandler, Kilian, and Fredrik Söderbaum. 2025. 'Populism and International Organizations: Beyond Backlash'. In *The Routledge Handbook of Populism and Foreign Policy*, edited by David Cadier, Angelos Chryssogelos, and Sandra Destradi, 308-326.

Sridharan, Eswaran. 2020. 'India in 2019'. *Asian Survey* 60 (1): 165–76.

St. John, Ronald Bruce. 2020. *Bolivia: Geopolitics of a Landlocked State*. London: Routledge.

Stefanowitsch, Anatol. 2019. 'Delivering a Brexit Deal to the British People: Theresa May as a Reluctant Populist'. *Zeitschrift für Anglistik und Amerikanistik* 67 (3): 231–63. https://doi.org/10.1515/zaa-2019-0022.

Stengel, Frank A., David Bruce MacDonald, and Dirk Nabers, eds. 2019. *Populism and World Politics: Exploring Inter- and Transnational Dimensions*. Basingstoke: Palgrave Macmillan.

Stephen, Matthew D., and David Skidmore. 2019. 'The AIIB in the Liberal International Order'. *Chinese Journal of International Politics* 12 (1): 61–91.

Stewart, Heather, Kalyeena Makortoff, and Patrick Wintour. 2019. 'May to Hail "Great Partnership" with US as Trump Visits No 10'. *The Guardian*, 3 June 2019. https://www.theguardian.com/politics/2019/jun/03/may-to-hail-great-partnership-with-us-as-trump-visits-no-10.

Stone, Diane. 2015. 'The Group of 20 Transnational Policy Community: Governance Networks, Policy Analysis and Think Tanks'. *International Review of Administrative Sciences* 81 (4): 793–811. https://doi.org/10.1177/0020852314558035.

Stone, Jon, and Andrew Woodcock. 2019. 'EU President Donald Tusk Accuses Boris Johnson of Playing "Stupid Blame Game" and Not Wanting a Deal'. *The Independent*, 8 October 2019. https://www.independent.co.uk/news/uk/politics/boris-johnson-donald-tusk-brexit-deal-quo-vadis-latest-a9147231.html.

Strategic Survey. 2003. 'Turkey: Tensions from Within and Without'. *Strategic Survey* 103 (1): 127–41. https://doi.org/10.1080/04597230312331339843.

Stratton, Allegra. 2008. 'Assad Confirms Turkish Mediation with Israel'. *The Guardian*, 24 April 2008. https://www.theguardian.com/world/2008/apr/24/syria.israelandthepalestinians.

Strazzari, Francesco, and Mattia Grandi. 2019. 'Government Policy and the Migrant Crisis in the Mediterranean and African Arenas'. *Contemporary Italian Politics* 11 (3): 336–54. https://doi.org/10.1080/23248823.2019.1644833.

Strezhnev, Anton, Beth A. Simmons, and Matthew D. Kim. 2019. 'Rulers or Rules? International Law, Elite Cues and Public Opinion'. *European Journal of International Law* 30 (4): 1281–302. https://doi.org/10.1093/ejil/chaa002.

Stuenkel, Oliver. 2010. 'Leading the Disenfranchised or Joining the Establishment? India, Brazil, and the UN Security Council'. *Carta Internacional* 5 (1): 53–63.

Subotic, Jelena. 2022. 'Antisemitism in the Global Populist International'. *British Journal of Politics and International Relations* 24 (3): 458–74.

Suleymanov, Ruslan. 2023. 'War in the Middle East Is Boosting Russia-Turkey Ties'. Carnegie Endowment for International Peace, 15 November 2023. https://carnegieendowment.org/russia-eurasia/politika/2023/11/war-in-the-middle-east-is-boosting-russia-turkey-ties?lang=en.

Sullivan, Kate. 2024. 'Trump Says He Would Encourage Russia to "Do Whatever the Hell They Want" to Any NATO Country That Doesn't Pay Enough'. *CNN*, 11 February 2024. https://www.cnn.com/2024/02/10/politics/trump-russia-nato/index.html.

Sullivan de Estrada, Kate. 2023. 'India and Order Transition in the Indo-Pacific: Resisting the Quad as a "Security Community"'. *Pacific Review* 36 (2): 378–405. https://doi.org/10.1080/09512748.2022.2160792.

Supreme Court of the Philippines. 2005. Senator Aquilino Pimentel, Jr. vs. Office of Executive Secretary. https://lawphil.net/judjuris/juri2005/jul2005/gr_158088_2005.html.

Supreme Court of the Philippines. 2019. 'Agreement between the Republic of the Philippines and the United States of America Concerning Military Bases'. 2019. https://elibrary.judiciary.gov.ph/thebookshelf/showdocs/35/12634.

Swinford, Steven. 2019. 'Election 2019: Boris Johnson Vows End to Migrants "Treating Britain as Their Own"'. *The Times*, 9 December 2019. https://www.thetimes.com/uk/politics/article/election-2019-johnson-vows-end-to-migrants-treating-britain-as-their-own-nczv7r97n.

Szczerbiak, Aleks. 2017. 'Should the EU Be Concerned about a Possible "Polexit"?' *LSE European Politics and Policy (EUROPP) Blog*. https://blogs.lse.ac.uk/europpblog/2017/09/08/should-the-eu-be-concerned-about-a-possible-polexit/.

Szent-Ivanyi, Balazs, and Patryk Kugiel. 2020. 'The Challenge from Within: EU Development Cooperation and the Rise of Illiberalism in Hungary and Poland'. *Journal of Contemporary European Research* 16 (2): 120–38. https://doi.org/10.30950/jcer.v16i2.1078.

Talbot, Ian, and Gurharpal Singh. 2009. *The Partition of India*. New Approaches to Asian History. Cambridge: Cambridge University Press.

Tarchi, Marco. 2015. *Italia populista. Dal qualunquismo a Beppe Grillo*. 2nd ed. Bologna: Il Mulino.

Taş, Hakki. 2014. 'Anti–Westernism in Turkey'. openDemocracy, 11 March 2014. https://www.opendemocracy.net/en/north-africa-west-asia/antiwesternism-in-turkey/.

Taş, Hakkı. 2015. 'Turkey—from Tutelary to Delegative Democracy'. *Third World Quarterly* 36 (4): 776–91. https://doi.org/10.1080/01436597.2015.1024450.

Taş, Hakkı. 2020. 'The Formulation and Implementation of Populist Foreign Policy: Turkey in the Eastern Mediterranean'. *Mediterranean Politics*, January, 1–25. https://doi.org/10.1080/13629395.2020.1833160.

Taş, Hakkı. 2022a. 'Continuity through Change: Populism and Foreign Policy in Turkey'. *Third World Quarterly* 43 (12): 2869–87. https://doi.org/10.1080/01436597.2022.2108392.

Taş, Hakkı. 2022b. 'Erdoğan and the Muslim Brotherhood: An Outside-in Approach to Turkish Foreign Policy in the Middle East'. *Turkish Studies* 23 (5): 722–42. https://doi.org/10.1080/14683849.2022.2085096.

Taş, Hakkı. 2022c. 'The Formulation and Implementation of Populist Foreign Policy: Turkey in the Eastern Mediterranean'. *Mediterranean Politics* 27 (5): 563–87. https://doi.org/10.1080/13629395.2020.1833160.

Taş, Hakkı. 2024. 'Populism and Civil–Military Relations'. *Democratization* 31 (1): 70–89. https://doi.org/10.1080/13510347.2023.2255976.

Tavory, Iddo, and Stefan Timmermans. 2014. *Abductive Analysis: Theorizing Qualitative Research*. Chicago: University of Chicago Press.

Taylor, Derrick Bryson. 2019. 'Trump Mocks Greta Thunberg on Twitter, and She Jabs Back'. *New York Times*, 12 December 2019, sec. U.S. https://www.nytimes.com/2019/12/12/us/politics/greta-thunberg-trump.html.

Enerji ve Tabi Kaynaklar Bakanlığı. 2022. *Türkiye Ulusal Enerji Planı*. Ankara: ETKB. https://enerji.gov.tr/Media/Dizin/EIGM/tr/Raporlar/TUEP/T%C3%BCrkiye_Ulusal_Enerji_Plan%C4%B1.pdf

TCMB. 2024. 'International Investment Position'. 2024. https://www.tcmb.gov.tr/wps/wcm/connect/EN/TCMB+EN/Main+Menu/Statistics/Balance+of+Payments+and+Related+Statistics/International+Investment+Position/.

Tekin, Funda, and Anke Schönlau, eds. 2022. *The EU-German-Turkish Triangle*. Turkey and European Union Studies. Baden-Baden: Nomos.

Tharoor, Shashi. 2019. '"Shehzada" Rahul & Ahmed "Mian" Aren't Routine Jibes on Congress, They Are Modi's Bigotry'. *ThePrint*, 20 April 2019. https://theprint.in/opinion/shehzada-rahul-ahmed-mian-arent-routine-jibes-on-congress-they-are-modis-bigotry/224135/.

Thiers, Consuelo, and Leslie E. Wehner. 2022. 'The Personality Traits of Populist Leaders and Their Foreign Policies: Hugo Chávez and Donald Trump'. *International Studies Quarterly* 66 (1). https://doi.org/10.1093/isq/sqab083.

Thompson, Mark. 2016. 'Bloodied Democracy: Duterte and the Death of Liberal Reformism in the Philippines'. *Journal of Current Southeast Asian Affairs* 35 (3): 39–68.

Thompson, Mark. 2020. 'Explaining Duterte's Rise and Rule: "Penal Populist" Leadership or a Structural Crisis of Oligarchic Democracy in the Philippines?' *Philippine Political Science Journal* 41 (1–2): 5–31.

Thorhallsson, Baldur, and Sverrir Steinsson. 2017. 'Small-state foreign policy'. In *The Oxford Encyclopedia of Foreign Policy Analysis* edited by Cameron Thies. Oxford University Press. https://doi.org/10.1093/acrefore/9780190228637.013.484

Timberman, David. 2019. 'Philippine Politics under Duterte: A Midterm Assessment'. 1 January 2019. https://carnegieendowment.org/2019/01/10/philippine-politics-under-duterte-midterm-assessment-pub-78091.

The Times of India. 2016. 'Modi Demonstrated Indian Leadership on Climate Change: White House'. 7 June 2016. https://timesofindia.indiatimes.com/india/modi-demonstrated-indian-leadership-on-climate-change-white-house/articleshow/52634055.cms.

The Times of India. 2019. 'PM's Poll Speeches on Pulwama, Balakot, Sabarimala under Study: EC'. 19 April 2019. https://timesofindia.indiatimes.com/elections/news/pms-poll-speeches-on-pulwama-balakot-sabarimala-under-study-ec/articleshow/68948074.cms.

The Times of India. 2020. 'Stand Firm: Foreign Minister Jaishankar Lays Out a Welcome Shift in China Policy'. 3 August 2020. https://timesofindia.indiatimes.com/blogs/toi-editorials/stand-firm-foreign-minister-jaishankar-lays-out-a-welcome-shift-in-china-policy/.

Tir, Jaroslav. 2010. 'Territorial Diversion: Diversionary Theory of War and Territorial Conflict'. *Journal of Politics* 72 (2): 413–25.

Tocci, Nathalie. 2012. 'Turkey's Neighbourhood Policy and EU Membership: Squaring the Circle of Turkish Foreign Policy'. *International Journal* 67 (1): 65–80.

Torres Armas, William G. 2004. 'La agenda contemporánea de la política exterior boliviana'. In *La complejidad de nuestras circunstancias: Diálogos sobre política exterior boliviana*, edited by Unidad de Análisis y Política Exterior (UDAPEX), 1–9. La Paz: Ministerio de Relaciones Exteriores y Culto and Konrad-Adenauer-Stiftung.

Toygür, Ilke, Funda Tekin, Eduard Soler i Lecha, and Nicholas Danforth. 2022. Turkey's Foreign Policy and Its Consequences for the EU. Brussels: European Union. https://www.europarl.europa.eu/thinktank/en/document/EXPO_IDA(2022)653662.

Tripodi, Paolo, and Andrés Villar. 2005. 'Haití: La encrucijada de una intervención latinoamericana'. *Revista fuerzas armadas y sociedad* 19 (1): 17–35.

TÜİK Turkish Statistical Institute. 2022. 'Foreign Trade Statistics, October 2022'. 29 November 2022. https://data.tuik.gov.tr/Bulten/Index?p=Foreign-Trade-Statistics-October-2022-45545.

TÜİK Turkish Statistical Institute. 2023. 'Russia the Biggest Source of Imports for Turkey'. 27 February 2023. https://data.tuik.gov.tr/Bulten/Index?p=Foreign-Trade-Statistics-January-2023-49621.

Tupaz, Voltaire. 2015. 'Aquino: 'Fair' Climate Change Deal for Poor Countries'. *Rappler*, 1 December 2015. https://www.rappler.com/nation/114512-aquino-leads-vulnerable-countries-in-calling-for-fair-climate-deal-cop21/.

Turhan, Ebru, ed. 2019. *German-Turkish Relations Revisited: The European Dimension, Domestic and Foreign Politics and Transnational Dynamics*. Baden-Baden: Nomos. https://doi.org/10.5771/9783748900191.

Tüyloğlu, Y. 2021. 'Turkish Development Assistance as a Foreign Policy Tool and Its Discordant Locations'. Stiftung Wissenschaft und Politik. Working Paper (April 2021). https://www.swp-berlin.org/publications/products/arbeitspapiere/CATS_Working_Paper_Nr_2_2021_Turkish_Development_Assistance_as_a_Foreign_Policy_Tool.pdf

Tüysüzoğlu, Göktürk. 2014. 'Strategic Depth: A Neo-Ottomanist Interpretation of Turkish Eurasianism'. *Mediterranean Quarterly* 25 (2): 85–104. https://doi.org/10.1215/10474552-2685776.

Ülgül, Murat. 2019. 'Erdoğan's Personal Diplomacy and Turkish Foreign Policy'. *Insight Turkey* 21 (4): 161–82.

Ülgül, Murat. 2024. 'Do Leaders Really Matter? The Failure of Ambitions in Turkish Foreign Policy'. *International Relations*. https://doi.org/10.1177/00471178241248554.

UN News. 2021. 'Philippines President Urges World to "Reverse Course" on Inequality'. 21 September 2021. https://news.un.org/en/story/2021/09/1100612.

UNGA. 2010. 'Budgetary and Financial Situation of the Organizations of the United Nations System, A/65/187'. https://unsceb.org/sites/default/files/imported_files/CEB%20Secretariat/Public%20Document/A-65-187_0.pdf.

UNGA. 2022. 'A/RES/ES-11/1'. 18 March 2022. https://undocs.org/Home/Mobile?FinalSymbol=A%2FRES%2FES-11%2F1&Language=E&DeviceType=Desktop&LangRequested=False.

United Nations Alliance of Civilizations. 2023. 'Who We Are'. *United Nations Alliance of Civilizations (UNAOC)* (blog), 2023. https://www.unaoc.org/who-we-are/.

United Nations General Assembly. 2010. 'General Assembly Official Records, 65th Session: 15th Plenary Meeting, Friday, 24 September 2010'. New York.

United Nations General Assembly. 2011. 'General Assembly Official Records, 66th Session: 13th Plenary Meeting, Wednesday, 21 September 2011, New York'. New York.

United Nations General Assembly. 2012. 'General Assembly Official Records, 67th Session: 15th Plenary Meeting, Friday, 28 September 2012'. New York. https://documents.un.org/doc/undoc/gen/n12/523/96/pdf/n1252396.pdf?token=BidCUGvO0pZpKhuUNo&fe=true.

United Nations General Assembly. 2014. 'General Assembly Official Records, 69th Session: 7th Plenary Meeting, Wednesday, 24 September 2014'. New York.

United Nations General Assembly. 2015. 'General Assembly Official Records, 70th Session: 15th Plenary Meeting, Monday, 28 September 2015'. New York.

United Nations General Assembly. 2019. 'General Assembly Official Records, 74th Session: 3rd Plenary Meeting, Tuesday, 24 September 2019'. New York.

United Nations General Assembly. 2021. 'General Assembly Official Records, 76th Session: 3rd Plenary Meeting, Tuesday, 21 September 2021'. New York. file:///C:/Users/Sandra%20Destradi/Downloads/A_76_PV.3-EN.pdf.

United Nations Peacekeeping. 2003. 'UN Mission's Contributions by Country'. https://peacekeeping.un.org/sites/default/files/december2003_5.pdf.

United Nations Peacekeeping. 2004. 'UN Mission's Contributions by Country'. https://peacekeeping.un.org/sites/default/files/dec2005_5.pdf.

United Nations Peacekeeping. 2005. 'UN Mission's Contribution by Country'. https://peacekeeping.un.org/sites/default/files/dec2005_5.pdf.

United Nations Peacekeeping. 2006a. 'Ranking of Military and Police Contributions to UN Operations'. https://peacekeeping.un.org/sites/default/files/jan06_2.pdf.

United Nations Peacekeeping. 2006b. 'UN Mission's Contribution by Country'. https://peacekeeping.un.org/sites/default/files/dec06_5.pdf.

United Nations Peacekeeping. 2019. 'Summary of Troops Contributing Countries by Ranking Police, UN Military Experts on Mission, Staff Officers and Troops'. https://peacekeeping.un.org/sites/default/files/02_country_ranking_november_2019.pdf.

United Nations Peacekeeping. 2024. 'Troop and Police Contributors'. 2024. https://peacekeeping.un.org/en/troop-and-police-contributors.

United Nations Peacekeeping. n.d. 'How We Are Funded'. United Nations Peacekeeping. Accessed 18 September 2024. https://peacekeeping.un.org/en/how-we-are-funded.

United Nations Security Council. 2018. 'Security Council, 73rd Year: 8362nd Meeting, Wednesday, 26 September 2018'. New York. https://digitallibrary.un.org/record/1644134?ln=en&v=pdf.

Urbinati, Nadia. 2019a. *Me the People: How Populism Transforms Democracy.* Cambridge, MA: Harvard University Press.

Urbinati, Nadia. 2019b. 'Political Theory of Populism'. *Annual Review of Political Science* 22 (1): 111–27. https://doi.org/10.1146/annurev-polisci-050317-070753.

Usta, Betül. 2023. 'Dünyanın umudu Erdoğan'. *Sabah,* 4 September 2023. https://www.sabah.com.tr/gundem/2023/09/04/dunyanin-umudu-erdogan.

Varadarajan, Siddharth. 2008. 'Dateline Vienna: Thirty Words That Saved the Day'. *Reality, One Bite at a Time* (blog), 8 September 2008. http://svaradarajan.blogspot.com/2008/09/dateline-vienna-thirty-words-that-saved.html.

Varga, Judit. 2020. 'Time for a Christian Conservative Green Policy'. *Politico,* 27 January 2020. https://www.politico.eu/article/christian-conservative-green-policy/.

Vasilopoulou, Sofia, Daphne Halikiopoulou, and Theofanis Exadaktylos. 2014. 'Greece in Crisis: Austerity, Populism and the Politics of Blame'. *JCMS: Journal of Common Market Studies* 52 (2): 388–402. https://doi.org/10.1111/jcms.12093.

Vatan. 2009. "Monşerler'den Davos Yorumu'. *Vatan,* 1 January 2009. http://www.gazetevatan.com/-monserler-den-davos-yorumu-220953-siyaset/.

Verbeek, Bertjan, and Andrej Zaslove. 2015. 'The Impact of Populist Radical Right Parties on Foreign Policy: The Northern League as a Junior Coalition Partner in the Berlusconi Governments'. *European Political Science Review* 7 (4): 525–46.

Verbeek, Bertjan, and Andrej Zaslove. 2017. 'Populism and Foreign Policy'. In *The Oxford Handbook of Populism,* edited by Cristóbal Rovira Kaltwasser, Paul A. Taggart, Paulina Ochoa Espejo, and Pierre Ostiguy, 384–405. Oxford: Oxford University Press.

Vihma, Antto. 2011. 'India and the Global Climate Governance: Between Principles and Pragmatism'. *Journal of Environment & Development* 20 (1): 69–94. https://doi.org/10.1177/1070496510394325.

Visnovitz, Péter, and Erin Kristin Jenne. 2021. 'Populist Argumentation in Foreign Policy: The Case of Hungary under Viktor Orbán, 2010–2020'. *Comparative European Politics* 19 (6): 683–702. https://doi.org/10.1057/s41295-021-00256-3.

Vitug, Marites, and Camille Elemia. 2024. *Unrequited Love: Duterte's China Embrace.* Manila: Ateneo de Manila University Press.

Voeten, Erik. 2020a. 'Populism and Backlashes against International Courts'. *Perspectives on Politics* 18 (2): 407–22. https://doi.org/10.1017/S1537592719000975.

Voice of America. 2011. 'Turkey's PM Warns against Cyprus EU Presidency'. *Voice of America,* 20 July 2011. https://www.voanews.com/a/turkeys-pm-warns-against-cyprus-eu-presidency-125968143/170778.html.

Volgy, Thomas J., and John E. Schwarz. 1991. 'Does Politics Stop at the Water's Edge? Domestic Political Factors and Foreign Policy Restructuring in the Cases of Great Britain, France, and West Germany'. *Journal of Politics* 53 (3): 615–43. https://doi.org/10.2307/2131573.

Vukovic, Sinisa. 2014. 'International Mediation as a Distinct Form of Conflict Management'. *International Journal of Conflict Management* 25 (1): 61–80. https://doi.org/10.1108/IJCMA-02-2012-0015.

Waisbord, Silvio. 2018. 'The Elective Affinity between Post-Truth Communication and Populist Politics'. *Communication Research and Practice* 4 (1): 17–34.

Wajner, Daniel F. 2021. 'Exploring the Foreign Policies of Populist Governments: (Latin) America First'. *Journal of International Relations and Development* 24: 651-680. https://doi.org/10.1057/s41268-020-00206-8.

Wajner, Daniel F. 2022. 'The Populist Way Out: Why Contemporary Populist Leaders Seek Transnational Legitimation'. *British Journal of Politics and International Relations* 24 (3): 416–36. https://doi.org/10.1177/13691481211069345.

Wajner, Daniel F., Sandra Destradi, and Michael Zürn. 2024. 'The Effects of Global Populism: Assessing the Populist Impact on International Affairs'. *International Affairs* 100 (5): 1819–33. https://doi.org/10.1093/ia/iiae217.

Wajner, Daniel F., and Philip Giurlando. 2024. 'Populist Foreign Policy: Mapping the Developing Research Program on Populism in International Relations'. *International Studies Review* 26 (1): viae012. https://doi.org/10.1093/isr/viae012.

Wajner, Daniel F., and Luis Roniger. 2019. 'Transnational Identity Politics in the Americas: Chavismo's Regional Legitimation Strategies'. *Latin American Research Review* 54 (2): 458–75.

Wajner, Daniel F., and Leslie Wehner. 2023. 'Embracing or Rebuffing "the International"? Populist Foreign Policy and the Fourth Wave of Populism in Latin America'. *Global Studies Quarterly* 3 (2): ksad026.

Waldner, David, and Ellen Lust. 2018. 'Unwelcome Change: Coming to Terms with Democratic Backsliding'. *Annual Review of Political Science* 21 (1): 93–113. https://doi.org/10.1146/annurev-polisci-050517-114628.

Walgrave, Stefaan, and Jonas Lefevere. 2013. 'Ideology, Salience, and Complexity: Determinants of Policy Issue Incongruence between Voters and Parties'. *Journal of Elections, Public Opinion & Parties* 23 (4): 456–83. https://doi.org/10.1080/17457289.2013.810630.

Walker, Peter. 2021. 'Cop26: Humanity 5-1 down at Half-Time on Climate Crisis, Says Johnson'. *The Guardian,* 29 October 2021. https://www.theguardian.com/environment/2021/oct/29/cop26-humanity-5-1-halftime-climate-crisis-boris-johnson.

Walker, Shaun. 2019. 'Classes Move to Vienna as Hungary Makes Rare Decision to Oust University'. *The Guardian,* 16 November 2019. https://www.theguardian.com/world/2019/nov/16/ceu-classes-move-to-vienna-orban-hungary-ousts-university.

Walker, Stephen G., and George L. Watson. 1989. 'Groupthink and Integrative Complexity in British Foreign Policy-Making: The Munich Case'. *Cooperation and Conflict* 24 (3): 199–212. https://doi.org/10.1177/001083678902400306.

Ward, Bradley, and Joseph Ward. 2022. 'Britain's Centralising State Makes It Vulnerable to Clientelism and Cronyism'. *British Politics and Policy at LSE* (blog), 27 January 2022. https://blogs.lse.ac.uk/politicsandpolicy/cronyism-and-clientelism-british-state/.

Ward, Joseph, and Bradley Ward. 2023. 'From Brexit to COVID-19: The Johnson Government, Executive Centralisation and Authoritarian Populism'. *Political Studies* 71 (4): 1171–89. https://doi.org/10.1177/00323217211063730.

Warren, Spenser A., and Sumit Ganguly. 2022. 'India–Russia Relations after Ukraine'. *Asian Survey* 62 (5–6): 811–37. https://doi.org/10.1525/as.2022.1799235.

Watson, Katy. 2019. 'A Tale of Two Trumps: Jair Bolsonaro Goes to Washington'. *BBC,* 20 March 2019. https://www.bbc.com/news/world-us-canada-47633940.

Webber, Esther. 2021. 'UK MPs Back Boris Johnson's Foreign Aid Cut despite Outcry'. *Politico,* 13 July 2021. https://www.politico.eu/article/uk-mps-back-boris-johnsons-foreign-aid-cut/.

Weeks, Jessica L. 2012. 'Strongmen and Straw Men: Authoritarian Regimes and the Initiation of International Conflict'. *American Political Science Review* 106 (2): 326–47. https://doi.org/10.1017/S0003055412000111.

Wehner, Leslie. 2020. 'The Foreign Policy of South American Small Powers in Regional and International Politics'. In *Handbook on the Politics of Small States*, edited by Godfrey Baldacchino and Anders Wivel, 259–77. Cheltenham: Edward Elgar. https://doi.org/10.4337/9781788112932.

Wehner, Leslie E. 2023. 'Stereotyped Images and Role Dissonance in the Foreign Policy of Right-Wing Populist Leaders: Jair Bolsonaro and Donald Trump'. *Cooperation and Conflict* 58 (3): 275–92.

Wehner, Leslie. 2025. 'Gradual Change in Foreign Policy: A Role-Theoretic Approach'. *International Studies Perspectives*: ekaf007. https://doi.org/10.1093/isp/ekaf007

Wehner, Leslie E., and Cameron G. Thies. 2021. 'The Nexus of Populism and Foreign Policy: The Case of Latin America'. *International Relations* 35 (2): 320–40. https://doi.org/10.1177/0047117820944430.

Wesslau, Fredrik. 2016. 'Putin's Friends in Europe'. ECFR, 19 October 2016. https://ecfr.eu/article/commentary_putins_friends_in_europe7153/.

Weyland, Kurt. 2001. 'Clarifying a Contested Concept: Populism in the Study of Latin American Politics'. *Comparative Politics* 34 (1): 1.

White, Jenny. 2013. *Muslim Nationalism and the New Turks*. Princeton, NJ: Princeton University Press.

White, Joshua. 2021. 'After the Foundational Agreements: An Agenda for US-India Defense and Security Cooperation'. Brookings. https://www.brookings.edu/articles/after-the-foundational-agreements-an-agenda-for-us-india-defense-and-security-cooperation/.

The White House. 2005. 'Joint Statement between President George W. Bush and Prime Minister Manmohan Singh'. 18 July 2005. https://georgewbush-whitehouse.archives.gov/news/releases/2005/07/20050718-6.html.

Winberg, Oscar. 2017. 'Insult Politics: Donald Trump, Right-Wing Populism, and Incendiary Language'. *European Journal of American Studies* 12 (2). https://doi.org/10.4000/ejas.12132.

Wintour, Patrick. 2021. 'UK Aid Cut Seen as Unforced Error in "Year of British Leadership"'. *The Guardian*, 23 April 2021. https://www.theguardian.com/global-development/2021/apr/23/uk-aid-cut-seen-as-unforced-error-in-year-of-british-leadership.

Winzer, Linda. 2023. 'Hoffmann: Klimaideologie kämpft gegen die Physik auf Steuerzahlerkosten'. *AfD Fraktion im Thüringer Landtag* (blog), 9 November 2023. https://afd-thl.de/2023/11/09/hoffmann-klimaideologie-kaempft-gegen-die-physik-auf-steuerzahlerkosten/.

The Wire Analysis. 2024. 'Modi Claims on "Divine" Origins: From Not "Born Biologically" to "Earn Punya from Good Deeds I Do"'. *The Wire*, 23 May 2024. https://thewire.in/politics/modi-claims-on-divine-origins-from-not-born-biologically-to-earn-punya-from-good-deeds-i-do.

Wivel, Anders. 2024. 'Foreign Policy Analysis and Realism'. In *The Oxford Handbook of Foreign Policy Analysis*, edited by Kaarbo and Cameron G. Thies, 97–114. Oxford: Oxford University Press.

Wlezien, Christopher. 2005. 'On the Salience of Political Issues: The Problem with "Most Important Problem"'. *Electoral Studies* 24 (4): 555–79. https://doi.org/10.1016/j.electstud.2005.01.009.

Wojczewski, Thorsten. 2020a. '"Enemies of the People": Populism and the Politics of (in)Security'. *European Journal of International Security* 5 (1): 5–24. https://doi.org/10.1017/eis.2019.23.

Wojczewski, Thorsten. 2020b. 'Populism, Hindu Nationalism, and Foreign Policy in India: The Politics of Representing "the People"'. *International Studies Review* 22 (3): 396–422. https://doi.org/10.1093/isr/viz007.

Wojczewski, Thorsten. 2020c. 'Trump, Populism, and American Foreign Policy'. *Foreign Policy Analysis* 16 (3): 292–311.

Wojczewski, Thorsten. 2023. *The Inter- and Transnational Politics of Populism: Foreign Policy, Identity and Popular Sovereignty*. Global Political Sociology. Cham: Springer International Publishing.

Wolff, Jonas. 2012. 'New Constitutions and the Transformation of Democracy in Bolivia and Ecuador'. In *New Constitutionalism in Latin America: Promises and Practices*, edited by Detlef Nolte and Almut Schilling-Vacaflor, 183–202. London: Routledge.

World Bank. 2024. 'GDP Growth (Annual %)—India'. World Bank Open Data. 2024. https://data.worldbank.org/indicator/NY.GDP.MKTP.KD.ZG?locations=IN.

Wright, Thomas. 2021. 'Advancing Multilateralism in a Populist Age'. Brookings. https://www.brookings.edu/wp-content/uploads/2021/02/FP_20210204_multilateralism_wright_v2.pdf.

Yeni Akit. 2016. 'Avrupa Erdoğan'dan korkuyor'. 24 April 2016. https://www.yeniakit.com.tr/haber/avrupa-erdogandan-korkuyor-165534.html.

Yeni Akit. 2022. 'Artık Türkiye'den korkuyorlar! Erdoğan'ın duruşu Alman gazeteciyi korkuttu'. 19 October 2022. https://www.yeniakit.com.tr/haber/artik-turkiyeden-korkuyorlar-erdoganin-durusu-alman-gazeteciyi-korkuttu-1700400.html.

Yeni Şafak. 2004. 'Denktaş'a herşeyi söyledim'. 1 January 2004. https://www.yenisafak.com/gundem/denktasa-herseyi-soyledim-2710394.

Yeni Şafak. 2017. 'Faşizm Avrupa'da kol geziyor'. 16 March 2017. https://www.yenisafak.com/gundem/fasizm-avrupada-kol-geziyor-2628971.

Yesilyurt, Nuri. 2017. 'Explaining Miscalculation and Maladaptation In Turkish Foreign Policy towards the Middle East during the Arab Uprisings: A Neoclassical Realist Perspective'. *All Azimuth: A Journal of Foreign Policy and Peace* 6 (2): 65–83. https://doi.org/10.20991/allazimuth.310151.

Yıldırım, Nilgün Eliküçük. 2024. 'The Uyghur Issue in Turkey-China Relations'. Istanbul: Heinrich Böll Stiftung.

Yılmaz, Zafer. 2020. 'Erdoğan's Presidential Regime and Strategic Legalism: Turkish Democracy in the Twilight Zone'. *Southeast European and Black Sea Studies* 20 (2): 265–87. https://doi.org/10.1080/14683857.2020.1745418.

Ylä-Anttila, Tuukka. 2018. 'Populist Knowledge: "Post-Truth" Repertoires of Contesting Epistemic Authorities'. *European Journal of Cultural and Political Sociology* 5 (4): 356–88. https://doi.org/10.1080/23254823.2017.1414620.

Zakharov, Aleksei. 2024. 'India-Russia Relations in Troubled Times: Steady but Stagnating'. IFRI, 2024. https://www.ifri.org/en/publications/notes-de-lifri/asie-visions/india-russia-relations-troubled-times-steady-stagnating.

Zambrana Marchetti, Juan Carlos. 2017. 'Soft "Nation-Building": The Economic Weapon Developed by the US in Bolivia'. *Bolivian Studies Journal* 23–24 (January): 189–338.

Zaytsev, Dmitry G., Valentina V. Kuskova, and Alexandra Kononova. 2021. 'The Power of Knowledge: How Think Tanks Impact US Foreign Policy'. *Foreign Policy Analysis* 18 (1): orab034. https://doi.org/10.1093/fpa/orab034.

Zeit. 2016. 'Erdoğan-Satire: Merkel erlaubt Strafverfolgung von Jan Böhmermann'. *Die Zeit*, 15 April 2016. https://www.zeit.de/politik/2016-04/erdo-an-satire-merkel-erlaubt-strafverfolgung-von-jan-boehmermann.

Ziemer, Henry, Tina Dolbaia, and Mathieu Droin. 2024. 'Russia and Iran in Latin America: Same Outlook, Similar Playbooks'. Center for Strategic and International Studies. https://csis-website-prod.s3.amazonaws.com/s3fs-public/2024-07/240725_Ziemer_Russia_Iran.pdf.

Zotti, Antonio, and Enrico Fassi. 2020. 'Immigration and Foreign Policy: Italy's Domestic-International Linkage in the Management of Mass Human Movements'. *Italian Political Science* 15 (1): 96–113.

Zuazo, Moira. 2009. *¿Cómo nació el MAS?: La ruralización de la política en Bolivia.* 2nd ed. La Paz: Fundación Friedrich Ebert.

Zürn, Michael. 2004. 'Global Governance and Legitimacy Problems'. *Government and Opposition* 39 (2): 260–87.

Zürn, Michael. 2014. 'The Politicization of World Politics and Its Effects: Eight Propositions'. *European Political Science Review* 6 (1): 47–71.

Zürn, Michael. 2018. 'Contested Global Governance'. *Global Policy* 9 (1): 138–45.

Zürn, Michael. 2019. 'Politicization Compared: At National, European, and Global Levels'. *Journal of European Public Policy* 26 (7): 977–95.

Index

For the benefit of digital users, indexed terms that span two pages (e.g., 52–53) may, on occasion, appear on only one of those pages.

Tables, figures, and boxes are indicated by an italic *t*, *f*, or *b*.